Communism's Shadow

■■■■■

Communism's Shadow

HISTORICAL LEGACIES AND CONTEMPORARY POLITICAL ATTITUDES

■■■■■

Grigore Pop-Eleches and Joshua A. Tucker

PRINCETON UNIVERSITY PRESS

Princeton and Oxford

Published by Princeton University Press, 41 William Street,
Princeton, New Jersey 08540

In the United Kingdom: Princeton University Press, 6 Oxford Street,
Woodstock, Oxfordshire OX20 1TR

press.princeton.edu

Cover photograph: Chuck Nacke / Alamy Stock Photo

Cloth ISBN 978-0-691-17558-4

Paperback ISBN 978-0-691-17559-1

British Library Cataloging-in-Publication Data is available

This book has been composed in Sabon LT Std

Printed on acid-free paper. ∞

Printed in the United States of America

10 9 8 7 6 5 4 3 2 1

Contents

■ ■ ■ ■ ■

For our most important legacies,
Sasha, Rica, Matthew, and Lia

■ ■ ■ ■ ■

Acknowledgments

■■■■■

"How does the past matter?" Five simple words, and yet at the same time an enormously complex question. This book is motivated by an over-arching desire to try to understand the answer to this question generally, but also to understand the effect of a particularly important past, perhaps the single greatest social experiment in the radical remaking of society in the modern era: Soviet communism.

Note that the question with which we begin is not "does the past matter?" but rather "*how* does the past matter?" We consider the former question fairly well settled: the past of course matters, and the communist past probably more so than most. But how it matters is another question altogether.

To date, much ink has been spilled on the question of how communist legacies have affected the development of post-communist institutions. When we started this project, though, there had been much less attention paid to the question of how communist legacies might have affected what political scientists call *political behavior*—the way in which individual cit-izens interact with politics, such as by participating in politics, evaluating political institutions and actors, and forming their own opinions about political issues and topics.

While our overall research agenda has taken us in all three directions, this book is focused on the last of these topics: how might the experience of communism have affected the ways in which citizens of post-communist countries think about such fundamental issues as democracy as a form of political rule, the role of markets as an organizing principle in the econ-omy, the responsibility of the state for individual social welfare, and the importance of gender equality in society? We were drawn to these ques-tions precisely because it was *communist* legacies that we sought to ex-amine: all these questions had important antecedents in Marxist-Leninist ideology.

Despite the importance of the topic—at least in our eyes!—we began the project with less of a roadmap that one normally does in political sci-ence. Therefore, we needed to put together new theoretical frameworks for understanding the potential effects of legacies on attitudes, figure out research methods that would be appropriate for testing our hypotheses, and collect what would turn out to be a great deal of data from a wide range of different sources to allow us to actually conduct our analysis. As a result, we are indebted to a large number of people who provided us with feedback as we sought to develop and refine our theoretical arguments, who critiqued our methodological choices and pushed us to further develop our techniques and statistical methods, and who assisted us with our data collection efforts. Indeed, all the survey data on which we rely for our analyses in this book—and much of the aggregate data as well—was collected by others and provided to the scholarly community as a public good. We are so very grateful for the efforts of all those involved in these projects, without whom this research simply would not have been possible.

Let us begin first by thanking the many institutions that invited one or the other of us—and occasionally both of us—to present our research from this project at various stages of development: the Center for Advanced Study in the Social Sciences at the Fundación Juan March (Spain); Central European University (Hungary); Columbia University; Duke University; ETH Zurich (Switzerland); the European Bank for Reconstruction and Development (UK); the European University Institute (Italy); Georgetown University; Harvard University; Hebrew University of Jerusalem (Israel); the Higher School for Economics (Russia); LUISS Guido Carli University (Italy); the New Economic School (Russia); New York University–Abu Dhabi (UAE); New York University–Shanghai (China); Oxford University (UK); the Program on New Approaches to Research and Security in Eurasia (PONARS); Rutgers University; Universitat Oldenburg (Germany); the University of Birmingham (UK); the University of California–Berkeley; the University of Michigan; the University of North Carolina–Chapel Hill; the University of Pittsburgh; the University of St. Gallen (Switzerland); the University of Wisconsin—Madison; Uppsala University (Sweden); and Vanderbilt University.

During these talks, we were fortunate to receive comments and feedback from more people than we can list here. With that caveat in mind, we do in particular want to thank: Laia Balcells; Pablo Barberá; Mark Beissinger; Nancy Bermeo; Michael Bernhard; Yitzhak Brudny; Noah Buckley; Joshua Clinton; Michael Donnelly; Daniela Donno; Grzegorz Ekiert; Patrick Emmenegger; Zsolt Enyedi; Geoff Evans; Steven Finkel; Steve Fish; Robert Fishman; Natalia Forrat; Timothy Frye; Barbara Geddes; Anastasia Gorodzeisky; Anna Grzymała-Busse; Steven Hanson; S. P. Harish; Tim Haughton; Jude Hays; Sarah Hobolt; Macartan Humphreys; Amaney Jamal; Andrew Janos; Krzysztof Jasiewicz; Kristin Kanthak; Herbert Kitschelt; Jeffrey Kopstein; George Krause; Alex Kuo; Jonathan Ladd; Pierre Landry; Margaret Levy; David Lewis; Oana Lup; Noam Lupu; Michael MacKuen; Anne Meng; Rebecca Morton; Ola Onuch; Laura Paler; Leonid Peisakhin; Maria Popova; Adam Przeworski; Markus Prior; Adam Ramey; John Reuter; Pedro Riera; Bryn Rosenfeld; Nasos Roussias; Arturas Rozenas; Ignacio Sánchez-Cuenca; Gwendolyn Sasse; Victoria Shineman; Kathryn Stoner; Gabor Toka; Daniel Treisman; Vera Troeger; Lucan Way; Jonathan Woon; Deborah Yashar; Alexei Zakharov; John Zaller; and Liz Zechmeister.

We are very thankful as well for a number of people who patiently answered our questions and offered suggestions regarding our application of statistical methods in this book: Christopher Achen; Nathaniel Beck; Kosuke Imai; John Londregan; Anja Neundorf; Richard Niemi; and Cyrus Samii. We also want to thank the following people who provided open source modules for Stata that we utilized in our analysis: Jens Hainmueller; Raymond Hicks; and Dustin Tingley.

We were extremely fortunate to have a number excellent research assistants over the course of this project: Kelsey Holland; Ari Mitropoulos; Djordje Modrakovic; Muthhukumar Palaniyapan; Toma Pavlov; and Alexander Peel. We are especially grateful to Dominik Duell and Marko Klašnja, both of whom worked as RAs for us while pursuing their PhDs in political science at NYU and now have their own tenure-track faculty positions; whether that says more about the value of working on this project or the amount of time it took us to finish this book we will leave to others to decide.

Our work benefited enormously from a book manuscript conference that was hosted at the Centre for Russian and Eurasian Studies at the University of Uppsala in Uppsala, Sweden, in the fall of 2012, without which this book would undoubtedly have been published earlier but would have been of lower quality. We were challenged by the participants at that conference to improve the manuscript on many dimensions, and while their suggestions were time consuming, we hope these people are as pleased as we are with the results of taking their comments seriously. We are very grateful to Li Bennich-Bjorkman for inviting us to Uppsala and organizing the conference, as well as to the Johan Skytte Foundation for funding it. We are also tremendously indebted to a wonderful collection of scholars who not only gave so generously of their time to read six chapters of the manuscript, but most of whom flew from around the world to join us in Uppsala for the two-day conference. We are very well aware of what a precious commodity time is, and we thank the following for generously spending some of their time helping us improve this book: Li Bennich-Bjorkman; Ted Brader; Scott Gehlbach; Henry Hale; Mark Kayser; Keena Lipsitz;

Radosław Markowski; Monika Nalepa; Sven Oskarsson; Graeme Robertson; and Jason Wittenberg.

We also wish to express our sincerest thanks to Milada Vachudova, who read significant portions of this manuscript at our request at multiple times throughout the project and gave us thoughtful advice for making the first two chapters more engaging, and Andrew Roberts, who out of the blue volunteered to read the entire manuscript at the same time we submitted it for consideration for publication and offered us thorough comments on each chapter.

We both benefited enormously from institutional support during the writing of this manuscript at NYU and Princeton. Tucker also served as a visiting professor at the Center for Advanced Study in the Social Sciences of the Fundación Juan March in Madrid, Spain, LUISS Guido Carli University in Rome, Italy, and at NYU-Florence while working on the project, and he thanks all three institutions for their support. Pop-Eleches was a visiting scholar at Nuffield College–University of Oxford and is grateful for the hospitality (and the feedback.) We thank our PhD students for their helpful and stimulating comments during discussions of the papers from this project that they were generous enough to read when we put the papers on their required reading lists.

We also wish to thank Eric Crahan and Princeton University Press—as well as two anonymous reviewers—for shepherding the manuscript through its final stages. The reviews were extremely helpful, and the support from Princeton has been excellent. We thank in particular Kathleen Kageff for copyediting, and Jill Harris at Princeton for overseeing the publishing process. Additionally, we thank Steven Moore for preparing the index.

Last but certainly not least, we wish to thank Tali Mendelberg, the editor of Princeton Studies in Political Behavior. Tali has gone above and beyond what we could have possibly expected from a series editor, which included giving us detailed comments on the entire manuscript. Her comments and suggestions were invaluable, and we believe the manuscript will be that much stronger for her involvement. It has been an absolute pleasure to work with Tali, and we cannot recommend the series strongly enough to other prospective authors.

Of course, none of this would have been possible without our friends and family to support us, distract us, entertain us, and challenge us throughout this process. We will spare you yet another list but do want to note that many (though certainly not all) of those friends have already been mentioned previously in these acknowledgements. We consider ourselves very fortunate to be able to work in a field with not only wonderful scholars but also wonderful people.

For Pop-Eleches writing this book involved the sometimes delicate intersection of academic interests and personal biography. Having grown up in communist Romania in the last two decades of Ceauşescu's increasingly surreal dictatorship, he has childhood memories that are a mosaic of pioneer songs and ubiquitous official propaganda during the day countered by evenings spent listening to Voice of America and Radio Free Europe (often by candlelight amid the frequent power cuts). Just as importantly, the family narratives he grew up with combined numerous stories of communist persecution and labor camps with an acknowledgment of the genuine social mobility that communism brought to many people. Last but not least, from an intellectual perspective, Pop-Eleches is grateful for the experience of watching the vast majority of Romanians voting for a thinly disguised communist successor party less than half a year after Ceauşescu's fall. While at the time it triggered a combination of bewilderment and disbelief, the Romanian election of 1990 (and the rhetoric surrounding it) were a first—and crucial—lesson that communist ideology could have a lasting effect even in one of Eastern Europe's most delegitimized communist regimes and after the immediate threat of repression was gone. Tucker grew up in New York, but as a Mets fan, he has some relevant experience with feeling as a child that top-down mismanagement had stifled the dreams of many, as well as having experienced a brief moment of euphoria in the mid-late 1980s followed by two and a half decades of trying to make sense of what happened next. We think this may have something to do with why he enjoys Pop-Eleches's communist-era jokes so much.

Before closing, we want to thank our parents, Robert, Linda, Grigore, and Renate, for all their support over all the years. Pop-Eleches also wants to thank his brother Kiki and his sister-in-law Cristina for many wonderful discussions of communist and post-communist politics over the past two decades.

Above all, we thank Keena and Ellie for their love, support, and generosity in allowing us to spend so much time on this project. This was a labor of love, but a labor nonetheless, and it would not have been possible without them.

Finally, we dedicate this book to our most important legacies, Sasha, Rica, Matthew, and Lia.

Country Code Abbreviations Used in Figures 4.1, 5.1, 6.1, and 7.1

■■■■■

Country Code	Country
AL	Albania
AM	Armenia
AZ	Azerbaijan
BA	Bosnia-Herzegovina
BG	Bulgaria
BY	Belarus
CZ	Czech Republic
DE	East Germany
EE	Estonia
GE	Georgia
HR	Croatia
HU	Hungary
KG	Kyrgyzstan
LT	Lithuania
LV	Latvia
MD	Moldova
MK	Macedonia
PL	Poland
RO	Romania
RS	Serbia
RU	Russia
SI	Slovenia
SK	Slovakia
UA	Ukraine

CHAPTER 1

Communism's Shadow

1.1. INTRODUCTION

More than a quarter century after the Leninist extinction in the former Soviet bloc, the specter—or at least the memory—of communism still haunts the region. Memories of Stalinism (both glowing and bitter) feature prominently in the political discourse of Russia and Ukraine, while new national-populist regimes in Poland and Hungary justify their political tactics at least in part in terms of the fight against communism, even as their opponents accuse them of having adopted much of the communists' mindset and tactics. Even if much of this language is intended simply as a rhetorical flourish, it suggests a deeper truth about the politics of the region: communism's shadow is still ever present in the hearts and minds of post-communist citizens.

Indeed, when analyzing a wide range of public opinion data from the first two decades after the collapse of communism, we find that post-communist citizens are, on average, less supportive of democracy, less supportive of markets, and more supportive of state-provided social welfare—but no more of supportive of gender equality—than citizens elsewhere in the world. (See Figure 1.1 on the following page.) Why?

The most intuitive answer to this question is that it is somehow a legacy of communism. But as popular as it has become to attribute outcomes of interest in post-communist countries to "legacies,"[1] and despite some recent theoretical efforts to conceptualize historical legacies more carefully (Beissinger and Kotkin 2014: 11–20; Wittenberg 2015), there is no clearly established theoretical or empirical blueprint for analyzing the effect of legacies on attitudes. Accordingly, we begin with two more theoretically precise potential answers to the question of "why": it may be because of the experience of *living through communism*; or it may be because of the experience *of living in a post-communist country*. While related—we do not expect to find truly large proportions of a population who *lived*

---

[1] The phrase "communist legacies" returns almost 1,700 citations on Google Scholar (accessed October 28, 2016).

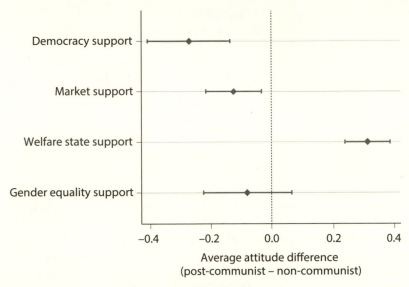

Figure 1.1. Post-communist Attitudinal Differences
This figure shows the difference in standard deviations (along with 95% confidence intervals) between the average attitudes of post-communist and non-communist respondents from the 2nd, 3rd, 4th, and 5th waves of the World Values Survey. The figure reveals that residents of post-communist countries have on average significantly lower support for democracy and markets and higher support for welfare states than their non-communist counterparts. Post-communist citizens are also somewhat less supportive of gender equality, but the difference is not statistically significant. For comparability, all dependent variables are standardized to have a mean of 0 and a standard deviation of 1. The estimates are based on models that include only the post-communist citizen indicator and a series of dummies for the year of the survey. For more details about the survey questions used to construct the dependent variables, see Chapter 3. For full regression results, see the electronic appendix.

through communism anywhere else than in post-communist world,[2] and (at least originally) most people *living in post-communist countries* had lived through some period of communist rule—they are not the same thing, and this is increasingly true as time passes and more people *live in post-communist countries* who did not *live through communism*. In addition, even people *living in post-communist countries* will have spent different numbers of years *living through* communist rule. Crucially, the two approaches have different implications for how we understand these attitudinal differences, how long we might expect them to persist, and the role

[2] Certain neighborhoods in London and Chicago notwithstanding.

that communist legacies play in structuring opinion on fundamental social, political, and economic issues. Furthermore, the answer to this question remains as relevant as ever, because it informs some of the most pressing issues in international politics, such as the future of the European Union project, the status of frozen conflicts in the former Soviet space, and Russia's relationship with the rest of Europe.

To the extent that differences in attitudes held by post-communist citizens are a function of people *living through* communist rule, then this would undoubtedly be a legacy of communism. Why might we expect *living through communism* to have an effect on attitudes toward democracy, markets, social welfare, and gender equality? For one, there is a long-standing literature on "political socialization" that argues that all political regimes—to one extent or another—seek to inculcate attitudes supportive of the regime into their citizens (Dennis 1968; Greenstein 1971; Greenberg 1973). In many cases, these efforts may be lackadaisical or passive, but Soviet communism clearly made an active attempt to create a new "Socialist Man" complete with a requisite set of beliefs about politics, economics, and social relations (Deutscher 1967). Thus, *living through* communist rule should be a promising candidate for explaining communist legacy effects on public opinion.

Indeed, communist regimes differed from most other flavors of authoritarian regimes by being not merely interested in ruling over citizens, but also trying to implement a particular project of shaping citizens' attitudes. Communist citizens were not simply expected to accept the rule of the communists, but rather additionally to embrace and embody the precepts of socialism.[3] Moreover, this was not just a stated goal: communist regimes took active steps to try to make sure these precepts were adopted, including in the schools, the workplace, and party meetings. As Ilie Moromete remarks in the Romanian novel *Moromeții* by Marin Preda, "these guys [the communists] are not content with just taking your cattle from the stable, they also make you sign that you gave it willingly" (Preda 1967: 261). Thus the idea that people who *lived through* communist rule would come to adopt attitudes in line with those the regime wanted its citizens to hold should not be that much of a stretch.

Of course, it is also possible that the experience of *living through* communism did nothing to affect the way that individuals thought about politics, economics, and basic social relationships in the post-communist era. Perhaps the experience of living under communist rule was simply relegated to the past once post-communism began, a relic of bygone times eclipsed by subsequent experiences. In that case we need a different explanation

---

[3] Of course, this desire was stronger under certain types of communist regimes than others, a point to which we return in much greater detail shortly.

for why post-communist citizens hold different attitudes on such fundamental political and economic questions than citizens elsewhere. If *living
through* communism does not hold the answer, then the next most likely
candidate would seem to be the fact that post-communist citizens are *living in* post-communist countries. After all, there are all sorts of appreciable ways in which post-communist countries differ from other countries.
Importantly, some of these ways will themselves be legacies of communism, but some will not.

How might we characterize these differences? To begin with, countries
"assigned" to experience communism—to use the parlance of experimental research design—were not assigned randomly. Soviet communism took
root—or was imposed—in particular geographic areas with particular social and political histories. If these geographic characteristics or historical
patterns of sociopolitical development were driving contemporary attitudes, then the observed differences in post-communist attitudes would
not in any way be a legacy of communism. For example, if attitudes toward
markets were simply a function of the geographic location of a country
(e.g., suppose that the colder the climate, the more likely citizens were to
oppose markets), then differences in attitudes between post-communist citizens and citizens from other countries would simply be due to the fact that
post-communist citizens are *living in* countries that have characteristics—
predating the communist experience—that are associated with opposition
to markets. The actual experience of having been ruled by communists
would be irrelevant; the divergence could be explained simply by the fact
that communists came to power in countries with features that—today—
are associated with a greater antipathy to markets.

Of course, the contours of post-communist societies were not exclusively shaped by factors that predate communist rule: both communist-era
and post-communist developments affect the nature of the countries that
post-communist citizens are *living in* now. At the time of any survey of
post-communist citizens' attitudes, post-communist citizens will be *living
in* countries with particular political institutions, economic conditions,
and sociodemographic characteristics: all these factors could explain divergence in attitudes from citizens living in other countries. After all, there
are already many theoretical arguments to explain why democracy and
markets are more popular among some people than others.[4] Maybe overeducated and underemployed people everywhere are more likely to oppose market economies. Or it may be the case that democracy is less popular

[4] On democracy, for example, see Chu et al. 2008; Duch 1993; Evans and Whitefield
1995; Gibson et al. 1992; Gibson 1995; Kitschelt 1992; Mishler and Rose 1996; Rose and
Mishler 1996; on markets, see Przeworski 1991; Gibson 1996; Stokes 1996; Earle and
Gehlbach 2003; Hayo 2004; Graham and Sukhtankar 2004; and Gabel 2009.

in countries with young, dysfunctional political institutions. And perhaps citizens in countries with poorly performing economies are more likely to turn against both democracy and capitalism. If post-communist countries have a disproportionately high number of overeducated and underemployed citizens, are governed by new and not particularly well-functioning political institutions, and experience greater economic turmoil, then all these characteristics of the society they are currently *living in* could explain why post-communist citizens hold systematically different attitudes toward politics and economics than citizens elsewhere. More generally, we can classify the relevant characteristics of the countries that post-communist citizen are *living in* at the time of the survey as falling into one of three broad categories: the *sociodemographic makeup* of society; *economic conditions*; and *political institutions and outcomes*. Any of these factors could explain why we observe—on average—post-communist citizens holding different attitudes about politics, economics, and social relations than citizens in other parts of the world.

This leads to an important and complicated question: to the extent that factors related to the countries that post-communist citizens are *living in* at the time of the survey could explain divergence in attitudes, would this then represent evidence that *communist legacies* are having an effect on post-communist attitude formation? Technically speaking, any characteristic of society in the post-communist era is a function of varying combinations of *communist-era* and *post-communist-era* developments; everything is therefore both a legacy of communism and a result of post-communism. However, some of these factors—for example, the sociodemographic makeup of society—are clearly more of a communist-era legacy than a feature of post-communist developments, while others—for example, electoral rules—are the opposite; still others—for example, unemployment levels in the 1990s—are probably a function of both communist legacies and post-communist policies. Thus, if our primary explanation for post-communist attitudinal divergence were to come from these contemporaneous indicators of the country post-communist citizens are *living in*, we would have to look very carefully at each relevant factor to assess the extent to which it could be credibly considered a communist legacy.[5]

If, however, we want to capture features of the countries that post-communist citizens are *living in* that are totally independent of post-communist influences, then we need to measure conditions as they were in these countries (and in the countries to which we are comparing them) on the eve of communism's collapse. If, for example, we think that the reason post-communist citizens are supportive of state-provided social welfare

---

[5] As will be discussed very shortly, this does not turn out to be a concern in this book in practice.

is because *communism* resulted in abnormally large spending on social welfare, then we would want to look at the relationship between state spending before communism collapsed and contemporary attitudes. To the extent that attitude divergence among post-communist citizens could be explained by the fact that they are *living in* a country where there was high spending on social welfare in 1989, this would be a strong candidate to be a legacy effect of communism.[6]

To end the suspense quickly, the primary empirical contribution of this book is to show that there is much stronger support for the claim that the attitudes of post-communist citizens toward democracy, markets, and state-provided social welfare are due to *living through* communism than *living in* post-communist countries, and thus these attitudes should be considered at least in part a legacy of communism.[7] This is not to say that conditions on the ground in post-communist countries are never useful for understanding the attitudes of post-communist citizens, but at least in these three issue areas, the incremental leverage from these factors is dwarfed by the effect of *living through* communism.

The empirical evidence to support this claim is motivated by a simple assumption: people who *live through* "more communism" (i.e., live more years of their life under communist rule) should exhibit "more" of (i.e., higher congruence with) the attitudes consistent with communist ideology.[8] This basic idea forms the core of our *living through communism* analysis in this book: an additional year of exposure should be correlated with additional support for the pro-regime attitude (i.e., less support for democracy and markets, and more support for state-provided social welfare and gender equality). However, it is crucial that we estimate the effect of years of exposure to communism independent of the age of respondent at the time she or he is queried about her or his opinions. Clearly, people

[6] The reason we cannot claim that this would definitively be a legacy of communism is that state spending on social welfare in 1989 could itself be a legacy of pre-communist conditions. However, as we will explain in detail in Chapter 3, when we actually test the effect of these "end of communism" variables, we will include pre-communist indicators in our models as control variables. If we could control for every aspect of pre-communism in our analysis, then our end-of-communism variables could be said to be exclusively picking up communist legacies. This is of course impossible in practice, but we do our best to control for as many pre-communist indicators as possible. In addition, as we detail later in this chapter, examining the differential effect of different sets of end-of-communism variables has the added advantage of allowing us to unpack which particular aspects of the communist project were potentially most responsible for the attitudes in question.

[7] Attitudes toward gender equality reveal a much more complex—but no less interesting—story for reasons that we will explain a bit later in this chapter and then in much more detail in Chapters 7 and 8.

[8] Here, less support for democracy, less support for markets, more support for social welfare spending, and more support for gender equality.

with many years of exposure to communism will typically be older than those with few years of exposure to communism, and thus it is necessary to ensure that assessments of the effect of exposure on attitudes are made while controlling for the age of the respondent.[9] This is one of the major advantages of employing large comparative cross-national survey data—crucially including multiple surveys from the same country—in our analyses: such a research design makes it possible to estimate an effect for exposure to communism while controlling for age.[10]

That being said, all exposure is of course not equal, so we also test a series of hypotheses based on the idea that the *intensity of exposure* might vary. Moreover, different people in different contexts might react to this exposure in different ways, so we similarly test a number of hypotheses related to variation in *resistance to exposure*.[11] We allow both *intensity* and *resistance* to be a function of both country-level factors[12] and individual-level factors.[13]

The empirical tests of our *intensity* and *resistance* hypotheses produce nuanced results.[14] On the one hand, for all four attitudes in question, there

[9]We thank Anja Neundorf and Dick Niemi for driving home the importance of this approach at a crucial time in the development of the project.

[10]Our identification strategy for estimating the effect of exposure while controlling for age is laid out in more detail in Section 3.3.3 of Chapter 3 but essentially relies on the fact that with multiple surveys from a given country, we will have examples of respondents with the same years of exposure and different ages, as well as the same age and different years of exposure, across different surveys. Moreover, the total number of years of exposure to communist rule is capped at a level fixed by history (and constant within countries), while age is not theoretically capped at any particular level and certainly varies across individuals even within countries. We can also gain leverage from the fact that communist rule started and ended in slightly different years in different countries even above and beyond the dramatic difference in start dates across East-Central Europe and the non-Baltic former Soviet republics. Note that doing so with a single cross-sectional survey in a single country where everyone had lived their entire life under communist rule would make such a task impossible, as age and exposure would perfectly co-vary if the period of communist rule was long enough.

[11]As explained in great detail in Chapter 3, we test both sets of hypotheses by interacting exposure to communism with the relevant *intensity/resistance* variable.

[12]E.g., in a communist context, was the individual living under a Stalinist regime (*greater intensity*)? Does the individual live in a country with a prior history of democratic rule (*greater resistance*)?

[13]E.g., in a communist context, was the individual educated under communism (*greater intensity*)? Is the individual Catholic (*greater resistance*)?

[14]The theoretical concept of *living through* rule by a particular regime—along with the idea that there can be variation in the *intensity of* and *resistance to* exposure to the regime and its precepts—is intended to be general enough to be applied to the study of the effects of any type of regime that attempts to inculcate a particular view of politics among its citizens. However, for the purpose of this book we introduce a specific set of hypotheses—presented in Chapter 2—to predict both micro- and macro-level factors that affected the *intensity* and *resistance* to Soviet communist regimes specifically (see Table 2.2 in Chapter 2).

are always at least some *intensity* and *resistance* hypotheses for which we find strong empirical support. To put this another way, we always learn more about the drivers of political attitudes by engaging in the exercise of testing our *intensity* and *resistance* hypotheses than if we had stopped simply at testing the average effects of a year of exposure to communist rule. Moreover, in the one opinion area where our generic exposure variable does not seem to work the way in which our *living through communism* model would predict—gender equality—we find a great of deal of empirical support for many of our *intensity* and *resistance* hypotheses. In other words, without the intensity and resistance hypotheses, we would have wrongly dismissed communist exposure as irrelevant to gender equality attitudes.

On the other hand, there is no single particular class of *intensity* or *resistance* hypotheses (e.g., country-level resistance hypotheses) for which we find consistent support across all our hypotheses, nor even a single hypothesis for which there is consistent support across all four opinion areas. This finding, in turn, demonstrates the importance of a rather wide-ranging approach to thinking about these *intensifying* and *resistance* hypotheses. It is not possible, therefore, to simply say "measure exposure and take account of this one particular variable and you will have the whole story." Nevertheless, the effort required to examine a varied set of *intensifying* and *resistance* hypotheses does seem worthwhile, precisely because it provides a richer account how communist exposure affected the attitudes we study in Chapters 4–7. Moreover, we do find a few factors—in particular Catholicism, urban residence, and pre-communist regime type—that have the effect predicted across three of the four issues we examine, although of course this could be a function of the particular issues examined in this book.[15] Perhaps the most striking finding, though, is the fact that even though we examine many different *intensifying and resistance* factors, it is extremely rare that we are able to find subgroups of respondents that are completely unaffected by exposure. Thus we can also

---

[15] We do, however, recognize that our testing of a wide range of *intensifying* and *resistance* hypotheses means that we are devoting a nontrivial amount of space in the book to demonstrate a large number of null results. However, it is now increasingly being recognized that political science has a publication bias in favor of positive results (Franco, Malhotra, and Simonovits 2014; Mullinix et al. 2015; see as well https://www.washingtonpost.com /news/monkey-cage/wp/2016/03/09/does-social-science-have-a-replication-crisis/). Given that we had theoretical reasons to expect to find support for these *intensity/resistance* hypotheses, we felt it was important to include the (many) null findings we encountered along with the positive ones that get more discussion in the text. It is still important, however, to be aware that operationalizing many of these hypotheses was challenging and, ultimately, sometimes resulted in less than optimal measures. So most of these null findings are probably safer interpreted as failing to provide evidence in support of the relevant hypotheses as opposed to definitively proving the null hypothesis.

conceive of these analyses as robustness checks to make sure that our find-ings of exposure effects are not driven solely by particular subsets of our respondents.

In addition, our goal is not so much to establish whether the past mat-ters or not, but rather to show *the way* in which factors that are related to the experience of communist rule in these countries can account for attitudes held in the post-communist era and the extent to which this can be predicted by theory. With this in mind, the primary analysis in each of our four main empirical chapters (Chapters 4–7) provides the empirical tests of whether *living through communism* or *living in a post-communist country* best accounts for post-communist attitudinal divergences. We also examine the *mechanisms* by which *living through communism* accounts for attitude formation through our analysis of *intensifying* and *resistance* hypotheses as the final part of our primary analysis. In addition, we sup-plement these primary analyses with additional, chapter-specific research drawing on other sources of data in an attempt to delve deeper into ad-ditional mechanisms by which these effects are transmitted, but which we cannot observe using our primary data source.

In the remainder of this chapter, we proceed as follows. In the next two sections, we develop more thoroughly the theoretical arguments underly-ing our *living through communism* (Section 1.2) and our *living in post-communist countries* (Section 1.3) approaches to studying regime legacy effects on public opinion. In Section 1.4, we discuss the implications of our choice of attitudes toward democracy, markets, social welfare, and gender equality to form the substantive basis of this book, noting the dimensions on which these issues do—and do not—vary in theoretically interesting ways. We then turn in Section 1.5 to providing a basic overview of the em-pirical strategy employed in the book (which is addressed in much more detail in Chapter 3). In Section 1.6 we lay out a brief summary of the most important substantive findings of the book, which leads to a more general discussion in Section 1.7 of the book's contributions to the literature. We conclude by outlining the remainder of the book in Section 1.8.

1.2. LIVING THROUGH COMMUNISM

Intuitively, the idea that *living through communism* might have an effect on one's attitudes toward politics, economics, and social relationships seems fairly obvious and indeed permeates much of the literature on post-communist politics. As we will discuss throughout this book, actually dem-onstrating that this is the case in a rigorous, falsifiable empirical frame-work is quite challenging. There is also surprisingly little theoretical work on *how* living through one type of authoritarian regime might affect attitudes following the collapse of that regime.[16] Fortunately, there is an extant literature in the study of political behavior in established democracies on the topic of "political socialization" that provides a nice base on which to build such a *living through* approach to the study of regime legacies on attitudes. In the remainder this section, we build on the brief introduction provided in the previous section to flesh out in a bit more detail the general contours of such a *living though* model, including beginning with a brief review of the political socialization literature. For now, though, we limit ourselves to general arguments underlying our *living through* approach; in Chapter 2 we go into much more detail regarding the specific hypotheses we test regarding the effects of *living through communism*.

Like many other aspects of the study of political behavior, the vast majority of the work on political socialization has been conducted in American politics, and this is especially true for the earliest work on the topic (Campbell et al. 1960; see Sapiro 2004 for a review, although see Mishler and Rose 2007). The term has been attached to a rather wide range of topics (Dennis 1968), but the most prominent have been in regard to the ways in which citizens pick up society's "prevailing norms,"[17] the ways in which children learn about politics,[18] and the manner in which parental partisanship is transmitted from parents to their children.[19] Although the last of these topics has come to predominate more recent work in the field in American politics, it is the first of these that is of most use to us in our current endeavor.

More specifically, there are four valuable observations from the existing literature on political socialization that we can use in attempting to craft a general model of how citizens are likely to internalize attitudes that are actively promulgated by a regime:

(1) There is clear evidence that individuals "acquire attitudes, beliefs, and values relating to the political system of which he is a member and to his own role as citizen within that political system" (Greenberg 1973: 3).

(2) This process can occur via multiple agents, some of the most important of which are schools (Dennis 1968; Jennings and Niemi 1968; McDevitt and Chaffee 2002; Campbell 2006).

[16]Although see our own earlier attempts to grapple with this question: Pop-Eleches and Tucker 2011, 2012, 2014.

[17]The term is from Greenstein 1971, but for a similar idea, see Greenberg 1973; Sears 1993; and Sears and Valentino 1997.

[18]Greenstein 1971; Sapiro 2004; and Prior 2010.

[19]Jennings and Niemi 1968; Zuckerman et al. 2007; and Jennings et al. 2009, although see McDevitt and Chaffee 2002, who turn the causal arrows around, arguing that we should be investigating whether parents pick up attitudes from their children, which they study by examining the effect of children's civic education programs at school on the political behavior of their parents.

(3) Socialization clearly varies across subsections of the population (Dennis 1968; Greenstein 1971; Visser and Krosnick 1998; Zuckerman et al. 2007; Eckstein et al. 2013).

(4) There remains an ongoing debate about whether these socialization processes happen primarily during childhood (the "impressionable years" hypothesis) or throughout one's life (the "lifelong openness" or "constant updating" hypothesis), but there is general agreement that the early years of one's life are important (Krosnick and Alwin 1989; Visser and Krosnick 1998; Sears and Valentino 1997; Prior 2010; D. Osborne et al. 2011).

In moving away from the American to the post-communist context, we are struck by the wide number of factors that have been proposed to us as we developed this research agenda as possible candidates to either strengthen or weaken the effect that a given year of living under communist rule might have on the political socialization of an individual. Even in the American context there are a number of these types of factors that have been considered, but from our reading of the literature it seems that most work really focuses only on one or at most two of these factors at a time (e.g., childhood vs. adult exposure, prevalence of political discussion in one's home), and thus the literature has not really had to develop a theoretical framework for thinking systematically about this type of variation. In the post-communist context, however, we not only have communist regimes in different countries; we also have different varieties of communism (e.g., Stalinism vs. reform communism) both within and across countries; individuals who were educated before, during, and after communism; and a wide range of religious traditions that had different relations with the officially atheistic communist state, to identify just a few potential sources of variation.

To avoid either (a) ignoring these many important sources of variation or (b) simply incorporating them into our analysis in a haphazard manner, we turn to the somewhat unlikely analogy of the causes of sunburn to motivate the *living through communism* model.[20] Surely, no one is going to develop sunburn without being exposed to the sun, and, correspondingly, we would expect the likelihood of doing so to increase as one spends more time in the sun. However, each additional hour of exposure to the sun is likely to have a larger effect on one's likelihood of developing sunburn if the exposure in question is to a blazing hot sun on a cloudless summer day than if it occurs on a hazy day during the fall late in the afternoon.[21] Similarly, we would expect for any given intensity of sunlight,

[20] We set aside the normative implications of conceiving of living through communism as being analogous to suffering from sunburn.

[21] We might also expect sunburn to be more severe over time as the levels of ozone in the atmosphere are depleted (Abarca et al. 2002).

each additional hour of exposure to have a greater effect on the likelihood of developing sunburn for an individual covered in tanning oil than an individual covered in sunscreen.[22] Thus we have a primary factor that predicts the likelihood of any given individual developing sunburn, *temporal exposure* to the stimuli (e.g., hours out in the sun), as well as two factors that can moderate the effect of that primary factor: the *intensity* or *strength* of that exposure (e.g., how strong the sunlight is); and *resistance* to that exposure (e.g., how much sunscreen a person is wearing).

The idea behind our *living through communism* model is simply to transfer this framework to exposure to the "message" of any given regime—like a Soviet communist regime—that is interested in actively transmitting a set of attitudes to its citizens. So instead of hours of sunlight, the *temporal exposure* is the time spent living under the rule of that regime.[23] Our simplest hypotheses will therefore be that each additional year of exposure to communist rule will increase the likelihood of the individual coming to hold the attitude that the regime wants to promote among its citizens, that is, that the "socialization" of the population by the regime will be successful.

However, much like exposure to sunlight, we are well aware that the *intensity* of any given individual's exposure to the regime's socialization efforts will vary. Crucially, our *living through* model allows for the fact that factors that *intensify exposure*—we will also use the term *strengthen exposure* interchangeably—can vary at both the country level and at the individual level. So some factors will intensify exposure for everyone living in a given country at a given time, whereas other factors will affect the intensity of exposure at the individual level.[24] In Chapter 2 we will provide specific hypotheses as to the types of factors that are germane for communist regimes, but for now consider just two examples to illustrate these different categories. At the *country level*, we might expect a state dominated by true believers in a regime's ideological vision (e.g., Stalinist communist regimes) to deliver a stronger dose of regime propaganda to its citizens than a state dominated by technocrats and careerists (e.g., post-totalitarian communist regimes [Linz and Stepan 1996]).[25] At the *individual level*, we might expect people who attended secondary school under communism to

[22] Or, interestingly enough, an individual drinking red wine regularly; see Matito et al. 2011; and http://www.cbsnews.com/8301-504763_162-20086913-10391704.html.

[23] For ease in interpretation and measurement, we will operationalize this concept as the number of years spent living under a communist regime, although one could of course use alternative measures of time.

[24] To be clear, this is what we mean by a "country-level" factor: something that affects equally everyone living in a given country at a given time. Technically, we probably should call this a "country-year" level factor (although quite a few of these country-level variables are invariant to time), but for simplicity's sake we will simply call it a country-level factor.

[25] This is not meant to question the strength of conviction of reformers in the potential of reform communism, but rather only to order communist regime types from more "extreme"

have gotten a stronger version of the regime's message than people who either attended secondary school before or after communist rule, or who dropped out of school before completing their secondary education. So in these cases, we would expect each year of *temporal exposure* to the regime to have a *larger* effect on developing the pro-regime attitude. To put this in the language of statistics, these are variables that we would expect to have a positive interaction with exposure in terms of holding the regime-endorsed attitude.

At the same time, there are other factors that we might expect—much like sunscreen—could increase an individual's *resistance* to regime socialization, regardless of the *intensity* of the exposure. So for example, at the *country level* Darden and Grzymała-Busse (2006) have argued that people who lived in countries where literacy was higher in the pre-communist era were more likely to have been raised on stories of national myths, and thus more likely to be able to resist communist indoctrination because of recourse to these nationalist stories. At the *individual level*, we might expect Catholics—who had access to a community and a set of organizations that were often hostile to communist regimes—to have had an additional buffer between themselves and the state, and therefore additional exposure to the regime's message would have correspondingly less influence on Catholics (Grzymała-Busse 2015; Wittenberg 2006). Alternatively, it could be the case that Catholicism increases individual-level resistance through a social identity mechanism, i.e., Catholics see "people like me" as skeptical of communism.[26] To reiterate, the point of this argument is not that people from more literate pre-communist countries or Catholics were necessarily going to be more opposed to the ideals underlying the Soviet communist project (although that would not be inconsistent with the model), but only that a given additional year of exposure to communism might have less of an effect on these people than on others, that is, that their *resistance* would be higher.

To be clear, these are only a few examples of the types of individual-level and country-level factors that we expect could affect the *intensity* of the regime message received by citizens and their likely *resistance* to that message. Most hypotheses within this framework of course need to be developed taking account of the peculiar features of actual regimes. Therefore, we devote a large part of Chapter 2 to fleshing out a *living through*

---

models to more moderate versions in their adherence to communist ideological principles (such as repudiating markets).

[26] For more on these types of "people like me" arguments related in particular to partisanship, see Green et al. 2002; and Achen and Bartels 2016. It is interesting to think about how social identities could be related to our concept of *resistance hypotheses*, which are largely about how individuals react to regime messages, but less so to our *intensity hypotheses*, which are more related to the strength of the message sent by the regime.

communism model that specifically identifies factors that we expect to enhance the effect of exposure to *communism* and increase resistance to *communist* socialization attempts; for a concise summary of these hypotheses, see in particular Section 2.3 and Table 2.2.

However, there are two individual-level variables that have received a great deal of attention in the literature and that are not necessarily context dependent. The first is age of exposure. There is a school of thought that suggests children are much more likely to be susceptible to political socialization than adults, although others have suggested that this is a lifelong process (Krosnick and Alwin 1989; Visser and Krosnick 1998; Sears and Valentino 1997; Mishler and Rose 2007; D. Osborne et al. 2011).[27] If we accept the premise that adults are more resistant to communist socialization, then we should expect to find that only living one's early formative years under communist rule would be related to the adoption of the attitudes associated with the communist paradigm (or at least that subsequent socialization effects would be much weaker). If the lifelong socialization model holds, we should see similar effects for years spent living under a communist regime throughout one's life. Of course, it is also possible that communist socialization—unlike the more commonly studied forms of political socialization in democratic regimes—has an effect on adults but not on children. This would fly in the face of a lot of what is assumed about the effect of communist schooling (Rosen 1964), but might be consistent with a view of the world where it is only as an adult that the incentives of adopting the groupthink pushed by an authoritarian (or especially a totalitarian) regime become apparent.[28]

Closely related is the topic of parental socialization, or the idea that children will take on the political opinions of their parents (Jennings and Niemi 1968; Beck and Jennings 1991; Achen 2002). However, it is important to note that parental socialization effects could cut in both directions depending on the attitudes of the parents toward the regime. Thus children of parents who were strongly supportive of communist rule might be more likely to adopt attitudes in line with communist ideology. But at the same time, children of parents who were long-term opponents of communist

---

[27]Interestingly, the only one of these works that focuses on a post-communist country (Mishler and Rose 2007, analyzing data from Russia) not only emphasizes the possibility of lifelong socialization but actually finds strong affects for what they call "adult relearning" in the post-communist context.

[28]As we discuss in more detail below in Section 1.6 and in Chapter 9, we actually find more evidence in favor of an adult exposure effect than a childhood exposure effect! Only in the case of gender equality do find an effect for child but not adult exposure. In the other three issue areas, there is a much larger effect for adult socialization; this is most extreme in the case of attitudes toward democracy, where there is apparently no effect for childhood exposure. See as well Mishler and Rose (2007).

rule could be expected to do exactly the opposite. Thus in the language of this book, we could expect parental socialization either to function as an *intensifier* of or to provide *resistance* to communist exposure, conditional on the political proclivities of the parents. In pragmatic terms, this means that an analysis of the effect of parental socialization as a moderator of communist exposure requires data that allows an estimate of the pro- or anti-communist nature of a respondent's parents. Unfortunately, this is not possible for our primary analyses because of the limitations of our data, but it is a topic to which we turn in the supplementary analysis in multiple chapters.

Taken together, all these *intensifying* and *resistance* variables can be thought of in two ways. First, they are potential modifiers of the effect of a year of exposure to communist rule on attitude formation. If we accept the notion that a year of communist exposure does not have the same effect on all individuals in all countries and at all time periods, then we need these *intensifying* and *resistance* variables (and the related hypotheses laid out in Chapter 2, Section 2.3) in order to better specify our *living through communism* model. However, there is another way to think about these variables, which is as a first step to better understanding the *mechanisms* by which exposure to communism translates into attitude formation. For example, if we find that youth exposure, communist schooling, and parental socialization (from pro-communist parents) all increase the impact of communist exposure on pro-regime attitudes, then it would suggest that the mechanism by which this occurs flows through traditional methods of political socialization such as schools and family life at a young age. If on the other hand the most important factors turn out to be pre-communist regime type, development, and literacy, then it would suggest that pre-communist conditions were paramount for conditioning the impact of exposure to communist rule. Alternatively, if we find that factors such as urban residence, being a male, Communist Party membership, and communist education predominate, then it might suggest that exposure to communist propaganda is an important mechanism for picking up pro-regime attitudes.

1.3 LIVING IN POST-COMMUNIST COUNTRIES

There are of course a wide variety of factors that could explain why opinions held by post-communist citizens on politics and economics appear to diverge from those held by people in other parts of the world that have nothing to do with the experience of having lived through communism. Collectively, we refer to these explanations as flowing from the fact that the people whose opinions are being surveyed are *living in post-communist countries.* Post-communist countries—like any collection of countries with some degree of commonality among them—will differ from other countries in appreciable ways.[29] Certainly it is possible that these characteristics could explain why citizens hold different opinions on politics, economics, and social relations.

As was already discussed previously in Section 1.1 of this chapter, the first place we want to look for potential distinguishing characteristics of post-communist countries is in the types of countries in which communist regimes came to power. In other words, the first test of the *living in* post-communist countries model will be to see if *pre-communist* conditions can explain why post-communist citizens hold different attitudes than people in other parts of the world. Setting aside the thorny question of the mechanism by which attitudes might be transmitted across generations, there are a number of features of pre-communist societies that we might expect to be correlated with attitudes in the post-communist era. In particular, levels of socio-economic development (e.g., wealth, literacy, urbanization), cultural history (e.g., religious tradition, imperial/colonization history), and prior regime type all would seem to be important factors (Bunce 2005; Bădescu and Sum 2005). Recent literature in both political science and economics has pointed as well to the role of geography (e.g., distance from the equator, being landlocked) in influencing long-run developments in both economics and politics (Sachs and Warner 1997; Hall and Jones 1999; Acemoglu et al. 2001; Easterly and Levine 2003; Collier and Hoeffler 2003; Rigobon and Rodrik 2005).

In addition to the strong theoretical rationale for including pre-communist conditions in our study, accounting for these factors in our analyses has two additional empirical advantages. First, as we go on to analyze all the other variables in our models that occur after the imposition of communist regimes (i.e., contemporaneous conditions, end-of-communism conditions, and exposure to communism), we can do so with greater confidence that our findings do not suffer from omitted variable bias. But perhaps even more importantly from the perspective of this book, looking at the correlation between attitudes and pre-communist conditions provides us with one completely clean test that could supply evidence that contemporary divergence in attitudes between post-communist citizens and citizens from other parts of the world are *not* a function of communist-era legacies. While obviously the quality of data from that far in the past makes this a difficult test, it is an important part of our empirical effort.

---

[29] We take up the question of why we focus on *post-communist* countries as opposed to a different collection of countries at the start of Chapter 2.

Of course, the most obvious candidates for demonstrating that the divergent attitudes of post-communist citizens are due to *living in post-communist countries* are the conditions on the ground at the time attitudes are being surveyed. Perhaps the simplest way this could occur would be if people's preferences, evaluations, and political behavior were a function of their *sociodemographic characteristics* and if post-communist countries had different sociodemographic makeups than other countries. Consider the following highly stylized example. Imagine a world with three income categories (high, medium, and low) and three education categories (post-secondary, secondary, and less than secondary). If all political preferences were a direct function of income and education, then we would expect societies with similar distributions of education and income to have similar distributions of political preferences. Now imagine that preferences for extreme forms of redistribution were largely concentrated among those with high levels of education and low incomes. If in Country A, which is non-communist, there are very few highly educated poor people (either because there are few poor people, or few highly educated people or because income is very highly correlated with education), then that country would have a very small proportion of the population supporting extreme forms of income redistribution. In contrast, if in Country B, which is post-communist, income was unrelated to education or if both poverty and higher education were both very prevalent, then we might find a much larger proportion of the population supporting extreme forms of income redistribution. This would hold despite the fact that in both countries, *individual preferences were generated in exactly the same manner* (and thus had nothing to do with *living through* communism): as a function of income and education. Thus, despite identical processes of individual preference formation, the aggregate nature of preferences across the whole society would be different, and we would find higher support for extreme redistribution in the post-communist country.

Moving beyond sociodemographic characteristics, we might also expect attitudes to be a function of *current economic conditions* (Mishler and Rose 1994, 1997, 2001; Tucker et al. 2002; Mason 1995). Consider again a highly stylized world, only now it is one in which one embraces markets as long as one's real disposable income has gone up in the past 12 months; conversely, if real disposable income has declined in the past 12 months, one is skeptical of markets. Now let us assume that in non-post-communist countries in the 1990s, at any given time 50% of citizens had incomes that were going up, while the remaining 50% had incomes that were going down. However, let us assume—not completely unrealistically—that post-communist economic transitions (Przeworski 1991; Svejnar 2000; Gould 2011) resulted in only 20% of the population of post-communist countries enjoying rising incomes, with 80% suffering from

falling incomes, in the same time period. Were we then to observe preferences for market versus state-run economies, we would find that citizens
in post-communist countries were much more likely to be skeptical of
markets (Pop-Eleches and Tucker 2014). This would again be the case
despite the fact that in all countries the determinants of attitudes toward
markets were identical (i.e., solely determined by change in income).

Similarly to the economic conditions argument, we might expect citizens' political views to be a function of the political and economic institutions with which they interact in the political world. Again, let us
consider a highly stylized example. Imagine that support for democracy
was simply a function of whether one lived under a parliamentary form
of government or presidential form of government. Let us suppose that in
the former case, the average citizen supports democracy "a lot" (imagine
this as a 4 on a 5-point scale), while the average citizen living in a presidential regimes supports democracy only "a little" (say 2 on a scale from
1 to 5). If the rest of the non-post-communist world is evenly split between presidential and parliamentary systems of government but the post-
communist world is made up exclusively of countries with presidential
systems of government,[30] then the data would reveal that the average post-
communist citizen supports democracy a little (say 2 on our 1–5 scale)
whereas the average citizen in the rest of the world supports democracy
somewhat (say 3 on our 1–5 scale). The key point from our perspective
is that this finding would have nothing to do with the fact that post-
communist citizens are somewhat less trusting of political parties because
of decades of single-party rule; instead, it would be a function solely of the
fact that post-communist countries have exclusively presidential systems
of government.[31]

As we noted earlier in this chapter in Section 1.1, assessing the extent to
which any of these contemporaneous characteristics—sociodemographic
characteristics, economic conditions, and political and economic institutions—are legacies of communism will require careful attention to the
particular variable in question. This is because once we get into the post-
communist era, any condition measured at that point in time will have at
least the potential of being in part a legacy of communism and in part
a function of post-communism. Take unemployment rates in the 1990s,
for example. The fact that many post-communist countries suffered from
high levels of unemployment in the 1990s was undoubtedly in part due to

[30] This is, of course, not the case in the real world, where plenty of post-communist
countries have parliamentary systems of government.

[31] Astute readers will notice that we have not provided a list of specific variables that
we will use in any of these categories. In order not to interrupt the flow of this introductory theory chapter, we have elected to hold off the discussion of individual variables until
Chapter 3, where we address data, models, and methods.

decades of decisions about how to organize the economy under communist rule, but at the same time variation in unemployment across countries and over time would certainly have been affected by decisions made by *post-communist* governments (Tucker 2006; Frye 2002; Hellman 1998; Przeworski 1991). Each variable (or set of variables) that was found to play an important role in explaining divergence in attitudes would therefore need to be assessed in a similar manner before one evaluated the extent to which it represented empirical evidence of a legacy effect. Thus to be clear, any variable measuring conditions at the time of a survey in the post-communist period could help explain post-communist citizens' attitudes without necessarily being a legacy of communism. Thus the legacy status of that variable hinges on the extent to which the variable in question was affected by communist-era versus post-communist-era developments. Of course, this question is relevant only following a statistical assessment of whether the variable did indeed help to explain attitudinal divergence in the first place.

As noted previously, if we want to assess the effect of variables that clearly do *not* reflect any post-communist influences, then we need to measure conditions at the *end of the communist era* and before the advent of post-communism. To the extent that we are thorough in controlling for *pre-communist* context, then our measure of the *end of communism* context should be a reasonably good proxy for developments under communism.

Moreover, as long as we focus on factors that are distinctly linked to the communist experience,[32] then examining the relative impact of *end of communism* variables on our dependent variables is a way of "unpacking" communism to see what exactly it was about communism that left behind a legacy. Was it the fact that communist governments were leftist or authoritarian? Or perhaps that communist countries were highly industrialized, had large state sectors, or had (relatively) lower levels of economic inequality? To address this question systematically, we will consider three sets of factors related to the communist experiences: developmental legacies of communism;[33] communism's redistributive/economic egalitarian policies;[34] and the authoritarian/leftist political character of communist regimes.[35]

---

[32] E.g., examining rainfall in 1989 makes little sense in this regard; examining industrialization, however, does.

[33] We include in this category urbanization, industrialization, expansion of primary education, efforts at expanding literacy, and economic development (see Table 3.1 in Chapter 3).

[34] We consider social welfare spending, size of the state sector, and income inequality (Gini coefficients) (see Table 3.1 in Chapter 3).

[35] In our analysis, we examine government left-right orientation and degree of authoritarianism both individually and interactively (see Table 3.1 in Chapter 3).

1.4. DEMOCRACY, MARKETS, SOCIAL WELFARE, AND GENDER EQUALITY

Of course, if we wish to examine the effect of communist-era legacies on post-communist attitudes, we need to choose actual attitudes to examine. Even to explore four sets of attitudes thoroughly has required us to write a fairly long book, so we had to consider our choice of issues carefully. Ultimately, our goal was to examine the most important potential communist-era legacies in the realm of public opinion: democracy, markets, social welfare, and social relations (for which we explore attitudes toward gender equality). Thus, we chose these topics because of their relevance to communist ideology, not because we were aiming to maximize variation on a particular characteristic of the issues that would allow us to test hypotheses regarding cross-issue variation. That being said, by exploring overtly political, economic, and social topics we are tapping into some of the most important areas of the study of public opinion formation generally.[36]

However, it is still useful to classify the issues we did choose to examine along theoretically relevant dimensions. Further, we can then use these classifications both to inform some of our expectations of variation in empirical findings across issues and to structure our interpretation of our findings. The three classifications we will consider are *centrality* to communist ideology (on which there is some variation, even though we "oversample" issues that score high on this dimension), divergence between *rhetoric and reality* in terms of on-the-ground implementation of relevant ideological tenets, and *popularity* of the issue among the populace. As we will go into greater detail on each of our four issue areas—democracy, markets, social welfare, and gender equality—in the following chapter, for now we limit ourselves to laying out how we see these issues varying along these three dimensions, along with a very brief discussion of the implications this holds for our remaining analyses.[37]

Table 1.1 lays out how we classify our four issues—democracy, markets, social welfare, and gender equality—along these dimensions. A few quick words of explanation are in order. First, despite the eventual popu-

---

[36] The one potentially "central" area of communist ideology this leaves out is the foreign policy dimension, which does not translate nearly as easily into a clear "legacy" position as the other four issues examined in this book. While "anti-Western" or "anti-American" attitudes could be an interesting subject for legacy analysis in future research, there was nothing inherent about communist doctrine that foretold an anti-Western foreign policy would emerge (given that Marx expected communist revolutions to start in the West).

[37] To be clear, as we are not using these categories for any actual hypothesis testing, these categorizations are simply loose approximations of how we think the issues differ along these dimensions, and thus should not be interpreted as a result of any sort of rigorous coding scheme.

Table 1.1. Classifying Issue Areas

	Ideological centrality	Match between reality and rhetoric?	Popularity
Democracy	High	High	Low
Markets	High	Medium-high	Uneven
Social welfare	Medium	Medium-high	High
Gender equality	Low	Medium-low	Uneven

larity and importance of social welfare spending in the post-totalitarian communist regimes, social welfare provision was not originally a central tenet of communist revolutionary doctrine but was gradually added—based at least in part on non-communist welfare state models—and over time became one of the more popular aspects of communist rule (Cook 1993; Hoffman 2011; Lipsmeyer 2003). Second, the classification of "reality matches rhetoric" for democracy is especially complicated, because—as we detail in Chapter 4—Soviet communist regimes often referred to themselves as "democratic"; the ultimate example here is the German Democratic Republic. To the extent that we interpret democracy from a Western liberal democratic perspective, though, there was a very strong congruence between the regime's rhetoric of opposition to democracy and the reality of no multiparty democracy. Accordingly, we have also coded the "popularity" of communist opposition to multiparty democracy as low on the grounds that so many of the efforts to fight back against—and eventually overthrow—communist rule were focused on efforts to increase political pluralism and, eventually, institute multiparty elections, but we realize that this may have varied quite a bit across the post-Soviet space. Markets are listed as "medium-high" congruence between rhetoric and reality because this varied substantially by country, although, as we detail in Chapters 2 and 5, even at their most open communist countries had much more extensive state control over of the economy than elsewhere. Moreover, as we discuss in Chapter 7, while in most cases communist regimes did not match their pro–gender equality rhetoric with consistent real-world action, there were important exceptions with respect to employment and, especially, schools. We also note that we have marked the popularity of gender equality as uneven to reflect the fact that while there were likely small portions of the population who felt this to be an important issue (especially among educated women), there were other portions of the population that were undoubtedly hostile to this idea.

Most importantly, though, readers should note that gender equality is distinguished from the other three issues along two of the three of the dimensions that we have highlighted: it was less central to communist ideology and has a greater gap between rhetoric and reality.[38] This leads to two important takeaway points. First, it should perhaps not be that surprising that we find different results when looking at attitudes toward gender equality than we do when analyzing the other three issue areas. Second, when we do find different results for gender equality, we do not have the research design in place to really disentangle whether this is due to its lack of centrality in communist ideology or because of the gap between rhetoric and reality in the actual development of gender equality. While this would be an excellent subject for future research—teasing out the relative importance of centrality, rhetoric versus reality, and popularity on the likelihood of an issue areas exhibiting signs of a legacy effect—our current study was not designed with this goal in mind.[39]

We leave thorough explanations of how to conceptualize and measure these four concepts—attitudes toward democracy, markets, social welfare, and gender equality—to the particular empirical chapters in which each is featured (Chapter 4–7, respectively). But with these four issue areas in hand, we can now turn to introducing our basic empirical strategy to examine the effect of communist-era legacies on public opinion in these areas in post-communist countries.

1.5. EMPIRICAL STRATEGIES

In this section we briefly lay out the empirical strategy we follow for answering the questions we have laid out above. This section is intended only to introduce readers to our general empirical approach; the entire purpose of Chapter 3 is to go into our methodological approach in much greater detail.

---

[38] The likely popularity of gender equality under communism relative to the other three issue areas is a bit more complicated. On the one hand, in Table 1.1, it is somewhat in the middle of the pack as "uneven" in terms of popularity. On the other hand, there are good reasons to suspect that (a) popularity is heterogeneously distributed and (b) we could probably make some pretty good predictions about subpopulations that are more and less likely to support gender equality. For more, see the discussion in Section 7.1 of Chapter 7.

[39] To reiterate, the issues areas were chosen largely because of centrality to communist ideology, and thus not to provide variation across levels of centrality, let alone the other categories. A research design that sought to disentangle the effects of centrality, gaps between rhetoric and reality, and popularity would seek to ensure both variation within these categories across cases, but also variation in combinations of the three sets of classifications across cases. This sort of study would require many more types of attitudes than we had space for in this book given the level of detail into which we decided to go for each issue area. It might be an interesting area for future research with a different sort of research design, but we would not be surprised if it was difficult to find appropriate questions for testing less central tenets of communist ideology on *existing* cross-national surveys; as it was, it was difficult for us to find enough questions in all cases to test the highly central issues we do test in this book.

1.5.1. Inter-regional Comparisons

In order to identify distinctive patterns of post-communist political attitudes, we use comparative survey data from both the post-communist world and, crucially, countries from outside of the post-communist world. Only by looking at the attitude or behavior in question both outside and inside the set of post-communist countries can we in fact determine whether there is a post-communist "difference" to be explained. The simplest and most direct way of doing so is to measure a quantity of interest in post-communist countries, measure the same quantity of interest in other countries, and then establish whether there is a statistically and substantively significant difference across the two.[40] So for example, if one wants to claim that there are lower levels of support for democracy in post-communist countries, then a first step would be to find a comparative survey project that measures levels of support for democracy cross-nationally—such as the World Values Survey, which we use here—then calculate the mean level of democratic support in post-communist countries, calculate the same values outside of the post-communist countries, and then compare the two.

In practice, rather than comparing the difference of means, we will run a multiple regression model with a *post-communist dummy variable* that uniquely identifies respondents who are being surveyed in post-communist countries. Our simplest models include only this dummy variable (plus control variables for the year of the survey) in order to establish that post-communist citizens indeed hold different attitudes; these are the models from which Figure 1.1 at the beginning of this chapter was derived. To test our *living in post-communist countries* models, we will then systematically add our pre-communist, contemporaneous (demographic, economic, and political), and unpacking communism variables to the model, in each case testing to see how the size and significance of the post-communist dummy variable is affected. To the extent that adding these variables reduces the size of the coefficient on the post-communist dummy variable, we can conclude the relevant *living in post-communist countries* variables are related to the post-communist attitudinal divergence. If it does not, we can dismiss that particular set of variables as being a potential source of the variation in attitudes between citizens of post-communist countries and citizens elsewhere. We also use this framework for initial exploration of our *living through* communism model by adding years of exposure to the analysis.[41]

[40] For the moment, we set aside the question of the appropriate reference group of "other countries"; depending on the question, it could include all other countries in the world, advanced industrialized democracies, other European countries, other new democracies, non-democracies, etc. This point is addressed in much greater detail in Chapter 3.

[41] To reiterate, this is only the briefest of summaries of the methodological approach, and there are a myriad of other factors at work here as well; we explain all of these in great details in Chapter 3; see especially Section 3.3.

1.5.2. Intra-regional Comparisons

For testing the *living through* communism model, we will also leverage variation *within* post-communist countries. These types of analyses will be most useful when we are interested in understanding the effect of variables that are hypothesized to increase either the *intensity* of or *resistance* to exposure to communism. There are both theoretical and methodological reasons for limiting these analyses to post-communist countries. We explain these in detail in Chapter 3, but the most intuitive explanation here is that many of our variables here make no sense outside of the post-communist context (e.g., how could you code a non-post-communist country in terms of whether communism was imposed from outside or came about as a result of homegrown movements?).

1.5.3. Intra-country Comparisons

All the previously described analyses will involve the pooling of survey data across multiple countries. While such a research design is justified by the fact that we need to compare the attitudes and behavior of ex-communist citizens to their counterparts in non-communist countries (as well as comparing attitudes and behavior across post-communist countries), such analyses will nevertheless raise concerns about the comparability of survey questions given cross-national cultural and linguistic differences in the absence of anchoring vignettes (King et al. 2003).

However, history has provided us with an interesting opportunity in this regard. The reunification of Germany in 1990 offers a methodological solution to this problem, because it allows us to compare the patterns of attitudes and behavior among East and West Germans, who share a common language and culture but of course differ in their exposure to communism. Since the two countries have had very similar—and in many cases identical—political institutions, such a comparison has the additional advantage of reducing the potential for omitted variable bias that may affect cross-country regressions. While demographic and developmental differences of course persist between West and East Germany, these are arguably captured by individual characteristics, such as household income, for which we can often control in our analyses. Thus, reunified Germany offers another opportunity to explore our hypotheses, only this time in a context that does not require cross-country analysis.[42]

---

[42] In certain limited instances, we may also be able to get similar within country leverage from analyses of Ukraine and Belarus, both of which include Western regions which were only incorporated into the Soviet Union after World War II and thus their inhabitants had shorter exposures to communism than their compatriots from the East. We do not take

1.5.4. Over-Time Comparisons

While our primary empirical analyses involve pooling all our empirical data and controlling for the year of the survey (see Chapter 3, Section 3.3 for details), there are other interesting questions to be asked about the temporal evolution of differences in post-communist attitudes, as well as regarding the relative importance of cohort effects. What is the half-life of communist attitudinal legacies and to what extent does it differ across different types of attitudes? To the extent that "normalization" (i.e., attitudinal convergence between citizens of post-communist and non-communist countries) occurs, is it the result of attitudinal changes in age cohorts that personally experienced communism, or is it largely driven by the generational replacement of communist with post-communist cohorts? With these questions in mind, we also provide over-time analysis that allows us to examine these effects in more detail; see Chapter 8 for details.

1.5.5. Data

We rely on a number different data sources for our analysis, all of which are explained in detail in Chapter 3 (see Section 3.4). These include two large cross-national survey data sets—the World Values Survey (WVS) and the European Bank for Recovery and Development's Life in Transition Societies (LiTS) surveys—as well two single-country panel studies: the Hungarian Household Panel Survey and the Political Attitudes, Political Participation and Electoral Behavior in Germany Panel Study (hereafter German Election Panel Study). For the cross-national surveys, we then supplement the survey data with our own original collection of country-level and country-year-level aggregate variables that measure pre-communist conditions, end of communist-conditions, and contemporaneous demographic, economic, and political conditions at the time of surveys.[43]

1.6. SUMMARY OF KEY FINDINGS

What do we learn from this enterprise? Many, many things of course (i.e., you should continue on to read the rest of the book!), but for now let us highlight five key overall conclusions. First and foremost, *living through*

---

advantage of such opportunities in this book but simply wanted to highlight them here as a potential source for future research (e.g., see Peisakhin 2015).

[43] To be clear, while the overall collection of aggregate-level data is novel, we of course draw on a wide-range of sources to put this collection together, all of which will be documented in a supplemental online codebook. See Table 3.1 and the online codebook for details.

communism does a much better job of accounting for the attitudinal divergence of post-communist citizens than *living in* post-communist countries. At least one of us began this project with a strong predisposition toward thinking that *living in* post-communist countries—and especially economic conditions in those countries—would very likely explain away the attitudinal differences between citizens in post-communist countries and citizens in the rest of the world. However, after years of gathering data to try to make our *living in* models as thorough as possible, we simply cannot come to this conclusion: no matter what we add to these models, the differences do not go away. This is not to say that taking account of the fact that our post-communist respondents are *living in* post-communist countries does not explain away some of the differences in attitudes: in every chapter, there is always at least one battery of variables that does reduce the size of the difference substantially. That being said, the difference never disappears, and, moreover, in three chapters we find that when we use our fully saturated *living in* a post-communist country model (pre-communist conditions, and contemporary demographic, economic, and political variables), the gap in attitudes is always larger than when we started with just a simple bivariate model not taking account of any of the differences. Moreover, we can always reproduce a similar effect in just the German case.

Closely related, we find that the theoretical concepts of *intensity of* and *resistance to* exposure in our *living through* communism model are indeed a useful vehicle for capturing the reality that not all years of exposure to communism were created equally. As noted earlier, it is not the case that all the hypotheses we tested using this framework are supported empirically. Still, we do find a number of hypotheses that are supported by the data, and far more than we would expect to find by chance alone. Moreover, we also find a few that are consistently supported by the data across multiple chapters (e.g., the effects of late-communist growth, being a Catholic, living in an urban residence) and some that are largely not supported by the data (e.g., late-communist liberalization, having had a native communist regime, having only a primary education).

Third, something very different is going on in the case of attitudes toward gender equality than for attitudes toward democracy, markets, and social welfare. Not only is there *not* a post-communist gender equality surplus, but to the extent that we do find differences in post-communist attitudes, they are actually in the opposite direction from what we would have expected: post-communist citizens are *less* supportive of gender equality. By contrast, we do find what we would expect from a regime legacy perspective in the case of attitudes toward democracy, markets, and social welfare, with post-communist citizens having consistently less supportive views of the first two and more supportive views of the last.

Our fourth major finding may be of particular interest to behavior scholars who have previously worked on the question of adult versus childhood socialization. As noted previously, the major fault line in this academic debate revolves around the question of whether socialization occurs *only* during *childhood* or whether it continues on throughout one's lifetime; we are not aware of academic work claiming that socialization occurs only in adulthood. Our findings, however, suggest that something different might be going on in non-democratic contexts, perhaps because success in one's adult life might be more dependent on adopting regime values. More specifically, we find that adult exposure has the predicted effect on attitudes toward democracy, markets, and social welfare, while the effect of childhood exposure is nonexistent in the case of democracy, and only half the size of the adult effect in the case of attitudes toward markets and social welfare (with the last effect being only marginally significant as well). Interestingly, it is only in the case of attitudes toward gender equality that we find an effect for child socialization and not adult socialization. This actually fits nicely with the idea that the "rhetoric but not reality" of gender equality was reflected in not finding a pro–gender equality bias among post-communist citizens: arguably it was only in the schools that the reality of gender equality was present alongside the rhetoric.

Finally, when analyzing the temporal evolution of post-communist attitudes, the patterns we encounter are remarkably heterogeneous. Thus, at one extreme, we observe a large and virtually unchanged post-communist bias for social welfare, which even extends to cohorts with minimal personal communist exposure and suggests strong cross-generational transmission mechanisms. At the other extreme, views on gender equality converged rather quickly after the first few transition years. Perhaps the most interesting pattern was with respect to democracy and market support, where the early transition years witnessed a significant worsening of the post-communist distrust toward democracy and capitalism (driven primarily by cohorts with extensive communist exposure) followed by a gradual convergence after 2000.[44]

1.7. CONTRIBUTIONS OF THE BOOK

Why study the effect of communist-era legacies on the attitudes of post-communist citizens? First, we believe it helps us understand the nature of post-communist politics better. Originally, the collapse of communism led observers to suggest that the region would be a tabula rasa on which new

---

[44] See Chapter 8 for analysis of over-time trends.

institutions could be painted and politics and economics would be accordingly reshaped.[45] Since that time, however, study after study has demonstrated the fact that we cannot hope to understand post-communist politics without first taking account of what was left behind by communism.[46] However, most of this literature has focused on how the communist past has shaped either institutions (e.g., post-communist party systems) or the interests and choices of political elites. By comparison, the role of communist legacies in shaping political attitudes and behavior of citizens, which are the main focus of the present study, has received much less attention.[47]

And while the topic of legacies generally has attracted quite a bit of attention among scholars of post-communist politics (Bernhard 1993; Haerpfer and Rose 1997; Stan and Turcescu 2000; Kopstein and Reilly 2000; Kurtz and Barnes 2002; Neundorf 2010), surprisingly little of this work has explicitly compared results in post-communist countries with results in other parts of the world.[48] Thus we hope that our work can provide another model for how to think about the study of legacies: that there are questions that are best answered by inter-regional comparisons either alone or in conjunction with intra-regional comparisons. In this book, we try to be very precise about the values of both approaches and the types of questions to which they ought best to be applied.

Beyond post-communist politics, however, the question of how the experience of living under one form of political regime affects attitudes held by those citizens after regime change is an important general topic. In political science, studies of the effects of the past on the present have been largely focused on the evolution of institutions (Thelen 1999; Pierson and Skocpol 2002; Acemoglu, Johnson, and Robinson 2001, 2002); until re-

---

[45] See, e.g., Di Palma 1990; Karl and Schmitter 1991. While taking Leninist legacies seriously, Geddes (1997) also argues that post-communist political attitudes were shaped decisively by newly constructed political institutions.

[46] Although undoubtedly an incomplete list, see, e.g., Jowitt 1992; Crawford and Lijphart 1997; Fish 1998; Bunce 1999; Kitschelt et al. 1999; Grzymała-Busse 2002, 2007; Bunce 2003; Ekiert and Hanson 2003; Kopstein 2003; Vachudova 2005; Tucker 2006; Wittenberg 2006; Pop-Eleches 1999, 2007; Kitschelt and Bustikova 2009; Nalepa 2010; Dolenec 2013; Carter et al. 2016.

[47] Although see Blanchflower and Freeman 1997; Alesina and Fuchs-Schündeln 2007; and Mishler and Rose 2007. To be clear, this is not to say there has not been important research on political attitudes and public opinion in post-communist citizens. See, e.g., Gibson and Duch 1993; Miller et al. 1994; Bahry et al. 1997; Cox and Powers 1997; Evans and Whitefield 1999; Anderson and O'Conner 2000; Brady and Kaplan 2012.

[48] Although see the debates about the comparability of post-communist and other third-wave transitions (Bunce 1995, 1998; Schmitter and Karl 1994). Two other recent publications have taken a more broadly comparative approach: Carter et al. 2016, who examine the likelihood of democratic survival of post-communist states as compared with other third-wave democratizing states; and Djankov et al. 2015, who examine the post-communist "happiness gap" using data from 82 countries.

cently less attention has been paid to the subject of how the past affects political attitudes.[49] The general methodological approach we lay out—to assess differences between citizens in terms of attitudes, to attempt to explain away as much of these differences by *living in* features, and then to attempt to directly study the effect of exposure to the old regime—holds promise for understanding the effect of other types of regime change, such as moving from colonial to post-colonial rule or from military dictatorship to democratic competition. Furthermore, the *living through communism* model is purposely designed from a set of general principles—that individuals are exposed to regimes for different periods of time (*temporal exposure*), and that there are factors that can *intensify* the effect of that exposure and other factors that may increase *resistance* to that exposure—so that it can be applied in contexts beyond the post-communist transitions. And while we do focus on applications of the *living through* model for studying the effects of communism in particular in the following chapter, even then some of the variables that we will posit to be important in the communist context—such as prior experience with democratic rule or religious affiliation—may have value in additional contexts as well.

It is also our hope that the individual empirical chapters on attitudes toward democracy, markets, social welfare, and gender equality will each on their own contribute to the relevant literatures on these topics. At the very least, we hope to provide some of the most systematic evidence to date of the determinants of these attitudes among post-communist citizens, which can serve as a baseline for comparison for studies being carried out in other areas. But more optimistically, we hope that will raise new and interesting questions for people interested in the determinants of these different attitudes. Similarly, we hope that Chapter 8 will contribute to the ongoing debates about the relevance of post-communism as an analytical category (Bernhard and Jasiewicz 2015), about how to judge whether the post-communist transition is over (Shleifer and Treisman 2004, 2014), and more broadly about the half-lives of authoritarian regime legacies and the dynamics of post-authoritarian attitudinal change (Roberts 2004; Bernhard and Karakoc 2007).

Moreover, the framework we present in this book could certainly also be applied to other aspects of post-communist political behavior beyond attitude formation. For example, elsewhere we have examined the effect of communist-era legacies on the evaluation of political parties (Pop-Eleches and Tucker 2011) and on civic participation (Pop-Eleches and Tucker 2013). Natural extensions of our approach here could be to examine participation in elections in post-communist countries (Pacek et al. 2009), the

---

[49]However, in recent years, a few studies have started to address the attitudinal effects of historical legacies more systematically (see, e.g., Peisakhin 2015).

incumbency disadvantage in post-communist countries (Roberts 2008; Pop-Eleches 2010; Klašnja 2015), and participation in protests (Robertson 2010). More generally, we can think about extending the framework beyond legacy effects on *attitudes* to effects on *evaluation* and *participation* as well.

Finally, we want to highlight the central puzzle that motivates us in writing this book. As communism collapsed in 1989, the enthusiasm for democracy in the region seemed as strong and vibrant as anywhere in human history. The fact that a few short years later a deficit in support for democracy emerged in the region is an important puzzle to be solved in its own right. The question of whether communism was successful in creating "Socialist Man"—a possible solution to this puzzle—also strikes us as an important question to be answered before we close the books on the communist experiment in Eurasia and Eastern Europe.

1.8. LAYOUT OF THE BOOK

The remainder of the book is laid out as follows. In Chapter 2, we elaborate further on the Soviet communist project and how it relates to our *living through communism* model, as well as why we have chosen to examine legacy effects in post-communist—as opposed to some other collection of—countries. In particular, we lay out the specific variables that we expect—based on the history of communism and how it developed in the former Soviet Union and Eastern Europe—to have potentially increased the *intensity* of the communist message to which citizens were exposed and the *resistance* that citizens might have had to that exposure.

In Chapter 3, we turn to questions of data and methodology. We have chosen to devote a specific chapter to this topic so as not to interrupt the flow the empirical chapters with repeated methodological discussions that are important across multiple chapters—as well as to allow readers who are not interested in these topics to move quickly through the materials—but also to reflect growing interest in the field of political science in methodological transparency. We divide the chapter into three parts. In the first part, we introduce in much greater detail the intuition behind our methodological approach; our hope is that for those not interested in the details of statistical analysis, this section will suffice to understand why we are carrying out the analyses we do in the remainder of the book. In the second part, we provide information regarding the modeling choices we made in our analyses, our justification for doing so, and a discussion of some of the consequences of these choices for how we ought to interpret our findings. The third part describes both the survey data sets we analyzed and the aggregate-level data we collected to augment these surveys.

Our hope here is that the section can function almost as a stand-alone reference section that is easily accessible at any time during the reading of the book.

In Chapters 4–7, we present our empirical analyses of the determinants of attitudes toward democracy (Chapter 4), markets (Chapter 5), social welfare (Chapter 6), and gender equality (Chapter 7). Each of these chapters follows a similar pattern with a set of analyses that are consistent across all four chapters, followed by supplementary analysis that is specific to each chapter and allows us to examine a specific question of interest in more depth, and in particular to begin exploring the question of the *mechanisms* by which exposure may have impacted attitude formation. In Chapter 8 we revisit findings from all four of these chapters with an eye toward the temporal evolution of attitudes and an examination of cohort-level effects. In Chapter 9, we conclude the book by considering our results in toto, addressing what they suggest both for our understanding of post-communist politics and for the study of legacy effects more generally.

Before moving on, we close with a few very quick words on terminology. One phrase that always comes into question in these types of studies is what exactly we mean by "post-communist countries." We are not interested here in whether terms like "post-communist" or "transition" imply some unalterable path toward one political outcome or another (Gans-Morse 2004; Roberts 2004). Instead, we merely use the term descriptively, as shorthand for identifying the successor states to the former Soviet Union, the former Yugoslavia, and the East European countries that at one time or another made up the old communist bloc.[50] Similarly, while there have been different types of "communist" experiences around the globe, we are referring particularly to the form of communism that took hold in Eastern Europe and the former Soviet Union. While it would probably be more accurate to refer to this as "Soviet communism" or "Soviet-style communism" (and indeed occasionally we do use these terms), for the most part we will simply use the more efficient "communism" as shorthand for this particular communist experience. Finally, throughout the book we will be comparing citizens from post-communist countries with citizens from countries in the rest of world. While the technically correct way to refer to these people is as citizens of "non-post-communist countries," we at times use the slightly more parsimonious phrase "non-communist" countries to refer to countries that are not former communist countries.[51]

---

[50]Essentially, this latter category is the former members of the Warsaw Pact plus the former Yugoslav republics.

[51]As will be explained in Chapter 3, we exclude China and Vietnam from any comparative analyses.

CHAPTER 2

Living through Communism

LEONID BREZHNEV'S MOTHER COMES TO VISIT HIM. BREZHNEV TAKES HER
TO SEE HIS INCREDIBLE OFFICE AT THE KREMLIN:

BREZHNEV: Mama, what do you think of my office?
MAMA: It's nice, Leonid.
HE TAKES HER TO SEE HIS HUGE APARTMENT IN MOSCOW:
BREZHNEV: Mama, what do you think of my apartment?
MAMA: It's nice, Leonid.
HE TAKES HER OUT TO HIS PALATIAL DACHA OUTSIDE OF MOSCOW:
BREZHNEV: Mama, what do you think of my dacha?
MAMA: It's nice, Leonid.
BREZHNEV: Mama, I've shown you my incredible office, apartment, and
    dacha, and yet you don't seem excited. Aren't you proud of me?
    Aren't you impressed with any of these things? What's the matter?
MAMA: They are all nice Leonid, but I'm worried about what's going to
    happen to you when the communists come to power!

—Soviet joke from the late 1970s[1]

2.1. INTRODUCTION

In the previous chapter, we laid out two different analytical frameworks
for how to explain the fact that post-communist citizens hold systematically different social, economic, and political attitudes than people elsewhere in the world. The first focused on the fact that post-communist
citizens today are *living in* a particular set of countries, with particular
pre-communist histories, particular developmental paths during the years
of communist rule, and particular sociodemographic characteristics, economic conditions, and political conditions and institutions at the time re-

[1] Note: We start this and each subsequent chapter with a communist joke on (more or
less) the topic of each chapter. Jokes are not only an important gateway into understanding
life under communism but are also a fascinating—and surprisingly uniform—communist
legacy (Davies 2007).

spondents were surveyed in the 1990s and 2000s. It is eminently possible that all we need to take account of in order to explain post-communist attitudinal divergence is precisely how these different features were related to the attitudes we examine.

We also introduced an alternative framework, which focuses on the possibility that these attitudes might in some way be a function of having *lived through* Soviet communist rule. Most of our discussion in the previous chapter of this theoretical approach was pitched at a sufficiently general level that it could be applied to *living through* any regime that had ended and was posited to have had a lasting effect on attitudes in the period of time following the collapse of that regime. We introduced readers to our basic hypothesis for testing the *living through* theory of legacy effects: more *exposure* to the regime (i.e., living through more years when that regime was in power) should be associated with stronger support for attitudes that were consistent with regime ideology. Further, we suggested that not all years of exposure would be equally influential, and not all individuals would respond to exposure in the same way. As a result, a more nuanced approach would involve identifying factors that could *intensify* the effects of exposure as well as factors that could increase *resistance* to that exposure.

Pitched at this level of generality, though, there is nothing about this argument that is peculiar to living through *communist* rule. We could just as easily apply this *living through* framework to legacy effects from living through military rule (e.g., suggesting that citizens with more exposure to a military regime would be more likely to harbor nationalist sentiments, that this effect would strongest among people who had served in the army, and that ethnic minorities and those who had studied abroad would be more likely to resist this message, etc.). We largely kept the introduction of the argument in Chapter 1 at this level of generality in order to introduce the basic idea to readers interested in the broader question of attitudinal legacies before we got into its appropriate implementation in the *communist* context.[2]

The purpose of this chapter, therefore, is to do just that: develop a more focused *living through Soviet communism* (hereafter *living through communism*) model to explain attitudinal divergence among post-*communist* citizens. As we have already introduced the four issue areas—attitudes toward democracy, markets, state-provided social welfare, and gender equity—in practice this means the focus of this chapter will be to identify

---

[2]The one major exception, of course, was Section 1.4, where we introduced the particular issues that we expected communist exposure to impact; these are of course specific to communist rule.

the factors that we expect to *intensify* or provide *resistance to* the effects of *living through communism*.

We take a two-part approach to doing so. In the second half of this chapter (Section 2.3), we present and motivate the *living through communism intensifying* and *resistance* hypotheses that we test in Chapters 4–7. But first (Section 2.2), we provide some general background on Soviet communism (hereafter simply "communism"). Of course, a vast literature has dealt with the subject of communism (e.g., Brzezinski 1989; Jowitt 1992; Kornai 1992; Verdery 1996; Tismăneanu 2009), so this will be at best a cursory overview. Our goals, therefore, for this section are modest and related specifically to the needs of the current book. First and foremost, we want to provide the necessary context to justify the particular *intensity* and *resistance* hypotheses we will present in Section 2.3. Second, we want the book to be accessible to people who know little about communism or post-communism, so Section 2.2 should also function as a quick primer for non-area-specialists on communism. Finally, from a methodological perspective, we want to take this opportunity to explain why exactly we are focusing on *post-communist* countries as opposed to, for example, more generally post-authoritarian countries, or, more specifically, Eastern European countries or former Soviet republics. While these three goals could ostensibly be pursued separately, in practice the material that each section would need to cover would overlap to such an extent that it makes more sense to just address all three simultaneously. Accordingly, we structure Section 2.2 around the theme of "why study post-communism?" but spill more ink on the topics of "institutional similarities" and "pre-communist divergence" than would be necessary without these other goals in mind.

2.2. WHY STUDY POST-COMMUNISM?

Post-communism is not the only analytically useful category for understanding the countries of the former Soviet bloc. We could move down the ladder of generality (e.g., by further subdividing ex-communist countries as a function of their pre-communist or communist developmental trajectories) or up the ladder (e.g., by analyzing transition countries as part of even broader categories such as post-totalitarian or post-authoritarian regimes). What, then, are our reasons for studying post-communism?

Aside from the intrinsic interest of understanding the legacy of what was arguably the largest-scale social and political experiment of the 20th century, studying political behavior in the former communist countries of Eastern Europe and Eurasia has a number of theoretical justifications and presents certain methodological advantages over studying the legacies of other types of political regimes or economic systems. These advantages include: (1) significant differences in pre-communist economic, political, and cultural legacies, which help disentangle communist legacies from alternative explanations; (2) a distinctive set of shared political and economic institutions, which set ex-communist countries apart from other post-authoritarian and developing countries; (3) a fairly high degree of exogeneity in both the rise and the fall of communism for most of the Soviet bloc countries; (4) an uninterrupted exposure to communist rule ranging from around 45 years for most of Eastern Europe to 70 years for the interwar Soviet republics (i.e., a strong treatment effect); (5) significant divergence in the economic and political trajectories after the fall of communism; and (6) several instances of significant within-country variation in the exposure to communism (specifically, Germany, Ukraine, and Belarus). In the remainder of this section, we address each of these in turn.

2.2.1. Pre-communist Differences

Of great advantage to our analytical effort is the fact that the post-communist countries entered into their periods of communist rule from a remarkably diverse set of prior conditions. Such diversity presents two distinctive analytical advantages for our efforts to assess the attitudinal and behavioral legacies of communism. First, this heterogeneity should make it easier to distinguish the legacy of communism from other competing explanations of political attitudes and behavior, such as accounts based on socioeconomic development, prior institutional legacies, or cultural factors. Second, the large "within-bloc" variation along many key drivers of attitudes and behavior means that our empirical setup represents a hard test of the systemic legacy of communism. To the extent that—despite their important differences—ex-communist countries exhibit significant commonalities in attitudinal patterns and significant differences compared to non-communist countries, we can be even more confident that communism played an important causal role in explaining these distinctive patterns than if such patterns were observed among countries that shared more similar developmental and political histories.[3]

The countries of the former Soviet bloc entered their communist periods with significant variations in socioeconomic development, political history, and cultural and religious backgrounds. This ranged from countries with remarkably high levels of socioeconomic development, literacy, and

---

[3]This is not to say that there is not attitudinal variation across different post-communist countries—see Figures 4.1, 5.1, 6.1, and 7.1 for more details. At the same time, addressing this within post-communist variation plays a major role in the research design, i.e., the country-level *resistance* and *intensifying* hypotheses.

even experiences with democracy in countries like Poland and Czechoslovakia, to areas in the Balkans, the Caucasus, and Central Asia where
most of the population was illiterate and reliant on subsistence agriculture
before the advent of communism. In addition, Eastern European and Eurasian communism took root in a part of the world with a wide degree of
cultural and religious variation that included Catholics, Protestants, Eastern Orthodox, and Muslims. We consider each of these factors in turn.

Perhaps the most significant distinction across the pre-communist landscape was socioeconomic development. Some of the communist countries—
especially those that had previously been part of the Prussian or Habsburg
empires such as Czechoslovakia and East Germany—had reached pre-
communist income, education, and industrialization levels that were on
par with much of Western Europe and superior to southern Europe and
most of the rest of the world (Gaidar 2012; Maddison 2009). In other
areas—especially in Central Asia and parts of the Caucasus and the Balkans—most people relied on subsistence agriculture at the time when the
communists took over. Moreover, literacy rates varied greatly across the
region. As Darden and Grzymała-Busse (2006: 113) document, in Central
and Eastern Europe numerous countries (including Czechoslovakia, Estonia, Hungary, Latvia, and Slovenia) had literacy rates above 90% at the
onset of the communist era. In contrast, Albania, Azerbaijan, and all five
of the Central Asian republics had literacy rates below 20%.

These countries had also traveled very different political paths on their
way to communism. Most significantly, while most of the Central and
Eastern European post-communist states were independent countries at
the onset of communist rule, most of the former Soviet republics were
part of the Russian empire. The only exceptions were Estonia, Latvia, and
Lithuania, which were independent, and Moldova, which was part of Romania in the interwar period. Moreover, prior to WWI, some of the now
post-communist countries were part of the Russian empire, others the
Habsburg or Prussian empires, and still others the Ottoman empire. In
addition, while a few Eastern European countries—especially Czechoslovakia and to a lesser extent Poland and the Baltic republics—had experienced reasonably democratic elections and governance in the interwar
period, most of the former Soviet republics and Albania had practically
no usable democratic past prior to entering communism.

Culturally, the former Soviet bloc included a broad mix of ethnicities,
religions, and cultural traditions. This included the predominantly Muslim and partially nomadic populations of Central Asia, the predominantly
Eastern Orthodox countries found in both the former Soviet Union and
the Balkans,[4] and the countries of East-Central Europe with their long

---

[4]This includes Russia, Ukraine, Belarus, Armenia, Georgia, Moldova from the former
Soviet Union and Bulgaria, Romania, Serbia, and Macedonia from East-Central Europe.

Western Christian traditions, including both majority Protestant and Catholic countries.[5] In addition to the range of religious traditions, there was also a great deal of variation in the degree of ethnic heterogeneity across these countries, ranging from the volatile ethnic mosaics of Yugoslavia to the relative ethnic homogeneity of Hungary or Estonia.

While some of these differences were subsequently modified by communist developmental and redistributive efforts, by 1989 the countries of the Soviet bloc still differed along a significant range of socioeconomic, political, and cultural dimensions, and these differences are strongly correlated with post-communist political trajectories (Bunce 1999; Janos 2000; Horowitz 2003; Kitschelt 2003; Pop-Eleches 2007). Thus, it was arguably no coincidence that Czechoslovakia, Hungary, and Poland, some of the countries with the region's highest levels of pre-communist socioeconomic development, not only experienced some of the largest anti-communist protest movements before 1989 (Ekiert 1996; Janos 2000) but also subsequently emerged as the region's liberal democratic frontrunners in the 1990s. Moreover, even in areas where communist development effectively erased pre-communist differences—especially in terms of education—it has been argued that post-communist political behavior seems to be shaped to a significant extent by pre-communist developmental patterns (Darden and Grzymała-Busse 2006).

2.2.2. Institutional Similarities

Having touched on important sources of differences in the pre-communist world, we now turn to the task of identifying institutional features that were *similar* across communist regimes. Indeed, it is these institutional similarities—combined with the fact that the regimes consciously self-identified as communist—that even allow us to speak of a communist regime "type," and, consequently, to discuss the possibility of a predicted consistent effect from *living through communism*. Determining whether these similarities were a direct result of communist ideology or more a function of the powerful influence of the Soviet Union as both an institutional model and an (implicit or explicit) enforcer of communism in the region is beyond the purview of our current project, but clearly the Eastern European and Eurasian communist countries shared several crucial economic and political institutional features that set them apart from many developmentally comparable countries. We focus here on five such similarities: (1) de facto *one-party regimes*,[6] led by a Marxist-Leninist

---

[5] As the joke goes: Poland, Ireland, and the Vatican are the three most Catholic countries in the world, in that order.

[6] A few countries, such as East Germany and Poland, nominally allowed the existence of multiple parties, but such parties were expected to—and almost always did—toe the official party line.

political party whose organization was closely intertwined—and often fused—with the state apparatus; (2) *greater penetration of all levels of society* by communist regimes compared to other authoritarian regimes; (3) the central role of *the state in the economy*; (4) a comparatively stronger emphasis on the *development of industry*, which in turn led to urbanization drives and a rapid expansion of primary and secondary and technical post-secondary education; and (5) societies that were decidedly more *equal* in terms of the relative distribution of wealth than most other societies (Haggard and Kaufman 2008). In the remainder of this section, we expand on each of these similarities in turn.

First—and perhaps most clearly—all the communist regimes were either de jure (or at least de facto) *one-party regimes*, led by a Marxist-Leninist political party whose organization was closely intertwined—and often fused—with the state apparatus. The prominent role of the Communist Party in communist regimes differed from the patterns of postwar authoritarian regimes in other regions, such as military regimes in Latin America (and parts of sub-Saharan Africa), monarchies (in the Middle East), or regimes with partially free multiparty competition (in parts of Latin America and Asia). While one-party regimes were not limited to the communist bloc, with a few notable exceptions[7] the non-communist one-party regimes were much less institutionalized (and were often not much more than the personal vehicles of authoritarian leaders).[8] Moreover, while cultural transformation was often subordinated to system-building priorities (Jowitt 1992: 82–83) and the role and nature of ideology varied across both time and space among the countries of the Soviet bloc, the propaganda efforts to reshape individuals and society along ideological lines (Ebon 1987; Hoffman 2011), and the central role of the party in these efforts, were much more prominent in communist regimes than in the non-communist world (democratic and authoritarian alike). Therefore, we should expect the legacy of the once dominant Communist Party and its ideology to affect both the institutional landscape of post-communist politics and the individual values and attitudes of individuals in ex-communist countries.

A second feature, driven to a great extent by the combination of institutionalization and ideological aspiration discussed above, was the much *greater penetration of all levels of society* by communist regimes compared to other authoritarian regimes. Even beyond the infamous mass "reeduca-

---

[7]Probably the most prominent exception is the KMT in Taiwan—a highly institutionalized political party that allowed very little political competition until the 1980s.

[8]This is true even of many of the pseudo-Marxist regimes sponsored by the Soviet Union in parts of the developing world (e.g., Angola, Tanzania, Yemen) as part of the Cold War ideological and military rivalry with the United States.

tion" campaigns and purges of Stalinism, the deep penetration of society by extensive networks of secret police agents and informers led to an unprecedented degree of state control over the daily lives (and thoughts) of individuals.[9] The effects of these surveillance and indoctrination efforts were exacerbated by the simultaneous repression and cooptation of most civil society organizations by communist regimes. Thus, churches were either subordinated to the political agenda of the regimes—and often infiltrated by secret police informers up to the highest levels—or severely limited in their activities and in some instances completely outlawed.[10] Meanwhile other intermediary organizations—such as labor unions, youth organizations, sports clubs, and cultural groups—were allowed to operate and often received generous state support but were subjected to tight ideological controls by the state and therefore did not provide opportunities for independent civic interactions. By contrast, most other authoritarian regimes were usually content to ward off political challenges, and while such concerns sometimes resulted in violent campaigns against certain parts of civil society—as in the case of unions in many Latin American military regimes—they nevertheless left more space in other parts of public life.

A third important feature that sets communist countries apart from the non-communist world is *the central role of the state in the economy.* While extensive state intervention in the economy (including in some cases prominent roles for state-owned enterprises in many key sectors) also featured prominently in some Western European democracies and in the import-substituting industrialization (ISI) models prevalent in many developing countries until the early 1980s, communist countries nevertheless stood out in their systematic suppression of private enterprise and in their heavy reliance on central planning, which produced a very different economic logic and a series of typically communist pathologies (Kornai 1992). Again, important variations in the scope and nature of the state's economic control existed within the Soviet bloc,[11] and in the 1980s there were significant differences in the extent to which communist governments

---

[9] Of course the aggressiveness and effectiveness of such efforts varied widely across time, space, and sector (Jowitt 1992), arguably peaking during the Great Terror of the 1930s in the Soviet Union and in the first postwar decade in Eastern Europe. While we will analyze the implications of such intra-regional variation throughout the book, for the purpose of the present discussion what matters is that (with the partial exception of the late Gorbachev years) communist regimes never abandoned this basic model of societal control.

[10] However—as we will discuss in the final section of this chapter—this varied across countries and religious denominations and even within the same denomination and country (Wittenberg 2006; Nalepa and Pop-Eleches 2015).

[11] The most prominent outlier was Yugoslavia's "socialist self-management," where enterprises were technically owned and controlled by workers' councils (albeit with a great degree of interference from the party).

embraced Gorbachev's limited economic reform efforts. But despite such differences, as late as 1989 the share of the private sector in overall economic output varied surprisingly little in most of communist Eastern Europe and Eurasia, largely ranging from about 5% in most Soviet republics, Czechoslovakia, and Albania to 15% in most of the Yugoslav republics (EBRD 2008).[12]

Fourth, driven by both ideological commitment to promote the industrial proletariat and by the demands of military competition with the West, the communist economies also differed from both advanced industrialized countries and even other late developers in *the nature of their economic development and modernization strategies*. In particular, communist countries stood out in their emphasis on industry, and especially energy-intensive heavy industry (at the expense of both agriculture and services) and in their relative neglect of consumer goods, whose variety and quality lagged far behind the sometimes impressive achievements in producer goods and military technology. Politically, these imbalances, combined with the widespread shortages of even basic goods, inevitably invited invidious comparisons to Western Europe and helped undermine the legitimacy of communist regimes (Janos 2000).

But beyond its immediate impact on living standards and regime legitimacy, the particular nature of communist economic development led to modernization strategies that produced peculiarly communist demographic patterns. On the one hand, the rush to promote industrialization pushed communist regimes to promote a rapid expansion of primary and secondary and technical post-secondary education, as well as—less successfully—urbanization. On the other hand, the ideological bent and the often narrowly technical nature of communist education, combined with the tight restrictions imposed on individual entrepreneurship, arguably put many Eastern Europeans in a difficult position in the post-communist period, where in the emerging market economies of the 1990s there was much less demand for their particular education and job skills. Similarly, many of the "one-factory" industrial towns promoted by communist central planners were highly vulnerable once the communist system of price controls and subsidies was dismantled, and indeed many of these towns suffered devastating drops in employment after the fall of communism, often leaving residents few options but to try to migrate, either internally—sometimes to the countryside in a remarkable trend of de-urbanization—or abroad. Thus, communism left behind a demographic landscape characterized by very specific opportunities and vulnerabilities, which differed from the so-

---

[12] The only partial outlier was Poland, where the private sector in 1989 accounted for 30% of the economy, largely because of the failure of large-scale collectivization of agriculture.

cial footprint of alternative development models and could be expected to shape the longer-term attitudes and behavior of its subjects in the post-communist period.

Fifth, true to its ideological aspirations of promoting social and economic equality among its citizens, communist regimes left behind more equal societies and more expansive welfare states than their non-communist counterparts. Thus, judging by a series of statistical measures, ranging from Gini coefficients of income inequality to access to education and health care, communist countries outperformed non-communist countries with similar levels of economic development. Rather than engaging in the debates over the extent to which these achievements justify the high human costs at which they were achieved, our focus here is on how they are likely to affect post-communist attitudes and behavior. A few points are worth noting: first, given that the transition to capitalism brought significant—though highly variable—increases in inequality to the former Soviet bloc countries, one would expect that in countries and periods of time with rapidly increasing inequality, citizens—and particularly transitional losers—would become much more receptive to the egalitarian rhetoric of communist parties (and some of their post-communist successors). Along similar lines, the legacy of generous communist-era welfare benefits created strong popular expectations about the state's responsibilities for caring for its citizens. The combination of economic liberalization and deep recessions in the early transition years resulted in a significant reduction of welfare benefits in many countries and created very difficult choices for politicians caught between demands for fiscal restraint (in the context of inflationary pressures) and the difficulty of scaling back preexisting social entitlement programs (Haggard and Kaufman 2008). This tension, which was to a great extent an institutional legacy of communism, may have played an important role in driving the chronic discontent of Eastern European citizens with post-communist political leaders. Finally, many welfare benefits under communism—including child care and public housing—were channeled through state-owned enterprises. This peculiarity of the communist welfare state arguably made it more difficult to disentangle welfare state reform from other aspects of economic reform.

Furthermore, the emphasis on egalitarianism extended—at least on a rhetorical level—beyond economic inequality to a commitment to gender and ethnic equality (Lapidus 1978; Slezkine 1994). While there was much more variation in the extent to which this rhetoric was matched by practice than in the case of single-party rule, economic redistribution, and the state provision of social welfare, the advent of communist rule brought with it an unprecedented—at least for these countries—entry of women into the workplace, access to abortion, and an end to legal discrimination against ethnic minorities (Lapidus 1978; Kligman 1998; Gal and Kligman

2000). It is worth noting, though, that this was never really accompanied by any commensurate effort in the area of gay rights (O'Dwyer 2012), often included in scales of social progressivism in comparative studies.

2.2.3. Exogeneity in the Rise and the Fall of Communism

A serious—and potentially intractable—challenge for studying the impact of political and economic regimes on subsequent attitudes and behavior is the possibility of reverse causation due to the endogeneity of political regimes. Thus, it is reasonable to argue that the emergence of certain types of economic and political regimes may be the consequence of prior economic and political attitudes among a country's citizens. For example, if citizens strongly value crucial aspects of democratic regimes, and if they are sufficiently organized and mobilized to act on these beliefs, then we would expect their countries to be more likely to democratize and/or less likely to revert to authoritarianism. To the extent that such values and behavioral proclivities are relatively stable over time, then any correspondence between current attitudes and recent regime characteristics may simply be the product of spurious correlation rather than evidence of regime legacies.

From this perspective, studying the effects of communism also has significant advantages because, for many of the countries of the former Soviet bloc, both the rise and the fall of communism was much more exogenous than for many other authoritarian regimes elsewhere around the world. Among the former Soviet republics, Russia was arguably the only one where communism arose endogenously, whereas in the other republics of the former Russian empire it was imposed as a result of the Red victory in the Russian civil war of 1917–21.[13] For the three Baltic states and Moldova, the incorporation into the Soviet Union and the imposition of communism were initially the direct result of the Ribbentrop-Molotov Pact between Nazi Germany and Soviet Russia, and later of the ability of Soviet troops to reconquer these territories following the German invasion of 1941. For the Eastern European satellite states, the rise of communism was indelibly tied to the presence of Soviet troops in most countries in the region in the aftermath of World War II, and this de facto power balance on the ground was sanctioned by the agreements of the Yalta Conference in early 1945, in which Churchill and Roosevelt agreed to Stalin's demands for control over Eastern Europe. Therefore, except for Albania and

---

[13] Even in Russia, much of the evidence suggests that the rise of communism was in many ways the product of a series of historical accidents rather than the inevitable conclusion of the type of historical forces that Marx had expected would lead to the victory of communism.

Yugoslavia,[14] and to some extent Czechoslovakia,[15] the rise to power of communist regimes in Eastern Europe was also largely exogenous, in the sense that it was driven by great power politics and the presence of Soviet troops rather than the economic and political preferences of the majority of citizens from the region.

The surprising collapse of Eastern European and Eurasian communism in 1989–91 was also more exogenous than the collapse of most other authoritarian regimes, and once again for reasons closely tied to the actual or threatened use of force by the Soviet army to uphold communist rule throughout the region. Here again, we need to distinguish between the events in the Soviet Union and those in its Eastern European satellite states. The timing of the collapse of communist regimes in Eastern Europe was arguably to a large extent the result of Gorbachev's abandonment in late 1988 of the Brezhnev Doctrine, which signaled that the Soviet Union would no longer use force or the threat of force (as in Hungary in 1956, in Czechoslovakia in 1968, and in Poland in 1981) to reverse political reforms in its Eastern European satellites. Following this crucial external signal the communist regimes of the Warsaw Pact countries collapsed with remarkable speed over the course of a single year, starting with the Polish Roundtable in the early spring of 1989 and ending with the fall of the Ceaușescu regime in Romania in December 1989. While the collapse of these regimes obviously had important domestic roots, including an erosion of political legitimacy and a range of economic difficulties in the 1980s, the timing of these events cannot be explained by domestic factors alone. Many of these problems had existed for years before 1989 without producing regime change. Furthermore, change happened almost simultaneously in countries whose recent communist experience had been as diverse as Hungary's relatively benign and prosperous "goulash communism" and the nightmare of Romania's neo-Stalinist Ceaușescu dictatorship. While it is true that Poland and Hungary were at the forefront of these changes, and that their earlier timing was hardly accidental,[16] what

---

[14]In both cases the communists took over as a result of anti-fascist military campaigns with genuine popular backing and minimal Soviet military involvement in 1944–45. As a result, the Soviet Union also had less of an influence on the subsequent development of communism in these countries (in particular in Yugoslavia after 1948 and in Albania after 1956).

[15]In Czechoslovakia, the Communist Party won the largest vote share in the reasonably free and fair 1946 elections, riding a wave of anti-fascist sentiment. Nevertheless, their vote share was still only around 38%, and their subsequent rise to absolute power was less the result of an increase in popular support than aggressive tactics on the part of the Czech communists to marginalize their non-communist coalition partners and to suppress the resulting dissent.

[16]We thank Milada Vachudova for this point and for her many other useful comments on the first draft of this chapter.

matters most for the purposes of our analysis is that over the course of about a year most Eastern European countries transitioned from communism to post-communism irrespective of their differences in pre-communist and communist trajectories.[17]

In the Soviet republics, the fall of communism was intertwined with the complicated and chaotic dissolution of the Soviet Union. Thus, technically, the transition to multipartyism was driven by Gorbachev's change in March 1990 of Article 6 of the Soviet Constitution, which effectively ended the political power monopoly of the Communist Party and paved the way for competitive elections later that year. The outcomes of these elections differed quite dramatically—with anti-communist popular fronts doing much better in the Baltics, Georgia, and Moldova than in the Central Asian republics—and arguably reflected different popular evaluations of the legitimacy of the communist regime. Nonetheless, Gorbachev's refusal to recognize the independence declarations of the Baltic republics, and the repeated violent interventions of Soviet troops against independence movements in the Soviet republics (e.g., Azerbaijan in January 1990, Lithuania in March 1990 and January 1991, etc.) suggest that the ultimate fate of communism in the region was once again decided by events in Moscow to a greater extent than by the preferences of Soviet citizens. While it is unclear for how long the Soviet Union could have been held together by force after the fall of Eastern European communism and the rapid rise of nationalist popular mobilization (Beissinger 2002), it seems very likely that the political trajectories of most former Soviet republics would have looked very different in the 1990s had the August 1991 hardline coup been successful or had the power struggle between Yeltsin and Gorbachev been won by the latter. As things turned out, the failure of the coup and Yeltsin's assertion of Russian independence effectively sealed the fate of Soviet communism and led to the emergence of fifteen newly independent countries in the fall of 1991. While the trajectories of these countries diverged quite dramatically over the following years, what matters for the current discussion is that all of them abandoned communism at roughly the same time,[18] and—with the partial exception of Russia—for reasons that were largely independent of the political attitudes of their citizens.

---

[17]The fall of communism in the two non–Warsaw Pact communist countries of Eastern Europe was slightly different: in Albania, where communism had survived under conditions of almost complete international isolation for most of the 1980s, the transition to multipartyism did not start until December 1990. Meanwhile, in Yugoslavia the timing of the transition to multiparty competition was quite similar to the rest of Eastern Europe but was driven primarily by ethnic rifts between Serbian, Croatian, and Slovenian factions within the League of Communists of Yugoslavia at the 14th Congress in January 1990.

[18]The high continuity of communist personnel and political repression in many of the former Soviet republics (especially in Central Asia) raises important questions about the

2.2.4. Regime Longevity

The communist regimes of Eastern Europe and Eurasia also stand out—at least in comparison to most 20th-century authoritarian regimes—in their remarkable longevity, ranging from roughly 45 years in Eastern Europe to over 70 years for the pre-WWII Soviet republics. Combined with their previously discussed ambitious efforts to revolutionize the societies and individuals over which they ruled, this longevity arguably gave communist regimes a unique scope for affecting the political attitudes and behavior of Eastern European citizens. Therefore, the communists had greater opportunities to root out or at least marginalize prior formal and informal institutions. While these efforts were only partially successful, they nevertheless had more profound consequences than similar efforts by other authoritarian and totalitarian regimes. Thus, even though the Nazi and fascist regimes arguably had similarly radical—though differently conceived—societal transformation ambitions, their execution was cut short by the defeat of the Axis countries in World War II, which capped the length of the fascist experiment at just over two decades in the case of Italy, and at less than 15 years for the other comparable regimes.[19]

Regime duration matters not only for the extent of institutional transformation, but also for the processes through which individual citizens are politically socialized. For shorter-lived authoritarian regimes, such as interwar fascist regimes or postwar Latin American military dictatorships, large proportions of the adult population of the country still had distinctive personal political memories of the preceding regimes by the time the authoritarian regimes collapsed. By contrast, even assuming that a 10-year-old could form political memories that would survive over 70 years of turmoil and repression, in the interwar Soviet republics such memories would have been limited to persons in their 80s and older, while in the Eastern European satellite states the corresponding age cutoff would have been around 55–60 years. Even if we allow for intergenerational transmission of political memories (see Darden and Grzymała-Busse 2006; Lupu and Peisakhin 2016) the much greater longevity of communist regimes

---

extent to which 1991 really represented genuine regime change (for much more detail, see Jones Luong 2002). Nonetheless, the marginalization of the role of communist parties and communist ideology in the new regimes, combined with the albeit gradual and uneven abandonment of central planning, suggest that even the most notoriously authoritarian of the former Soviet republics (especially Uzbekistan and Turkmenistan) represent new breeds of authoritarian regimes rather than continuations of Soviet communism.

[19]Technically the authoritarian Spanish and Portuguese regimes that were installed prior to WWII lasted over three decades, but the extent to which they can be accurately characterized as fascist in the post-WWII years is debatable, especially given the broad international disavowal of fascism in the decades that followed WWII.

effectively meant that the average resident of an interwar Soviet republic was two generations further removed from the pre-communist past than a German citizen would have been from the pre-fascist past in 1945.

In addition to allowing us to test the individual-level effects of a much larger "dose" of authoritarian/totalitarian rule, the communist social experiment provides us with two additional analytical advantages. First, it provides dramatic within-country individual-level variation in the extent to which citizens were exposed to communism, ranging from people who had been born and lived for 70 years under a communist regime, to others who were born just as communism collapsed and thus had no direct personal experience with the system. Second, the coexistence among the post-communist transition countries—and sometimes even in the same country (see below)—of regions that had experienced 45 versus 70 years of communism means that we can systematically test the effects of authoritarian/totalitarian regime duration on a scale that would not be possible elsewhere in the world.

2.2.5. Post-communist Divergence

To the extent that political attitudes are shaped by a combination of an individual's personal experience of the political sphere, then, with the partial exception of the few months immediately following the collapse of communism, we should expect that any survey-based evidence of post-communist exceptionalism would reflect not only the influence of communism, but also that of the post-communist transition. To the extent that the nature of this transition was both highly uniform across ex-communist countries and very different from the experience of non-communist countries during the same period, this fact would raise important doubts about our ability to draw inferences regarding the direct individual-level effects of communism as opposed to indirect effects via economic and institutional legacies. These concerns are particularly salient given the shared—and significant—challenges facing ex-communist countries in their transition away from one-party states and command economies (Orenstein 2001). Moreover, these challenges resulted in high political uncertainty, and significant economic and social costs, which were on average much more severe than those inflicted by the economic and political reform efforts undertaken during the same time period in other parts of the developing world.

While in our statistical tests we will try to address this issue in a number of ways—including through the use of survey data from the very early transition period and by controlling for indicators of well-established differences in economic and political performance—the task is simplified by the fact that following the collapse of communism the former communist countries experienced very different economic and political trajectories (Stark and Bruszt 1998; Hellman 1998; Fish 1997; Janos 2000; Frye 2002; Bunce 2003; Ekiert et al. 2007; Pop-Eleches 2007; Stoner and McFaul 2013). While even a brief inventory of these differences is beyond the scope of the present discussion, it is worth noting that after 1990 some countries (such as Poland) underwent rapid economic and political reforms in an effort to emulate Western markets and democratic institutions; others (such as Romania and Slovakia) underwent similar transformations, but over a longer period and via lengthy detours of economic and political populism; while others still (such as Uzbekistan and Turkmenistan) went in an entirely different economic and political direction altogether. At the same time, the socioeconomic and political outputs of the last two decades have varied widely across almost all politically salient performance indicators, ranging from economic output, monetary stability, unemployment, inequality, and life expectancy to criminality, governance, and state capacity (Svejnar 2000; Frye 2002, 2010). Finally, the international context of these domestic transformations has also varied dramatically, with some countries benefitting from the powerful incentives of European integration (Vachudova 2005; Schimmelfennig and Sedelmeier 2005; Schimmelfennig 2007), while others were affected by regional conflicts such as the Afghan war or the dissolution of Yugoslavia.

This significant post-communist divergence means that to the extent that substantial ex-communist attitudinal commonalities persist beyond the early transition years, such evidence would significantly strengthen our confidence in the causal impact of the communist experience on citizen politics. Moreover, this diversity provides us with greater analytical leverage for understanding how the relatively uniform experience of communism interacts with the sharply contrasting post-communist developments to produce particular attitudinal configurations.

2.2.6. Within-Country Variation

The dramatic reconfiguration of Eastern European borders in the aftermath of World War II provides us with an additional analytical tool for studying the impact of communism on subsequent economic and political behavior: the existence of significant within-country variations in the length of communist exposure for several of the post-communist countries. Such subnational variation has become an increasingly popular alternative in comparative politics for dealing with the potential shortfalls of cross-country comparisons, which may be more prone to omitted variable bias.

In the post-communist context, the most visible instance of such a "natural experiment"—though there was very little that was natural about it—was the partition and subsequent reunification of Germany, which meant that by the 1990s East Germans differed from their West German compatriots through their experience of 45 years of communist rule but shared not only a common language, culture, and history, but also—increasingly—similar economic and political institutions. Therefore, a number of studies have used comparative survey data from East and West Germany to study the impact of communism while minimizing the risk of omitted variable bias (see Alesina and Fuchs-Schündeln 2007; Dalton 1994; Neundorf 2009). Other instances of such analytically valuable border changes also occurred in several former Soviet republics, which include territories that belonged to the Soviet Union in the interwar period along with more recent territorial acquisitions during and after World War II. The most prominent such division is between eastern and western Ukraine, which has produced a deep and durable political cleavage,[20] but similar differences exist between Eastern and Western Belarus, between Transnistria and the rest of Moldova, and between Kaliningrad and the rest of Russia.

While such subnational comparisons are important complements to cross-national survey analyses, and will be employed in all our empirical chapters, we do not claim that the former are necessarily methodologically preferable to the latter. Even though, as mentioned, subnational comparisons help reduce the omitted variable concerns that usually plague even many well-specified cross-country statistical comparisons, they do not eliminate them entirely. To take the German example, East Germans do not differ from West Germans just in their experience of communism and in potentially observable variables such as income, but prior to the unification of Germany in 1871, most of what eventually became East Germany was part of Prussia, a state with a very different political history and culture than many of the states that eventually became part of West Germany, such as Bavaria or Saarland. Moreover, comparisons focused on subnational variation in a single country run into potentially serious external validity limitations: even if it turns out that East Germans prefer larger welfare states or hold different democratic values than their West German counterparts, it is unclear whether one would be justified in concluding that communism had similar effects elsewhere in Eastern Europe and the former Soviet Union. For example, East Germans had a reputation for being much more ideologically committed to communism in the

---

[20] See, e.g., Arel (1995); Craumer and Klem (1999); Birch (2000); Kubicek (2000); Barrington (2002); Katchanovski (2006); Darden and Grzymała-Busse (2006); Kulyk (2011); and Peisakhin (2015).

late 1980s than their Eastern European neighbors, which suggests that they may have experienced and processed communism differently than their communist comrades elsewhere in Eastern Europe.[21]

2.3. LIVING THROUGH *COMMUNISM*: INTENSITY AND RESISTANCE HYPOTHESES

Having laid out the rationale behind our decision to examine the effect of legacies on attitudes in *post-communist* countries (as opposed to other collections of countries) as well as highlighting a number of distinctive features of the experience of *communist* rule, in this section we now turn to the task of identifying the appropriate *intensifying* and *resistance* hypotheses for *living through communism*. While a few of these will draw on more general arguments that could be applied to legacy models of *living through* other types of regimes, most are drawn from a logic related specifically to features of communist rule discussed earlier in this chapter. As a reminder, our four basic hypotheses—that is, the ones modified by the *intensity* and *resistance* hypotheses and explained in detail in the previous chapter in Section 1.4—are that the longer an individual is exposed to communist rule, (a) the less likely an individual will be to support democracy,[22] (b) the less likely an individual will be to support markets, (c) the more likely an individual will be to believe the state should provide social welfare, and (d) the more likely an individual will be to have views in line with gender equality.

In the remainder of this section, we proceed systematically through the different factors we believe could *intensify* the effect of exposure and then those that could provide *resistance* against the effect of exposure to

---

[21]Other examples include the trauma of living in a divided city (Berlin), the greater salience of the Western consumption model through the proximity of West Germany, the particular patterns of communist-era economic transfers (marked by significant outflows in the 1950s but balanced by significant Soviet subsidies later on), etc.

[22]Our prediction regarding support for democracy is intended to be *in general* as a form of government, and not the *performance* of democracy in one's own country. While it is of course impossible to rule out the fact that evaluations of the latter affect attitudes regarding the former, these are distinctly different concepts that can be measured with different questions (Evans and Whitefield 1995; Torcal and Montero 2006; Neundorf 2010). To be clear, it is not the case that we think the basic legacies framework we have advanced in this manuscript cannot be used to measure *evaluation* questions such as how an individual views the performance of democracy in her country. Indeed, we have previously published work applying our general framework to the question of evaluating political parties (Pop-Eleches and Tucker 2011) and intend to pursue this topic again in the future. However, the purpose of this current book is to look solely at the underlying attitudes associated with fundamental tenets of Soviet-style communism, and for this reason we concentrate here on attitudes toward democracy generally.

communism.[23] Before doing so, a few additional words of explanation are in order. First, the method for testing the effect of these *intensifying* and *resistance* factors will be addressed in much more detail in the following chapter, but the basic idea is that we will initially test the effect of years of exposure directly, and then test the level of support for our *intensity* and *resistance* predictions by interacting these factors with years of exposure and seeing if the *interactive effect* is in the expected direction.[24] Second, it is important to note as well that both factors work independently of one another: factors that *intensify* the effect of a year of exposure to communism are expected to do so independent of the level of resistance of any given individual; factors that increase *resistance* are expected to do so independent of the intensity of exposure.[25] Finally, we need to reiterate that we expect factors that can *intensify* the effect of exposure to communism could vary at the country level or at the individual level; the same holds for factors that affect *resistance* to communist exposure. Thus the remainder of the section is divided into four parts: country-level factors that are predicted to *intensify* the effect of exposure to communism; individual-level factors that are predicted to *intensify* the effect of exposure to communism; country-level factors that are predicted to increase *resistance* to the effect of exposure to communism socialization, and finally individual-level factors that are predicted to increase *resistance*.[26]

---

[23] To reiterate a point made in the first chapter, *intensifying* factors and *resistance* factors are not just two sides of the same coin. Returning to the sunburn analogy, anyone can put on suntan lotion, regardless of whether they are out in a part of the world where the ozone layer provides more or less protection from the sun. Thus you could experience high resistance in an area where you are getting intense exposure or low resistance in an area with intense exposure; the same holds for weak exposure. Thus our intensity and resistance variables are meant to tap into distinct effects on how additional temporal exposure to communism (i.e., more years living under communism) affects one's attitudes.

[24] The one exception here concerns type of communism (e.g., Stalinist vs. reformist) and age of exposure, which we analyze by decomposing years of exposure into its relevant constituent parts, i.e., we include years of childhood exposure and years of adult exposure as separate variables. See Chapter 3 for more details, especially Sections 3.3.3 and 3.3.4.

[25] Put another way, we are not attempting to model a triple interaction effect between exposure, intensity of exposure, and resistance to exposure. Instead, we are simply going to test the model by looking at the two interactive effects (exposure × intensity of exposure; exposure × resistance to exposure) separately. The former approach is a potentially interesting direction for future research, but beyond the scope of what we are attempting to analyze here.

[26] As a reminder "country-level" implies that the variable is the same for all people living in a given country at a given time-period, not that the variable is by definition time invariant. Some country-level variables do vary over time (such as whether the country is currently being ruled by a reformist communist regime or a Stalinist communist regime), whereas others (such as literacy levels in the pre-communist era) are in fact time invariant.

2.3.1. Country-Level Intensifying Variables

We begin first with factors that we expect could *intensify* the effect of a given year of exposure to communism that vary at the country level. We start with regime-level factors. One of the most prominent aspects of diversity within the communist experience was the systematic variation between different "types" or "phases" of communist rule. To put this most starkly, we might expect that someone who came of political age in Moscow under Stalinism in the early 1950s to have been exposed to somewhat different propaganda and policies than someone who came of age under Gorbachev's perestroika.

With the goal of effectively capturing these different phases, Table 2.1 breaks down the communist experience into five subcategories that represent different "types" of communist experiences. As with any attempt at classification,[27] we face a trade-off between level of detail, comparability, and parsimony. Thus we do not mean to claim that Stalinism in Albania in the 1980s was exactly the same thing as Stalinism in Romania in the early 1950s, but at the same time we hope that the classification scheme represents a useful first step in identifying different types of communist-era experiences.

Table 2.1. Communist Experience by Year and Country

Country	Transition to communism	Stalinist	Neo-Stalinist hardline	Post-totalitarian	Reformist
Bulgaria	1945	1946–53	1954–89		1990
Czechoslovakia	1945–47	1948–52	1953–67, 1969–89		1968
East Germany	1945–48	1949–62	1971–89		1963–70
Hungary	1945–47	1948–53	1957–60	1961–89	1954–56
Poland	1945	1946–56	1982–83	1963–81, 1984–87	1957–62, 1988–89
Romania	1945–47	1948–64	1971–89		1965–70
USSR*	1918–20	1928–52	1953–55; 1965–69	1970–84	1921–27, 1956–64, 1985–91
Yugoslavia	1945	1946–48			1949–90

* The Baltic republics and western Ukraine were coded as starting communism in 1945, and exposure to regime subtypes was adjusted accordingly.

[27] For an interesting alternative approach at classifying communist regimes, see Janos (2000).

Our five-fold classification scheme works as follows.[28] First, we consider the initial years in which countries were in the process of installing communist systems of government. The next category is the Stalinist period, essentially the high-water mark of communist orthodoxy and repression. With the exception of Albania, the communist countries then all moved beyond Stalinism, and we break down these "post-Stalinist experiences" into three categories. "Neo-Stalinist" refers to regimes that moved beyond Stalinism, but essentially still pursued hardline policies (e.g., low dissent tolerance, an active repressive state apparatus but without widespread terror, active security services, etc.). The concept of "post-totalitarianism" is taken from Linz and Stepan (1996) and refers to communist regimes where the communist monopoly on power was still in place, but true believers in the ideology were few and far between, with most party members now associating with the party for careerist as opposed to ideological reasons.[29] Post-totalitarian regimes are also known for the tacit trade-off of political power for economic security; limited pluralism was tolerated so long as the state was not directly targeted. Finally, reformist communism refers to periods like the Prague Spring, Gorbachev's perestroika, and Poland's various flirtations with greater political openness and independent trade unions like Solidarity (Brzezinski 1989; Ash 1990; Sakwa 1990; Janos 2000). Our expectation here is simply that the *intensity* of the effort on the part of communist regimes to actively inculcate their citizens with the underlying values of Soviet communism decreases across the categories from Stalinist to neo-Stalinist to post-totalitarian to reformist.[30]

In addition to assuming that the effect of a year of exposure might vary based on the type of communism to which one was exposed, we might also reasonably expect that there was a cumulative effect of regime efforts at socialization from having spent more years under hardline rule. Therefore, we also test—at the regime level—whether there is a stronger effect for a year of exposure in countries that spent a *larger proportion of the communist period with Stalinist or neo-Stalinist* regime types, which we refer

---

[28] We were surprised to find that no one else had previously attempted this sort of classification and are much in debt to the many people who offered us suggestions on the classification scheme following various presentations of our research and a post soliciting feedback on *The Monkey Cage* blog. We in particular thank Andrew Janos, Radosław Markowski, and Maria Popova, who also provided us with written comments and suggestions.

[29] See as well the discussion in Shlapentokh (1989) about the gradual shift away from the public to the private sphere in these types of regimes.

[30] In some cases, it might be desirable to draw a more nuanced argument about intensity decreasing in a non-monotonic manner, e.g., we might think that as the political legitimacy of communist regimes decreased there would be correspondingly more of a need to emphasize the economic benefits of communism, and thus we might actually see *particular* socialization efforts increasing during, for instance, post-totalitarian years. For now, we leave the discussion of such types of arguments to the actual empirical chapters in which they are analyzed.

to as "hardline rule." In addition, Kitschelt (1999) proposes that post-communist countries can be subdivided on the basis of whether their bureaucratic organization is more or less based on traditional patronage ties as opposed to what he calls a "bureaucratic authoritarian" model. Thus one might suppose that in countries where the bureaucratic authoritarian model predominates, communist messages would be more likely to be amplified than in countries where government was run along more traditional patrimonial principles. For this reason, we also test if there is an intensifying effect for *bureaucratic authoritarianism*.

Finally, we note the importance of variation in the extent to which different communist regimes "let up on" hardline communism in the final decades of communist rule. This could be realized both in terms of more tolerance of markets outside of the control of the state (*late-communist economic liberalization*) as well as a growing tolerance of political pluralism and decreasing use of political repression (*late-communist political liberalization*).[31] In both cases, we expect the net effect to be to reduce the *intensity* of the effect of communist exposure. For markets, this effect is postulated to work primarily by undercutting the seriousness of the regime's message: if markets are being tolerated by a regime that is supposedly anti-market, then what does this say about the regime's commitment to its own philosophy generally? In the case of political liberalization, the effect could be even more direct, in the form of reduced emphasis on political propaganda and greater tolerance of political dissent.[32]

2.3.2. Individual-Level Intensifying Variables

In addition to factors that vary across countries and over time, we need to consider the fact that there might also be individual-level factors that will affect the *intensity* of one's exposure to communism, or, to put it another way, that certain individuals were simply more likely to have been exposed to communist messages and propaganda over the course of their lives.

[31] While it is fairly easy to construct a comparative measure of late-communist political liberalization using existing cross-national measures of regime type, commensurate measures do not exist for economic liberalization under communist rule; the one candidate would be the European Bank for Recovery and Development's economic liberalization indexes, but these did not start until 1989, when the economic transition was already under way in some post-communist countries. For this reason, we include *late-communist economic liberalization* in our theoretical discussion here, but not in our empirical tests, and, correspondingly it is bracketed in Table 2.2.

[32] Note, however, that we think political liberalization could also simultaneously reduce *resistance* to communist exposure, for reasons we explain in the following section, thus producing two contradictory effects that could cancel each other out.

Perhaps the single most obvious candidate for increasing the intensity of exposure to communist ideology is whether or not the respondent was a *member of the Communist Party*.[33] Party membership could have this effect either directly through simply exposing one to more Communist Party rhetoric, or indirectly through convincing party members that adopting party ideology would be beneficial to their own personal career advancement, or even by functioning as more of a selection mechanism to identify individuals more predisposed to communist ideology in the first place. In this latter case, of course, it would be harder to claim a causal impact for party membership, but we should still expect to see a relationship between party membership and larger effects for years of exposure to communist rule; a different research design would be needed in any case for teasing out the causal impact of party membership.

A second candidate is place of residence. Jowitt (1992: 81–82), in particular, has argued that because of their single-minded focus on rapid industrialization, communist regimes achieved much greater penetration in urban settings. To the extent that this is correct, we would therefore expect *urban residents* to be more affected by communist exposure than rural residents.

A third individual-level factor that ought to predict the amount of exposure to communist ideals and propaganda is whether or not an individual is a *male*. We propose two potential mechanisms for this effect. First, the armed forces—like schools—were certainly a vehicle for communist socialization, and the armed forces of Soviet communist countries were almost entirely made up of men (Gambolati 1975; Kenez 1985; Hoffman 2011). Second, we would expect the workplace—especially under communist regimes, focused as they were on the workplace as a location for political organization—to be places where individuals would have greater exposure to communist ideals and propaganda, especially compared to their own homes (Remington 1989; Hoffman 2011; Berkhoff 2012). And because of the fact that—despite significant progress in female workforce participation—women in communist countries were still more likely than men to stay home and not enter the workforce, we have a second reason for suspecting that exposure to communism would have a greater effect on *males*.[34]

---

[33] Unfortunately, although not surprisingly, the cross-regional World Values Survey does not ask respondents whether they are/were members of the Communist Party, as the question would be less useful in a broader global sample. Thus our party membership analysis is relegated to our supplemental analyses using alternative data sources in Chapters 5 and 6.

[34] For a related argument, see Shabad and Slomczynski (1999), who argue that "political identities" in post-communist Poland are related to forms of labor force participation under communism. While occupation under communism represents a potentially interesting intensifying variable, we currently lack the data to test such a hypothesis.

Finally, *parental socialization* could also *intensify* the effect of exposure to communist rule on pro-regime attitudes, but only conditional on the parents themselves being pro-regime. This actually can lead to all sorts of interesting hypotheses and tests, for example comparing the relative impact of mothers versus fathers, or of having one parent who is pro-regime but not the other. Teasing out the regime orientation of a respondent's parent from most surveys is a challenging task, however. One useful proxy could be parental Communist Party membership, and thus we rely on such data when available.[35] However, even questions about parental membership in the Communist Party rely on self-reported measures one step removed from the actual individual in question, so the gold standard here is really household surveys, where all members of a household are surveyed in the same study.[36]

2.3.3. Country-Level Resistance Variables

We now turn to the types of factors that we would expect to generate varying levels of *resistance* to communist regime socialization efforts. Recall that these are factors that we expect to reduce the marginal impact of an extra year of exposure to communism, regardless of the intensity of that exposure. We begin with three country-level factors that capture key elements of pre-communist economic and political development.

First, Darden and Grzymała-Busse (2006) and Darden (2011) point to the importance of *higher literacy rates* before the onset of communism as an important factor that moderated citizens' experiences with communism. Their argument is that the higher the literacy rates before communism, the more likely it will be that that citizens were familiar with national myths. These "national identities" can therefore serve as an alternative reference point to the "Socialist Man" identity.[37] From this vantage point, we would predict that higher pre-communist literacy rates would therefore signify a larger percentage of the country with access to these types of national myths during communist rule, and correspondingly overall higher levels of resistance to communist socialization.

A second set of country-level characteristics that could shape the way in which communism is viewed in a country concern the pre-communist political trajectories of different countries and regions. Thus, in some countries,

---

[35] Again, there are no questions regarding Communist Party membership on the World Values Survey, unfortunately.

[36] Unfortunately, it is our sense that most household surveys tend not to focus on political issues; we were, however, fortunate to be able to find some questions on attitudes toward unemployment and social welfare in the Hungarian Household Panel Survey, which we analyze in Chapter 5 and Chapter 6, respectively.

[37] Russia is of course in its own category in this regard.

communism followed a period of *interwar democracy*.[38] In these countries, we suspect communism may look somewhat worse in comparison to the previous regime (i.e., citizens were not just moving from one form of non-democratic regime to another) than in other countries that had not previously experienced democratic (or even quasi-democratic) rule. Therefore, in the countries that had enjoyed a period of interwar democracy, we would expect the effects of exposure to communism to be reduced.

Third, following a similar logic, we might expect that people who lived in countries that had enjoyed greater economic success prior to the onset of communism might be less receptive to communist socialization. To put this in the language of our hypotheses, we would expect greater *resistance* among citizens of countries with *higher levels of pre-communist development*. The logic here hinges on the idea that citizens in these countries would have less reason to be "thankful" for communism than people who lived in countries that were worse off prior to the onset of communism and its concomitant attention to economic development.

Next we turn to a number of communist-era variations that could explain why citizens of some countries may have been more receptive to communist socialization efforts. One such factor is how well the economy performed under communism. Conceptually, there are two ways that seem intuitively plausible for how we might think about the economy "performing well" under communism. One approach would be to take a long-range view, and assume that resistance will be lower in countries with *more economic growth under communist rule*. However, if post-communist citizens are more myopic, it is possible that they will view their years of interacting with communism through the prism of only the most recent years of economic development. Thus another way we could attempt to separate out countries where communism may have been seen in a better economic light would be by identifying countries where the *economy performed better in the final decade of communist rule*. In both cases, we would expect a more positive economic experience with communism to strengthen the effect of communist exposure.

Along similar lines, and building on Jowitt's distinction between independent and "derivative" regimes (Jowitt 1992: 47), we focus on the fact that for some countries, communism was essentially a *homegrown* affair. Here, we might expect citizens to be more receptive to communism, and thus to have less resistance to communist socialization, than those living in countries where communism was imposed by external forces (i.e., the Soviet army). In particular in Russia, communism was not only homegrown but was also associated with a period of superpower status.

---

[38] We measure the quality of interwar democracy by using the average Polity score in a country from 1920 to 1939.

Finally, there was rather significant cross-country variation in the degree to which repression continued to be a key component of communist rule as time passed (Linz and Stepan 1996). Here, the expectation is that in countries in which the communist regime maintained a more antagonistic relationship with the larger population to the bitter end, citizens might be that much more resistant to incorporating any of the regime's precepts in their own worldviews once communism collapsed. Put another way, there could be a "nostalgia effect" of continuing to reflect communist socialization after the collapse of communism in regimes where people look back on their most recent memories of communism with a more pleasant eye. In this way, late-communist liberalization could reduce resistance to communist socialization. We already somewhat tap into this with our characterization of different regime types (discussed in Section 2.3.1), but taking stock of how closed the regime remained at the very end of the communist era gives us a chance to explore this particular aspect of communist rule more directly. Recall, though, that in Section 2.3.1, we noted that it is possible that as a consequence of liberalization—or perhaps as an additional result of the same factors that gave rise to the liberalization—the quantity and intensity of communist propaganda (as well as the seriousness with which such message were viewed) could have decreased. Thus we are left with opposite predictions: late-communist liberalization could reduce resistance to communism socialization, but it also could reduce the intensity of that exposure as well.

2.3.4. Individual-Level Resistance Variables

Finally, we turn to individual-level factors that could strengthen resistance to communist socialization. Before doing so, it is important to mention one important caveat, which is that there could likely be other relevant factors that we are unable to measure with the data at our disposal. One would be the extent to which the respondent is an "economic winner" in the post-communist era (Tucker et al. 2002; Pacek et al. 2009). Further, there are certainly a number of personality traits that would be interesting to assess vis-à-vis resistance.[39] Thus for now, we simply note that economic winners and personality would be interesting categories to include among individual-level *resistance* hypotheses, but ones that we will not pursue in this book.

The first individual-level factor we do consider is the age at which one receives exposure to communism. As discussed in Chapter 1, there is a line

---

[39] For recent work in political science applying personality traits to political behavior, see, for example: Mondak and Halperin 2008; Mondak 2010; Mondak et al. 2010; Gerber et al. 2010; Gerber et al. 2011; Greene and Robertson 2016.

of argument in the political socialization literature proposing that people
are more open to socialization as children than later in life (Krosnick and
Alwin 1989; Visser and Krosnick 1998; Sears and Valentino 1997; D. Osborne et al. 2011). Within our *living through communism* framework,
then, this suggests we might find more *resistance* to communist regime
socialization efforts among adults than among children.[40]

Another factor that could increase individual-level *resistance* to communist socialization is *additional education*. Here a straightforward hypothesis would be that individuals with lower levels of education would
be more likely to accept regime pronouncements at face value than those
with additional years of schooling. We can think of this as either a selection effect—naturally curious people with more inclination to question
the world around them might be more likely to seek out higher education—or as a result of the additional schooling itself, in which students
with more years of education would likely have received more instruction
in the types of skills necessary to support critical thinking, especially in an
environment in which access to information was limited.

The situation is potentially more complex in the case of post-communist
countries, as not all education is created equal. For example, we might expect that *resistance* would be especially likely to have been increased by
pre-communist education (Darden and Grzymała-Busse 2006). By contrast, communist-era education provided the state with an additional opportunity to socialize children and young adults. So it is actually possible
that *communist education* would reduce resistance to future subsequent
socialization effects, thereby leading to stronger exposure effects. Therefore, even though such an analysis raises some methodological challenges,[41]
in Chapters 5 and 7 we present supplementary analyses that address the
variation in socialization effects for education received under different
political regimes.

Combining all our different discussions of education, therefore, we
have a number of related hypotheses about the role of education. Addi-

---

[40] It is worth noting that this argument has nothing to do with communism in particular,
and therefore could be applied to *living through* models anywhere.

[41] The ideal way to test these predictions would be to separately interact both communist
education and pre-communist education with years of exposure to communism while controlling for age. Unfortunately, because pre-communist education had to take place prior to
the advent of communism, the people who received pre-communist education are almost
all from Eastern Europe and correspondingly received between (approximately) 42 and
45 years of exposure to communism, which is simply not enough variation to estimate a
convincing model. We can, however, test the direct effects of pre-communist education on
attitudes and compare these with the direct effects of communist education. While outside
the framework of our *living through communism* model as specified here, such an approach
is consistent with the idea of trying to unpack the *mechanisms* by which *living through communism* affects attitude formation; see Section 1.2. in Chapter 1.

tional education generally is predicted to *increase resistance* to regime socialization, but having been educated under communist rule is predicted to *reduce resistance*. Finally, having been educated under pre-communist rule is predicted to *increase resistance*.

Third, to return to a theme from the beginning of this chapter, it is possible that followers of particular religious denominations would be more likely to resist communist imprinting. This could be because the actual doctrinaire teachings of the religion were more hostile to communism or, as Wittenberg (2006) has demonstrated, because religious institutions actually provided a bulwark against communist attempts at indoctrination. To explore this possibility, we subdivide post-communist citizens into five groups based on their self-identified religious denomination in the surveys: Protestants, Catholics, Eastern Orthodox, Muslims, and other (almost entirely atheists). While the very fact that respondents self-identify with a certain religious denomination may itself reflect a greater willingness/ability to resist communist indoctrination, we expect to see differences across religious denominations. In particular, we expect that Catholics and to a lesser extent Protestants would be more resistant to communist teachings than Eastern Orthodox and Muslims owing to the fact that Catholic and to some extent Protestant churches were on balance less accommodating to communist regimes than their Orthodox and Muslim counterparts. Furthermore, we would expect any resistance effect related to religion to be more pronounced among frequent attenders of religious services than among those who either do not attend religious services or do so only rarely.

Finally, we need to consider the fact that *parental socialization* could also contribute to *resistance* to communist exposure. We expect this effect to be strongest among the children of dissidents and/or parents actively repressed by the communist regime, but there is no reason not to expect an effect simply from the cumulative effect of years of negative comments about communists and communism around the dinner table, as one of us experienced firsthand growing up in Romania in the 1970s and 1980s. Thus *parental socialization* joins *late-communist political liberalization* in being identified as both a potential *intensifying* and *resistance* variable. However, in the case of *parental socialization* we do have theoretical expectations for when the effect should be more of an *intensifying* one (pro-communist parents) and more of a *resistance* one (anti-communist parents).

2.4. CONCLUSIONS

Tying all the preceding arguments together, Table 2.2 concisely presents the various factors that we propose could either strengthen or weaken the effects of exposure to communism.

Table 2.2. A Living through Communism Model

	Country level	*Individual level*
Intensifying factors	Types of communism (Stalinism (+), neo-Stalinism (+), post-totalitarian (−), reform communism (−) Higher proportion of hardline communist rule (+) Bureaucratic authoritarianism (+) [Late-communist economic liberalization] Late-communist political liberalization (−)	Urban residence (+) Male (+) Communist Party membership (+) Parental socialization (+ parent communist supporter)
Resistance factors	Pre-communist literacy (−) Interwar democracy (−) Pre-communist development (−) Communist economic success (+) Externally imposed communism (−) Late-communist political liberalization (+)	[Economic winners] [Personality traits] Childhood exposure (+) Pre-communist education (−) Communist education (+) Additional years of education (−) Religion: denomination (− Catholic, Protestant) and attendance (−) Parental socialization (− parent communist opponent)

Note: This table concisely summarizes our *intensifying* and *resistance* hypotheses. To facilitate the comparison with the statistical tests in Chapters 4–7, in this table a "+" represents a prediction that more of that factor will be associated with an additional year of exposure to communism having a *larger* effect in the direction predicted by communist ideology; a "−" suggests that an additional year of exposure to communism will have a *smaller* effect. So a "+" for intensity corresponds to more intensity and a larger predicted exposure effect, but a "+" for resistance corresponds to *less* resistance, and therefore a larger predicted effect for communist exposure. Note that late-communist political liberalization is predicted to possibly both strengthen exposure effects via increased *intensity* and weaken exposure effects via increased *resistance*. Similarly, parental socialization is predicted to increase intensity of exposure when one's parent was a communist supporter, but to increase resistance when one's parent was a communist opponent. Variables in [brackets] are those that are discussed in the text as having theoretical relevance but that we are unable to test empirically given our data.

Three points are worth noting. First, this is clearly not the only *living through communism* model that one could write down. Despite the fact that we have even tried to consider factors that we cannot currently test (e.g., personality traits), we are sure that other observers could identify additional factors that might moderate the effect of *living through communism*. That being said, as with all modeling exercises there are trade-offs between parsimony and thoroughness, and, as will become apparent in Chapters 4–7, testing even the effects of this many different variables is a time-consuming exercise. Overall, we believe the model laid out in Table 2.2 does a reasonably good job of moving beyond the original naive assumption—that any year of communist exposure in any country at any time is equivalent to any other year of communist exposure in any country at any time—to explore a wide range of factors that might *intensify* the effect of or provoke *resistance* to exposure to communism. Further, this list of factors was developed as a result of presenting earlier versions of our research to a large number of audiences, and the final compilation of factors listed above represents many valuable suggestions from many patient people.

Second, even to the extent that readers may disagree with any particular factors either included in or excluded from Table 2.2, the approach of thinking about legacy effects from *living through* rule by a particular regime—and *living through communism* specifically—as a function of years of *exposure*, factors that *intensify* this exposure, and factors that provide *resistance* to that exposure is one that could be replicated elsewhere without necessarily duplicating all the specific hypotheses we test in this book. Indeed, the very way we have introduced our *living through* legacy approach—generally in Chapter 1, and then applied to communism here in Chapter 2—is a reflection of the fact that we think the variables that populate Table 2.2 ought to vary across different regime types.[42]

Finally, it is important to note that Table 2.2 is not a statistical model, but a rather a concise statement of a set of hypotheses generated by a particular theoretical framework. Some of these factors undoubtedly covary (e.g., pre-communist literacy and interwar democracy), and tap into

---

[42]While we obviously think the variables we have presented here are the most appropriate ones in the communist context—otherwise the table would have different variables in it!—we would not be surprised to find scholars who think other factors are more important than the ones we have identified. And while we have included a few factors here that we do not measure in the empirical sections of this manuscript, it is undoubtedly the case that our choice of factors has been affected by the feasibility of data collection and data availability.

similar dimensions (e.g., Eastern Europe vs. former Soviet Union).[43] For now, this is fine, as we are just trying to create a thorough inventory of the specific hypotheses we will test as part of our assessment of the effects of *living through communism*. Correlation across independent variables in actual statistical models of course presents some challenges for how we interpret the results of our analyses, and it is to this and the many other methodological challenges of testing both our *living through communism* and *living in a post-communist country* explanations for the divergence in post-communist political attitudes to which we turn in the following chapter.

[43] We return to this question of the difference of effects in Eastern Europe and the former Soviet republics in Section 9.4.2 of Chapter 9.

■ ■ ■ ■ ■

CHAPTER 3

Methods and Data

QUESTION TO RADIO YEREVAN: Is Marxism-Leninism an art or science?
RADIO YEREVAN ANSWERS: It is probably an art. If it had been a science,
they would have tried it on animals first.

—Soviet joke from the 1980s

3.1. INTRODUCTION

The goal of this book is to document differences (or the lack thereof) in
opinions about fundamental political, economic, and social issues between
citizens in post-communist countries and those in the rest of the world and
to assess the extent to which these differences are due to communist-era
legacies. More specifically, we want to understand the extent to which *living in a post-communist country* and/or *living through communism* can
account for these attitudinal differences, and we want to do so in a rigorous, transparent, and falsifiable manner. The point of this chapter—much
in the spirit of all the recent moves in the field of political science toward
greater methodological transparency—is to be as explicit as possible about
the methodological and data choices we made in order to accomplish those
goals.

The chapter is divided into three parts. In Section 3.2, we introduce
the general ideas behind the methods that we employ in the book. In Section 3.3, we then discuss the more specific modeling decisions we made in
implementing the basic methodological approach described in Section 3.2.
The point of this section is not to discuss individual variables and how
they were coded, but instead to address categories of variables (e.g., "pre-
communist control variables") and why they appear in the models they do.
Moreover, for the most part we will avoid discussion of chapter-specific
modeling decisions (i.e., decisions pertaining to supplementary analyses
that appear only in single chapters, including Chapter 8, which features a
different set of analyses from Chapters 4–7) and leave those to the individual chapters in which they appear. This is also where readers can find a

description of our identification strategy for estimating the effect of years of exposure to communism while controlling for the age of the respondent.[1] In Section 3.4, then, we discuss the data, including both the surveys we use in our analysis (3.4.1) and the aggregate-level data we collected to supplement those surveys (3.4.2).[2]

That being said, we have designed the flow of the book in a way that hopefully makes reading this chapter optional. If you are reading this now and are not particularly interested in our methodological choices and simply want to get on with learning more about our findings, you should be able to jump ahead to Chapter 4 at this point and still be able to follow our analysis. In addition, this chapter is meant to be modular: if you are interested in data but not statistical methods, feel free to jump ahead to Section 3.4.[3] Finally, we hope that this chapter can be read out of order—and in a way function almost like a glossary—whereby if you get into the thick of one of the empirical chapters and then want to know why we made certain choices, you should be able to jump back and read the relevant sections of this chapter at that point in time.

3.2. GENERAL METHODOLOGICAL APPROACHES

The goal of this section is to provide an overview of the rationale underlying the primary statistical analysis that is found in each of the next four chapters (i.e., the first three tables in Chapters 4–7).[4] Roughly speaking, this breaks down into two categories: the *living in a post-communist country* analysis and the *living through communism* analysis. We describe each of these in turn.

---

[1] See Section 3.3.3. We largely do so by drawing on the fact that we have multiple surveys carried out at different points in time for almost all the countries in the primary analyses. We also gain leverage from the fact that communism took hold and ended in slightly different years in different countries, as well as the much more significant difference in the onset of communism across East-Central Europe and the non-Baltic former Soviet Union.

[2] Readers are also invited to see Pop-Eleches and Tucker (2014), where we address many of the more technical methodological points covered in this chapter in greater detail.

[3] For those of you who grew up in the United States in the 1980s, you can think of this as a "Choose Your Own Adventure" chapter: *If you'd like to immediately learn more about post-communist attitudes toward democracy, turn to Chapter 4. If you'd like to continue thinking about statistical models, proceed to Section 3.2. If you'd prefer to seize the sword of power and fight the dragon on your own, turn to page 370.*

[4] To reiterate, the additional analyses found in the latter parts of these chapters that differ from chapter to chapter will instead be introduced as they occur.

3.2.1. *Living in Post-communist Countries Analysis*

To recall, the goal of the *living in a post-communist country* approach is twofold. First, we want to identify whether or not there is a systematic difference in the attitude in question between citizens in post-communist countries and citizens in the rest of the countries included in our analysis. Second, we want to see if—having identified such a difference–any of our proposed *living in a post-communist country* variables can account for this difference.[5] In other words, can we explain this attitudinal discrepancy solely by taking account of the characteristics of the countries in which our respondents are living without recourse to any measure of an individual's actual experience of living through communism?[6]

Accordingly, we begin with a simple model that approximates a bivariate correlation. The dependent variable in this—and all the remaining—models will be our measure of the attitude in question at the time of the survey. To be clear, all the surveys employed in our study were carried out in the years *following* the collapse of communism, so we are examining attitudes among citizens of *post-communist* countries.[7] Whenever possible, we try to use an index composed of multiple questions for our dependent variable to avoid being overly reliant on a single question; details on how each specific dependent variable is constructed as well as basic descriptive statistics are provided in each chapter.[8] The model contains a dummy variable that identifies whether or not the respondent is a resident

[5] In Chapter 7, we find in our initial analysis of attitudes toward gender equality that there is *not* a systematic difference in our simplest model. Nevertheless, we still proceed with the remainder of our analysis in order to check—as seemed warranted at that point based on the findings in Chapters 4–6—whether or not the predicted difference appears once we, for example, take account of the pre-communist context.

[6] As will be addressed in greater detail below, we measure most of these characteristics at the aggregate level but do take advantage of a richer source of data to measure demographics at the individual level.

[7] This is also why we drop Vietnam and China from our analysis, as is discussed later in this chapter. Also, technically we should note that all of the former Soviet Republics were not actually "post-communist" countries at the time of the 1990 surveys, though the transition was well underway in many of these countries, especially in the Baltic republics. There were no surveys of post-Soviet states carried out in 1991, and by 1992 all the countries were actually post-communist.

[8] The one case in which we were unable to use an index was in our World Values Survey analysis of support for social welfare, for reasons we explain in more detail in Chapter 6, Section 6.2. In both the markets and gender equality chapters, we can use an index although we have fewer variables with which to work than we would have preferred. For this reason, we explored some different ways to compose our indexes—essentially whether to include variables in a continuous format or as a combination of dichotomous variables (e.g., high support for a position, low support for a position)—to see which produced the most reliable index (i.e., the highest Cronbach's alpha).

of a post-communist country, and the coefficient on this post-communist dummy variable represents our simplest estimate of the difference in attitudes between citizens in post-communist countries and those in the rest of the sample. The reason we do not simply report a correlation coefficient or a difference in means is because we do include year-fixed effects for the years in which the survey took place (as we do in every one of our cross-national analyses).[9]

To this baseline we then add blocks of variables designed to measure, in turn, pre-communist conditions in each of the countries, and then contemporaneous demographic, economic, and political conditions. Pre-communist conditions, as well as contemporary economic and political conditions, are all measured at the aggregate level, that is, each respondent in a given country-year gets the same value for those measures. The pre-communist conditions are, by definition, time invariant (i.e., they do not depend on the year in which the survey takes place); the contemporary economic and demographic conditions vary by year of survey but are again constant for each respondent in each country-year survey. Demographic variables, on the other hand, are measured at the individual level.[10]

We first add pre-communist conditions, then, in turn, add contemporaneous demographic, economic, and political conditions, first separately (by block) and then jointly.[11] What we are looking for here is the effect of including these variables in the model on the post-communist indicator (or "dummy") variable. We want to see both what this does to the magnitude of the coefficient for the post-communist indicator variable, as well as what it does to the statistical significance of the estimate.[12] Intuitively, what we are checking is whether by taking account of these other differences, say for example in the level of literacy in countries before the 1920s,

---

[9] We do this primarily to control for any global trends across time (e.g., the development of faith—or the loss thereof—in the "Washington Consensus") and to take account of the fact that the mix of communist and non-communist countries in the World Values Survey varies across years.

[10] These include education, income, rural/urban residence, and gender; although see footnote 31 of this chapter for details on the one exception in this regard, ethnolinguistic fractionalization. Pre-communist demographic conditions, such as literacy, are of course measured at the aggregate level, as in the proportion of the population that is literate.

[11] There is of course collinearity across these blocks—which is why we first enter them into our analysis separately before presenting a fully specified model—as well as within the blocks. The collinearity within blocks would be problematic if we were attempting to disentangle the effect of, for example, unemployment and inflation on the attitude in question. However, since our focus is simply on whether adding the block of variables eliminates the effect of the post-communist dummy variable, the fact that individual economic variables correlate with one another is essentially beside the point.

[12] In doing so, we will not stick to a particular cutoff of statistical significance (.05 or .01) but rather discuss the relative size of coefficients and standard errors in different models.

the post-communist differential in the attitude in question disappears.[13] So to continue with this example, if we found that there was a large democratic deficit in post-communist countries, but once we controlled for pre-communist literacy that deficit disappeared, we might very well conclude that the reasons citizens in post-communist countries were less supportive of democracy was *not* because of communist rule, but rather because people living in countries that had low literacy in the 1920s tended to be less supportive of democracy for reasons having nothing to do with communism, and it happens to be the case that communism took root in countries with disproportionately low-literacy rates in the 1920s.[14]

While controlling for contemporaneous variables that characterize *living in a post-communist country* is theoretically important if we want to disentangle the impact of communist legacies from other potential drivers of political attitudes, in statistical terms it raises concerns about post-treatment bias. In particular, given that by definition these variables are measured after the end of the "treatment" (i.e., communism), they are likely to be affected by both communism and other factors (such as the nature of IMF conditionality in the 1990s, EU integration incentives, policy decisions made by post-communist governments, etc.), which means that our estimates of the effect of communism from a model that includes post-communist controls will be biased. In a sense the issue is a question of semantics: if we interpret the post-communism dummy as a country-level variable, then post-treatment bias concerns apply for the reasons discussed

[13] When applied to the post-communist variables, one can think of this approach as broadly equivalent to a basic mediation analysis along the lines of the Baron and Kenny (1986) method of testing whether "we can make the effects go away" by adding particular variables (that in turn need to be affected by communism). However, note that in almost all cases, we are not engaging in a full-fledged mediation analysis both because these *living in a post-communist country* variables are not our main theoretical focus in this book and because the large number of variables would make systematic mediation tests for all the *living in a post-communist country* variables quite impractical. Moreover, a proper mediation analysis would require a careful discussion of the extent to which communist legacies were really responsible for particular post-communist developments—e.g., whether the high inflation experienced by many transition countries was due to communism or due to the adjustment strategies chosen in the wake of its collapse—which would get us into debates that are well beyond the scope of the present book. That being said, we do report the results of a standard mediation analysis for exposure to communism as part of our tests of the *living through communism* model using the approach of Hicks and Tingley (2011) and Imai et al. (2009) in Chapters 4–6.

[14] It is of course possible that some of the contemporaneous variables are in fact a function of pre-communist conditions. Again, this would be more of a concern if we were trying to somehow measure the direct and indirect effects of pre-communist conditions on our outcome variables. Instead, our goal is simply to see if the different blocks of variables explain away the post-communist attitudinal difference. Nevertheless, this is part of the reason we include our pre-communist control variables in all the subsequent *living in a post-communist country* analyses.

above. If, however, we interpret it as an individual-level indicator (that tells us whether a particular individual lives in a post-communist country), then we do not need to be concerned that this particular individual's residence would affect the aggregate-level economic and political country in his or her country of origin. Unfortunately, there are no real statistical fixes for post-treatment bias (King 2010). Thus, we use a two-pronged methodological approach. In the first table of our four main empirical chapters, we present the statistical models *with* contemporaneous variables as part of our *living in a post-communist country* analysis in order to satisfy the interests of readers who want to know whether post-communist attitudinal patterns can be attributed to the peculiar economic and political context of the turbulent transition years. However, to assuage the concerns of those who worry about post-treatment bias, we then drop the country-level contemporaneous variables from the model specifications used in the subsequent analyses.[15]

In addition to the cross-national analysis, we also rerun our models using data from just the German portion of the World Values Survey. The advantage of doing so is that Germany has citizens who experienced communism (those who lived in East Germany) and citizens who did not experience communism (those who lived in West Germany). Restricting our data to just Germany allows us to sidestep the potential concerns about survey response comparability and omitted/unobservable differences that may cause problems for cross-country regressions. These models are run solely with the individual-level demographic control variables, the year-fixed effects, and the post-communist dummy variable (capturing respondents from the Eastern Bundesländer). While there are of course many reasons why Germany might not be a "typical" post-communist country, this approach does give us the opportunity to address concerns about omitted country-level variables and the cross-cultural comparability of survey questions in cross-national public opinion surveys.[16]

---

[15] Note, however, that even though post-treatment bias concerns also apply at least in part to individual demographic controls (which may also be the product of both communist and post-communist influences, although see our previous discussion about post-treatment bias if we conceive of the post-communist dummy variable as an individual-level characteristic), we nevertheless continue to include the individual-level demographic control variables in the analyses related to communist exposure because we worried that dropping them would result in severely under-specified models given the extensive literature about the effects of various sociodemographic factors on political attitudes.

[16] One potential concern is that when people are interviewed in, for example, Munich in 2006 and coded as living in West Germany, they may have grown up in East Germany and in fact have been exposed to communism. This, unfortunately, is always going to be a problem with any attempt to study legacies using survey data (unless surveys explicitly ask about a respondent's origin) and at the end of the day is part of the inherent measurement error in such data. Indeed, this is a potential problem in our larger cross-national analyses,

3.2.2. *Living in Post-communist Countries:*
Unpacking Communism Analysis

Our next set of analyses employs the same basic framework as the original *living in a post-communist country* analysis—we add variables to a base model and observe whether the addition of these variables changes the effect of the post-communist dummy variable—but with a slightly different purpose in mind. Here, we attempt to measure discernible characteristics associated with the most important ways in which communism is thought to have remade these societies, and then observe whether taking account of these particular characteristics can explain away the attitudinal differences we observe. However, in an effort not to measure the effect of changes under post-communism, and in a sense get our "purest" measure of the effects of communist rule, we measure these "results of communism" not at the time of survey, but as they were in 1989, when communist rule came to end in Eastern Europe.[17]

We designed these analyses by attempting to model the set of variables that would give us the best opportunity to observe the way in which communist rule could have changed societies either from the pre-communist version of their own country or as compared contemporaneously to non-communist countries: in other words, how might communism have "mattered"? To illustrate the intuitive thinking behind the approach, consider the communist emphasis on reducing inequality. If the state of the world was such that people in countries with less inequality were also less supportive of markets, then perhaps the reason that we find less support for markets in post-communist countries could be because communism reduced

---

although of course we expect a far smaller proportion people to have moved from a non-post-communist country to a post-communist one (or vice versa) than we do to have moved internally in Germany; still, this is another reason why we use the German analysis as a supplementary test as opposed to as our primary form of analysis. However, in Chapter 5 we take advantage of the fact that a different survey carried out only in Germany (the German Election Panel Study) allows us to measure both where people grew up and where they were presently living at the time of the survey to explicitly leverage these differences in our analysis; see Section 5.7 in Chapter 5 for more detail.

[17]Here we faced a trade-off between accurately capturing the exact moment when communism came to an end in each post-communist country and using a much more complex coding rule for the data. In particular, even if we did divide up the post-communist countries and use data from 1989, 1990, and 1991 for different countries, we would face the perplexing question of which of these years we should use to draw the data for the rest of the (non-post-communist) countries in the analysis. So here we side with parsimony and simply use 1989, when the collapse of communism started, as the reference point. To the extent that we are trying to capture only the effects of communist rule, we run these models using just the pre-communist control variables (plus our survey-year-fixed effects) in addition to the end-of-communism variables but drop all the contemporaneous variables, including the individual-level demographic indicators.

inequality in these countries. If this was the case, then by adding a measure of inequality in 1989 to our models, we could test whether having a more equal society at the end of the communist period can explain the post-communist attitudinal differential in terms of markets.

The key point here is that if we are able to adequately control for conditions before communism took hold, then measuring conditions at the end of the communist period should give us our best opportunity to measure cleanly the effect of not simply having been living in a post-communist country at the time of the survey (which is what the dummy variable picks up), but of the various attributes of communist rule. Accordingly, we add blocks of variables to the model that are designed to account for four major characteristics of communist rule: development, redistribution/egalitarianism, non-democratic rule, and leftist ideology.[18]

3.2.3. Living through Communism: Inter-regional Analysis

Having addressed our *living in a post-communist country* methodological approach, we now turn our methodology for studying the effects of *living through communism*. In doing so, we turn our focus to examining the relationship between exposure to communist rule *at the individual level* and the attitude in question (e.g., do more years of exposure to communism make one more likely to oppose democracy?). We go about this in two different ways. The first approach builds directly on the method of analysis utilized to test the effect of *living in a post-communist country* (described in Section 3.2.1, above) but involves three important changes.

First, we begin with a base model that includes our pre-communist control variables and demographic characteristics of the respondent including, importantly, the age of the respondent. We include pre-communist controls here because—as in all our analyses—we want to account for factors that were present in these countries before the advent of communism. We include our demographic controls in the analysis because now that we are switching our emphasis to individual levels of exposure, we

---

[18] For the former two categories, we use these variables measured in 1989; for the latter two, we use the average values over the decade and a half prior to the collapse of communism. More specifically, we used the average number of years that a country was run by a regime classified as Left by the Database of Political Institutions from 1975 to 1989 and the average Polity regime score for 1975–89. In the case of the Polity scores, we find similar results using different time windows or using Freedom House Democracy scores, but we chose to present the results using Polity to be consistent with the pre-communist regime measure (which could not be calculated using Freedom House data).

want to make sure to control for all individual-level characteristics that could be influencing attitudes.[19]

Second, we add to this model a measure of years of exposure to communism, which becomes our primary focus. This measure is calculated by taking into account the year of the survey, the age of the respondent, and the country in which he or she lived; the value is set at zero for people who do not live in post-communist countries.[20] The primary test of our *living through communism* model, then, is to observe the coefficient on this variable. If the coefficient is in the correctly predicted direction and is statistically and substantively meaningful, then it would suggest that additional years of exposure to communism are associated with more congruence with the attitude (e.g., support for social welfare) in question.

The third difference from the *living in a post-communist country* analysis is that we also run these exposure models using country-fixed effects (i.e., including a series of dummy variables to pick up respondents' country of residence).[21] Normally, we would address this in the following section as part of our modeling discussion, but there is actually a substantive reason for addressing it here, which is that we are essentially measuring the effect of exposure in two different ways. In the standard analysis, we are leveraging cross-country variation in exposure, which includes the difference in exposure between citizens in post-communist countries and citizens in non-post-communist countries, but also the differences between citizens in different post-communist countries that had longer versus shorter spells of communist rule. In the country-fixed-effects models, however, we are examining variation in exposure across individuals only *within* countries. These fixed-effects specifications provide us with a more conservative estimate of exposure effects and, as we address in greater detail below, in some cases produce estimates that approximate more closely the results from running the models using hierarchical linear models.

---

[19] Of course, the most crucial demographic variable that we need to control for is age, or else our attempts to measure exposure will end up largely picking up the effect of being old in the post-communist era; how this is implemented and the methodological rationale behind our way of doing so is explained in detail below in Section 3.3.3. Note as well that, as discussed above, we drop the contemporaneous political and economic aggregate-level variables from these analyses so as to avoid problems of post-treatment bias.

[20] We exclude from our analyses anyone living in communist countries outside of Eastern Europe, the former Soviet Union, and Mongolia. In practice, the only countries in the World Values Survey that fall into this category are China and Vietnam; the rationale for doing so is explained later in this chapter in Section 3.3.5.

[21] Adding country-fixed effects means that we need to remove the post-communist dummy variable from our analysis because it perfectly co-varies with a linear combination of post-communist countries' country-fixed effects.

Having examined the effect of exposure directly, our next step is to assess the effect of the various *intensifying* and *resistance* factors in moderating the effect of exposure. We explore most of these using intra-regional analysis (described below in Section 3.2.4), but for two of these variables—communist regime type and adult versus childhood socialization—we continue to use the inter-regional analysis setup. We do this because individuals can have exposure to different types of communist regimes, and can have exposure to communism as both an adult and as a child. Further, the number of years of exposure to communism as an adult and as a child will vary at the individual level (and the same holds for exposure to different types of communist regimes). Thus modeling these effects using interactive variables—as we do for the remaining *intensifying* and *resistance* variables (and describe in detail in the following section)—seemed not to be the best way to take advantage of the richness of the data. Given that total years of exposure is equal to the sum of exposure to the different regime types (Stalinist + neo-Stalinist + post-totalitarian + reformist) or at different points of one's life (adult + childhood exposure), we chose instead to simply include multiple exposure variables in the models.[22] This in turn allowed us to continue to use the inter-regional analysis set up we had used for the generic *living through communism* model.

Before we turn to the methodological approach for the remaining *intensifying* and *resistance* variable—which will focus only on survey respondents in post-communist countries—it is important to address the question of why we continue to include non-post-communist countries at all in our first set of analyses of the effects of *living through communism*, given the fact that all respondents in non-post-communist countries are coded as having zero years of exposure to communism. We do so primarily for two methodological reasons. First, by continuing to maintain the structure used in our *living in post-communist countries* analysis, we can more directly compare the results for these analyses with the results from our *living through communism* analysis. In particular, this allows us to continue to include a post-communist dummy variable in our (non-fixed-effects) *living through communism* analysis, and thus measure the effect of adding exposure to communism to our models on the post-communist attitudinal differential in much the same way as we did, for example, with pre-communist characteristics. These models are then the basis for a more

---

[22] For the rest of our intensifying or resistance variables—regardless of whether they are coded at the individual level or the aggregate level—each individual will be assigned to either one category (e.g., highest level of education, lives in a country with the lowest quintile of pre-communist literacy) or to one value on a continuous scale (e.g., has a pre-communist per capita GDP of X), and thus are modeled as interactive effects.

formal mediation analysis to establish the extent to which individual communist exposure can account for the post-communist attitude differential.[23]

But even more importantly, including non-post-communist countries in the analysis gives us much more data from which to identify an exposure effect while simultaneously estimating the effect of age. Indeed, as we describe below in Section 3.3.4, when we limit our analysis only to respondents from post-communist countries, we will use a constrained regression with a fixed coefficient for the effect of age precisely because estimating both variables simultaneously leads to less stable estimates when relying only on respondents from post-communist countries. So there are pros and cons to both approaches; neither is a perfect fix.[24]

3.2.4. Living through Communism: Intra-regional Analysis

For our remaining *intensifying* and *resistance* variables, the value of the variable is fixed for each individual (e.g., you live in a country with a certain literacy level in the 1920s, or you are in an urban area, or you are a Catholic, etc.), and therefore the appropriate form of analysis is to interact each of these variables in turn with years of exposure. However, many of these aggregate-level variables make little sense out of the post-communist context (e.g., what would late-communist liberalization mean for a country that was not ever under communist rule?), so we now restrict our analysis to *only post-communist countries*. This has methodological implications for how we set up our models (discussed below in Section 3.3.4), but for now we focus on questions of interpretation.

Given that we are now interacting years of exposure with our intensifying and resistance variables, the key variable of interest is now the *interaction* between years of exposure and the variable in question; in other words, we want to ascertain whether years of exposure has a *different effect* on people in the different categories hypothesized to increase the intensity of exposure or resistance to exposure. Recall from the previous

---

[23] We run the formal mediation analysis using the medeff command in Stata 13.1 (Hicks and Tingley 2011), which compared to other mediation routines in Stata has the advantage of allowing the use of both weights and sample restrictions.

[24] Importantly, though, our country-fixed-effects models essentially approximate dropping all the non-post-communist countries from the analysis anyway. Since these models are measuring only within-country variation in years of exposure—and there is no within-country variation in exposure in the non-post-communist countries—then including these countries in the analysis cannot have an effect on the estimate of the exposure variable except to the extent that they affect the coefficients on other individual-level variables (such as age). So readers who would have preferred us exclude the non-post-communist countries from these analyses entirely can simply focus on the results from the country-fixed-effects version of the models.

chapter that these hypotheses make predictions regarding both aggregate-level factors (e.g., the effect of exposure to communism should be stronger in countries where it was *homegrown* as opposed to *imposed*) and at the individual level (e.g., the effect of exposure to communism should be stronger for people with *lower levels of education*). In order to test these hypotheses, we want to observe whether a year of exposure has a larger effect (in the direction predicted by the *living through communism* model, e.g., less support for democracy or markets) for residents of countries where, for example, communism was homegrown, in our aggregate example, or a larger effect on people with less education, in our individual example.[25] By looking at the *difference* between the predicted effect of a year of exposure across the categories within each intensifying/resistance variable, we will then be able to assess the level of support for each of the intensifying and resistance hypotheses in turn.[26] Collectively, though, assessing all these hypotheses will give us the opportunity to understand in a more nuanced way how exposure affects the attitude in question.

3.3. MODELING DECISIONS

Having laid out the basic logic behind our methodological approach, our next task is to explain the explicit modeling decisions we have made in each of these cases. By definition, then, this section will be more technical than the previous one and represents our attempt to be as transparent as possible about both what analyses are presented in the remainder of the book and why we made the specific modeling choices we did.

---

[25] The one area where the interpretation of these interactions effects is not straightforward is for the variables measuring late-communist economic and political conditions. The problem lies in the fact that while strong economic growth in the 1980s may lower the resistance to communist exposure in that decade, it obviously cannot retrospectively lower resistance to the exposure that some citizens of communist countries experienced in the 1960s and 1970s. Therefore, the interactions for those models need to be interpreted somewhat differently, in the sense that it is conceivable that solid late-communist performance would reinforce earlier communist socialization, while weak performance in the 1980s could undermine the effects of earlier socialization.

[26] As many before have argued, the best way to assess interactive effects is graphically, and so we will follow this path as well by displaying the predicted effect for a year of exposure in the different categories suggested by the relevant intensifying or resistance variables (Brambor et al. 2006). For all the aggregate variables, we will display the effect in two categories (e.g., homegrown vs. imposed communism, high pre-communist GDP vs. low pre-communist GDP); we do the same for some of the individual variables (e.g., male vs. female, urban vs. rural), but in some cases we have more than two categories (e.g., religious denomination, highest level of education).

3.3.1. Modeling the Living in a Post-communist
Country Analysis

Most of our data is multilevel in nature, with country-specific indicators (e.g., literacy rates pre-1920), country-year indicators (e.g., unemployment in the year of the survey), and individual-level variables (e.g., educational achievement of the respondent) (Snijders and Bosker 1999; Gelman and Hill 2007). Despite its hierarchical nature, we opted to employ a simpler analysis: ordinary least squares regression with clustered standard errors. We feel confident doing so for four reasons. First, we have so many Level 1 observations (i.e., survey respondents) for each Level 2 observation (i.e., the country's unemployment rate) that there is very little analytical leverage to be gained as part of a trade-off for the added complexity of running a hierarchical model. Second, in all our analyses, we cluster the standard errors at the country-year (survey) level, which adjusts the standards errors to account for the much smaller number of Level-2 (country-year) observations and patterns that an ordinary least squares (OLS) analysis might miss. Third, we also use equilibrated survey weights in all our analyses that combine any within-country survey weights with a cross-country component that adjusts for sample size differences across countries; this ensures that each country-survey affects the overall results the same amount, regardless of whether certain surveys had a larger N than others.[27] Finally, we have at various points throughout the project run robustness tests of particular sets of results and have never found that rerunning our analyses using hierarchical models produces results that noticeably differ in substantive terms from what we find with OLS.[28]

As mentioned in the previous section, we begin the *living in a post-communist country* analysis by adding variables measuring pre-communist conditions to our base model. Our goal was to control for as many aspects as possible of the cultural, political, and developmental context in which Soviet communism took root. The challenge here is that data from the pre-1920s era is of course harder to come by than data from the post-communist era. With these constraints in mind, we include data on pre-communist wealth, urbanization, and literacy in an effort to take account of pre-communist development, the religious denomination of the majority of the population and colonial legacy to take account of pre-communist cultural and institutional influences (Janos 2001; Acemoglu et al. 2001),

---

[27] In other words, if one country happened to sample twice as many respondents, it would not have twice as large a commensurate effect on the overall results.

[28] In addition, for this book we have rerun the primary *living in a post-communist country* models (the first tables in Chapters 4–7) and *living through communism* models (the third tables in Chapters 4–7) using hierarchical models, and we include these results in the electronic appendix. We thank in particular Nathaniel Beck for numerous discussions on this topic.

and pre-communist Polity regime scores to take account of the political context. In addition, we also include a number of geographic indicators—distance from Greenwich, England, distance from the equator, average altitude, and whether the country is landlocked—that prior research has shown to be related to political and economic development.[29] One important point to note about all these variables is that—by definition–they are coded at the *country* level, not at the country-year level, as pre-communist history does not change based on whether a survey is conducted in 1995 or 2005. A full list of these variables can be found in Table 3.1.

For contemporary political, economic, and demographic variables (all also listed in Table 3.1), we rely on many of the usual suspects. The main point to note is that our economic and political variables are coded at the country-year level and our demographic variables are coded at the individual level.[30] We have more details on particular variables and how they are coded below in Section 3.4, but for now two additional points are worth noting. First, we include religion as one of our demographic variables in two different ways, distinguishing both denomination and frequency of attendance at religious services. Second, we felt strongly that it was important to include a measure of corruption as part of our *living in a post-communist country* analysis, but it could have been included as part of either the political or economic set of variables. We ultimately chose to include the corruption measure as part of our political variables because we saw corruption more as an "institutional" feature of society more than a particular economic outcome. As readers will discover in the ensuing chapters, the distinction between adding economic and political variables that capture *living in a post-communist country* to the models does not end up being one of the main substantive conclusions of the book; had this been the case, we would likely have carried out additional tests to see if shifting corruption from the political to economic set of variables would have made much of a difference.[31]

---

[29] See for example Sachs and Warner (1997); Hall and Jones (1999); Acemoglu et al. (2001); Easterly and Levine (2003); Collier and Hoeffler (2003); and Rigobon and Rodrik (2005).

[30] The one exception here is ethnic diversity, which we include as part of our demographic control variables and which is actually coded at the country level because the data we use here—James Fearon's ethnolinguistic-fractionalization index—is coded only at the country level (Fearon 2003). It is obviously not ideal to have to rely on a single variable here, but compared to many of the other variables in the study, ethnic diversity (generally) does change relatively slowly.

[31] Readers should also note that we do *not* include individual-level sociodemographic variables in our controls in all our *living in a post-communist country* models precisely because these variables are one of our blocks of post-communist characteristics to be tested. They are, therefore, included in the model where we introduce post-communist demographic characteristics (see Table 3.1, as well as the first tables in Chapters 4–7, Model 3)

Table 3.1. Living in a Post-communist Country Variables

Pre-communist variables (*country-level*): Urbanization 1920s; Landlocked; Distance from equator; Distance from Greenwich; British colony; French colony; Spanish colony; German empire; Habsburg empire; Russian empire; Ottoman empire; Other European colony; Mean elevation; Log GDP/capita 1914; Literacy 1920s; Average Polity score 1900–1915; Average Polity score 1900–1915 × Overseas colony; Overseas colony pre-WWI; Imperial territory pre-WWI; Muslim majority; Christian majority

Post-communist demographic variables (*all individual-level except Ethnic fractionalization*): Ethnic fractionalization; Post-secondary education; Secondary education; Primary education; HH income; Town resident; City resident; Large city resident; Male; Age; Religious attendance often; Religious attendance never; Atheist

Post-communist economic variables (*country-survey-level*): GDP change since previous year; Unemployment; Inflation (Log); GDP as % of GDP in 1989; Income inequality

Post-communist political institutions variables (*country-survey-level*): Corruption index; Health and education spending as % of GDP, Freedom House Democracy Score; Proportional representation electoral system; Mixed electoral system; Majoritarian electoral system; Presidential system; Parliamentary-presidential system; Parliamentary system*

End of communism sociodemographic variable (*country-survey-level*): Urbanization in 1989; Primary school enrollment 1989, Literacy 1989; Energy intensity 1989; Industry as % of GDP in 1989; Log GDP per capita 1989

End of communism social welfare indicators (*country-level*): Health and education spending as % of GDP 1989; Income inequality 1989; State sector size 1989

End of communism political variables (*country-level*): Average Polity score 1975–89; Average left-wing party share of government 1975–89

* The electoral system and governing system variables are mutually exclusive and exhaustive categories; thus one category is always omitted when these dummy variables are include in regression analyses. For consistency, we generally omit majoritarian electoral system and parliamentary system.

One other methodological issue related to our *living in a post-communist country* analysis warrants mention at this time. One of the concerns with cross-country analysis is that we can never control for all the factors that distinguish countries from one another in any statistical model. One way to account for this concern is to conduct statistical analyses only within a single country, but for the purpose of our study that would have meant restricting our analysis to Germany, the only country with intra-country variation in

and in our full models with all the *living in a post-communist country* variables (Models 7 and 8 in the first tables in Chapters 4–7).

having a communist past. Doing so would have come at the cost of more limited external validity, which is why we opted to include a Germany-only analysis alongside the cross-country analysis to function as a kind of robustness check. Another option would have been to include country-fixed effects in all the models—which we do employ in our inter-regional analysis of the effect of *living through communism*—but by doing so we would lose the ability to analyze cross-national variation. Indeed, using country-fixed effects for our *living in a post-communist country* analysis would essentially undermine the main point of the analysis, which is to distinguish attitudes in one set of countries (post-communist countries) from attitudes in other countries.

We do, however, test the robustness of our pre-communist findings using a relatively new methodological technique. Following Hainmueller (2012), we use entropic balancing to create a set of weights that allow us to match the treatment group (post-communist countries) to the control group (non-post-communist countries) along a number of the key developmental characteristics included as controls in the original model (see Table 3.1). This approach has the advantage of relaxing the linearity assumptions implicit in our parametric regression model but comes at the cost of reducing the number of characteristics on which we can match the two groups.[32] With this trade-off in mind, we employ entropic balancing primarily as a robustness test, but in each of the following four chapters, we are reassured when the entropic balancing models produce largely the same findings as we find in our standard parametric analysis of our pre-communist variables.

3.3.2. Modeling the Living in a Post-communist Country Unpacking Communism Analysis

Our modeling choices for the "unpacking communism" analysis are exactly the same as for the *living in a post-communist country* analysis: we employ ordinary least squares analysis with country-year (survey) clustered standard errors and equilibrated survey weights. Again, the goal is to see what happens to the coefficient on the post-communist dummy variable when we add different clusters of variables—here, clusters tied to the primary features of communist rule (development, redistribution/low inequality, non-democratic rule, and leftist ideology). The key distinction, however, from the *living in a post-communist country* analysis is that instead of adding variables that measured conditions before the onset of communist rule or contemporaneously with the survey, we are instead now attempting to capture conditions *at the end of communist rule but before the onset of post-communism.*

---

[32] The tests were run using the ebalance routine in Stata 13.1 (Hainmueller and Xu 2013).

To do so, we measure conditions as they were in 1989. For most variables, this means simply taking the aggregate-level statistic for the year of 1989. However, for two variables—level of democracy and leftist ideology—sampling conditions in 1989 seemed less valuable than measuring conditions during the last period of communist rule. Remember that we are measuring conditions both in post-communist countries and outside of post-communist countries, and what we are trying to do is answer questions such as "can the fact that post-communist countries had been ruled by leftist regimes under communism account for the differences we see in post-communist attitudes?" By definition, communist countries will be coded as "leftist" for any summary measure of rule under communism, so the question becomes what exactly it is we are measuring in all other countries. For both ideology and political openness we settled on using average values in the decade and a half (i.e., 1975–89) preceding the collapse of communism because such averages are arguably better at capturing the political environment experienced by citizens of particular countries than a short-term snapshot in a single year.[33]

One final point to note is that—as with the previous *living in a post-communist country* analysis—we still do not include demographic control variables in these analyses. The reason we do so here is because most of the variables we are including in these analyses (e.g., education under communism, literacy under communism, economic development under communism) are trying to pick up the effects of communist policies that were intended to alter the sociodemographic composition of the population. Thus controlling for sociodemographic characteristics at the time of the survey—in addition to introducing post-treatment bias—would also in effect be somewhat akin to measuring the effects of communism twice. We do, however, include our pre-communist control variables in these analyses, precisely because controlling for conditions before communism took hold and then measuring conditions when communism collapsed represents our best estimate of the "pure" effect of communism (i.e., net of pre-communist starting positions).

3.3.3. Modeling the Living through Communism Inter-regional Exposure Analysis

To reiterate, the difference between the setup of the *living through communism* analysis and the *living in a post-communist country* analysis is that we are now adding a measure of years of exposure to communism to our analysis. This variable is coded on an individual-level basis and is

---

[33]Thus, if a country (such as Brazil) was authoritarian until the mid-1980s and then democratized, we would want to capture that fact rather than just call it democratic in 1989. Similar points can be made about having a leftist party in power.

calculated using each individual's age and country of residence to estimate the number of years that the individual was six or older while her country was under communist rule. Therefore, if communism ended in one's country of residence in 1989 and someone was 25 years old at the time of a 2005 survey, the respondent would be coded as receiving 4 years of communist exposure (at ages 6, 7, 8, and 9). However, if respondent was only 20 years old at the time of the 2005 survey, she would be coded as having no years of exposure to communism. Thus, *years of exposure* is a function of the start and end dates of communism in one's country, one's age, and the time of the survey. Residents of non-post-communist countries are all coded as having had 0 years of exposure.

While the setup is largely the same as in the *living in a post-communist country* analysis, our focus in interpreting the findings now changes, with our primary emphasis being on the direction and significance of the coefficient on the exposure variable; our expectation is that more years of exposure will lead to greater support for the regime position on the issue in question (e.g., anti-markets, pro–social welfare, etc.). Since we still include the post-communism dummy and the age variable in the non-fixed-effects model specifications,[34] the exposure variable represents a fairly conservative estimate of the role of communist socialization effects, net of the effects of living in a post-communist country and of the fact that respondents with longer communist exposure tend to be older. As discussed in the previous section, we run each of our models a second time using country-fixed effects; in these models we drop the post-communist dummy variable because it is a linear combination of the country-fixed effects from the post-communist countries.[35] We also repeat the analysis four times, once for exposure, once for exposure by regime type, once for exposure by time of life (i.e., adult versus childhood exposure), and once interacting adult and childhood exposure.[36] While our expectation remains

[34] In line with the convention in age-period-cohort (APC) models, our regressions include age and dummy variables for the survey year in addition to exposure indicators to disentangle the different dimensions of temporal variation; for more details, see Pop-Eleches and Tucker (2014).

[35] Indeed, once we include country-fixed effects, it is impossible to include any dummy variable in our models that single out a particular set of countries, because that would always represent a linear combination of the country dummy variables from those particular countries.

[36] Childhood exposure is coded as years of exposure between ages 6 and 17, while adult exposure is coded as years of exposure from age 18 up. Total exposure is simply the sum of child and adult exposure. Given the length of the communist experience—especially in the former Soviet Union—this gives the child-exposure variable a peculiar distribution. Most respondents will simply have had a full 12 years of exposure as children. Those who have had fewer than 12 years will either be young (people who were younger than 17 when communism collapsed in their country) or old (people who were at least 7 years old upon

that more years of exposure will increase support for the relevant attitude in question, we are now also interested in whether these effects differ across the predicted subcategories, for example, whether we observe a larger effect for Stalinist exposure than for reformist communist exposure. To assess the empirical support for this claim, we can simply observe the relative size of the coefficients for, in this example, Stalinist exposure and reformist exposure, as well as the statistical significance of any difference between these coefficients.

Our "base model" for these analyses (i.e., the model to which we add years of exposure) includes pre-communist control variables because they predate any communist exposure. We also continue to control for individual-level demographic characteristics in order not to introduce unnecessary omitted-variable bias into our analyses. We do not, however, include contemporaneous political and economic indicators in an effort to avoid introducing post-treatment bias.

One final point worth reiterating is our identification strategy for finding an effect for years or exposure while controlling for the age of respondents. The challenge is that if we were to use a single survey from a single country, age would be very highly correlated with years of exposure to communism because of the way that the exposure variable is constructed. However, even within a single survey this correlation is not perfect for two reasons. First, there is a ceiling effect for exposure among the older respondents (those born seven or more years before the start of communism), since exposure cannot be higher than the total years the country was under communist rule. Obviously this ceiling effect is not very important in the interwar Soviet republics (because there are relatively few respondents born pre-1910 in post-communist surveys), but it matters considerably more for the post-WWII Eastern European communist regimes.[37] Conversely, exposure is coded as zero for all respondents who were five or younger when communism fell, and this group becomes a larger part of the survey samples in later surveys.

---

the advent of communist rule in their country). Of course, citizens of non-post-communist countries will have 0 years of exposure. As will become clear in the ensuing chapters, we find less support for the effect of childhood exposure than the extant political socialization literature would have led us to expect in a number of the chapters, which led us to wonder whether there might be something mechanical about the distribution of this variable that prevent positive findings. This concern, however, was at least somewhat mitigated when we did finally see substantively and statistically significant findings in the gender equality chapter in line with the received wisdom regarding child socialization, suggesting that there was nothing mechanical about the distribution of child exposure that prevented statistically significant findings.

[37] For example, in the 1990 WVS survey for Bulgaria the ages for respondents with the maximum communist exposure (45 years) varied from 50 to 90.

When pooling data from multiple surveys from multiple years from multiple countries, though, there are several important additional sources of leverage for disentangling the effects of age and communist exposure. First, we can take advantage of the fact that communism did not start and end at the same time in all countries, especially when comparing Eastern European and interwar former Soviet republics. Thus, even among the former communist countries, respondents of the same age in a given survey year will have had different years of exposure to communism (e.g., a 70-year-old Russian surveyed in 1999 will have had significantly more exposure to communism than a 70-year-old from Poland surveyed in 1999 owing to the earlier start date and later end of communism in the former country as opposed to the latter). Second, in some cross-national survey series, such as the World Values Survey, there are multiple countries that were surveyed multiple times over time periods spanning almost two decades. Therefore, if we compare respondents from the same country across different years, we can also get respondents of the same age different lengths of communist exposure (e.g., a 40-year-old surveyed in 1992 will have had 10 more years of exposure to communism than a 40-year-old in the same country surveyed in 2002). Taken together, these factors allow us to estimate an effect for exposure even controlling for age, a fact we go into in significantly greater detail in an article on this methodological approach that was part of a special issue on age-period-cohort analysis in *Electoral Studies* (Pop-Eleches and Tucker 2014).[38]

3.3.4. Modeling the Living through Communism Intra-regional Exposure Analysis

Our assessment of our remaining intensifying and resistance variables follows the same basic approach as our analysis of the regime-type and time-of-life exposure analysis: we have a base model to which we add years of exposure, and then we examine our results to see if the effect of exposure is moderated by our intensifying and resistance variables as predicted. As noted above in Section 3.2.3, once we move beyond regime type and time-of-life exposure, the rest of our intensifying and resistance variables are of the type that each respondent will be assigned to a single category (e.g., religious attendance) or value on a continuous scale (e.g., interwar average Polity score in one's country of residence). Thus, the appropriate modeling technique is to interact years of exposure with the proposed

---

[38] Interested readers should see the article, but one interesting takeaway is that we do not actually need that many waves of surveys in each country to identify an estimate for exposure. We thank Anja Neundorf and Dick Niemi for their invitation to participate in the conference leading up to the publication of the special issue.

modifying variable (i.e., the intensifying or resistance variable). This leads us to make three important methodological changes for these analyses.

First, we now—for the first time—limit our analysis to data from post-communist countries. We do so because of strong theoretical concerns about the comparability of certain measures between communist and non-communist countries. To give a couple of examples, what would "late-communist political liberalization" mean outside the context of post-communist countries? We measure this using a country's Polity score in the decade and a half leading up to 1989, but we do so in order to distinguish post-communist countries where the regime opened a bit toward the end of the communist era from those where it did not; outside of the post-communist world this would simply indicate whether a country was democratic or not in the 1989. The United States, for example, would score high on this category but was in no way a communist country that was opening up a bit. In a similar vein, only countries that had ever experienced communism could be coded as having homegrown versus imposed communism; there is not even a way to code a country like that United States in that categorization.

More generally, once we move away from "years of exposure" as a non-interacted variable—where we can code people outside the communist world as having zero years of exposure, and which was still the case in our inter-regional analysis set up when we could break down individuals into years of exposure in different categories—to models where we need to interact years of exposure with distinct features of the communist experience, it becomes increasingly difficult to justify continuing to leverage the data from the non-post-communist countries in our analysis. While there are some intensifying and resistance variables for which we could code people in non-post-communist countries (e.g., highest level of education attained), the trade-off here would be bouncing back and forth between different data sets for the analysis of different intensifying and resistance variables, which would make comparisons arguably more difficult to justify. Thus we made the decision to limit all our intensifying and resistance analyses that included interactive variable to only the post-communist cases.

However, this change in samples raises some methodological challenges owing to the fact that in the post-communist only sample, age and communist socialization are much more highly correlated than in the global sample, thereby leading to more unstable statistical results.[39] Therefore, our methodological change is that we now employ *constrained* regression

---

[39]This is the case because in the global sample we have so many people of all ages with no exposure to communism. Once we restrict the analysis to just the post-communist countries, this correlation becomes higher. To be clear, we can still identify our models for all the reasons discussed in the previous section, but the results are less stable.

analysis instead of standard regression analysis,[40] in which we constrain the age coefficient across all the models to the estimate obtained from running a model regressing our variable in question (e.g., support for democracy in Chapter 4, support for markets in Chapter 5, etc.) on age (and a battery of demographic controls) in the full sample of *non-communist* countries. We then set the coefficient for age in our main regression (run on the post-communist surveys only) to the coefficient estimate for the age variable obtained from the first regression. Thus, the model is run still controlling for age, which allows us to estimate the attitudinal effects of additional years of communist exposure net of the age of the respondent, but without having to simultaneously estimate effects for age and exposure using only the post-communist data.

Note that there are basically two options for how to "set" age for the constrained regression analysis: estimate age on the full data set; and estimate age using just the non-post-communist countries. The advantage of this latter option is that it ensures that our estimate of the effect of age on our variable in question is entirely uncontaminated by any of effect of communist exposure. As "age independent of exposure" is what we would be trying to estimate by including age in a regression model in the first place, we opted to generate our coefficient for age in this matter. Thus the coefficient on age in these models can be interpreted as the effect of age on the attitude in question untainted by any exposure to communism, but in practice running the model on the full dataset or only the non-post-communist countries tended to generate very similar coefficients for age in all cases (arguably because ex-communist countries accounted for only about a quarter of the overall respondents in the WVS surveys we analyzed).[41]

The third change is that since we are we now including only data from the post-communist countries, we no longer have any reasons to include our pre-communist control variables (other than the case where the pre-communist indicator is the intensifying or resistance variable being tested as a moderator in the model). Recall that the point of including the pre-communist control variables in the prior base models was to control for where communism took root and how those countries differed from countries where communism did not arise in period of time before the communist era; with only communist countries in the sample, these variables are no longer needed.[42] As we continue to exclude all contemporaneous

---

[40]These analyses are performed using the cnsreg command in Stata 13.1. We thank Larry Bartels for this suggestion.

[41]However, we would expect this choice to matter more in surveys where ex-communist countries are overrepresented (e.g., in the EBRD Life in Transition Societies surveys).

[42]There is also a pragmatic dimension to this decision: similar to the age/exposure relationship, many other pre-communist control variables become much more highly corre-

Table 3.2. Intensifying and Resistance Variables

Country-level variables: Literacy in the 1920s; Pre-communist GDP per capita; Average polity scores 1920–39; Economic growth over entire communist period; "Native" communist regime; Installed communist regime; Proportion of years under communism with "hardline" communist rule;* Economic growth 1981–88; Polity score in 1989

Individual-level variables: Catholic, Protestant, Eastern Orthodox, Muslim, other religion; Religious attendance; Religious attendance interacted with denomination; Primary education; Secondary education; Higher education; No education; Sex; Residence**

* Years of rule under Stalinism and neo-Stalinism as proportion of total years under communist rule.

** Religion, education, residence, and sex are mutually exclusive and exhaustive categories; thus one category is always omitted when these dummy variables are include in regression analyses. For consistency, we generally use "other" religion, no education, female, and rural resident as our omitted category.

variables to avoid post-treatment bias, our intra-regional exposure analysis models therefore consist only of years of exposure, age (constrained), the variable for which we are testing whether there are either resistance or intensifying effects, and our individual-level control variables. While this choice leads to statistical models that are underspecified compared to the first set of regressions, this does not affect the estimates for the main coefficients in which we are interested: individual communist exposure and the interaction terms between exposure and individual or country-level moderating variables.[43]

Table 3.2 concisely lists all the different intensifying and resistance variables. One final point to note is that since we are now primarily interested in the interactive effect between each of these variables and years of exposure, we follow the advice of Brambor et al. (2006) and display our results for these analyses in the text of book in graphic format. While we provide more detail on exactly how these figures are constructed the first time one appears in Chapter 4, the basic idea is that we will display the marginal

---

lated (e.g., such as interwar literacy and economic development) when we limit ourselves to only the post-communist countries. Similarly, we also would encounter degree of freedom constraints more quickly for aggregate-level variables with the more limited set of post-communist cases, especially for pre-communist indicators at the country level (as opposed to at the country-survey level).

[43] Additionally, we no longer report country-fixed-effects models in these sections. In the case of the country-level *intensifying* and *resistance* variables, this would basically be impossible because the country-fixed effects would be linear combinations of our country-level variables. We report the results from the individual level interactions in the same manner for consistency's sake.

effect of an additional year of exposure for a respondent in the 5th and 95th percentile for each variable (which, for categorical variables, and of course dummy variables, essentially means the highest and lowest categories) as well as confidence intervals around that estimate.[44] This allows for an easily interpretable overview of which intensifying/resistance variables do indeed lead to different effects for years of exposure, and whether these differences are in the correctly predicted direction. The tabular version of the regression results are available in the electronic appendix, and, when relevant, we will discuss the statistical significance of the effects in the text of the chapter.

3.3.5. Other General Modeling Points

In this final section on modeling choices, we address modeling choices that run across our different forms of analysis.

The first modeling issue that permeates all the different analyses is the question of missing data, which primarily affects a few of the country-level variables used in the *living in post-communist countries* analyses. We approach this in two ways. As a first cut, we identified a small number of microstates (Andorra, Iceland, Luxembourg, and Malta) and non-independent territories (Puerto Rico and Taiwan) that had missing data for a broad range of indicators (because many data sources do not report statistical data for very small or non-independent countries). In order to ensure that the results of our *living in a post-communist country* tests were comparable across different model specifications, we excluded these countries from all our tests. While doing so leads to a small but noticeable reduction of the sample size, we felt that—with the partial exception of Taiwan—the substantive loss of doing so was minimal given that most of these countries were only marginally comparable to the post-communist countries in our sample.

The second component of our approach is that in the few cases where we were unable to fully code our aggregate-level variables, we mean replace the missing variables and then add a dummy variable to identify the cases where this mean replacement takes place.[45] This means that the coefficient on the variable in question is estimated only using the cases for which we actually have data without forcing list-wise deletion.[46] Obviously we do not use this approach for any of our dependent variables.

A second issue concerns the reference group of countries to which we compare attitudes in post-communist countries. In our primary analysis,

---

[44]These are estimated using the margins command in Stata 13.1.

[45]We also applied this approach to a few individual-level demographic variables in the World Values Survey.

[46]We thanks Chris Achen and Larry Bartels for suggesting this approach. For other applications, see Pacek et al. 2009; and Powell and Tucker 2014.

we include in this group any country included in the World Values Surveys that was *not* still a communist county at the time of the survey (i.e., we drop Vietnam and China). The reason for doing so was simply that while we clearly could not include these countries as "post-communist," it made even less sense to put them in the non-communist reference category when the goal was to see if, for example, the effect of communist rule was to make people less supportive of markets than people in "other" countries. Put another way, if communism made people less supportive of markets, then we should not expect people in post-communist countries to be less supportive of markets than people still living in communist countries.

However, this still leaves open the questions of what countries should be included in our non-communist reference category. Four options seemed viable. The first would be to compare post-communist attitudes to those of citizens in "advanced industrialized democracies," which in turn could be limited to European countries if we wanted to control for history and geography a bit more. The second option would be to take the opposite approach and compare post-communist attitudes to those held by people from countries that were *not* living in advanced industrialized democracies. To be clear, both of these approaches strike us as defensible and interesting. It would be interesting to know if and why post-communist citizens held attitudes that differed from either of these subgroups of countries, and indeed one set of our analyses (those involving data from the EBRD's LiTS collection) takes the former approach by necessity, as the only non-post-communist countries in that dataset are from Europe.

A third option would be to try to compare the post-communist countries to a set of non-communist countries that approximate most closely what the ex-communist countries might have looked like if they had never been under communist rule. While such an approach can be approximated by comparing East to West Germany, applying this counterfactual logic to the full set of ex-communist countries is obviously much more difficult. One could do so on a geographic basis, by selecting neighboring non-communist countries such as Austria, Greece, Turkey, or Iran, or one could select on the basis of pre-communist developmental indicators, which might throw a number of other late-developing countries into the mix (including parts of Latin America and East Asia). While we did not explicitly create such a counterfactual sample, given that doing so is bound to be arbitrary and controversial, our entropic balancing analysis described earlier in this chapter essentially creates such a synthetic comparison group and has the additional advantage of being tailored to the particular mix of countries in a particular set of tests based on the WVS surveys.[47]

---

[47]Thus, beyond the "philosophical" question of how much Finland and how much Afghanistan to throw into the mix, a meaningful comparison would need to be tailored to the particular country composition of the post-communist sample for any given analysis. In

However, for our primary analysis utilizing the World Values Survey data set, we decided to use all the available data—that is, every country (besides the still technically communist China and Vietnam and the non-independent/microstates mentioned above) for which the relevant questions allow us to code our dependent variables—in our analyses. The reason was simply that we did not have a compelling theoretical reason to want to compare attitudes in post-communist countries only to other advanced industrialized democracies, European countries, or other transition countries. The theoretical arguments we have advanced in the previous chapters all related to the overall effect of communism, not of communism compared to some other particular form of historical development or political experience. From this vantage point, then, the goal of trying to take advantage of all the data we had available seemed most appropriate. Furthermore, dropping countries in nonrandom ways could introduce bias into our analyses, and by adopting an a priori rule of using whatever data we had available in the World Values Survey we are able to avoid concerns that we somehow cherry-picked which countries to include in order to generate more interesting findings. Of course, this does not mean that countries were selected into the World Values Survey at random—a point we discuss below—but at least it removes the concern that our decision of which countries to include in our study could be a source of bias in our findings.

A final point that needs to be addressed is the issue of measurement error due to asking survey questions in the post-communist period when we are interested in people's experiences in the communist era. One issue that compounds this problem is migration. Most of the data we analyze comes from surveys that do not ask people if they were born in different countries.[48] That means for a certain portion of our respondents, we may be incorrectly attributing the number of years they spent living under communism rule, as well as the correct "country variables" in our *intensifying* and *resistance* analyses. Unfortunately, this is unavoidable; we simply need to accept it as a source of measurement error.[49] A similar issue is at play in our measure of religious attendance. The questions on our surveys ask people about current religious attendance practices, while

---

other words, if we have more Czech and Hungarian respondents, then Austria would be a more relevant comparison; but if we have more Central Asian respondents in the mix, then perhaps Afghanistan, Turkey, or Iran would be the more useful reference groups.

[48] The one exception is the German Election Panel Study, and we do actually take advantage of this fact as part of our supplementary analysis in Chapter 5.

[49] However, the type of migration that is most relevant for our discussion here—that of Eastern Europeans to Western Europe—is likely to lead to more conservative estimates of the post-communist attitudinal differential since Western European samples will have been "contaminated" by communist attitudinal legacies.

what we are really interested in is religious attendance under communist rule. Nevertheless, we feel comfortable that religious attendance at time *t+1* is probably the best proxy we can have for religious attendance at time *t*, but again we want to acknowledge that this will inevitably lead to some people being labeled incorrectly.[50]

3.4. DATA

Having explained our general methodological approach (Section 3.2) and the modeling choices we made to implement that approach (Section 3.3), we conclude this chapter by providing a more detailed discussion of the data analyzed in the remainder of the book. We divide this section into two parts. In the first part, we provide descriptions of the two large-scale cross-national surveys and the two single-country panel surveys that we use for our analysis in the following five chapters, as well as addressing their advantages and disadvantages. In the second part, we describe the aggregate-level data collection we have put together to supplement the two cross-national survey collections in our statistical analyses, thus allowing us to implement our methodological approach. While we leave a description of every single variable we use to the data codebooks (in the electronic appendix), we will use this section to provide some additional discussion of a number of variables where coding decisions or data collection was not necessarily straightforward.

3.4.1. Survey Data Sets

In the following five chapters, we draw on survey data from four different survey projects. To be very clear, this is all secondary analysis: in none of these cases did we collect the survey data ourselves, which means that we did not have the opportunity to participate in the design of the survey. Nevertheless, we consider ourselves extremely fortunate that so many people put so much time into both carrying out and conducting these surveys *and* making them publically available for secondary analysis by scholars. Two of the data sets—the World Values Survey (WVS) and the European Bank for Recovery and Development's Life in Transition Societies (LiTS) surveys—are cross-national surveys; the other two datasets

---

[50]The biggest concern here would be if we were measuring religious attendance of people in the present who were too young to attend religious services under communism. Fortunately, this will not be a problem given the set up of our analysis. Recall that we are interested in the *interactive* effect of religious attendance and years of exposure to communism; respondents too young to have attended religious services under communism will by definition not have had any exposure to communist rule.

we analyze—the Hungarian Household Panel Survey (TARKI 1997); and the German Election Panel Study (Falter et al. 2012)—are single country panel studies.

3.4.1.1. WORLD VALUES SURVEY (WVS)

The WVS is the workhorse of our book, as we use the WVS in every single empirical chapter for our primary analysis. The reason is simple: the global and temporal coverage of the WVS is unparalleled for any survey of political attitudes. Carried out under the supervision of Ronald Inglehart of the University of Michigan, the WVS has been deployed in a continuously expanding sample of countries from all geographic regions for more than three decades.

The advantage of working with the WVS is that we are able to include so many countries in our analyses over so many years; in addition, most of the countries in the data set are surveyed in multiple waves of the survey. As discussed above in Section 3.3.3, this feature of multiple surveys of individual countries in different waves of the study plays a very important role in our identification strategy. Furthermore—as also discussed previously—the WVS has countries from all over the world, therefore increasing the external validity of our analysis. A final advantage of working with the World Values Survey is that it is a very well known and widely used data set in the scholarly community that has already generated large numbers of scholarly publications.[51]

Another significant advantage of the WVS data is that the surveys included questions on the full range of attitudes that we analyze in this book. Moreover, with the partial exception of the analysis about welfare state attitudes in Chapter 6,[52] the WVS includes multiple questions tapping into the attitudes in which we are interested. This allowed us to construct standardized multi-item indexes with reasonably high reliability scores for our cross-national statistical tests.[53] Additional details about the survey questions and additional measurement decisions for each of the dependent

---

[51] A Google Scholar search for "World Values Survey" produces more than 20,000 results, and the WVS website at one point featured a 200-page-long selective list of publications based on WVS survey data.

[52] As we discuss in Chapter 6, in addition to the main survey question we use in the analysis, some surveys included two additional related questions. However, the two questions were asked in a very small proportion of the surveys, and they produced a low-reliability index (alpha below .7), so we decided to analyze the single survey question with broad geographic and temporal coverage for our main analyses in Chapter 6.

[53] We used the alpha command (with the standardized option) in Stata 13.1 to calculate the indexes and used .7 as the cutoff for acceptable index reliability.

variables are discussed in the introductory sections of the relevant empirical chapters.

Working with the WVS data, however, of course has some disadvantages as well. As a decentralized academic survey-research project—surveys are carried out and supervised by country-specific teams—there is less control that each survey is administered in the same way than one would have in a project carried out in a more centralized manner. From our perspective, this is most problematic because not all questions are asked on all surveys. This is often the case across waves of surveys, but in the case of the WVS we have found this variation even within waves. This problem manifests itself in two ways that are of direct importance for our study. First, the democracy indicators that we use to calculate our dependent variable in Chapter 4 were not asked in Wave 2 (1990–94) of the survey, so our democracy analysis begins with 1995 and utilizes data only from Waves 3 (1995–98), 4 (1999–2004), and 5 (2005–9) of the WVS; this is in contrast to our markets, social welfare, and gender equality analysis, which rely on Waves 2–5 of the WVS.[54] However, across the waves certain country teams chose not to ask the gender equality questions, so our results in Chapter 7 are based on a smaller number of observations than our results in Chapters 4–6.

More broadly, the reliability and comparability of cross-national survey data has long been the subject of debate in political science, and given its particularly broad geographic reach and decentralized structure, these problems are likely to be exacerbated in the World Values Survey. Since the best way to address such issues—through survey vignettes (King et al. 2003)—was obviously not an option for our current analysis, we tried a number of alternative approaches. First, as discussed earlier, we report a series of tests based solely on the East versus West Germany comparison, where the cross-cultural comparability of survey questions is not a concern, and we are reassured by the fact that these tests produce for the most part very similar results to the cross-national tests. Second, in Chapter 4 we test whether respondents from different countries understand democracy differently, and while we do find some systematic differences, we show that

[54] Readers familiar with the World Values Survey will note that the sixth wave of the survey (2010–14) was released before we completed the writing of this book. We do not, however, include surveys from that wave in our study for both theoretical and pragmatic reasons. Theoretically, we felt that the global financial crisis of 2008–9 would create a whole host of reasons to potentially expect different patterns in the Wave 6 data, which we felt best to leave to future research. Pragmatically, the data were released quite late in the life of the project. Realistically, incorporating the new wave of data would have delayed the publication of the book substantially, especially because of the fact that we supplement all our analyses with aggregate-level data that we collect from variety of different sources. Finally, there is a certain aesthetic appeal to exploring the first two decades of post-communist public opinion.

our substantive findings are not affected if we account for these different democratic conceptions (or, for that matter, if we base our dependent variable only on survey questions that do not include the word "democracy" in the actual question). Third, for the exposure tests we also report results from model specifications with country-fixed effects, and given that the results are largely similar to the models without fixed effects for our primary analysis, this increases our confidence that our findings are not an artifact of cross-national differences in how respondents understand survey questions.[55] Finally, to address concerns about the comparability of the household income question across different surveys in the World Values Survey, we adopted the method proposed by Donnelly and Pop-Eleches (2016) to obtain cross-nationally and cross-temporally valid income measures.

3.4.1.2. LIFE IN TRANSITION SOCIETIES (LITS) SURVEYS

The EBRD's Life in Transition Societies (LiTS) survey is the second large cross-national survey data set on which we draw in our study. Relative to the WVS, the LiTS surveys have much smaller coverage: the data we utilize are drawn from two waves of surveys (2006 and 2010) in 27 countries, of which only five are non-post-communist countries, and all of which are located in Europe.[56]

However, the LiTS survey has two main advantages for our study relative to the WVS. First, the coverage of post-communist countries is excellent, including 22 countries total, all of which are included in both waves of the survey. Second, the surveys contain a series of questions about whether the respondent had ever been a member of the Communist Party and whether their mother and/or father had belonged to the Communist Party, which the WVS survey—not surprisingly for a cross-national survey not expressly focused on communist or post-communist countries—does not contain.[57] This gives us the ability to explore not only the effect of Communist Party

---

[55]The gender equality results for communist regime type exposure are one notable exception.

[56]There is a third wave of the LiTS survey that was conducted during the writing of this book, but its results were not yet publicly available when we completed the analysis for this book.

[57]Unfortunately, the LiTS surveys do not ask *when* or for how long either the respondent or the respondent's parents were members of the Communist Party. Thus is it is possible that in some cases we are picking up people here who were not members of the Communist Party under communist rule but did join subsequently. While on face value this seems fairly unlikely—the big movement in Communist Party membership after the collapse of communism was away from Communist Party membership, and indeed in numerous countries the Communist Party largely ceased to exist and was replaced by a social democratic successor party—it is still logically possible. As one safeguard, we do recode as "not a Communist Party member" anyone who reports on the LiTS survey that they were a member of the Communist

membership as a potential mechanism for communist socialization, but also the effect of parental CP membership. Furthermore, the LiTS surveys include questions about the educational achievements of both respondents and their parents. Therefore, the LiTS surveys give us an opportunity to do some additional analysis of parental socialization.

The main disadvantage of the LiTS data, and the reason why we use the WVS survey instead of the LiTS data for our primary analysis, is simply the coverage. The first survey was carried out in 2006, which means that we are missing attitudinal data from the first decade and a half of the post-communist transition. Furthermore, the LiTS surveys include only a very limited number of non-post-communist countries in the study: Germany, France, Italy, Sweden, and Turkey, with only Turkey included in both survey waves. This means that the LiTS surveys were much less useful for establishing the extent of post-communist attitudinal exceptionalism than the much broader sample of the WVS.[58]

3.4.1.3. SINGLE-COUNTRY PANEL SURVEYS

Although the LiTS data set contains questions about parental education and Communist Party membership, the ideal data for studying parental socialization is a household survey of multiple members in the same household. Thus, we were very fortunate to come across the Hungarian Household Panel Survey (HHPS), a yearly panel survey from 1992 to 1997 that included over 8,000 respondents from almost 2,700 households in Hungary. The panel has two other unique advantages for the purpose of our analysis of parental socialization. First, the survey includes interviews with all adult members of the household, thereby allowing us to analyze the temporal evolution of political attitudes across multiple generations. Second, unlike most other public opinion surveys, the HHPS includes respondents starting at the age of 16, which allows us to analyze an additional two years that may be crucial for understanding the "impressionable" period of political socialization.

Of course, the disadvantage of working with a single country panel survey is that we have respondents only from a single post-communist country, and thus do not have a control group of non-post-communist respondents.

Party but were under the age of 18 when communism collapsed, as such individuals could have joined the Communist Party only in the post-communist era.

[58] In Chapter 7, we also report on a supplementary analysis we conduct using the International Social Survey Programme (ISSP). The ISSP is an annual cross-national survey. As we do not actually present any tables or figures from the analysis in the text of the book (they are relegated to the supplemental appendix), in the interests of space we are referencing the data in this chapter only in this note; interested readers should see the website of the project: http://www.issp.org/.

Obviously, a multicountry panel survey with non-post-communist coun-
ties would solve this problem, but we are not aware of any cross-national
political panel survey. We can, however, draw on the unique history of
Germany here again to find a single-country panel survey with respondents who were and were not exposed to communist rule. The German
Election Panel Study (GEPS) which interviewed over 8,000 German citizens in 1994, 1998, and 2002 (including over 4,400 respondents who were
interviewed in at least two of the waves), is therefore our final source of
survey data in this book. Crucially, the GEPS surveys people in both the
former East Germany and West Germany, thus giving us access to a panel
of both post-communist and non-post-communist citizens within the same
country.

The disadvantage of single-country studies is of course the generalizability of the findings.[59] Again, this is why we keep the WVS data at the
center of all our analyses. However, as the WVS data are not suitable for
analyzing questions on topics such as Communist Party membership and
parental socialization, we believe there is value in turning to single-country
panel and household studies that allow us to explore some of these interesting questions, even if it is in a less generalizable fashion. We think
of it a bit as triangulating between different data sources to get at our
question of interest: we would not write a book using data only from the
Hungarian Household Panel Survey and claim that it represented a broad
view of the effect of communism, but we do believe it is valuable to take
questions raised by our most wide ranging analyses and put these questions to data in the one post-communist country where we can actually
test them.

3.4.2. Aggregate-Level Data

The most time-intensive data-related aspect of our analysis was the collection of the broad range of country-level statistical indicators we used for
the *living in a post-communist country* analyses. While for many of the
contemporary economic and political indicators the process largely involved merging the appropriate variable from the relevant data source—
for example, the inflation and growth statistics from the World Bank's
World Development Indicators database or regime data from the Polity IV
database—the task was more complicated for other variables, particularly
for historical indicators.

---

[59] One other issue is that neither of these surveys had a particularly wide breath of political questions on them, as neither was an explicitly political survey. This unfortunately limited
the use to which we could put these data and also forced us to construct dependent variables
that did not match our WVS dependent variables as closely as we would have liked.

We are not going to go through every single variable in our aggregate-level collection—for a full list, see Tables 3.1 and 3.2—but a number of the variables warrant a bit of extra discussion:[60]

Literacy in the 1920s: This variable tries to capture an important aspect of the developmental differences between the countries included in the World Values Surveys. We chose to focus on the 1920s because doing so allows us to get a comparative snapshot before the massive communist literacy drive started to affect literacy rates in the Soviet Union while at the same time allowing us to take advantage of the better post-WWI data coverage for many Eastern European countries (since many of them had not been independent before 1914). Nonetheless, the quality and coverage of literacy statistics for many developing countries was rather limited during this time period. Therefore, rather than using a continuous measure of the share of the adult population that was literate, we created a five-point measure based on 20%-wide literacy "bins."[61] While doing so leads to some loss of information for countries where more detailed literacy statistics were available in the 1920s, it allows us to code countries where precise statistics were not available but where we know that literacy was below 20% during the 1920s without falsely implying precision not warranted by the data.

Colonial/imperial legacies: While much of the cross-national work on the effects of imperial/colonial legacies focuses on the impact of British, French, and Spanish empires, these categories were less relevant for the Eastern European and Eurasian countries. Therefore, based on data from Mayer and Zignago (2011), we also coded a broader set of imperial dummy indicators for empires that mattered more for the ex-communist countries, namely the German, Habsburg, Ottoman, and Russian empires. Note that for the many countries that belonged to multiple empires over the course of their histories we did not assign a dominant imperial background, but rather coded each of the empires of which they had ever been part.

Pre–World War I regime: To capture the significant cross-country differences in the extent of political liberalization/democratization prior to the advent of communism, we calculated the average Polity regime score

---

[60]In addition, it is worth addressing one variable we did *not* include in measures of contemporary economic variables, which was GDP per capita. The reason we did not do this was because of the fact that because we already included household income as an individual level characteristic, we felt that adding GDP per capita would essentially be double-counting current income. Moreover, GDP per capita in the 1990s and 2000s was actually remarkably strongly (approximately 0.8) correlated with GDP in 1914, which we do include as one of our pre-communist variables.

[61]Thus, the variable is coded as 1 if literacy was below 20%, 2 if literacy is 20–40%, etc.

for the 1900–1915 period. The main dilemma here was how to deal with the countries that were not independent prior to World War I and for which—understandably—there are no pre-independence regime scores in the Polity database. Since we did not want to treat such observations as missing, we adopted the following approach. For countries that were fully integrated provinces of different empires—as in the case of most territories of the Habsburg and Russian empires—we simply used the average regime score for the relevant empire for the 1900–1915 period. We do so because the political rights (or lack thereof) of an imperial subject were arguably very similar for the center and the periphery of these empires: for example, Slovaks and Romanians in the Austro-Hungarian empire had very similar individual political rights as Austrians or Hungarians (even if their collective rights were different). By contrast, the same logic does not apply for overseas colonies: thus, British colonial subjects in Africa did not enjoy the same political rights as British citizens. Therefore, we coded overseas colonies as having the lowest possible regime score (−10) to reflect the fact that they had very little direct say in their political affairs.[62] However, to capture the possibility that the experience of political exclusion may differ across residents of an overseas colony and the subject of an independent authoritarian regime, we also included an interaction term between the Polity regime score average for 1900–1915 and a dummy variable capturing overseas colonial status.

GDP as proportion of 1989 GDP: This variable is intended to measure the change in the overall state of the economy since the collapse of communism. It is calculated by multiplying the annual GDP change rates from 1990 until the year prior to the survey using data from World Development Indicators.[63] There are a few cases where we do not have GDP data from 1989; in these cases we calculate the change from the first year that the data is available after 1989.

Corruption. This variable has already been discussed once in this chapter because of the fact that it is probably the hardest of all our variables to categorize as either a political or economic characteristic. But it is also a challenge because the most widely used cross-national time-series on cor-

---

[62] Of course, such an approach does not do justice to the variation in political rights between different overseas colonies—for example, India under British rule was allowed a number of non-trivial forms of local representative institutions (Varshney 2001)—but unfortunately we are not aware of a data source that captures such differences in a consistent cross-national fashion. However, we hope that at least some of the differences in colonial-era political rights will be captured by the imperial legacy variables discussed above.

[63] Thus, for a country that had a 10% growth rate in 1990 and 1991, the variable would take a value of 1.21 (=1.1*1.1) for a 1992 survey.

ruption—Transparency International's Corruption Perception Index and the Corruption Control measure from World Governance Indicators—has very limited data coverage for the early 1990s. Since corruption is an important *living in a post-communist country* variable in our analyses—especially for support for democracy and support for markets—we did not want to jettison the measure altogether.[64] With this in mind, we created an index based on the two indicators above and the *corruption* measure from the International Country Risk Guide, which has coverage starting in the mid-1980s for most countries in our sample.

Social welfare spending: Somewhat to our surprise, it proved to be enormously difficult to locate consistent cross-national welfare spending data, especially relative to the amount of academic literature that seems to have been written on the topic. As a result, we ultimately ended up building this variable ourselves using the following approach: given that the coverage for overall welfare spending was significantly smaller than for two of its largest components—public health care and education spending—we calculated an indicator that measures the sum of public spending on these two items as a percentage of GDP in the year prior to the survey (as well as for 1989 for the analyses in the second tables of *Chapters 4–7* about unpacking the effects of communism).[65] In doing so, we drew on data from a variety of data sources, but the vast majority of our data comes from the World Development Indicators and, in the case of the post-communist countries, from the Transmonee database (UNICEF 2014).

Catholicism: Finally, for the record we want to note (simply because we have gotten this question multiple times during presentations of our research) that our measure of Catholics in the intra-regional *resistance* analysis is not simply functioning as a dummy variable for Polish citizens. While it is true that over three-quarters of the Polish respondents self-identified as Catholics, Poles represent fewer than 20% of the self-identified Catholics in WVS surveys carried out in post-communist countries. In fact, Croatia actually has a larger percentage of self-identified Catholics (83%) than Poland in the WVS, and Slovenia, Slovakia, and Lithuania all have over two-thirds of respondents self-identifying as Catholics in the WVS. Moreover, all our results using Catholics as a moderating variable are robust to excluding Poland from the analysis.[66]

[64] And indeed, before we added a measure of corruption to the analysis, this was one of the most frequent questions we encountered when presenting our research.

[65] In cases where spending data was not available for the preceding year, we used data for up to four years prior, and, where no pre-survey data was available, for up to two years after the year of the survey.

[66] Results are available in the electronic appendix.

3.5. CONCLUSION

In conclusion, we want to reiterate that while we realize this chapter may not have made for the most scintillating reading, we feel it has accomplished three important goals. First, we have laid out our general methodological approach in a clear way so that those not familiar with statistical analysis should be able to understand why we are running the tests we run and using the data we use in the next five empirical chapters. Second, we want to embrace the growing movement in political science research of methodological transparency and thus have attempted to provide as much detail as possible regarding the actual statistical models employed and data analyzed for those who are not familiar with (or simply not interested in...) reading and rerunning Stata do files. Third, we want this chapter to serve as a reference when reading the next five chapters so that if questions arise about particular methodological choices, data sets, or even particular variables, readers could easily know where to turn for answers.

And with that, we are ready to turn to the analysis!

CHAPTER 4

■ ■ ■ ■ ■

Democracy

NICOLAE CEAUȘESCU ADDRESSES A MEETING OF THE CENTRAL COMMITTEE OF THE COMMUNIST PARTY.

CEAUȘESCU: "Comrades, I've been thinking that maybe Romania would benefit from having a new leader."
[THE ROOM IS PERFECTLY QUIET.]
CEAUȘESCU: "So I would like to propose to you my comrade and life partner, Elena Ceaușescu!"
[EVERYONE IS LOOKING DOWN. NO ONE SAYS ANYTHING.]
CEAUȘESCU: "I see, you probably think that she's not that much younger than me and perhaps we need a younger leader. So I propose to you my son, Nicu Ceaușescu!
[EVERYONE IS STILL LOOKING DOWN. NO ONE SAYS ANYTHING.]
CEAUȘESCU: "You tricksters! You just can't bear to see me go!"

—Romanian joke, late 1980s

4.1. INTRODUCTION

The collapse of communism generally—and in much of East-Central Europe in particular—was accompanied by overwhelming enthusiasm for democracy (Stoner and McFaul 2013; Fish 1995). Indeed, it is possible to call the anti-communist movements that swept through Eastern Europe largely pro-democracy movements: if there was a single common demand of all opposition forces, it was for the various communist parties in the region to give up their respective monopolies on power (Roeder 1993; Stark and Bruszt 1998). And yet, we began this book in Chapter 1 by noting that there is a systematic *deficit* in support for democracy among post-communist citizens. For those who remember the heady days of 1989 (e.g., Ash 1993), this result would not have been predictable (although see Jowitt 1992: 300–304). So why is this case?

The theoretical frameworks we presented in Chapters 1 and 2 suggest two possible explanations: the effect of *living in post-communist* countries, or the effect of *living through communism*. In this chapter, therefore, we present the first empirical tests of our two legacy models. Along with the attitudes toward markets, which will be analyzed in the next chapter, the extent to which citizens of post-communist countries support democracy has been one of the most important questions of the post-communist transition experience. Moreover, the transition toward democracy—or at least away from communist one-party rule—was for most Eastern Europeans the most visible aspect of the early post-communist period. Within a few months of the dramatic collapse of their communist regimes, the citizens of most Eastern European countries—as well as a number of the republics of the former Soviet Union—had the chance to experience their first genuinely contested multiparty elections in over four decades, if ever. Despite some early predictions that the legacy of communism would cast a long shadow on the region's subsequent political performance (Jowitt 1992), which were echoed and expanded by subsequent work on the challenges of post-communist democratization (Tismăneanu 1998; Howard et al. 2006; Pop-Eleches 2013), it is only more recently that the individual-level (anti-) democratic legacies of communism have been subjected to more systematic analysis. Much of this work has focused on whether ex-communist citizens are less civically and politically active (Howard 2002, 2003; Letki 2004; Bernhard and Karakoc 2007; Pop-Eleches and Tucker 2013; Ekiert and Kubik 2014). Within ex-communist countries, citizens with greater personal exposure to communism have been shown to be less satisfied with democracy (Neundorf 2010). In this chapter, however, we approach the topic from the perspective of support for general democratic values, exploring whether communist-era legacies can explain why, as illustrated in Figure 1.1 of Chapter 1, citizens in post-communist countries on average have lower levels of support for democracy than citizens from the rest of the countries included in the World Values Survey.

There is a long-standing debate in political science regarding the drivers of popular *support for democracy*, and more specifically about the relative importance of economic considerations, political performance, and cultural factors. Thus, whereas several authors have traced patterns of democratic support to individual and societal variations in economic conditions (Przeworski 1991; Kitschelt 1992; Dalton 1994; Mason 1995; Fidrmuc 2003), others have instead emphasized the importance of political performance and especially citizens' evaluations of the functioning of basic democratic institutions (Evans and Whitefield 1995; Rose et al. 1998; Chu et al. 2008). Still another strand of the literature focuses on the role of political culture in shaping democratic regime support (Almond and Verba 1965; Inglehart 1990).

Somewhat surprisingly, there has been very little explicit discussion about the extent to which communist legacies can help explain the patterns of democratic support in the region.[1] In part, this may be due to the fact that most of the contributions to this debate relied on surveys from only a single country or region, and that one of the few explicitly cross-regional analyses (Chu et al. 2008) does not include data from the ex-communist countries.[2] One exception in this respect is previous work by one of us (Pop-Eleches 2009), which identifies a significant post-communist deficit in democratic values but explains it largely in terms of the peculiarities of communist modernization efforts. Meanwhile, Rosenfeld (2016) identifies state employment, which is one of the key legacies of communism, as an important factor behind the weak middle-class support for democracy in many ex-Soviet countries, but she does not frame the discussion as an explicit communist legacy. Mishler and Rose (2007) analyze survey data from Russia and find that—in line with a communist socialization perspective—older cohorts were less supportive of the new regime, but their primary focus is on post-communist learning, which they argue has a greater impact on democratic attitudes.[3] Finally, Neundorf (2010) analyzes the impact of communist socialization, but her focus is on satisfaction with democracy rather than democratic support.[4]

Our analysis in this chapter speaks directly to these debates, in the sense that we test the explanatory power of hypotheses derived from all three of these scholarly traditions. However, we do so from the very specific perspective of our concern for the mechanisms through which

---

[1] Although see the various sources mentioned previously in this chapter that address post-communist distinctions in closely related areas such as civic participation; one exception is Pop-Eleches and Tucker (2014), where we previously addressed the issue of the post-communist deficit in support of democratic values, but in that case by relying solely on data from post-communist countries.

[2] Rose et al. (1998: 99–103) do include some comparative survey evidence from EU countries, but they do not analyze the differences between Eastern and Western Europe from a communist legacy perspective.

[3] The interpretation of their findings is complicated by the fact that the meaning of supporting Russia's new political regime is somewhat ambiguous given that during the time period covered by their surveys (1993–2005) Russia's regime was not fully democratic and in fact drifted toward renewed authoritarianism after 2000. For a related but different take on support for authoritarian values in post-communist Hungary, see Todosijevic and Enyedi (2008), who examine the relationship between left-right self-placement and authoritarianism.

[4] While democratic satisfaction is interesting in its own right, it is conceptually separate: thus, it is possible to hold liberal democratic values while being dissatisfied with democratic developments in one's own country (Achen and Bartels 2016: 8) and conversely to be satisfied with the state of democracy without embracing democratic values fully. (For an interesting analysis comparing ideal commitments to democracy to evaluations of real democracy in post-communist countries, see Evans and Whitefield 1995.) Empirically, factor analysis confirms that democratic satisfaction has much higher uniqueness and a lower factor loading on the main factor than the democratic support indicators, which suggests that there is no compelling statistical reason for lumping the two types of indicators together.

communist legacies affect post-communist political attitudes. Thus, we analyze both economic conditions and political institutions through our inclusion of measures of contemporaneous economic conditions and political institutions (see Models 4 and 5, respectively, of Table 4.1 in particular) when assessing the effects of *living in post-communist countries*. Moreover, we also tap into the "cultural" strand of this literature in two ways. First, the *pre-communist variables* in our *living in post-communist countries* model can certainly be interpreted as picking up underlying cultural elements from the region that predate the communist era. But in addition, our *living through communism* model can also be thought of as capturing exposure to Soviet culture.[5]

To understand the impact of communism on subsequent democratic attitudes, we begin with the authoritarian and often totalitarian nature of communist regimes over the course of their four to seven decades in power. Unlike many other authoritarian regimes, communist regimes went beyond the traditional repression of political opponents and launched—despite some important variations across both time and space—massive efforts to penetrate deep into civil society and into the private lives of individuals (see Section 2.2.2 of Chapter 2). This deeper penetration, combined with their longer duration—at least compared to most fascist regimes in Europe or military dictatorships in Latin America or Africa—suggests that we should expect the anti-democratic character of these regimes to be reflected more powerfully in the democratic preferences of post-communist citizens.

However, it is important to note that despite Marx's emphasis on the key role of the dictatorship of the proletariat in the transition from capitalist to communist society (Marx 2008: 39), communist regimes differed from most other authoritarian regimes in the 20th century in that they actually claimed to be democratic.[6] These pretensions went beyond the use of "democracy" in a variety of official names (including the "German Democratic Republic"), to include regular elections, which in some countries (e.g., Poland and East Germany) even gave voters a choice between multiple parties, albeit with outcomes that were never really in question

[5] Indeed, the sense that there was a Soviet "culture" that supported the values we associate with communism in this book is in some ways the purest interpretation of why additional exposure should be associated with a greater likelihood of holding that value. Of course, as we have laid out in Section 1.2 of Chapter 1, our goal is to go beyond simply positing that there were elements of Soviet culture that inculcated support for these attitudes and instead point to particular mechanisms that account for the effects we find to be associated with communist exposure. That being said, the general approach of analyzing the effects of *living through communism* has a shared intellectual heritage with the idea of regimes fostering a particular political culture among their citizens.

[6] In the 21st century, however, claiming to be democratic has become a hallmark of authoritarian regimes—and especially competitive authoritarian regimes (Levitsky and Way 2002, 2013)—more generally.

until 1989. Perhaps more importantly for the present discussion was the fact that communist regimes often referred to themselves as "people's democracies," whose democratic nature supposedly derived from the fact that their leaders governed in accordance with the interests of the majority of the people. However, by the 1980s most of these democratic claims sounded increasingly hollow,[7] and much of the negotiations between communist regimes and their opponents in the late 1980s and early 1990s revolved around the extent to which the former were willing to accede to political liberalization and eventually full-blown democratization (Roeder 1993; Stark and Bruszt 1998).

Thus, despite these pretenses to the contrary, there is little doubt that by the late 1980s communist regimes were seen not only by their opponents, but also by most citizens and even by most regime insiders (Kotkin 2010), as essentially authoritarian in nature. Therefore, the most straightforward expectation from a *living through communism* legacy perspective would be that citizens of former communist countries would exhibit weaker support for democratic values in the wake of the collapse of communism. Of course, it is also conceivable that post-communist citizens, driven by their rejection of the deeply compromised communist regimes, would be so excited to be rid of communism that they would embrace democratic values with greater fervor than their non-communist counterparts.[8] If this resistance mechanism had ended up predominating—and much of the democratic optimism of the early 1990s was implicitly or explicitly built on this expectation—then we should have expected a democratic surplus among citizens of Eastern Europe and the former Soviet Union. However, given that we have already demonstrated in Table 1.1 of Chapter 1 that there is a post-communist democratic *deficit*, our task in this chapter is to explain this weaker democratic support among post-communist citizens.

The remainder of this chapter is organized as follows: first, we demonstrate that a democratic deficit exists among post-communist citizens and that this deficit holds across a broad cross-national sample of countries even if we account for pre-communist differences. Next we examine the extent to which these differences in democratic support can be explained by the fact that these citizens were *living in post-communist* countries. We find that while post-communist contemporaneous conditions shape

---

[7]While some of the early communist redistributive efforts and developmental achievements had given a certain validation that communist regimes represented rule for the people (if not necessarily by the people), by the 1980s the increasingly visible lifestyle differences between communist elites and average citizens had largely delegitimized these claims.

[8]Put another way, perhaps the "counterfactual" of non-democratic rule would be both more real and more viscerally disliked among citizens of post-communist countries with memories of the reality of communist rule than among citizens in other countries where the concept was more hypothetical.

democratic attitudes, they do not fully account for the democratic deficit (see Table 4.1).[9] Nor does taking account of conditions at the end of communism—intended to be our most direct measure of the legacy effects of communism on society as a whole—which instead actually *increase* the size of the deficit (Table 4.2). Instead we show that individual exposure to communism—and especially exposure as an adult—has an important and lasting impact on democratic support (Table 4.3).

However, the anti-democratic effects of communist exposure were not uniform but were moderated by several of our intensifying and resistance factors. Thus, living in a country that had been wealthier, more literate, or more democratic before communist rule provided some resistance to these socializing effects, while living in a country with a greater proportion of hardline communist rule magnified the effect of exposure (see Figure 4.2). In addition, we find that having higher education or being a Catholic also provided resistance to these exposure effects (Figure 4.3). Conversely, living in an urban area and—somewhat surprisingly—being female intensified the effects (Figure 4.3). In the final section we tackle the potential complications introduced into our analyses by the peculiar history of the use of the word *democracy* under communist rule, including the question of whether post-communist citizens understand democracy differently, and whether these different democratic conceptions help explain the differences in democratic support.

4.2. LIVING IN POST-COMMUNIST COUNTRIES AND ATTITUDES TOWARD DEMOCRACY

To establish whether there is a systematic difference in attitudes toward democracy between post-communist citizens and their counterparts in countries that have never experienced communism, we rely on data from three waves (1994–98, 1999–2004 and 2005–9) of the World Values Survey, which yielded 164 surveys from 83 countries (including 52 surveys from 24 post-communist countries).[10] To assess democratic support, we create

[9] Indeed, while some factors reduce the size of the deficit, others increase it, and the net result of all our pre-communist and contemporaneous *living in post-communist countries* variables is that the deficit ends up being roughly the same size as in our simple bivariate model. Note, however, that in the HLM models in the electronic appendix the boost from controling for pre-communist factors in model 2 is weaker. As a result, even though the effects of adding post-communist controls are similar in the HLM and OLS models, the magnitude of the post-communist democratic deficit is smaller, and in the fully saturated model it falls short of achieving statistical significance (though it is still positive).

[10] Unfortunately from our perspective, the questions we use to create our democracy index were not asked in the 1990–93 wave of the World Values Survey, and thus we have fewer surveys on which we can draw in this chapter than in the next two. As a reminder, we use ordinary least squares (OLS) regressions and with robust standard errors clustered

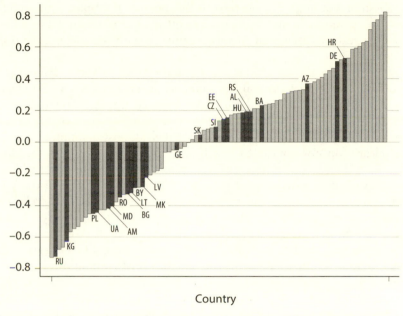

Country

Figure 4.1. Average Support for Democracy by Country: Post-communist vs. Non-communist
This figure lists the country-level averages in democratic support of post-communist countries (dark-gray bars) compared to those of non-communist countries (light-gray bars) based on the 3rd, 4th, and 5th waves of the World Values Survey (1995–2008). In calculating the averages we used any individual-level weights, and we also applied equilibrated weights to adjust for different sample sizes across surveys for different years in any given country. The figure shows that while only Russia and Kyrgyzstan rank toward the very bottom of the global democracy support distribution, most ex-communist countries are below average, and very few are in the top third of the most pro-democratic countries. The dependent variable is an index of seven survey questions (see the electronic appendix for details) which was standardized to a mean of 0 and a standard deviation of 1. For the full set of country codes, see the list of country code abbreviations on page xv.

a standardized democracy index based on seven WVS survey questions that ask respondents to evaluate different statements about democracy and alternative ways of ruling the country (see the electronic appendix

at the country-year level for our statistical analysis; we also use equilibrated survey weights in all our regressions that combine any within-country survey weights with a cross-country component that adjusts for sample size differences across countries. For much more detail on our statistical methods and approach, see Section 3.3 of Chapter 3 in particular, and all of Chapter 3 generally.

for question wording).[11] Conceptually, the measure is tapping into a preference for democratic rule as opposed to other types of regimes, as well as a belief that democracy is an effective regime type for producing desirable outcomes.

Figure 4.1 breaks down the average level of support for democracy by country, with post-communist countries in darker gray. To be clear, this is aggregated data—and thus says nothing about individual level variation—and it is raw data, so we are not taking account of any other factors while presenting these data. Nevertheless, post-communist countries clearly do not appear to just be randomly placed across the distribution. There are very few post-communist cases in the top third of countries most supportive of democracy (the right-hand side of the figure), and post-communist countries are clearly overrepresented (relative to their overall prevalence in the data) in the lower third (the left-hand side of the figure). Still, it is clearly not the case that all post-communist countries are on the left side of the figure, and nor are all countries with lower average levels of support for democracy post-communist. It is also interesting to note that while the two post-communist countries with the lowest average level of support for democracy are Russia and Kyrgyzstan, the next grouping of countries seems rather evenly distributed between countries that are now in the EU (e.g., Poland, Romania, Bulgaria, Latvia, and Lithuania) and former Soviet republics (e.g., Ukraine, Armenia, Moldova, and Belarus), which suggests that the anti-democratic effects of communist regimes were quite widespread in the region.

Turning to our statistical analysis, we begin with the results in Table 4.1, which indicate that citizens of the former communist countries were indeed on average less supportive of democratic forms of government than their non-communist counterparts. In the most basic specification in Model 1, which includes only the post-communism dummy variable and a set of survey year dummies to capture temporal effects, we identify a statistically significant negative effect of post-communist citizenship on democratic values, and this effect is moderately large in substantive terms: more than a quarter (27%) of a standard deviation of the democracy support index.

---

[11]Cronbach's alpha for the index was .72 for the WVS index, which is quite reasonable for this type of survey questions. The variable originally had a mean of −.03 and a standard deviation of .66, which we standardized to have a mean of 0 and a standard deviation of 1. Moreover, factor analysis confirmed that all the questions loaded on a single main factor, and we were not able to improve the alpha statistic by dropping any variables from the index. In the final section of the chapter, we present robustness tests using only those components of the index that do *not* contain the word "democracy"; see the penultimate section of this chapter. For question wording, see the electronic appendix.

Table 4.1. Living in a Post-communist Country and Attitudes toward Democracy

	(1)	(2)	(3)	(4)	(5)	(6)	(7)	(8)
Post-communist	-.273**	-.530**	-.532**	-.390**	-.436**	-.410**	-.264*	-.315**
	(.069)	(.098)	(.087)	(.120)	(.116)	(.120)	(.131)	(.048)
Year dummies	Yes	Yes	No	Yes	Yes	Yes	Yes	Yes
Pre-communist variables	No	Yes	No	Yes	Yes	Yes	Yes	No
Post-communist demographics	No	No	No	Yes	No	No	Yes	Yes
Post-communist economic outcomes	No	No	No	No	Yes	No	Yes	No
Post-communist political institutions	No	No	Yes	No	No	Yes	Yes	No
Pre-communist & year entropy balancing	No	No	Yes	No	No	No	No	No
Countries	All	All	All	All	All	All	All	Germany
Observations	227,373	227,373	227,373	227,373	227,373	227,373	227,373	6,018
R-squared	.028	.104	.077	.136	.113	.115	.156	.100

Note: This table demonstrates that post-communist citizens are less supportive of democracy than citizens in the rest of the world, even when controlling for pre-communist conditions (Models 2 and 3) and contemporaneous demographic characteristics, economic conditions, and political institutions (Models 4–7); similar results can be found from analyzing only data from Germany comparing East and West Germans (Model 8). The dependent variable is an index of seven survey questions (listed in the electronic appendix) which was standardized to a mean of 0 and a standard deviation of 1. The list of independent and control variables can be found in Table 3.1 of Chapter 3. Full regression results are in the electronic appendix. The data utilized in these analyses are from the 3rd, 4th, and 5th waves of the World Values Survey. Robust standard errors in parentheses: ** p<.01, * p<.05, # p<.1.

In Model 2, we include our pre-communist variables, which, as a reminder, control for a range of geographic and historical factors that set Eastern European and Eurasian countries apart from the rest of the world.[12] Interestingly, including the pre-communist control variables, far from explaining away the democratic deficit in post-communist countries, actually results in a post-communist democratic support deficit that is almost *twice as large* as in the baseline model. In other words, the deeper structural and historical differences between the post-communist countries and the rest of our sample would actually lead us to expect to see *more* support for democracy in these countries were we to ignore everything that happened after 1917/1945. Indeed, taking account of these factors suggests that simply living in a post-communist country—once we control for pre-communist conditions—is enough to reduce one's level of support for democracy by over half a standard deviation in our index.

To test the robustness of our results in Model 2, in Model 3 we present the results of a test using entropy balancing, a preprocessing technique that creates a set of weights designed to achieve covariate balance between the treatment and the control groups that we discussed in more detail in Chapter 3 (Hainmueller 2012). Since the resulting control group (composed of non-communist countries) very closely resembles the pre-communist developmental profile of the treatment group (ex-communist countries), we can run a simple weighted regression using the entropy weights but including only the post-communist indicator variable in the main regression. Even though we were unable to use the full battery of pre-communist developmental controls among the balancing criteria,[13] the procedure nevertheless allows us to match ex-communist countries to a synthetic control group that looks very similar along a number of crucial developmental and geographic characteristics including pre-communist urbanization and literacy, as well as longitude, latitude, and terrain. Comparing the results of the entropy balancing test in Model 3 to those from the standard OLS models with pre-communist controls in Model 2 suggests that the results are virtually identical, which gives us greater confidence in the robustness of our main estimation procedure.

In the next four models, we introduce variables that measure the demographic characteristics of our survey respondents,[14] economic con-

---

[12] See Table 3.1 in Chapter 3 for a list of these variables.

[13] This is at least in part due to the fact that no set of weights can deal with the fact that some of the colonial legacy variables are completely absent in either the treatment or the control group (e.g., there are no French or Spanish colonies among the post-communist countries).

[14] E.g., education, household income, residency, religious attendance. See Table 3.1 in Chapter 3 and the codebook in the electronic appendix for full list and details.

ditions,[15] and political institutions.[16] We begin by adding each of these blocks of variables separately, so the relevant comparison for Models 4–7 is Model 2. Adding demographics and religiosity in Model 4 leads to a modest reduction in the size of the deficit and an improvement in model fit, but given that our variables capture individual-level demographic conditions at the time of the survey, it is unclear how much of this effect is due to the demographic footprint of communism and how much to the traumatic social transformations of the post-communist transition. More importantly for our discussion, the post-communist democratic support deficit continues to be large and statistically significant, although it falls by about 25% from Model 2. So the contemporary demographic profile of the citizens of post-communist countries can explain some, but far from all, of the democratic deficit.

In Model 5 we include a series of post-communist economic performance indicators to test whether the post-communist democratic deficit could be the result of the traumatic economic transitions that post-communist countries were undergoing at the time of many of the surveys.[17] We find moderate support for this "Weimar hypothesis": thus, controlling for economic conditions explains approximately 14% of the democratic support gap in Model 2. This is less than the effect of demographic conditions, although it remains nontrivial.

In Model 6 we control for political institutions and outcomes, with similar results. Including these controls in the model reduces the size of the post-communist dummy variable from Model 2 by a bit more than 20%, placing it between the demographic and economic effects.

Combining all three of these controls—that is, including the full set of post-communist demographic, economic, and political contemporaneous variables associated with *living in post-communist countries*—results in a fairly large drop in the post-communist democratic deficit compared to Model 2, where we included only our pre-communist control variables. Altogether, the *living in post-communist countries* contemporaneous variables, reported in Model 7, reduce the democratic deficit by roughly 50% compared to Model 2, thus explaining away a good deal of the difference,

[15] E.g., unemployment, inflation, growth. See Table 3.1 in Chapter 3 and the codebook in the electronic appendix for full list and details.

[16] E.g., corruption index, health and education spending as % of GDP, regime type, electoral system. See Table 3.1 in Chapter 3 and the codebook in the electronic appendix for full list and details.

[17] As Walder et al. (2015: 444–45) note, "All but one of 28 post-communist nations suffered immediate economic downturns, but the severity and depth of these recessions usually went far beyond prior expectations. . . . Sharp recessions in the first states to emerge from the revolutions of 1989 were followed by much deeper economic crises in new states that emerged from the breakup of the Soviet Union." See as well Kornai 1994; Hellman 1998; Frye 2002; and Tucker 2006.

but certainly not all of it. In addition, the goodness of fit of the model also increases noticeably. That being said, the post-communist democratic deficit in Model 7 is still larger than the simple bivariate difference identified in Model 1. Put another way, controlling for all the contemporary demographic, economic, and political indicators is almost enough to balance out the increase in the estimated post-communist democratic deficit caused by taking account of pre-communist conditions.[18]

In Model 8, we restrict our focus to a within-country analysis of Germany to isolate the effects of the 45 years of communist rule in the areas that belonged to the former East Germany (GDR).[19] Model 8 not only confirms the existence of a democratic deficit among the residents of the ex-communist regions of Germany but suggests that the effect is nearly identical to the one found in Model 7, where we controlled for all the *living in post-communist countries* contemporaneous effects, thereby strengthening our confidence in the robustness of our cross-national findings.

4.3. LIVING IN POST-COMMUNIST COUNTRIES: UNPACKING THE EFFECTS OF COMMUNISM

We turn next to the ways in which communism may have affected the country *at the aggregate level* as a possible explanation for why post-communist citizens are less supportive of democracy.[20] As explained in detail in the previous chapter (Section 3.2.2), we do so by adding a series of aggregate level indicators that measure conditions *at the time of communism's collapse* related to distinctive features of communist rule: the developmental legacies of communism; the redistributive/economic egalitarian character of communism, and the political characteristics of communist regimes.[21]

---

[18] Note, however, that in the HLM models presented in the electronic appendix the reduction in the deficit due to accounting for post-communist controls is greater than the boost from pre-communist controls, though it does not eliminate the deficit completely.

[19] Testing the model on a single country allows us to control for a host of cultural and institutional similarities that may not have been captured even by the extensive sets of controls we used in the cross-national regressions above (see the relevant discussion in Section 3.2.1 of Chapter 3).

[20] This is not to be confused with the *individual-level* effect of *living through communism*, which we explore in the following section.

[21] As discussed in detail in the previous chapter (Section 3.2.2), measuring these variables at the time of communism's collapse ensures that we are not picking up effects of post-communist developments. To the extent that we can adequately control for pre-communist conditions, this type of analysis represents our best attempt at clean legacy effect measurement in the *living in post-communist countries* framework.

Table 4.2. Communist System Features and Support for Democracy

	(1)	(2)	(3)	(4)	(5)	(6)
Post-communist	−.530**	−.635**	−.577**	−.653**	−.575**	−.822**
	(.098)	(.122)	(.110)	(.127)	(.102)	(.148)
Urbanization 1989		−.295				
		(.197)				
Primary school enrollment		.004#				
		(.002)				
Literacy 1989		5.239				
		(4.723)				
Energy intensity		−.006				
		(.004)				
Industry as % GDP		.001				
		(.003)				
Log GDP per capita 1989		−.153*				
		(.065)				
Health & education spending 1989			−.012			
			(.014)			
Income inequality 1989			−.006			
			(.005)			
State sector size late 1989			.022			
			(.031)			
Average regime score 1975–89				−.008		−.009
				(.006)		(.007)
Left government share 1975–89					.120	.187*
					(.082)	(.077)
Average regime score 1975–89 × Left government share 1975–89						−.007
						(.012)
Year dummies	Yes	Yes	Yes	Yes	Yes	Yes
Pre-communist controls	Yes	Yes	Yes	Yes	Yes	Yes
Observations	227,373	227,373	227,373	227,373	227,373	227,373
R-squared	.104	.111	.109	.105	.105	.107

Note: This table demonstrates that post-communist citizens are less supportive of democracy than citizens in the rest of the world, even when controlling for conditions at the time of communism's collapse, including developmental legacies (Model 2), redistributive/egalitarian policies (Model 3), and the political orientation of communist regimes (Models 4–6). The dependent variable is an index of seven survey questions (listed in the electronic appendix) which was standardized to a mean of 0 and a standard deviation of 1. The list of independent and control variables can be found in Table 3.1 of Chapter 3. Full regression results are in the electronic appendix. The data utilized in these analyses are from the 3rd, 4th, and 5th waves of the World Values Survey. Robust standard errors in parentheses: ** p<.01, * p<.05, # p<.1.

As in the previous set of analyses, we rely on the model with pre-communist controls as our point of reference (i.e., Model 1 in Table 4.2 is the same model as Model 2 in Table 4.1). We then sequentially add in developmental legacy variables[22] in Model 2, redistributive/egalitarian variables[23] in Model 3, and political variables[24] in Models 4–6.[25] Somewhat surprisingly, each of these sets of variables results in a net *increase* in the size of the post-communist democratic deficit. Thus, far from explaining away the demographic deficit, taking account of the political, economic, and demographic effects of the communist experience—to the best of our ability to measure them—only heightens the difference in attitudes toward democracy between post-communist citizens and those found in the rest of the world.[26]

How should we interpret the inability of these models to reduce the post-communist democratic deficit even after accounting for indicators of communist developmental, economic, or political policies in the final years of the Cold War period? One possibility would be to point to the limitations of the statistical indicators we use, given that they capture only a relatively limited time period (largely the last decade of communism), and given that some observers have raised reasonable doubts about the validity of communist-era statistical indicators (Aslund 2002). However, whatever their limitations, these indicators nonetheless capture real differences between communist and non-communist countries in the 1980s (such as the fact that communist countries were non-democratic, had leftist governments, and had comparatively high levels of literacy and industrialization), and therefore we do not think that their lack of explanatory power can be blamed entirely on measurement problems. Instead, we favor a second explanation, which maintains that even though our indicators include some of the important "ingredients" of communism—leftist ideology, long authoritarian spells, statist economic policies—they

---

[22] Urbanization, primary school enrollment, literacy, energy usage, industry as % of GDP, and log GDP per capita.

[23] Health and education spending, income inequality, and state sector size.

[24] Average level of Polity regime score from 1975 to 1989 and percentage of years under a left-wing government.

[25] See Table 3.1 in Chapter 3 and the codebook in the electronic appendix for full list and details on all the variables.

[26] One interesting finding in Model 6 is that having a higher share of leftist governments in the final 15 years of the Cold War leads to higher levels of support for democracy. Note, however, that this direct effect of a leftist government is *after* controlling for whether the country is communist or not. Since there is no variation in the percentage of leftist governments within post-communist countries (in the period from 1975 to 1989, they are all coded as left-wing), the variable is simply picking up the fact that there are higher levels of support for democracy in non-post-communist countries that had leftist governments during that time period than those that did not.

do not add up to the full communist "recipe."[27] In other words, the experience of communism may not be reducible to living in literate, industrialized societies with large state sectors led by leftist parties in an authoritarian fashion. Perhaps this problem could be addressed in future work by looking at additional interactions between some of these variables to try to capture the distinctiveness of communism better (e.g., is communism distinctive because it is an authoritarian regime with generous welfare states in formerly underdeveloped societies?), or by trying to capture additional aspects of communism in a quantitative fashion (e.g., the use of ideology in education or propaganda at the workplace). However, in this book we take a different approach and in the next section instead focus on testing our alternative theoretical framework: the effects of actually *living through communism*.

4.4. LIVING THROUGH COMMUNISM AND ATTITUDES TOWARD DEMOCRACY

To examine the effect of *living through communism* on attitudes toward democracy, we begin with Model 1 of Table 4.3, which contains the precommunist controls and the contemporaneous individual demographic control variables from Model 4 of Table 4.1, but with an added simple measure of *years of exposure* to communist rule that captures the number of years from age six on that a respondent spent living under communist rule.[28] Recall that—as discussed in more detail in Section 3.3.3 of Chapter 3—in line with age-period-cohort modeling approaches, we include both a measure of the respondent's age and survey year dummy variables in all the models. Thus our estimates for the effect of exposure on attitudes toward democracy are *controlling for* the age of the respondent and the year of the survey.[29]

The results in Model 1, which are confirmed by the fixed-effects specification[30] in Model 2, indicate that in line with our expectations, an additional year spent living under communist rule reduces a respondent's

[27]To take this metaphor one step further, as bakers know very well, the same ingredients can produce very different results following from even minor variations in how these ingredients are combined and interact with each other.

[28]Recall that we do not include contemporaneous aggregate-level variables in these models in an effort to avoid post-treatment bias in our analysis (see the discussion in Chapter 3, Section 3.2.1 for more detail). In the second of each pair of models, we replace the post-communist dummy variable with country-fixed effects.

[29]See Section 3.3.3 of Chapter 3 for an extended discussion of the features of our data that allow us to identify the effect of exposure while still controlling for age.

[30]We cannot include the post-communist dummy variable in the fixed-effects models because it is a linear combination of the country dummy variables.

Table 4.3. Living through Communism and Attitudes toward Democracy

	(1)	(2)	(3)	(4)	(5)	(6)	(7)	(8)
Total communist exposure	-.0068** (.0010)	-.0069** (.0008)						
Stalinist exposure			-.0060# (.0036)	-.0115** (.0016)				
Neo-Stalinist exposure			-.0119** (.0033)	-.0066** (.0019)				
Post-totalitarian exposure			-.0117** (.0042)	-.0051** (.0019)				
Reform communist exposure			-.0010 (.0026)	-.0046** (.0015)				
Childhood communist exposure					.0016 (.0028)	-.0013 (.0019)	.0059 (.0038)	.0021 (.0027)
Adult communist exposure					-.0070** (.0010)	-.0070** (.0008)	-.0056** (.0017)	-.0059** (.0012)
Child × Adult communist exposure							-.0002 (.0001)	-.0001 (.0001)

	(1)	(2)	(3)	(4)	(5)	(6)	(7)	(8)
Post-communist citizen	-.2014#		-.1788		-.2787*		-.3168*	
	(.1196)		(.1285)		(.1231)		(.1235)	
Age	.0029**	.0033**	.0029**	.0033**	.0030**	.0034**	.0030**	.0034**
	(.0005)	(.0004)	(.0005)	(.0004)	(.0005)	(.0004)	(.0006)	(.0004)
Year dummies	Yes	Yes	Yes	Yes	Yes	Yes	Yes	Yes
Country dummies	No	Yes	No	Yes	No	Yes	No	Yes
Pre-communist controls	Yes	No	Yes	No	Yes	No	Yes	No
Demographic controls	Yes	Yes	Yes	Yes	Yes	Yes	Yes	Yes
Observations	227,373	227,373	227,373	227,373	227,373	227,373	227,373	227,373
R-squared	.138	.192	.140	.192	.138	.192	.138	.192

Note: This table demonstrates that additional exposure to communism is correlated with less support for democracy even after controlling for age. In each pair of models, the first model includes a dummy variable indicating whether the respondent lives in a post-communist country (for comparability with Tables 4.1 and 4.2) as well as pre-communist country-level control variables, while the second table model uses country-fixed effects and, accordingly, drops the dummy variable and pre-communist country-level control variables. Models 3 and 4 examine the differential effect of exposure by type of communist regime, and Models 5–8 examine differential effect of exposure during childhood (age 6–17) and adulthood (18+). The dependent variable is an index of seven survey questions (listed in the electronic appendix) standardized to a mean of 0 and a standard deviation of 1. The list of independent and control variables can be found in Table 3.1 of Chapter 3. Full regression results are in the electronic appendix. The data utilized in these analyses are from the 3rd, 4th, and 5th waves of the World Values Survey. Robust standard errors in parentheses: ** p<.01, * p<.05, # p<.1.

predicted support for democracy in the post-communist period. The result is highly significant (at p<.001) and is quite large in substantive terms: thus, the difference between a respondent with the full dose (e.g., 45 years) of Eastern European communism and one who was six or younger when communism fell (and therefore should be minimally affected by personal exposure) accounts for .3 points on the democracy index in Model 1 (or three-tenths of a standard deviation on the index), which is *larger* than the estimate of the post-communist dummy variable from the bivariate specification in Model 1 of Table 4.1 and practically the same size as the estimate of the post-communist dummy variable in the fully specified Model 7 (including all pre-communist and contemporaneous control variables) in the same table.[31] For comparative purposes, the magnitude of this exposure effect is about 50% larger than the democratic support difference between a respondent who completed secondary education and one with no education at all, and about 25% larger than the difference between post-secondary and secondary education.

The other results worth noting from Model 1 in Table 4.3 is that the size of the post-communist citizen variable is only marginally significant and is about half the size compared to the baseline model (Model 4 in Table 4.1). This suggests that controlling for exposure accounts for roughly half the post-communist effect on democratic attitudes. This finding was confirmed by more formal mediation analysis, which indicated that about 46% of the post-communist citizen effect is mediated by the communist exposure variable.[32] Another way to interpret this result is that since this model specification controls for years of communist exposure, the coefficient for the *post-communist citizen* variable now captures the democratic deficit of someone living in an ex-communist countries but who has had no personal exposure to communism past the age of six. While for such a person the post-communist deficit is indeed smaller, it nonetheless does not disappear completely, which suggests that the post-communist democratic deficit could extend to future generations.[33]

Next we consider whether the impact of exposure varies with the *intensity* of the exposure and/or the degree of *resistance* that individuals

[31] The predicted effects are obviously potentially larger among residents of the interwar Soviet republics, who could have up to 25 years of additional exposure.

[32] See the electronic appendix for the full output of the mediation analysis, which was conducting using the medeff command in Stata 13.1 (Hicks and Tingley 2011).

[33] To the extent that this continued deficit represents a legacy of communism, it raises the interesting question of how it could be transmitted to future generations not exposed to communism. In later chapters, we look at one possible mechanism, which is parental transmission. But it is also possible that this could be driven by more general nostalgia effects that we cannot measure, such as growing up in a country where anytime things go wrong people talk about how life was better under communism, and thus a generation with no personal exposure to communism picks up attitudes consistent with communist ideology.

have to that exposure. As an initial step, in Models 3 and 4 we investigate the first possible dimensions along which communist exposure could be expected to yield heterogeneous effects on democratic attitudes: the type of communist regimes under which people lived (see Table 2.1 in Chapter 2).[34]

In interpreting the results in Model 3 and Model 4 on the exposure effects across different types of communist regimes, recall that our baseline expectation here is that the effects of exposure to communism will be strongest under Stalinist regimes, then neo-Stalinist, then post-totalitarian, and finally weakest under reform communism. The empirical support for this expectation is mixed. Thus, Model 3 (without country-fixed effects) is consistent with the idea that the effect of exposure is weakest under reform communism but offers no evidence that the effect is strongest under Stalinism. Meanwhile, the country-fixed-effects specification in Model 4, which mirrors our findings using hierarchical models in the electronic appendix, does show the strongest effect for Stalinist exposure—as well as coefficients ordered in line with our expectations—but the effects for neo-Stalinism and, especially, post-totalitarian and reform communism are all very similar and are not statistically distinguishable from one another. So taken together, the two sets of analyses are at least vaguely consistent with our expectations, but not what we would call strong evidence that exposure to different types of communist regimes had differential impacts on attitudes toward democracy. Perhaps more importantly, all the coefficients on all of the exposure variables remain in the correct direction (negative) and, for the fixed-effects model, all remain statistically significant and substantively meaningful.

As a next step, we examine whether adults have more resistance to communist regime socialization than children. We do so by splitting our years of exposure variable into two separate variables for years of exposure to communism as a child (ages 6–17) and years of exposure to communism as an adult (ages 18 and older).[35] Quite surprisingly, we find the exact opposite from what the political socialization literature led us to expect. According to both models, the effects of adult exposure were negative and highly significant (at $p<.01$). Conversely, childhood exposure

---

[34] As discussed in Chapter 3 (Section 3.2.3), we include variables that break down years of exposures into mutually exclusive categories (e.g., years of Stalinist exposure vs. years of reform communist exposure) that vary at the level of the individual in our inter-regional analysis. For all other factors—both aggregate and individual—that we interact with years of exposure, we conduct our analysis using only intra-regional analysis (see Tables 4.4 and 4.5). We do so because these are not variables that we expect to "modify" the effect of exposure, but rather are essentially different ways to categorize years of exposure.

[35] Total exposure is equal to child plus adult exposure. For more details on these variables, see the discussion in footnote 37 of Chapter 3.

had a statistically inconclusive effect and pointed in the wrong direction in Model 5, while in the fixed-effects specification in Model 6 it was negative but still nowhere near statistically significant.

In Models 7 and 8, we repeat the child versus adult exposure analysis but also include an interaction effect between the two to test whether early and adult communist exposures reinforce each other. While the interaction terms fall short of achieving statistical significance at conventional levels, they are nevertheless negative, suggesting that perhaps longer childhood communist exposure intensifies the anti-democratic effects of adult exposure and vice versa.[36] Overall, these findings suggest that regime preferences get solidified later in a person's life—a pattern that is at odds with predictions suggesting that adults should be more resistant to socialization than children. The findings are more compatible with previous hypotheses suggesting that socialization would be more of a lifelong process, but even these theories never predicted an effect *only* in the adult years and not in the years of childhood.

What could explain this surprising finding? Perhaps it is the case that even in regimes that place a great deal of attention on inculcating a particular worldview among their citizens, childhood—despite the indoctrination potential of schooling—is a period when politics is simply less relevant in one's life. Adults living under communism, however, were more likely to be more deeply incorporated into communist political structures and power relations. This more constant contact at a time in one's life when people realized the cost and benefits of toeing (or not) the party line may have led to a more *intense* socialization experience.[37] Another possible explanation, which we discuss more in depth in the final chapter of the book (see Section 9.3), is that communist education was effective not so much at indoctrinating students as it was in suppressing their ability to resist the state/party later in life.

Having analyzed the effect of our two "subtype" exposure variables, we now turn to the remaining variables that according to the *living through communism* model are predicted to either increase the *intensity*

---

[36] In fact, in Model 8 the conditional effect of childhood exposure was at least marginally significant (at .05 one-tailed) for individuals with very long adult communist exposures (over 60 years). Conversely, in Model 7, early communist exposure has a modest positive effect (marginally significant at .15 two-tailed) for respondents without any adult communist exposure.

[37] As will become apparent in the following chapters, we find somewhat similar results regarding adult vs. childhood socialization in the markets and social welfare analyses, where both adult and childhood exposure have the predicted effects, but the size of the effect for adult exposure is twice as large as the effect for childhood exposure. Only in the gender equality analysis do we find early exposure having the predicted effect but *not* adult exposure.

of or *resistance* to communist exposure, and, consequently, also move to our intra-regional analysis. For the sake of clarity in the presentation of results, rather than first discussing either *intensity* or *resistance* variables, we instead first examine country-level factors that affect both *intensity* and *resistance* (Figure 4.2) and then turn to the individual-level factors (Figure 4.3).[38]

4.4.1. Country-Level Moderators of Exposure Intensity and Resistance on Attitudes toward Democracy

We present the results of our interaction analyses visually in the text of the chapter (see Figures 4.2 and 4.3), with tables similar to the ones previously presented in this chapter in the electronic appendix; full regression results also continue to be included in the electronic appendix. As discussed in Chapter 3, the reason we do this is because interpreting interaction effects from regression tables is always complicated, and therefore the figures more easily and intuitively convey the information necessary to assess our *intensifying* and *resistance* hypotheses.

With that mind, let us briefly explain exactly how to read Figure 4.2. Each pair of results (e.g., low pre-communist literacy and high pre-communist literacy, imposed communism and homegrown communism) shows the estimated conditional marginal effect of a year of exposure to communism on a person living in a country that meets that condition (e.g., in a country with low pre-communist literacy for the first row, in a country with high pre-communist literacy in the second row). The dot represents the estimated marginal effect of one additional year of exposure taking into account both the coefficient of the exposure variable and the coefficient of the variable interacting exposure with the country-level effect in question, while the lines represent 95% confidence intervals around these estimates.[39] As we already know the effect of an average year of

---

[38] Readers should recall that for reasons discussed in Section 3.2.4 in Chapter 3, we now restrict ourselves to only survey respondents from post-communist countries, utilize constrained regression analysis (with age constrained), and drop our pre-communist control variables.

[39] This is calculated using the lincom command in Stata 13.1. Note that the statistical significance of the interaction effects cannot be determined precisely from Figures 4.2 and 4.3. While estimate pairs with non-overlapping confidence intervals are always statistically significant from each other, overlapping confidence intervals do not necessarily imply lack of significant differences as long as the intervals of one estimate do not overlap with the other estimate. For example, the interaction term between pre-communist democracy (regime) and exposure is significant at .05 two-tailed even though the confidence intervals in Figure 4.2 overlap slightly. Meanwhile, for pre-communist literacy, the confidence intervals overlap to a greater extent (but do not fully include the other estimate points in the pair), and the interaction effect is still close to, although definitely outside, traditional cutoffs for

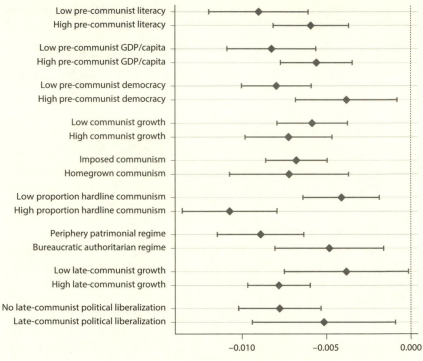

Communist exposure effects on democracy support

Figure 4.2. Communist Exposure and Democracy Support: Country Moderators
This figure reports the marginal effects of a single year of exposure to communism in different types of country contexts. The results indicate that negative communist exposure effects on democratic support were significantly stronger in countries with low pre-communist literacy, GDP/capita, and democracy, as well as for countries with lengthy periods of hardline communism, in peripheral patrimonial regimes and countries with high late-communist economic growth. In interpreting the substantive size of these effects it is important to keep in mind that the median number of years of exposure to communism in the analyses that produced this figure was 28 years, while the 90th percentile was 55 years for a resident of the former Soviet Union and 45 years for a resident of East-Central Europe.

exposure (see Table 4.3, Model 1), what we are primarily interested in here is how the effects of a year of exposure matter across each of the pairs of categories.[40]

---

significance (.13 two-tailed). Therefore, readers interested in the statistical significance of the interactions should consult the full regression tables in the electronic appendix.

[40]To generate the pairs, we estimate marginal effects of an additional year of communism at the 5th and 95th percentiles of the variable with which we are interacting years of

Starting from this perspective, we can begin assessing the support for our different *intensifying* and *resistance* hypotheses. The clearest differences can be found in two political variables: the proportion of years a respondent's country was under Stalinist and neo-Stalinist rule ("proportion hardline communism"), and levels of interwar democracy ("precommunist democracy").[41] Turning to the former (sixth pair from the top), we find that in a country that—all else equal—had spent 90% of its communist experience under either Stalinist or neo-Stalinist rule, the predicted effect of an added year of exposure to communism in decreasing support for democracy is more than two and a half times the size of the effect in a country that has spent only 6% of its communist period under Stalinist or neo-Stalinist rule. Similarly, the effect of an additional year of communist exposure in a country with an average Polity score of -7.375 (i.e., low level of democracy) from 1920 to 1939 results in twice as large of a decrease in support for democracy is in a country with an average Polity score of 7 (i.e., high level of democracy) from 1920 to 1939 (third pair from the top). Both of these interaction effects are statistically significant at .05 or better and are in the predicted direction: interwar democracy appears to provide resistance against anti-democratic communist socialization, while more years of exposure to hardline communism intensifies the effect of exposure.

In contrast, there is no meaningful distinction in the effect of a year of communist exposure in a country where communism was externally imposed as opposed to being homegrown (fifth pair from the top), in countries where there was more or less overall economic growth under communism (fourth pair from the top) or in countries where there was more versus less political liberalization in the last decade of communism (bottom pair). In all three of these cases, the standard error of our estimate for the interaction effect between the variable in question and communist exposure was larger than its coefficient, suggesting very low confidence in any real effect, as confirmed by our estimates of the marginal effects in Figure 4.2. This is surprising, as we would have expected homegrown Russian, Albanian, and Yugoslav communism to have been (at least initially) more effective in shaping the political values of its citizens,

---

exposure. In practice, for categorical variables such as pre-communist literacy, this means setting the variable to its highest and lowest categories.

[41] Prior experience with democracy varied from fairly robust in several countries in the region (Czechoslovakia, East Germany, Poland, and the Baltic states) to non-existent in the interwar Soviet republics and several Balkan countries. While the communists tried and largely (but not fully) succeeded in destroying the institutional vestiges of pre-communist democracies, we would nevertheless expect the availability of prior democratic memories (or myths) to shape both the resistance to communist political narratives and the post-communist embrace of democratic values.

and therefore to lower the resistance to communist exposure. However, our findings do not confirm this expectation, suggesting that the initial differences in legitimacy did not translate into noticeably greater receptiveness toward communist socialization (at least with respect to democratic values).

For the remaining three country-level variables we find effects that point in the predicted direction but were not very strong in substantive and statistical significance terms. Perhaps most interestingly from the perspective of the prior theoretical discussion, the socialization effect of communist exposure is about 50% higher in countries with low levels of pre-communist literacy than countries with high levels of pre-communist literacy (first pair in Figure 4.2).[42] While we have to be careful about inferring individual-level mechanisms from aggregate-level data, this finding is consistent with Darden and Grzymała-Busse's (2006) argument about the greater obstacles to communist indoctrination for citizens who had previously been exposed to different political narratives through pre-communist education systems. Along similar lines, communist exposure effects were almost 50% stronger in countries with low levels of pre-communist GDP/capita than in countries with higher pre-communist GDP. Given that the magnitude of these results is on a par with pre-communist literacy, this greater resistance to communist indoctrination of societies that were highly economically developed may reflect not only the importance of pre-communist political socialization as an ideological antidote to communism, but also the fact that the appeals of the developmental and political project of communism may have been stronger in less developed societies, therefore possibly resulting in citizens who were more likely to embrace its anti-democratic values as well. Or to put in the language of the *living through communism* model, the effect of exposure appears to have been reduced where greater pre-communist economic progress *increased the resistance* of citizens to the communist regime's political project (i.e., in the manner predicted by the model).

Interestingly, we find a very similar result when we look at growth in the last decade of communism. Here we are picking up the effects of the divergence between countries that weathered the economic crisis of the 1980s relatively well (e.g., East Germany and the Soviet Union) versus those that suffered crippling recessions (e.g., Poland, Yugoslavia, and especially Romania). To reiterate, our expectation is that communist economic success should *reduce resistance* to the effects of communist

---

[42] The interaction effect is even marginally significant. While the table in the electronic appendix reports the results of two-tailed tests for p-values, we actually have a pretty compelling a priori expectation in the case of pre-communist literacy, which means a one-tailed test would be appropriate, which would result in a p-value of <.10.

exposure, and thus we would expect to find a negative coefficient for the interaction effect. This is indeed what we find: a year of exposure in a country with higher late-communist growth results in about 50% more communist anti-democratic socialization than a year of exposure in a country with low late-communist growth, and the interaction effect is at least marginally significant (.07 two-tailed). Again, economic benefits from communism seem to increase its appeal.

Overall, the results in Figure 4.2 (and in the table in the electronic appendix) confirm that the extent to which Eastern European and Eurasian societies were affected by communist indoctrination efforts was shaped in predictable ways at the country-level by both pre-communist economic and political trajectories and by differences in communist economic performance. As expected, citizens of countries that entered communism with considerable democratic experience and with higher levels of socioeconomic economic development seem to be less affected by additional years of communist exposure in their attitudes vis-à-vis democracy. Homegrown as opposed to imposed communism, however, had no effect, and nor did overall growth throughout the communist period. Finally, political developments in the last decade of communist rule seem to have had no effect on either strengthening or weakening the communist socialization effect of an additional year of exposure, but *economic* developments in that final decade did.

Taken together, we find that while not all our predicted *intensifying* or *resistance* effects at the aggregate level were supported by the empirical data, all the cases where effects appeared to be statistically or substantively meaningful were indeed in the correctly predicted direction based on our *living through communism* model. Thus, where effects are present, they are the types of effects that we expected to find.

4.4.2. Individual-Level Moderators of Exposure Intensity and Resistance on Attitudes toward Democracy

Since the *living through communism* model predicts that the effects of communist exposure are likely to be modified not just by characteristics of the macro-environment but also by the particular individual circumstances of a respondent, in Figure 4.3 (and in the related table in the electronic appendix) we analyze the interactions between communist exposure and the individual-level *intensifying* and *resistance* characteristics identified in Chapter 2. We again restrict the analysis in this model to citizens of post-communist countries and therefore also use the same constrained linear regression approach we employed for the tests in Figure 4.2.

As a first step we interact communist exposure with different types of self-declared religious denomination, with the expectation that Catholicism

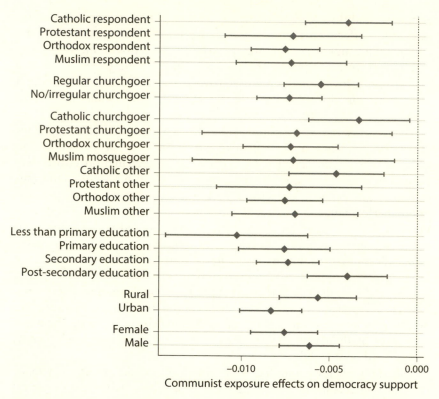

Figure 4.3. Communist Exposure and Democracy Support: Individual Moderators
This figure reports the marginal effects on democracy support of a single year
of exposure to communism in different types of individuals. The results indicate weaker negative communist exposure effects on democracy support among
Catholic respondents (among both frequent churchgoers and non-churchgoers)
and stronger negative exposure effects among less educated individuals and urban
residents. The dependent variable is an index of seven survey questions (listed in
the electronic appendix) which was standardized to a mean of 0 and a standard deviation of 1. The list of independent and control variables can be found in Table 3.1
of Chapter 3. Full regression results are in the electronic appendix. In interpreting
the substantive size of these effects it is important to keep in mind that the median
number of years of exposure to communism in the analyses that produced this
figure was 28 years, while the 90th percentile was 55 years for a resident of the
former Soviet Union and 45 years for a resident of East-Central Europe.

and to a lesser extent Protestantism will increase *resistance* to communist
exposure. Our analysis confirms this is the case for Catholics, but not for
Protestants: an additional year of communist exposure has an approximately 50% larger anti-democratic effect among Protestant, Muslim, and
Eastern Orthodox respondents than for Catholic respondents. These dif-

ferences do not necessarily reflect the differences in democratic sensibilities of different religions toward democracy,[43] but rather, we suspect, the more independent political stance of the Catholic Church vis-à-vis the communist regimes compared to their Orthodox, Protestant, and Muslim counterparts.

Interestingly, though, this finding does *not* seem to be entirely (or even primarily) driven by church *attendance*. An additional year of exposure to communism did have a slightly larger (20%) effect on Catholics who did not attend church regularly than those who did, but the difference is not statistically significant, and, moreover, even Catholics who did not attend church regularly seem to exhibit a great deal more *resistance* toward communist socialization than Muslims, Protestants, and Eastern Orthodox regular church attenders. One possible explanation for this Catholic phenomenon could be that it was driven by the role of the pope in opposing communism, something that would have been widely known to Catholics even outside of regular church attenders. Moreover, it is possible that a consistent message of resistance emanating from the Catholic Church could have reached those who only occasionally came to church (e.g., for major holidays) or even those who had relatives with more consistent contact with the church.

This pattern of church attendance being largely unrelated to the effect of exposure on attitudes toward democracy is, if anything, even stronger among Protestants, Muslims, and Eastern Orthodox. Indeed, despite the fact that there is limited evidence in this regard among Catholics, it was actually a larger difference than for the other three groups. The direct comparison of church attendance across all religious denominations—illustrated in the second grouping of effects in Figure 4.3—confirms the modest nature of this effect, which is at best marginally significant (at .1 one-tailed).

In the fourth grouping of effects in Figure 4.3, we focus on the effects of education, which should by all accounts play a crucial role in the political socialization process. Recall, though, that we had a number of different predictions regarding education: the effects of pre-communist education; the effects of communist education, and the effects of overall level of education generally. We address the first two of these categories in Chapters 5 and 7, but for now we examine whether or not higher levels of education lead to more *resistance* to communist exposure. The results in Figure 4.3 are actually remarkably clear in that regard: the higher the level of education, the smaller the size of the effect of an additional year of exposure to communism on anti-democratic attitudes. To be clear, even higher education

[43] Thus, Muslims in post-communist countries actually appear to be significantly more favorable to democratic systems than their Catholic counterparts among respondents with short communist track records. In the following chapter, however, we will show that Muslims also exhibit resistance to socialization in regard to markets in a similar manner to what we have identified in this chapter for Catholics.

did not completely inoculate one against socialization, but the effect of an additional year of exposure on someone with post-secondary education is only about half as large as for someone with less than primary education. The one exception to this rule is that the effects of primary and secondary education on exposure are practically indistinguishable, so the major action here is when we move from essentially no education to some education, and then from some education to higher education.

Next, we test whether Jowitt's (1992) argument about the greater political penetration of communist regimes in urban settings is confirmed in terms of the relative impact of communist exposure on democratic values. As illustrated in the next to last set of factors in Figure 4.3, the moderately large and statistically significant interaction effect between urban residence and communist exposure suggests that urban residents indeed exhibited almost 50% higher communist socialization effects for the same degree of temporal exposure. These findings support Jowitt's theory, which is remarkable given that urban residents had greater access to alternative sources of information, and therefore, like respondents with a higher education, may have been better equipped to resist communist indoctrination efforts.

Finally, because of the greater exposure of men to communist socialization in both the workplace and the army, we expected that being male should *intensify* the effect of communist exposure. The results of our analysis contradict this hypothesis: while the conditional effects of communist socialization were negative and statistically significant for both men and women, the anti-democratic effects of exposure were *weaker* among men.[44] As a result the democratic gap between men and women was larger among respondents with extensive communist exposure, but not in the direction we hypothesized.

Looking across all the individual-level *intensifying* or *resistance* variables, we find that this framework is indeed useful for getting a more nuanced picture of the effect of exposure to communism on lack of support for democracy, although not uniformly across the board. Catholicism and higher levels of education seemed to increase resistance to the socializing effect of communist exposure, although the effect of religious attendance was limited to Catholics and was only marginally important. Furthermore, as Jowitt predicted, urban respondents seemed to have had an intensified socialization experience but—contrary to expectations—exposure to communism had a larger effect on women than on men.[45]

Taking the last three sections together, we have our first complete assessment of the *living in post-communist countries* and *living through*

---

[44] This effect is marginally significant, with p=.06, albeit in the opposite direction from what we expected.

[45] Although perhaps this will be less surprising to fans of the US-based FX network television show *The Americans*, where Keri Russell's sleeper spy character does seem to be more of a true believer than her husband.

communism approaches to exploring the presence of legacy effects on attitudes of post-communist citizens. The findings are quite clear: on balance taking account of the fact that our survey respondents were *living in post-communist countries*, with peculiar pre-communist histories, socioeconomic economic outcomes from the communist experience, and with particular post-communist demographic profiles, economic conditions, and political institutions only partially accounts for the systematically lower levels of support for democracy among residents of these countries.[46] The experience of *living through communism*, however, had exactly the effect predicted: additional years of exposure to communism—even after controlling for age—led to less support for democracy. While not all the modifiers (especially at the country level) were significant, we nevertheless found clear evidence of uneven exposure effects at both the country and the individual level along the lines predicted by our theoretical expectations about intensifying and resistance factors.

4.5. EXTENSION: CONCEPTIONS OF DEMOCRACY

As briefly mentioned in the introduction to this chapter, there are good reasons to expect that the peculiar nature of communist "popular democracies" would shape not only citizen support for democratic politics but also their very understanding of democracy. Thus, Rohrschneider (1999), using public opinion surveys from the early to mid-1990s, shows that even though both East and West German citizens regarded liberal democratic rights as key components of democracy, the former showed considerably higher concern for social egalitarianism in their understanding of democracy. Given that we could expect democratic conception differences to be even greater in ex-communist countries with weaker pre-communist democratic traditions than East Germany, this raises questions about the validity of cross-national comparisons of democratic support measures. In other words, what does it mean to say that post-communist citizens are less supportive of democracy if their understanding of democracy is different than that of their non-communist counterparts?[47]

---

[46] This conclusion is based on comparing the fully saturated form of the model (Model 7 in Table 4.1) with the bivariate version of the model (Model 1). To be clear, once we control for pre-communist conditions (Model 2), then adding the full combination of contemporary demographic, political and economic variables does reduce the size of the democratic differential almost in half; it does not, however, make it disappear entirely. As mentioned earlier, the effects of the living in post-communist countries model were somewhat stronger in the HLM version of the test (see electronic appendix).

[47] We address a similar question with regard to left-right self-placement elsewhere (Pop-Eleches and Tucker 2010).

Table 4.4. Drivers of Democratic Conceptions

Variables	(1) Government tax rich and subsidize poor	(2) Religious authorities interpret laws	(3) Choose leaders in free elections	(4) People receive unemployment aid
Panel 1. Results without additional controls				
Post-communist	−.297	−.455	.314#	.942**
	(.345)	(.386)	(.163)	(.249)
Observations	60,097	58,488	61,030	60,570
R-squared	.002	.004	.003	.019
Panel 2. Results with individual and country-level controls				
Post-communist	1.022*	−.111	.229	.848**
	(.444)	(.371)	(.228)	(.270)
Observations	60,097	58,488	61,030	60,570
R-squared	.061	.198	.042	.079

Note: This table demonstrates that while post-communist citizens do have different conceptions of democracy from citizens in other countries, it is not as systematic as one might expect. Moreover, post-communist citizens seem just as likely to equate democracy with free elections and even more likely to equate democracy with civil rights, two findings we would not have expected if post-communist citizens' conception of democracy was overly influenced by the notion that communist regimes were "people's democracy." The dependent variable in each case is a 10-point scale asking the respondent how much he or she agrees that the factor at the top of the column was a characteristic of democracy. Panel 1 presents simple bivariate regressions with standard errors clustered at the country year and equilibrated survey weights; Panel 2 contains a more complete set of control variables (as in Table 4.3) Full regression results are in the electronic appendix. The data utilized in this analysis are from 5th wave of the World Values Survey. Robust standard errors in parentheses: ** $p<.01$, * $p<.05$, # $p<.1$.

To address these concerns we use a set of questions from the fifth wave (2005–9) of the World Values Survey, in which respondents were asked for a number of items to rate on a 10-point scale how essential each item was as a characteristic of democracy (see the electronic appendix for full question wording). As a first step we run a series of weighted and county-year clustered OLS regressions where we simply regress each item on the post-communism dummy variable (top panel of Table 4.4). As in the case of the democratic support regressions, we then supplement these simple bivariate models with a set of more fully specified models (lower panel of Table 4.4) along the same lines as those we have used to model exposure

(5)	(6)	(7)	(8)	(9)	(10)
Army takes over when government is incompetent	Civil rights protect people's liberty	Economy is prospering	Criminals severely punished	People can change the laws in referendums	Women same rights as men
−.240	.676**	.808**	.515	.516*	.495**
(.332)	(.245)	(.296)	(.309)	(.205)	(.170)
58,664	59,376	60,133	60,518	59,045	61,042
.001	.012	.017	.005	.007	.008
.682	.812**	1.420**	1.485**	.799**	.380#
(.500)	(.293)	(.265)	(.281)	(.242)	(.215)
58,664	59,376	60,133	60,518	59,045	61,042
.127	.071	.103	.080	.048	.089

effects in the interregional analyses (i.e., as in Table 4.3), that is, the pre-communist country-level variables and contemporaneous individual-level demographic characteristics.[48]

The results in both sets of regressions confirm that post-communist conceptions of democracy differ in some significant ways from those of non-communist respondents, and the results are broadly in line with theoretical expectations: thus, post-communist respondents were significantly more likely to consider state aid for the unemployed and a prospering economy as an essential component of democracy. In both cases the effect is fairly large: on a 10-point scale, these variables account for a predicted change of 0.9 points and 0.8 points, respectively, in the bivariate models, and 0.8 points and 1.4 points in the more fully specified models. In addition,

[48] Given that the democratic characteristics questions were only asked in a single survey wave, we have to slightly reduce the number of country-level controls in order to avoid the multicollinearity problems that arise with over-fitted models. Rerunning the model with the full set of pre-communist controls results in practically the same coefficient for the post-communist dummy variable in both specifications in Table 4.5, but because of multicollinearity standard errors are somewhat higher.

the fully specified model suggests that post-communist citizens were also more likely to see taxing the rich as a component of democracy.

On the other hand, these more economic conceptions of democracy do *not* come at the expense of what we would consider the more traditional procedural or liberal elements of democracy. Post-communist citizens are no less likely to think that democracy involves choosing leaders in free elections and are actually more likely to think that referenda could be used to change the law. Moreover, ex-communist citizens are also *more* concerned about a number of liberal aspects of democracy, such as equal rights for women and civil liberties protections. While some of these aspects, such as social security and gender equality (which we revisit in much greater detail in Chapter 7) are in line with communist-era principles, the emphasis on civil liberties and the endorsement of popular referenda are arguably more reflective of reactions against the abuses and the paternalism of communist regimes. Finally, it is worth emphasizing that for one of the more fundamental threats of democratic collapse—accepting intervention by the army against incompetent governments—post-communist citizens were statistically indistinguishable from their non-communist counterparts. So overall, the concern that perhaps post-communist citizens see democracy solely as a set of economic rather than political principles is not substantiated by these data.

That observation notwithstanding, it is still worth examining whether and how differences in conceptions of democracy affect democratic support patterns and—crucially from our perspective—whether these differences can help explain the post-communist democratic deficit. For example, if citizens who see a prospering economy as a key component of democracy tend to be less supportive of democracy, and given that we know that ex-communist citizens are more likely to see economic prosperity as a crucial element of democracy, then it is conceivable that the democratic deficit could disappear once we account for such different democratic conceptions.[49] To test whether this is the case, in Table 4.5 we first estimate a baseline model (along the lines of Model 4 in Table 4.1 with individual demographic and pre-communist country controls) using only data from the surveys for which the democratic conceptions questions were asked. In Model 2 we add the ten democratic conception indicators discussed in Table 4.4.

The results of the baseline regression in Model 1 confirm that the post-communist democratic deficit for the 2005–9 survey wave is similar to the deficit we found in the corresponding model using the full set of surveys

---

[49] Of course, if we were to find that this is the case, then that would not necessarily refute the importance of communist legacies but would suggest a particular cognitive mechanism for why ex-communist citizens profess weaker democratic support.

Table 4.5. Democratic Conceptions and Democratic Support

	(1)	(2)
Post-communist	–.401*	–.432**
	(.195)	(.142)
Democracy = governments tax the rich and subsidize the poor.		.009*
		(.004)
Democracy = religious authorities interpret the laws.		–.030**
		(.004)
Democracy = people choose their leaders in free elections.		.068**
		(.007)
Democracy = people receive state aid for unemployment.		–.004
		(.004)
Democracy = the army takes over when government is incompetent.		–.082**
		(.005)
Democracy = civil rights protect people's liberty against oppression.		.038**
		(.011)
Democracy = the economy is prospering.		.016**
		(.006)
Democracy = criminals are severely punished.		–.005
		(.006)
Democracy = people can change the laws in referendums.		.031**
		(.006)
Democracy = women have the same rights as men.		.021**
		(.006)
Pre-communist controls	Yes	Yes
Individual demographic controls	Yes	Yes
Observations	52,942	52,942
R-squared	.141	.285

Note: This table demonstrates that while post-communist citizens do have different conceptions of democracy from citizens in other countries, the differences do not explain away the post-communist deficit in support for democracy. The dependent variable is an index of seven survey questions (listed in the electronic appendix), which was standardized to a mean of 0 and a standard deviation of 1. The list of independent and control variables are similar to those used in Model 4 of Table 4.1 and can be found in the electronic appendix along with the full regression results. The data utilized in this analysis are from 5th wave of the World Values Survey. Robust standard errors in parentheses: ** $p<.01$, * $p<.05$, # $p<.1$.

for 1995–2009 (Model 4 in Table 4.1).[50] Turning to the results in Model 2, we find that democratic conceptions matter for explaining democratic support patterns: not only are several of the individual democratic conception variables individually significant predictors of democratic support (and their signs are in the expected direction), but adding them to the model specification leads to a significant improvement in the explanatory power of the model (the R-squared statistic doubles from .14 in Model 1 to .29 in Model 2). However, the most important finding for our purposes is that accounting for differences in conceptions of democracy does not in any way explain away the post-communist democratic support deficit: thus, in Model 2, the size of the post-communism coefficient is virtually unchanged compared to the baseline results and continues to be negative, substantively large, and highly statistically significant. In other words, even though post-communist citizens differ somewhat from citizens elsewhere in the world in terms of what they see to be essential elements of democracy, these differences cannot account for their lower overall support for democracy in the post-communist period.

As a final step to test whether simply including the word "democracy" in the survey questions is contaminating our analysis, we reconstruct our democratic support index by excluding all of the questions from the index in which the actual word "democracy" appears. To do so, we construct an alternative three-item index, which includes two of the questions from the original index—asking about the desirability of army rule and rule by a strong leader—as well as an additional question about having experts rather than the government ruling the country.[51] Doing so has the advantage of eliminating the potential validity concerns related to the different democratic conceptions discussed above even beyond the solutions applied in Table 4.5. Moreover, given the heavy normative emphasis on democracy in the post–Cold War era, one may worry about whether answers to direct questions about democracy would elicit truthful responses. On the other hand, however, the resulting three-item index has a considerably lower reliability than our original index, even though the two indexes are correlated at .66.

In Table 4.6 we start with the same baseline specification as in Table 4.5 (pre-communist controls plus individual-level demographic characteristics) and then rerun the models using the alternative three-item democracy

[50] We return to the question in variation in the size of the deficit in different time periods in much greater detail in Chapter 8.

[51] This question is not included in the original democracy index because its inclusion would lower the reliability of the index and because it is less obviously an anti-democratic alternative than army rule or a strong leader. We include it here out of interest in not relying solely on two variables in the index, but also because adding it to the index in this case actually increases the alpha of the scale across the full dataset.

Table 4.6. Robustness Test Using an Alternative Democracy Index

Variables	(1)	(2)	(3)	(4)
	7-item democracy index	3-item democracy index	7-item democracy index	3-item democracy index
Post-communist	–.384** (.119)	–.408** (.120)	–.317** (.045)	–.233** (.025)
Pre-communist controls	Yes	Yes	No	No
Individual demographic controls	Yes	Yes	Yes	Yes
Countries	All	All	Germany	Germany
Observations	220,276	220,276	5,957	5,957
R-squared	.138	.153	.100	.069

Note: This table demonstrates that purging our democracy index of the questions that include the actual word "democracy" does not change our overall findings. The dependent variable is an index of seven survey questions (listed in the electronic appendix) that was standardized to a mean of 0 and a standard deviation of 1 for Models 1 and 3; for Models 2 and 4 it is an index of three items not containing the word "democracy." The list of independent and control variables are similar to those used in Model 4 of Table 4.1 and can be found in the electronic appendix along with the full regression results. The data utilized in this analysis are from 3rd, 4th, and 5th waves of the World Values Survey. Robust standard errors in parentheses: ** p<.01, * p<.05, # p<.1.

index discussed above.[52] The results confirm that our findings about the existence of a substantively large and statistically significant democratic support deficit are not simply driven by biases inherent in question wording: thus, Model 2, which uses the three-item democracy index, reveals a post-communist democratic deficit that is highly significant and of a slightly larger magnitude than the one in the baseline Model 1, which uses the seven-item democracy index.[53] The similarity also holds when we restrict the analysis to within-country variation between East and West Germans in Models 3 and 4, although here the size of the coefficient falls a bit (but remains in the correct direction and statistically significant). Therefore, we can be quite confident that despite different conceptions of democracy,

[52] The coefficients differ slightly from those in Table 4.1 because the sample was restricted to observations for which data was available for both the seven-point and the three-point democracy indexes.

[53] While the two coefficients are not strictly comparable, the two variables nevertheless had very similar means and standard deviations.

possible normative biases in cross-national responses to survey questions about support for democracy, and even ways of thinking about the meeting of the word democracy itself, the patterns discussed in the rest of this chapter are not simply an artifact of these factors.

4.6. CONCLUSIONS

In this chapter we have analyzed the mechanisms underlying the large and temporally resilient democratic values deficit among residents of post-communist countries. While we have shown that a number of pre-communist and post-communist demographic, political, and economic factors affect democratic support patterns, these features of *living in a post-communist country* alone cannot account for the significant democratic deficit of post-communist citizens.[54] When we attempt to unpack the effect of communism at the aggregate level by measuring conditions at the end of the communist period, the democratic deficit only grows. By contrast, we find very strong support for the effects of exposure to communism at the individual level: the extent of the democratic deficit increases substantially with the length of time a given individual spent living in a communist regime, even after controlling for a citizen's age. The data, therefore, strongly suggest that the legacy of *living through communism* contributed to anti-democratic attitudes in the post-communist period.

Our analysis in this chapter has also illustrated the value of digging deeper to get a more nuanced understanding of the individual- and country-level contexts that moderate the effects of communist exposure. Turning first to factors predicted to *intensify* the impact of communist socialization, we find fairly strong evidence that the anti-democratic effects of communist exposure were more pronounced in countries with a greater proportion of years spent under the rule of hardline communist regimes. Along the same lines we also find some—albeit less robust—evidence that the effects of exposure were weaker in reform-communist regimes and stronger in Stalinist regimes. However, we find much weaker support for other country-level intensifiers, such as the possibility of weaker socialization effects in countries with late-communist political liberalization or in less ideologically focused patrimonial regimes. In terms of individual-level intensifiers, we find evidence for Jowitt's (1992) contention that living in urban areas would result in an intensified socialization effect, but the

---

[54]To reiterate, in our HLM robustness test, the coefficient on the post-communist dummy variable does drop below conventional levels of statistical significance in the fully saturated model, despite otherwise exhibiting similar patterns to the OLS analysis; see the electronic appendix for details.

other individual-level intensifying hypothesis we tested in this chapter—that socialization effects would be stronger among men, who had more opportunities to come in contact with the regime—is actually falsified by the data, which reveal a stronger socialization effect for women.

With respect to *resistance*, our analysis provides fairly consistent support for the hypothesis that pre-communist developmental differences shaped subsequent country-level differences in resistance/receptiveness to communist socialization efforts. Thus, we find significantly weaker communist exposure effects in countries with greater pre-communist democratic track records, as well as to a somewhat lesser extent in countries with higher pre-communist literacy and economic development levels. Communist-era country-level predictors of resistance are somewhat weaker, though as expected we do find that stronger economic growth in the late-communist period translates into stronger exposure effects, suggesting that the political message of communist regimes resonated more strongly in countries whose command economies performed somewhat better in the last decade of communism.

At the individual level, we find relatively strong individual-level support for two of the *resistance* hypotheses, with Catholics—and particularly Catholic churchgoers—as well as those with higher education levels experiencing smaller anti-democratic effects from each additional year of exposure to communism. However, when we assess the effect of *childhood* versus *adult* exposure, we find that it is adult exposure that has a consistent, systematic, and statistically significant effect on attitudes toward democracy, while childhood exposure does not. This finding is at odds with expectations based on the literature on political socialization in the United States.

In the final section of the chapter, we addressed a number of potential concerns about the cross-national comparability of survey questions tapping into democratic support. We show that while post-communist citizens indeed have somewhat different conceptions of democracy—placing a heavier weight on economic aspects but also on gender equality, popular participation, and civil liberties—these differences in conceptions of democracy cannot account for the democratic deficit discussed in this chapter. Nor do our findings seem to be sensitive to an alternative construction of the dependent variable that excludes survey questions that explicitly mention democracy and may therefore be sensitive to normative biases.

With these results in hand, we can move beyond the political sphere of democracy to questions of economic and social preferences as well. We turn to the first of these questions—attitudes toward the market—in the following chapter.

CHAPTER 5

Markets

An old lady walks into a butcher shop in Romania in the mid-1980s and asks for a kilo of pork. When told that there isn't any, she asks for a kilo of ham. When told that there isn't any ham either, she asks for beef for a roast, but once again it's not available. After a few more unsuccessful inquiries, the old lady finally storms off in a huff. The butcher turns to his assistant and says: "She's really annoying, but, by God, what a memory she has!"

—Romanian joke, late 1980s

5.1. INTRODUCTION

If the contrast between single-party rule in communist countries and Western-style multiparty democracy was the clearest political difference between Eastern and Western Europe during the Cold War, surely the division between capitalism and communism's approach to state management of the economy was the biggest *ideological* distinction. After all, Marxism—despite its political implications—was in its essence an argument for a different system of economic management, one in which capital would no longer exploit labor and a benevolent state under the leadership of the Communist Party would oversee the economy for the benefit of all.[1] Of course, as discussed in Chapter 2, there are all sorts of qualifications in terms of how this played out in the actual communist experience (Janos 2000), but if nothing else, Marxism-Leninism was certainly a critique of capitalism.

Further, the decision of how far and fast to go in embracing markets as a means of organizing economic activity has been absolutely central to the post-communist transition experience. In the early days of post-communism, the most important debates revolved around whether market reforms should be embraced all at once using "shock therapy" or through a more incremental "gradualist" process (Sachs and Lipton 1990; Murrell

---

[1] Or, as another communist-era joke put it: "Capitalism is all about the exploitation of man by man. By contrast in communism it's the other way around."

1993; Popov 2007).[2] Perhaps the preeminent public policy decision faced by the new post-communist governments concerned whether and how to move public property—where it was owned and managed by the state—into the hands of private citizens (Lipton and Sachs 1992; Appel 2004; Gould 2011). And even as the initial phase of post-communist transitions passed, the extent of marketization of the economy would continue to be important as countries prepared for EU accession (Vachudova 2008, 2009; Herzog and Tucker 2010; Grabbe 2014) and dealt with the aftermath of the 2008 global economic crisis.

Thus, in our continuing exploration of how communist legacies might affect attitudes in post-communist countries, we now turn to attitudes toward market-based economies. Simply put, our expectation is that—in line with the core arguments of Marxism-Leninism—citizens in post-communist countries will be less supportive of market-based economic systems—and therefore more in favor of state intervention in the economy—than citizens not living in post-communist countries (Marx and Engels 2002 [1848]; Marx 2012 [1867]; Lenin 1999 [1902]). And the data from the World Values Survey do indeed show that in a simple bivariate analysis, post-communist citizens are indeed less likely to support market-based approaches to the economy than citizens in the rest of the World Values Survey countries, thus making it a suitable subject for testing whether these distinctions can be explained by *living in a post-communist country, living through communism*, or neither. Further, as the reverberations of the global economic crisis continue to raise questions about the commitment of citizens to markets the world over, the question of whether we might expect post-communist citizens to be particularly fickle in their attachment to markets takes on renewed importance.[3]

What do we find? Building on the results in the previous chapter, the *living in a post-communist country* model explains away little of the difference between attitudes among post-communist citizens and those in the rest of the world regarding the market (see Table 5.1). In fact, adding our pre-communist or contemporaneous *living in a post-communist country* variables gives us a *larger* distinction in attitudes than in our simple bivariate model.[4] Conversely, and also similar to the findings in

---

[2] Although see Gould (2011) for an interesting argument that the more relevant distinction is actually whether insiders or outsiders oversaw the privatization process.

[3] For example, in 2007 Jacques Rupnik wrote in regard to Poland, "When economic results turned out to be generally positive, people became used to markets much more readily than they came to embrace democracy" (Rupnik 2007: 20). If this commitment, however, was less firm than it appeared on the surface, would it be able to survive a pronounced period of economic dislocation? While this book does not explore the post-2009 period, an understanding of the extent of communist legacies in structuring attitudes toward markets pre-crisis would seem to be an important prerequisite for such research.

[4] These patterns are also confirmed in the HLM tests presented in the electronic appendix.

the previous chapter, we continue to find strong evidence in support of the *living through communism* model (Table 5.3).

With the mounting accumulation of empirical evidence in support of our primary predicted observable implication of the *living through communism* model—that additional years of exposure to communism leads to more support for opinions associated with basic principles of communist ideology—we embark on a new empirical direction in the latter half of this chapter by exploring a number of channels through which communist exposure could have translated into opposition to markets.

Before doing so, we follow a pattern similar to the previous chapter. In Section 5.2, we introduce our measure of attitudes toward the market and assess the effect *living in a post-communist country* on differential attitudes toward markets when accounting for pre-communist conditions and our measures of contemporaneous demographic, economic, and political factors. In Section 5.3, we then analyze the effect of controlling for conditions at the end of the communist era that were related to some of the key characteristics of communism, including its developmental legacies, emphasis on reducing inequality and redistribution, left-wing ideology, and non-democratic rule. In Section 5.4, we test the effect of exposure to communism, including variables we have hypothesized could *intensify* the effect of or provide *resistance* to communist exposure at both the aggregate and individual level.

In Sections 5.5, 5.6, and 5.7, however, we depart from the analysis in Chapter 4 by taking advantage of additional sources of data that allow us to conduct supplementary analyses not possible with the World Values Survey. First, in Section 5.5, we draw on data from the 2006 and 2010 European Bank for Recovery and Development *Life in Transition Surveys* (LiTS) to test the impact of three potential channels through which Eastern Europeans may have been socialized into the political value system promoted by the communist regimes: the role of communist education, Communist Party membership, and cross-generational transmission of values by family members educated under communism or belonging to the Communist Party. In addition, we test whether recipients of pre-communist education were more resistant to communist ideology and whether such resistance was transmitted within families. In section 5.6 we use data from the early transition period (1992–1997) on parents and children from the same household from the Hungarian Household Panel Survey (HHPS) to analyze how parental socialization affects both the transmission of communist economic values and the resistance to official indoctrination. Finally, in Section 5.7 we use data on migrants from the 1994 German Election Survey to attempt to disentangle some of the effects of communist socialization from those of residence in a post-communist country.

5.2. LIVING IN POST-COMMUNIST COUNTRIES AND ATTITUDES TOWARD MARKETS

As in the previous chapter, we begin by conducting our analyses using data from the World Values Survey, although we can now analyze data from four survey waves (1989–93, 1994–98, 1999–2004, and 2005–9), which includes 201 surveys from 84 countries (including 67 surveys from 24 post-communist countries). Our dependent variable is an index that is largely drawn from a single question asking respondents where they place themselves on a 10-point scale between "private ownership of business should be increased" (1) and "government ownership of business should be increased" (10). We supplement this question with an additional item that unfortunately was asked only in a single wave of the survey (the third wave), which again used a 10-point scale to ask respondents to choose between "the state should give more freedom to firms" (1) and "the state should control firms more effectively" (10). The resulting "market support index" is standardized to a mean of 0 and a standard deviation of 1 and has a Cronbach's alpha of .70.[5]

Figure 5.1 presents the average level of support for our market index displayed by country. As is clearly discernible here, it is of course not the case that all post-communist countries have a lower average level of support for markets than all other countries. What we do observe, though, is that only two post-communist countries (Albania and Macedonia) placed near the top of the distribution in terms of their support for the market. There is also a rather large clump of post-communist countries in the lower part of the index, dominated primarily by countries from the former Soviet Union (e.g., Moldova, Russia, Armenia, Ukraine, and, perhaps more surprisingly, Poland).

[5] We use the first item to create two separate dummy variables: a "private ownership" supporter for people who rank themselves as a 1, 2, or 3 and a "government ownership" supporter for people who rank themselves as an 8, 9, or 10. In a similar fashion, we create two additional dummy variables from the second item for pro-firm freedom (1, 2, 3) and anti-firm freedom (8, 9, 10). We do so because coding the variable in this way increases the Cronbach's alpha on our index above .70, which simply entering the data as a continuous variable does not. Moreover, visual inspection of the government ownership variable reveals a strong tri-modal distribution around opposing, supporting, and being in the middle (the three modal responses are 5, 1, and 10). Recoding as essentially three dummy variables (with "no opinion" as the omitted category) therefore seemed to be an appropriate strategy. That being said, our index correlates with the government ownership variable at -.94. Not surprisingly then, rerunning the analysis using just the private ownership question in its 10-point scale format returns very similar results to those found in the remainder of the chapter.

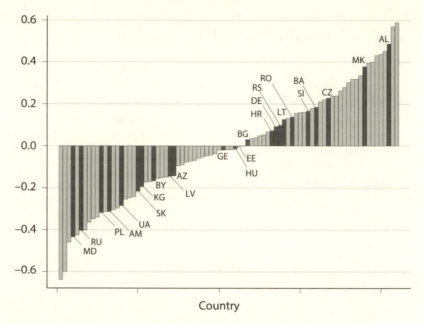

Country

Figure 5.1. Average Support for Markets by Country: Post-communist vs. Non-communist
This figure lists the country-level averages in market economy support of post-communist countries (dark-gray bars) compared to those of non-communist countries (light-gray bars) based on the 2nd, 3rd, 4th, and 5th waves of the World Values Survey (1990–2008). In calculating the averages we used individual-level weights, and we also applied equilibrated weights to adjust for different sample sizes across surveys for different years in any given country. The figure shows that while only Russia and Moldova rank toward the very bottom of the global market support distribution, ex-communist countries are over-represented in the lower half of the distribution, and very few are in the top quarter of the most pro-market countries. The dependent variable is an index of two or four items (depending on the survey wave) standardized to a mean of 0 and a standard deviation of 1. The data utilized in these analyses are from the 2nd, 3rd, 4th, and 5th waves of the World Values Survey. For the full set of country codes, see the list of country code abbreviations on page xv.

Three important points need to be addressed before we proceed with our empirical analysis. First, although there obviously was variation in the degree of state control of the economy across communist countries (de Melo et al. 2001), this was dwarfed by the variation in state control of the economy separating communist countries from non-communist countries. As discussed in Chapter 2, the share of economic output produced by the public sector in communist countries ranged from 85% to 95% (EBRD

2008). Even the most statist social democracies of Western Europe rarely approach 25% of economic output generated by the public sector, and many others (such as the United States) are closer to 5% (Estrin 2007). Thus the emphasis by communist regimes on state socialism as an alternative form of economic organization to capitalism was indeed marked by real, on-the-ground, economic realities. Under communist regimes, state ownership of the means of production was actually widespread,[6] agriculture was collectivized,[7] and massive government bureaucracies did indeed exist to actively manage economic activity.[8] So when respondents are asked questions about state involvement in the economy, our understanding is that this is indeed tapping into a reality with which people were familiar, whereas in the previous chapter we had to wrestle with the idea of what a "people's democracy" might have meant. Whatever its ambiguities, communism was certainly a massive experiment in state management and ownership of the economy.

Second, in interpreting the survey responses, we need to keep in mind that economic conditions were changing dramatically in post-communist countries throughout the period of our study. Thus, when respondents were asked questions about the relative merits of market-based versus state-managed economic systems, they were not doing so in an economic vacuum. The economic circumstances of post-communism were continuously changing and in many cases had fluctuated dramatically since the collapse of communism (Hellman 1998; Frye 2002). We address these circumstances in two ways. Most directly, in Table 5.1, Model 4, we introduce measures of contemporary economic conditions into our analysis (as we did in Table 4.1 in the previous chapter as well). Should it be the case that the post-communist "market support deficit" (i.e., the fact that post-communist citizens are less supportive of market-based economies than citizens in other countries) was simply a function of economic conditions at the time of our surveys, we would expect the deficit to disappear in this specification of the model. As it turns out, the deficit in this model is practically identical to the deficit in the model with pre-communist control variables, suggesting quite strongly that contemporaneous economic conditions were not the driving force behind a lack of support for market economics. As discussed in Chapter 3, we do not continue to include these contemporaneous economic conditions in the subsequent analyses in the chapter in an effort to avoid post-treatment bias in our models. However,

[6] See, for example, Ticktin (1973); Nove (1990); Ericson (1991); Goldman (1991); and Kornai (1992).

[7] See, for example, Millar (1974); Conquest (1986); Hunter (1988); and Pryor (2014), although note the exception of Poland (Gorlach 1989).

[8] See, for example, Neustadt (1947); Manove (1971); Gregory (1990); Gregory and Tikhonov (2000); and Ellman (2014).

we do include year dummies in all our analyses, which should pick up any *global* economic trends that are not specific to the post-communist context.

The final point we need to address—which builds on the previous two—is the fact that unlike the democracy indicators that essentially query respondents on their *level* of support for a given concept, the survey items we are forced to rely on in this chapter ask about *relative levels* of marketization, that is, should there be *more* or *less* private (or government) ownership of businesses; as well as *more* or *less* freedom for firms. To be clear, this was not a deliberate choice—we would have preferred to rely on questions that were more directly comparable with those in the previous chapter—but these were the only questions asked repeatedly on the World Values Survey related to markets.[9]

Nevertheless, we felt comfortable going forward with analyzing this dependent variable for two main reasons. First, to the extent that the move from absolute levels to relative levels complicates our analysis, it should bias us *against* finding a significant difference in attitudes in the predicted direction (i.e., less support for markets in post-communist countries). Thus, if we assume that for most of the period under study here post-communist countries had much larger state sectors than other countries, then the types of errors this would enter into the data (e.g., mistakenly coding a post-communist citizen as pro-market because he or she wants a little more private ownership in a country with extensive government ownership or a non-post-communist citizen as anti-market because he or she lives country with minimal government ownership and would just like a little more government ownership) would both bias *against* finding an anti-market post-communist differential.

Second, we confirmed the robustness of our main findings below in a separate analysis—reported in greater detail in the electronic appendix—where we used data from three waves (1990, 1996, 2006) of the International Social Survey Programme (ISSP) to replicate the key findings from the WVS-based analysis below using a different set of survey questions. The ISSP survey questions asked respondents whether they favored or opposed a series of government interventions in the economy, including wage and price controls and assuming a direct role in managing various economic sectors, and thus avoid the aforementioned concerns with the variables included in the WVS surveys. While the much smaller set of both post-communist and non-communist countries in the ISSP surveys precluded

---

[9]The alternative options—to drop the examination of markets entirely or rely on a completely different dataset for this chapter—struck us as an even less desirable research strategy.

us from running the same set of models and including the same variables as in the WVS tests, our analysis nevertheless confirms the main findings discussed in Sections 5.2 and 5.4 below: thus, we find a significant and robust anti-market bias among citizens of post-communist countries, and we show that longer personal communist exposure (and particularly adult communist exposure) was associated with more anti-market attitudes.

With these points addressed, we can now turn to assessing our empirical findings. Starting again with the *living in a post-communist country* framework, Model 1 of Table 5.1 confirms what the visual inspection of Figure 5.1 suggested: at the individual level, there is indeed a systematic market support deficit among post-communist citizens. As our index is standardized to a mean of 0 and a standard deviation of 1, the magnitude of this effect is about 12.5% of a standard deviation: substantively meaningful, although less than half the size of the democratic differential in our initial bivariate analysis in the previous chapter.[10]

Interestingly, though, the size of the deficit more than doubles once we include our pre-communist control variables (Model 2).[11] To reiterate, this means that based on the characteristics of the countries in which communism took hold *before* the communist period, we would actually expect citizens in post-communist countries on average to be *more* supportive of a market economy. Model 3 of Table 5.1 shows the robustness of this finding to using non-parametric modeling with entropic balancing: the size of the coefficients on the post-communist dummy variables is practically the same in both Models 2 and 3.

In Model 4, we add controls for individual-level demographic characteristics of all survey respondents. This results in an improvement in model fit by roughly one-third (the R-squared goes from 0.06 in Model 2 to 0.08 in Model 4) and an approximately 25% decline in the size of the coefficient on the post-communist dummy variable from Model 2 (although still leaving a coefficient that is 70% larger than the simple bivariate regression in Model 1). Thus, as in the previous chapter, we can explain some—but far from all—of the deficit in support for the attitude in question (here, markets) using demographic characteristics.

Interestingly, controlling for contemporaneous economic outcomes has almost no effect on the post-communist deficit in support for markets. This is especially surprising given that we are now directly considering an

---

[10] Note, though, that for the fully saturated model, the size of the market differential is actually a bit over two-thirds of the size of democracy differential (Model 7 in Tables 5.1 and 4.1).

[11] It is worth noting that the raw data in Figure 5.1 does not reflect these pre-communist controls.

Table 5.1. Living in a Post-communist Country and Attitudes toward Markets

	(1)	(2)	(3)	(4)	(5)	(6)	(7)	(8)
Post-communist	-.125**	-.288**	-.261**	-.212*	-.295**	-.161#	-.218*	-.176#
	(.047)	(.082)	(.084)	(.090)	(.083)	(.100)	(.096)	(.099)
Year dummies	Yes	Yes	No	Yes	Yes	Yes	Yes	Yes
Pre-communist controls	No	Yes	No	Yes	Yes	Yes	Yes	No
Post-communist demographics	No	No	No	Yes	No	No	Yes	Yes
Post-communist econ outcomes	No	No	No	No	Yes	No	Yes	No
Post-communist polit institutions	No	No	No	No	No	Yes	Yes	No
Pre-communist & year entropy balancing	No	No	Yes	No	No	No	No	No
Countries	All	All	All	All	All	All	All	Germany
Observations	262,299	262,299	262,299	262,299	262,299	262,299	262,299	8,857
R-squared	.022	.057	.018	.077	.061	.062	.083	.079

Note: This table demonstrates that post-communist citizens are less supportive of markets than citizens in the rest of the world, even when controlling for pre-communist conditions (Models 2 and 3) and contemporaneous demographic characteristics, economic conditions, and political institutions (Models 4–7); similar results can be found from analyzing only data from Germany comparing East and West Germans (Model 8). The dependent variable is an index of two or four items (depending on the survey wave) standardized to a mean of 0 and a standard deviation of 1. The list of independent and control variables can be found in Table 3.1 of Chapter 3. Full regression results are in the electronic appendix. The data utilized in these analyses are from the 2nd, 3rd, 4th, and 5th waves of the World Values Survey. Robust standard errors in parentheses: ** p<.01, * p<.05, # p<.1.

economic preference. It would stand to reason that support for markets would be lower in countries where economic conditions were worse, as was certainly the case in many post-communist countries in the 1990s. One possible explanation could be that the initially negative comparative performance of the ex-communist countries was balanced out by the subsequent economic recovery after the late 1990s, when many Eastern European countries grew faster than the rest of the world. If that was the case, then we should see an initial increase in the post-communist market deficit in the early to mid-1990s followed by a decline starting in the late 1990s.[12]

In contrast to our findings regarding economic conditions, adding political institutions to the analysis (Model 6), despite not greatly improving model fit (R-squared of .064 vs. .059 in Model 2) does have a rather substantial effect on the size of the post-communist dummy variable, reducing it by almost 40%. It is important to note here that our list of political and institutional variables includes our measure of corruption, which has a strong and statistically significant effect on support for the market (see full results in the electronic appendix). Thus, part of the difference in attitudes toward markets between post-communist countries and other countries in the world is likely due to having had less success in addressing problems related to corruption in the post-communist word, which not surprisingly undermines popular support for markets. Nevertheless, we still find a difference between the two sets of countries that is larger than in our simple bivariate test.

Model 7 in Table 5.1 confirms that even after adding all our *living in a post-communist country* variables simultaneously, there is still a meaningful market support deficit among post-communist citizens. It is about 25% smaller than what we found when simply controlling for pre-communist characteristics, but almost 75% larger than in the simple bivariate analysis with year dummies. Again as well, our single-country result from Germany (Model 8) yields a similarly sized (albeit marginally significant) effect in the same direction, suggesting that East Germans were on balance less supportive of markets even once we control for demographic differences. Thus, as in the previous chapter, we are unable to explain away the post-communist deficit in support for markets using country-level variables associated with *living in a post-communist country* and demographic characteristics of respondents, suggesting that once again we

---

[12] And indeed, this is exactly what we do find when we explore the temporal evolution of these deficits in Chapter 8; see Figure 8.1b.

need to examine the effects of communism more directly. We start with the aggregate-level characteristics of post-communist countries at the time of communism's collapse.

5.3. LIVING IN POST-COMMUNIST COUNTRIES: UNPACKING THE EFFECTS OF COMMUNISM

As previously, we begin by trying to unpack the various developmental, redistributive, and political effects of communism by measuring conditions in 1989, at the end of the communist era. In Model 1 of Table 5.2 we replicate the results from Model 2 of Table 5.1. This model specification includes our pre-communist control variables and year-of-survey dummy variables, thus allowing us to get our best estimate of the aggregate-level effects due to *communism*. Recall that our goal here is to see if we can model the distinguishing features of the communist experience to see if (a) these factors have interesting direct effects on attitudes toward the market (and therefore that "more" of this variable could explain the attitude in question) and (b) if controlling for these factors leads to the elimination of the post-communist market support deficit (and therefore suggests that these factors represent mechanisms through which communism shaped economic preferences).

The results in Table 5.2 are actually a bit more interesting than the commensurate results from the previous chapter on attitudes toward democracy, where attempts to control for communism's distinguishing effects actually led to an *increase* in the size of the democratic deficit in all cases. Starting with Model 2, we examine the effect of communism's developmental footprint through urbanization, industrialization, increased schooling and literacy, and overall wealth. Including these variables has a modest effect on the post-communist dummy variable, but at least it is in the correct direction, reducing the size of the differential by about 12%. Potentially more interesting is that it identifies statistically significant correlations between two sociodemographic characteristics of a society and *less* support for markets that are both hallmarks of the communist experience: having higher levels of urbanization and having industry represent a greater proportion of economic output in 1989. Given that communism increased both urbanization and industrialization, this might be one potential pathway of the manner in which communism decreases support for markets.

Adding our redistribution measures (health and education spending, income inequality, and size of state sector) in late 1989, however, does nothing to explain away the post-communist market support differential; on the contrary, it increases the size of the difference by about 40% in Model 3. Moreover, while higher health and education spending is associated with

Table 5.2. Communist System Features and Attitudes toward Markets

	(1)	(2)	(3)	(4)	(5)	(6)
Post-communist	−.288**	−.251**	−.397**	−.191#	−.342**	−.324**
	(.082)	(.073)	(.082)	(.099)	(.078)	(.109)
Urbanization 1989		−.393**				
		(.119)				
Primary school enrollment		.001				
		(.001)				
Literacy 1989		.002				
		(.002)				
Energy intensity		5.503				
		(4.067)				
Industry as % GDP		−.010**				
		(.002)				
Log GDP per capita 1989		.090*				
		(.043)				
Health & education spending 1989			−.017#			
			(.010)			
Income inequality 1989			−.001			
			(.002)			
State sector size late 1989			.053**			
			(.017)			
Average regime score 1975–89				.007#		.006
				(.004)		(.005)
Left government share 1975–89					.153**	.151**
					(.049)	(.048)
Average regime score 1975–89 ×						−.006
Left government share 1975–89						(.007)
Year dummies	Yes	Yes	Yes	Yes	Yes	Yes
Pre-communist controls	Yes	Yes	Yes	Yes	Yes	Yes
Observations	262,299	262,299	262,299	262,299	262,299	262,299
R-squared	.059	.065	.061	.059	.060	.060

Note: This table demonstrates that post-communist citizens are less supportive of markets than citizens in the rest of the world, even when controlling for conditions at the time of communism's collapse, including developmental legacies (Model 2), redistributive/egalitarian policies (Model 3), and the political orientation of communist regimes (Models 4–6). The dependent variable is an index of two or four items (depending on the survey wave) standardized to a mean of 0 and a standard deviation of 1. The list of independent and control variables can be found in Table 3.1 of Chapter 3. Full regression results are in the electronic appendix. The data utilized in these analyses are from the 2nd, 3rd, 4th, and 5th waves of the World Values Survey. Robust standard errors in parentheses: ** p<.01, * p<.05, # p<.1.

lower market support, the coefficient for state sector size (which is a five-category variable with higher values representing larger state sectors) is actually in the opposite direction, with citizens in countries with a larger state sector in 1989 being more supportive of markets.[13]

In Model 4, we control for how democratic the country was in the decade and a half before the collapse of communism. Almost by definition, post-communist countries are going to score much lower on this index—in the reported results we use the Polity scores, but we get similar findings when using Freedom House scores as well[14]—and therefore with Model 4 showing a positive relationship between living in a more democratic country and having a higher level of support for markets, it is not surprising that this variable reduces the size of the market support deficit by almost 30%. That being said, the coefficient on the dummy variable remains negative and statistically significant and is still larger that the bivariate coefficient from Model 1 of Table 5.1.

Model 5 leads to the most surprising effect in the entire table: controlling for pre-communist characteristics and the year of the survey, having had a more left-wing governments in the decade and a half leading up to the collapse of communism was related to *more* support for market economies. Since the post-communist countries had left-wing governments during that period of time, this unsurprisingly means that the addition of the left-wing government measure increases the size of the post-communist market support deficit. While one might suppose that this was being driven by citizens in democratic regimes with left-wing governments encountering "gentler" markets and thus liking them more, the interaction effect between regime type and left-wing governments (Model 6) actually shows that the effect is stronger in *less* democratic countries (recall that Polity is coded from −10 to 10) and weaker in more democratic countries. So the more democratic the country, the less having a left-wing government increases support for markets, but the less democratic the country, the more it does so. As a result, incorporating both regime type and government ideology (and the two interacted with one another) in the model, far from explaining away the market support deficit among post-communist citizens, actually enhances it further. This might be an instance where the fact that we are measuring preference for change

---

[13] Note that this effect may be due to the survey question wording (discussed earlier in the chapter): as the question measures preferences for changing the status quo, we would expect more pro-market preferences in a countries with larger state sectors even if the distribution of preferences about the absolute size of the state sector is identical to countries with smaller state sectors.

[14] The average country-year score between 1975 and 1989 for a citizen in a post-communist country was a −6.7 score on Polity's −10 to 10 scale, while for respondents not living in a post-communist country it was 3.5.

as opposed to levels might be creeping into our results; it is possible that citizens in countries that already had left-wing governments feel a need for more pro-market changes, whereas citizens in countries with right-wing governments may have preferred a little less exposure to markets.

Taken together, it seems that much of what made communism distinctive at the country level cannot explain why post-communist citizens are less supportive of markets. To be clear, there are some exceptions: living in a country with higher levels of urbanization, industrialization, spending on health and education, and being less democratic are all associated with being less supportive of markets. But none of these factors is enough to erase the distinction between citizens in post-communist countries and those in other countries, and incorporating most of them together tends to increase the size of the deficit.

Thus we arrive at roughly the same point we were in the previous chapter: despite including pre-communist, contemporaneous, and end-of-communism control variables in our models—as well as individual social-demographic characteristics—we still find a persistent gap in market support between citizens inside and outside of the post-communist world, which points again to individual exposure to communist rule as a possible explanation. It is to this topic that we turn in the following section.

5.4. LIVING THROUGH COMMUNISM AND ATTITUDES TOWARD MARKETS

Table 5.3 presents our initial analysis of the effect of exposure to communism (controlling for age) on attitudes toward markets. As in Chapter 4, we run each of these models twice, once with the post-communist dummy variable (and a battery of country-level controls) and once with country-fixed effects. We continue here with our inter-regional analysis—that is we are still including respondents from countries both inside and outside of the post-communist world—and accordingly the sample size remains the same as in Tables 5.1 and 5.2.

Models 1 and 2 reveal exactly what the *living though communism* model predicts: additional exposure to communism—controlling for age— results in lower support for markets, just as it did for democracy in the previous chapter. Not only are both of these coefficients statistically significant, but also they are substantively large and, in fact, almost 50% larger than the effect for a year of exposure on attitudes toward democracy. A full dose of exposure to Eastern European communism (45 years), for example, would result in an estimated decrease of close to –0.45 on our market support index. By comparison, this effect is about 30% larger than the predicted effect of moving from the 5th to the 95th percentile on the income scale among the WVS respondents in our sample.

The other finding worth noting is that whereas in the baseline model (Model 4 of Table 5.1) the effect of the *post-communist citizen* variable had been negative and significant, once we control for communist exposure in Model 1 of Table 5.3 the *post-communist citizen* coefficient turns positive (albeit insignificantly so). In other words, residents of ex-communist countries without personal exposure to communist regimes after the age of six do not exhibit (at least on average) the type of anti-market bias associated with communist ideology and reflected in the attitudes of their older compatriots. Thus, it appears that personal communist exposure completely accounts for the post-communist anti-market bias (and more!)—a conclusion that is confirmed by more formal mediation analysis.[15]

Turning to Models 3 and 4 of Table 5.3 we find once again greater differences between the fixed-effects and the non-fixed-effects specifications in the models focusing on communist regime subtypes. If we focus on Model 3, we find the somewhat surprising result that Stalinism has no effect on attitudes toward the markets, but that the other three—and especially post-totalitarian exposure—have large effects. This is broadly consistent with a "nostalgia" view of socialization, whereby exposure to gentler communism is more likely to result in socialization effects, but before we make too much of this finding it is important to note that it is not robust at all to including country-fixed effects. In the fixed-effects specification, as well as in the HLM models in the electronic appendix, the effect is actually largest for Stalinist exposure and smallest for post-totalitarian exposure, although all the coefficients are fairly close to one another and in no case can we reject the null that they are the same.[16] Taken together, the results suggest that there is little systematic evidence for different effects of exposure to different types of communist regimes.

[15] See the electronic appendix for the full output of the mediation analysis, which was conducted using the medeff command in Stata 13.1 (Hicks and Tingley 2011). The analysis indicates that communist exposure accounts for 150% of the initial difference between post-communist and non-communist countries. Since this number is over 100%, it confirms that taking account of communist exposure causes the direction of the post-communist dummy variable to flip, which is what we also observed in the simpler analysis presented in Models 1 and 2.

[16] The closest is the distinction between the effect of Stalinist exposure and post-totalitarian exposure, but even this difference is only marginally significant.

Our comparisons of adult and childhood exposure in Models 5–8, however, are much more interesting and differ in important ways from what we found in Chapter 4, where the only significant effects were from adult exposure and there was no interaction effect between adult and childhood exposure. Here, we find noticeably different results. When we do not model the interaction effect (Models 5 and 6), we find substantively and statistically significant effects for both early and adult exposure, although the effect for adult exposure is nearly twice as large, and we have greater statistical confidence in these effects as well. However, when we include the interaction effect between childhood and adult exposure, we find that the direction of childhood exposure flips, but we end up with a statistically significant interaction effect. This means that for people who were exposed to communism only as children there is actually a *positive* effect on support for markets for each additional year of exposure as a child, but that growing up under communism enhances the *negative* effect (i.e., strengthens the expected anti-market effect) for each year of adult exposure to communism. So experiencing communism as a child does not necessarily inculcate anti-market sentiments but does prime individuals to be more likely to develop those views as an adult, compared to adults who did not grow up under communism.

One important caveat is worth noting here. In practice, the only people in our surveys who would have had been exposed to communism as children but not as adults would have been born in the 1970s or 1980s, a time when skepticism about communist propaganda was higher in many places than in earlier years. So it is possible that had communism ended owing to some exogenous shock earlier (say in the early 1960s), the early socialization effects could have been different. So it may not be that we have identified some universal rule about the effect of childhood exposure to communism without adult exposure per se, but rather one that was peculiar to the particular time period that yielded the experience of being exposed to communism as a child but not as an adult.[17]

Having found strong evidence to support the hypothesis that increased exposure to communism is on average linked to lower support for markets, we now move on to consider whether the extent to which this exposure is either *intensified* or *resisted* in predictable ways by country-level variables (Figure 5.3) or individual-level variables (Figure 5.4). As a

---

[17] Note, though, that we did not find this effect in the previous chapter, nor do we find it in subsequent chapters. So it would be difficult to conclude that this was simply a methodological artifact of the way in which we have structured our analysis.

Table 5.3. Living through Communism and Attitudes toward Markets

	(1)	(2)	(3)	(4)	(5)	(6)	(7)	(8)
Total communist exposure	-.0106** (.0009)	-.0099** (.0007)						
Stalinist total exposure			-.0004 (.0026)	-.0119** (.0019)				
Neo-Stalinist total exposure			-.0134** (.0020)	-.0093** (.0015)				
Post-totalitarian total exposure			-.0251** (.0031)	-.0077** (.0021)				
Reform communist total exposure			-.0075** (.0019)	-.0101** (.0015)				
Early communist exposure					-.0050* (.0024)	-.0038* (.0017)	.0065* (.0032)	.0064* (.0025)
Adult communist exposure					-.0106** (.0008)	-.0099** (.0007)	-.0071** (.0013)	-.0068** (.0009)
Early communist exposure × Adult communist exposure							-.0004** (.0001)	-.0004** (.0001)

Post-communist	.1024		.1862*		.0465		-.0602	
	(.0887)		(.0799)		(.0942)		(.0957)	
Age	.0023**	.0019**	.0020**	.0019**	.0024**	.0021**	.0023**	.0020**
	(.0004)	(.0003)	(.0004)	(.0003)	(.0004)	(.0003)	(.0004)	(.0003)
Year dummies	Yes	Yes	Yes	Yes	Yes	Yes	Yes	Yes
Country dummies	No	Yes	No	Yes	No	Yes	No	Yes
Pre-communist controls	Yes	No	Yes	No	Yes	No	Yes	No
Demographic controls	Yes	Yes	Yes	Yes	Yes	Yes	Yes	Yes
Observations	262,299	262,299	262,299	262,299	262,299	262,299	262,299	262,299
R-squared	.0802	.1041	.0834	.1042	.0804	.1043	.0806	.1045

Note: This table demonstrates that additional exposure to communism is correlated with less support for markets even after controlling for age. In each pair of models, the first model includes a dummy variable indicating whether the respondent lives in a post-communist country (for comparability with Tables 4.1 and 4.2) as well as pre-communist country-level control variables, while the second table model uses country-fixed effects and, accordingly, drops the dummy variable and pre-communist country-level control variables. Models 3 and 4 examine the differential effect of exposure by type of communist regime, and Models 5–8 examine differential effect of exposure during childhood (age 6–17) and adulthood (18+). The dependent variable is an index of two or four items (depending on the survey wave) standardized to a mean of 0 and a standard deviation of 1. The list of independent and control variables can be found in Table 3.1 of Chapter 3. Full regression results are in the electronic appendix. The data utilized in these analyses are from the 2nd, 3rd, 4th, and 5th waves of the World Values Survey. Robust standard errors in parentheses: ** $p<.01$, * $p<.05$, # $p<.1$.

reminder, when specifying models that interact exposure with other variables, we move to our intra-region analysis and include only surveys from post-communist countries.[18]

5.4.1. Country-Level Moderators of Exposure Intensity and Resistance on Attitudes toward Markets

Recall that in the previous chapter we found the strongest moderating effects for *political* variables (namely experience with interwar democracy and the proportion of years under communism spent under Stalinist and neo-Stalinist rule). Interestingly, when we turn to attitudes toward the market, the two variables that have the biggest moderating effect on exposure are two *economic* variables: overall growth during the communist period (fourth pair of rows in Figure 5.2) and growth during the final decade of communism (seventh pair). In both cases we find much larger negative effects for a year of exposure to communism on attitudes toward markets in countries that had enjoyed higher levels of growth under communism. The only other statistically significant interaction effect is interwar democracy (third pair), with a year of exposure to communism having a smaller anti-market effect in interwar democracies (i.e., countries with higher interwar Polity 2 scores) than in countries with weaker or no interwar democratic experiences. In contrast to the previous chapter, though, there is no discernible effect from having spent more years under hardline communist rule (sixth pair) on the effect of a year of exposure on attitudes toward the market.

Also notable for the lack of any interaction effect at the country level are pre-communist literacy levels (first pair in Figure 5.2) or pre-communist wealth (second pair); in both cases, even though the coefficients are positive (indicating weaker exposure effects in more developed countries), the effects are far from statistically significant (see electronic appendix for more details). Thus there does *not* in this case seem to be any significant additional resistance from living in a country with higher levels of pre-communist literacy. There also appears to be little effect related to living in a periphery patrimonial regime as opposed to a bureaucratic authoritarian regime (seventh pair).

The two remaining variables—imposed versus homegrown communism (fifth pair) and late-communist political liberalization (last pair)—both have substantive effects worth noting, although their interaction coefficients do not achieve traditional levels of statistical significance. The anti-market effect of a year of communist exposure was about 25% larger in a country with homegrown communism than in a country where communism was imposed

---

[18]In addition, as addressed in Chapter 3, in the intra-regional analysis we employ constrained regression analysis; see Section 3.3.4 for details.

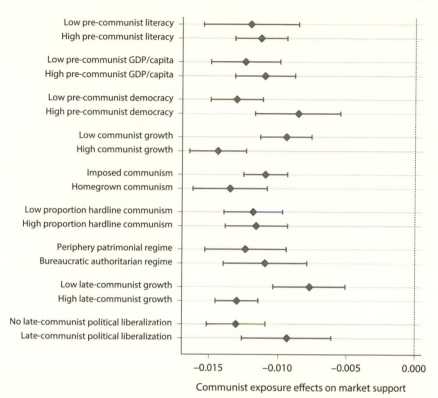

Figure 5.2. Communist Exposure and Market Support: Country Moderators
This figure reports the marginal effects on market support of a single year of exposure to communism in different types of country contexts. The results indicate that negative communist exposure effects on market support were stronger in countries with low pre-communist democracy, as well as for countries with high overall and late-communist economic growth, and countries without late-communist political liberalization. The dependent variable is an index of two or four items (depending on the survey wave) standardized to a mean of 0 and a standard deviation of 1. The list of independent and control variables can be found in Table 3.1 of Chapter 3. Full regression results are in the electronic appendix. The data utilized in these analyses are from the 2nd, 3rd, 4th, and 5th waves of the World Values Survey. In interpreting the substantive size of these effects it is important to keep in mind that the median number of years of exposure to communism in the analyses that produced this figure was 28 years, while the 90th percentile was 55 years for a resident of the former Soviet Union and 45 years for a resident of East-Central Europe.

from the outside, and the effect was about 40% higher in a country with no late-communist political liberalization than in a country with significant late-communist political liberalization. Note, however, that while this latter effect is in line with the hypothesis that political liberalization would be associated with a weaker *intensity* of the communist ideological message, it is at odds with the resistance-based version of this hypotheses, whereby having a gentler (here, liberalized) form of communism is predicted to make individuals more receptive (i.e., have a lower *resistance*) to the anti-market message of the communist regime.[19] The direction of the effect for homegrown versus imposed communism, however, is what we expected from a *resistance* perspective: socialization effects were stronger in countries with homegrown communist regimes, suggesting that—for markets at least—the effects of *living through communism* were strengthened in countries where communist rule may have been seen as more legitimate.

Taken together, we again find support for our theoretical expectations that country-level effects could enhance or reduce the effect of a year of exposure to communism. While we find mixed results for the particular individual moderators, it is interesting to note that in our first exploration of an *economic* attitude, it is two economic variables that have the most significant effects in this regard.

5.4.2. Individual-Level Moderators of Exposure Intensity and Resistance on Attitudes toward Markets

The effects of our individual-level intensifying and resistance variables on the effect of a year of exposure on attitudes toward the market are concisely summarized in Figure 5.3 (with regression tables in the electronic appendix).

Let us first consider the effect of religion. Recall that in the previous chapter Catholicism provided *resistance* against socialization in terms of attitudes toward democracy, and that church attendance did not seem particularly important in this regard. Figure 5.3 reveals a substantially different picture for attitudes toward the market. First of all, it is Muslims who have statistically significantly more *resistance* to anti-market exposure effects than adherents of any other faith (p<.05 vs. Catholics, p<.01 vs. Protestants and Orthodox). Thus a year of exposure to communism had the smallest effect on Muslims in decreasing support for markets. Catholicism does still seem to provide more resistance than being

---

[19] We realize that there can be something unsatisfying about a finding that confirms one hypothesis if it reveals a positive relationship and a different one if it reveals a negative relationship. That being said, we want to be clear that it is possible to falsify both hypotheses simultaneously, which would be the case if the analysis reveals no relationship (i.e., an insignificant interaction effect).

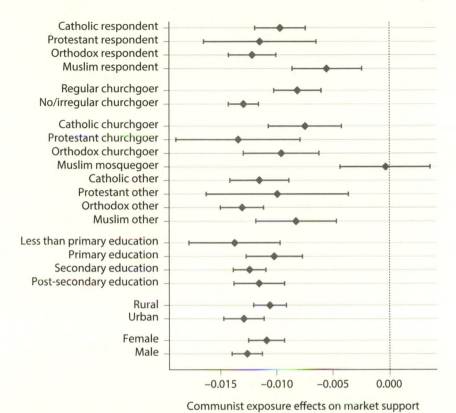

Communist exposure effects on market support

Figure 5.3. Communist Exposure and Market Support: Individual Moderators
This figure reports the marginal effects on market support of a single year of exposure to communism in different types of individuals. The results indicate weaker negative communist exposure effects on market support among Muslim respondents and churchgoers as well as among females and rural residents. The dependent variable is an index of two or four items (depending on the survey wave) standardized to a mean of 0 and a standard deviation of 1. The list of independent and control variables can be found in Table 3.1 of Chapter 3. Full regression results are in the electronic appendix. The data utilized in these analyses are from the 2nd, 3rd, 4th, and 5th waves of the World Values Survey. In interpreting the substantive size of these effects it is important to keep in mind that the median number of years of exposure to communism in the analyses that produced this figure was 28 years, while the 90th percentile was 55 years for a resident of the former Soviet Union and 45 years for a resident of East-Central Europe.

Protestant and Orthodox, but these differences are not statistically significant for the former.

Second, church (or mosque) attendance seems to be extremely important in providing resistance to socialization effects in terms of anti-market attitudes, with an additional year of exposure to communism having a two-thirds larger effect on those who did not attend (or attended irregularly) religious service than those who attended regularly.[20] However, this effect was not uniform across religious denominations. Thus, whereas in the case of Protestants, anti-market exposure effects on churchgoers were actually insignificantly stronger than for non-churchgoers, for the other three main denominations the effects were in line with the overall pattern of religion promoting resistance. In the case of Muslims who regularly attend religious services, the resistance effect is so strong that it completely wipes out any socialization effect of an additional year of exposure to communism on anti-market attitudes.

Turning to education, we find a substantially different pattern than in the previous chapter in all respects save one. Recall that our expectation here is that additional education will provide greater *resistance* to communist socialization, resulting in a smaller negative effect for each additional year of exposure to communism on attitudes toward the market. When we observe Figure 5.3 (and the corresponding table in the electronic appendix), we do indeed find that respondents who have not completed primary education experience the largest anti-market exposure effect, but the effects for primary education, secondary education, and higher education are all bunched closely together, and none is statistically distinct from the others at conventional levels of statistical significance.[21] So perhaps the most we can say here is that we once again have some suggestive evidence that socialization effects are marginally stronger among those with the least education.

In contrast, our findings for the relative strength of socialization efforts in rural versus urban areas are similar to the previous chapter and again confirm Jowitt's (1992: 81–82) contention that socialization effects should be stronger in urban areas: the anti-market effect of an additional year of exposure to communism is more than 20% larger for urban residents than for those living in rural areas (and the difference is significant

[20] Of course, as noted in Chapter 3, it is important to keep in mind that the surveys ask about contemporaneous rather than historical church attendance, so these results should be interpreted accordingly.

[21] The difference between primary education and no education has a p-value of .11, which is close to conventional levels of significance (especially if we think of this as a one-tailed test where our expectation is that the effect would be stronger [i.e., more negative effect] for no education as opposed to primary education, in which case the p-value would be .055). The p-values are higher for all other combinations of coefficients.

at .05). When we turn to gender, though, we find a different result from the democracy chapter: now, in line with our original theoretical expectations, the effect of a year of exposure to communism is larger (here, by approximately 17% [p<.01]) for men than women.

Taken together, the analysis of the individual-level moderating factors actually produces quite a lot of evidence that is consistent with the expectations of our *living through communism* model. We again find heterogeneous exposure effects across individuals: men and urban residents experience *intensified* exposure effects, while those who attend religious services more frequently (especially among Muslims but also among Catholics and to some extent Orthodox) and those with at least some education appear to have higher levels of *resistance*.

However, the findings as to which particular *intensifying* and *resistance* factors matter are not exactly in line with our findings from the previous chapter. For example, higher education provided additional resistance to socialization regarding anti-democratic attitudes, whereas in the case of markets it did not. Conversely, in the previous chapter we found no real effect for church attendance, while here we do. And while Catholics were more resistant to exposure than Protestants and Orthodox in both chapters, Muslims were more resistant to the anti-market than to anti-democratic influence of communist socialization. Finally, while gender moderated the effects of communist exposure in both chapters, the effect is in different directions (i.e., the correctly predicted direction here and the opposite in the previous chapter).

5.5. COMMUNIST SOCIALIZATION CHANNELS: FAMILY, EDUCATION, AND COMMUNIST PARTY MEMBERSHIP

While our empirical analysis has identified a number of factors that can either intensify or attenuate the effects of communist exposure, we have so far been somewhat limited in our ability to test some of the key mechanisms that may account for the heterogeneous effects of communism on political attitudes by the questions included in the WVS. In this section we therefore turn to another source of data, the EBRD *Life in Transition Survey* (LiTS), to analyze three important potential socialization mechanisms: *families and intergenerational transmission*; different types of *education*; and *Communist Party (CP) membership*.

As briefly discussed in Chapter 3, the LiTS data we analyze consists of two waves of surveys (2006 and 2010) in virtually all post-communist countries, as well as a handful of non-communist countries for comparison. In addition to their remarkable geographic coverage of the post-communist world, these surveys are an important complement to the World Values

Survey because they include two types of questions that were not asked in the WVS. First, in addition to the standard questions about the educational attainment of the survey respondent, the LiTS also recorded the education of the respondent's parents. This allows us to assess not only the direct impact on the respondent of having received a communist versus non-communist education, but also the extent to which such educational effects are transmitted across generations (Darden and Grzymała-Busse 2006). Second, the surveys also included questions about whether the respondent had ever been a member of the Communist Party and whether the respondent's mother and/or father had belonged to the Communist Party. This information, which is unfortunately (although understandably) lacking from the more global WVS, allows us to test both the direct socialization effects of *individual* Communist Party membership and the extent to which such indoctrination was passed on within *families*.

The dependent variable we used for this analysis was an index based on seven survey questions that touched on different aspects of state intervention in the market economy, including preference for a market or a planned economy, support for privatization versus re-nationalization, guaranteed state employment, price controls for food and utilities, and state ownership of utilities and large businesses.[22] The resulting index is coded such that higher values indicate greater support for markets over state intervention. In addition to our main variables of interest, discussed in greater detail below, our regressions control for demographic characteristics of the respondent, including gender, religious affiliation and attendance, type of residence (urban vs. rural), highest educational attainment, and an income-asset index.[23]

Since we are once again interested in how different factors moderate the effects of communist exposure, we use the same types of constrained regressions as in the preceding section and constrain the coefficient for age in our main regressions (which are restricted to ex-communist countries) to the value we obtain in a separate regression run only on the non-communist countries. The only difference compared to the statistical approach in the previous section is that in addition to year dummies we also

[22] We used questions q305_2, q305_2, q305_3, q305_4, q305_5, q305_6, q309, and q310 (while LiTS also included other potentially relevant questions, their inclusion lowered the reliability of the index). The Cronbach's alpha reliability score for the index was .724. See the codebook in the electronic appendix for details.

[23] This index captures whether the household received income from wages and/or pensions, as well as whether the household had (1) a car, (2) a bank account, (3) a cell phone, (4) a computer, and (5) internet access. The index has a Cronbach's alpha of .77.

included country-fixed effects.[24] As in the previous section, we present the key empirical findings in a series of figures, while the full regression tables are available in the electronic appendix.

5.5.1. Individual and Parental Education Effects

Before discussing the results presented in Figure 5.4, let us briefly place education and family socialization in the context of our *living through communism* model from Chapter 2. As far as individual education is concerned, we can think about it in two—not necessarily exclusive—ways. First, education could act as a one-time ideological shock that is largely independent of the length or nature of subsequent communist exposure, leading to more pro-communist attitudes for those who experienced a communist education and to more anti-communist attitudes for people who experienced pre-communist education. If that were the case, we should observe an anti-market impact among individuals who received communist education, but there should be no interaction effect between communist education and exposure. Alternatively, however, communist education may simply reduce resistance to subsequent exposure: in this case, the effects of communist education on economic attitudes would be modest for individuals with short personal exposures to communism but would be larger among those with longer exposure.

Similarly, the effects of parental education could work in two possible ways in shaping the political attitudes of their children. Thus, parents with pre-communist (communist) education may impart pro-market (anti-market) attitudes on their children, and this initial push could be largely independent of subsequent socialization experiences. Alternatively, parents with pre-communist (communist) education could increase (lower) the resistance of their children to communist socialization, in which case the differences would be once again much more pronounced among individuals with long personal communist exposures than among those with shorter exposures.

Given the discussion above, we are therefore interested in both the *direct* and the *indirect* effects of individual/parental education on market attitudes. Thus, unlike in Figures 5.2 and 5.3, in Figure 5.4 we present both the direct effects of education as well as the conditional effects of different types of education for individuals with low versus high communist exposure.[25]

---

[24]We did so because, unlike in the previous section, where we were interested in cross-country differences, here our main focus is on within-country individual differences. However, the results are robust to dropping the country-fixed effects.

[25]Note that we did not include interaction effects between pre-communist personal education and communist exposure. While from a theoretical perspective it would have been

The direct effects of different types of education are largely in line with our theoretical predictions: respondents who received a pre-communist education are more likely to be pro-market both compared to the base category of respondents without an education and compared to those educated under communism (significant at .05). Furthermore, the differences between pre-communist and communist education were also transmitted across generations, and according to Figure 5.4 the effects were actually slightly stronger for parental education differences. While the magnitude of these effects was not large (6–9% of a standard deviation of the DV) they were not trivial either: thus, the predicted difference in market support between an individual with a pre-communist education and a parent with pre-communist education and another individual with a communist education and a parent with communist education would be equivalent to the predicted difference between respondents at the 25th and 75th percentile of the income-asset index distribution.

Judging by the nature of the interaction effects in the rest of Figure 5.4, it appears that both individual and parental communist education are important primarily through their impact on resistance to subsequent communist exposure rather than as intrinsic ideological shocks. Thus, individual communist education had an insignificant positive effect on market attitudes among individuals with short personal exposures to communism, but the effects of communist exposure are roughly 50% stronger for those with communist education, and as a result communist education recipients were noticeably more anti-market among individuals with long communist exposures (marginally significant at .03 one-tailed).

Turning to parental socialization, we find a similar and even more pronounced pattern for parental communist education: whereas children of communist-educated parents were significantly more pro-market among those with short communist exposure,[26] the effect turns significantly negative for those with long communist exposure because of the much stronger negative effects of communist exposure among those whose parents

---

interesting to test whether pre-communist education functions as a one-time ideological shock or by providing greater resistance against subsequent communist socialization, our data do not lend themselves to such a test, because by definition anyone who experienced at least some pre-communist education was at least six years old at the time of the communist takeover, which means that all such respondents had the maximum personal exposure within their respective countries. Since respondents of the interwar Soviet republics would have had to be over 95 years old by 2006 to have received pre-communist education, the only variation in communist exposure among recipients of pre-communist education was due to the slight differences in the duration of Eastern European communist regimes.

[26] This counterintuitive effect probably picks up the fact that the children of communist-educated parents were better positioned to take advantage of market opportunities in the post-communist period (though it is also compatible with a revolt against their parents among younger respondents).

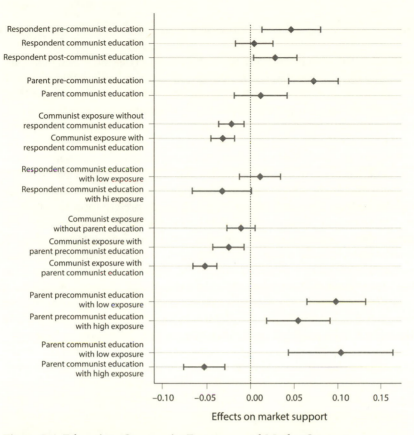

Effects on market support

Figure 5.4. Education, Communist Exposure, and Market Support
This figure illustrates the combined effects of different types of education and
communist exposure on market support. The first set of estimates indicates that
respondents with a pre- or post-communist education are more pro-market
than those with a communist education. The second pair shows that respondents
whose parents had a pre-communist education are more pro-market than those
with communist-educated parents. The third pair shows that communist exposure
has a stronger anti-market effect for those with a communist education, while the
fourth pair shows that communist education only matters for those with long
communist exposure. The fifth set shows that communist exposure primarily affects those with communist-educated parents. The sixth pair shows that parental
pre-communist has stronger pro-market effects for those with lower communist
exposure. The final pair suggests that having communist-educated parents is
associated with pro-market attitudes toward those with low exposure and anti-
market attitudes for those with high exposure. Full regression results are in the
supplemental online appendix. The data utilized in these analyses are from the
2006 and 2010 waves of the EBRD *Life in Transition Surveys*. In interpreting
the substantive size of these effects readers should keep in mind that the communist exposure effects reported in this figure are for 10 years of exposure to communism. The median number of years of exposure to communism in the analyses
that produced this figure was 22 years, while the 90th percentile was 45 years.
Where exposure is used as a moderator, it was set at the 5th and 95th percentile
of the actual distribution for that particular group of respondents.

were schooled under communism (compared to respondents whose parents were either schooled before communism or did not attend school). In other words, it appears that communist-educated parents shape their children's subsequent political preferences not through outright direct indoctrination but by weakening their resistance to subsequent communist socialization efforts.

By contrast, the effects of pre-communist parental education reveal a very different pattern. Thus, the conditional effects of communist exposure among individuals whose parents were educated before communism are more mixed: on the one hand, respondents with pre-communist educated parents were only about half as likely to be affected by communist exposure as their counterparts with communist-educated parents (and the difference is statistically significant at .05), and as a result the contrast between the two groups is most pronounced among respondents with long periods of communist exposure. On the other hand, children of recipients of pre-communist education experienced on average stronger anti-market communist exposure effects than respondents with parents without any education.[27] As a result, the second-to-last pair of coefficients in Figure 5.4 suggests that the attitudinal impact of having a parent educated before the communist takeover was almost twice as large among respondents with relatively short communist exposure as among those with long communist exposure (and the difference is statistically significant at .05). From this perspective, then, pre-communist parental education can be interpreted as a large initial ideological "shock" in favor of the market, which gets partially eroded—but not completely eliminated—by subsequent communist exposure.

5.5.2. Individual and Parental Communist Party Membership Effects

At least in theory, the function of the communist parties in the former Eastern bloc was not just simply as a power transmission mechanism deeply intertwined with the state apparatus, but also as a political socialization mechanism for its members and, at least indirectly, for the broader society. While socialization efforts through the party and its affiliated organizations—especially youth organizations for different education stages, such as pioneers' organizations or communist youth organizations (Komsomol)—affected broad swaths of society, arguably the most intense effects should be observed among actual Communist Party members and

---

[27]This is because respondents whose parents had been educated before communism tended to be older on average than those with uneducated parents.

their families. Of course, Communist Party membership was not necessarily associated with true ideological conviction—many people joined largely because doing so was a prerequisite for career advancement in many professions or because they were pressured to do so by their bosses—but even among such opportunists we may expect to see attitudinal effects either through the socialization that occurred during the mandatory regular party meetings and activities or from a "pocketbook" perspective given the fact that CP members were generally better off than the rest of the population.

Studying the socialization effects of CP membership using postcommunist survey data raises two potential inferential problems. The first concerns the reliability of self-reported Communist Party membership data: given that the LiTS questions about CP membership were asked directly (rather than through the use of list experiments or other techniques designed to address sensitive topics), we may be concerned about underreporting to the extent that there may be a negative stigma attached to admitting to membership in the former ruling party. While such concerns cannot be completely dismissed for particular individuals, the aggregate responses to the questions in the LiTS surveys are roughly line with the official CP membership statistics.[28]

The second difficulty lies in disentangling the socialization effects of Communist Party membership from the likely selection mechanisms underlying CP membership. Thus, to the extent that individuals with procommunist political attitudes were more likely to apply and/or be admitted to the Communist Party, we may observe attitudinal differences between CP members and nonmembers even if the socialization effects of membership itself were very weak. The ideal setup for such a task would be a panel survey that followed cohorts of Eastern European youths from before they were eligible for CP membership and then compared the attitudes of eventual CP members to nonmembers both before and after joining the party. While our post facto survey data does not lend itself to such analysis, we can nevertheless tease apart the effects of selection and socialization by analyzing the nature of the interaction effect between CP membership and communist exposure. Thus, to the extent that attitudinal differences are primarily driven by selection effects, then the magnitude of the CP ideological differential should be very similar irrespective how long an individual was a member of the CP. If, on the other hand, individuals join primarily for instrumental or other non-ideological reasons but are then influenced

[28] For example, according to the LiTS surveys, 23.9% of Romanian respondents who were 18 and older in 1989 reported having been CP members, a figure that is very close to the official membership share in Romania in 1989 (Cioroianu 2007).

by party indoctrination, then we should see minimal attitudinal differences for CP members who were members for a brief period but large and growing differences among respondents with longer CP membership tenures.[29]

The first set of results in Figure 5.5 provides some tentative evidence that CP membership matters: respondents were more likely to express anti-market attitudes almost two decades after the collapse of communism if either they or one of their family members had been CP members prior to 1989. However, the effects are fairly small in substantive terms (about 2.5% of a standard deviation of the DV) and are at best marginally significant.

However, to the extent that former Communist Party members still held more anti-market attitudes than their compatriots, the nature of the interaction between CP membership and communist exposure length suggests that the effects were driven by CP socialization rather than selection bias. Thus, as illustrated in the third pair in Figure 5.5, for former CP members with relatively short exposure, there is no discernible impact on attitudes toward markets, which suggests that CP members were not more opposed to markets than nonmembers when they joined the party. By contrast, for CP members with long personal exposure to communist regimes (and presumably with longer periods of CP membership) the effects were roughly twice as large as for the average CP member, and the difference was at least marginally significant (.05 one-tailed). Furthermore, as illustrated by the second pair in Figure 5.5, the anti-market effects of communist exposure were about 50% stronger for CP members than for nonmembers (though the difference in effects fell short of achieving statistical significance).

The final two pairs of rows in Figure 5.5 suggest that despite the fairly modest direct socialization effects of Communist Party membership, there may have been a stronger indirect ideological effect due to family transmission dynamics. Thus, the last pair of estimates in Figure 5.5 shows that while for short communist exposures the offspring of families with CP ties were somewhat more pro-market than their counterparts from nonparty families, long communist exposure respondents with family members in the CP exhibited a large and statistically significant anti-market bias. What explains these highly uneven effects of family ties to the Communist Party? The second-to-last pair of estimates suggests that the reason for this con-

[29] Ideally we would use data on the length of CP membership, but since the question was not asked in the LiTS survey we instead use overall communist exposure, which should be fairly highly correlated with CP membership tenure (since very young individuals could obviously not have been members for very long, and since few individuals joined the Communist Party very late in life). Note as well that both selection and socialization effects could be at work, with those more predisposed to share communist ideological positions being more likely to join in the first, but then also coming to resemble party orthodoxy even more closely owing to the socialization effects of party membership.

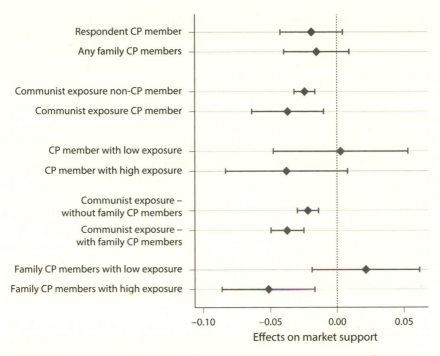

Figure 5.5. Communist Party Membership, Communist Exposure, and Market Support

This figure illustrates the combined effects of Communist Party membership and communist exposure on market support. The first pair of estimates indicates that both CP members and individuals with relatives in the Communist Party were marginally more anti-market. The second pair suggests that the effects of communist exposure were somewhat stronger for CP members than for nonmembers (but the difference was not statistically significant). The third pair shows that contrary to the selection hypothesis CP members with low communist exposure were not anti-market, but in line with the socialization hypothesis CP members with high communist exposure were more anti-market than nonparty members. The last two pairs suggest that the anti-market effects of communist exposure were stronger among respondents with family members in the CP and, conversely, that having a family members in the CP matters more for those with high exposure. Full regression results are in the electronic appendix. The data utilized in these analyses are from the 2006 and 2010 waves of the EBRD *Life in Transition Surveys*. In interpreting the substantive size of these effects readers should keep in mind that the communist exposure effects reported in this figure are for 10 years of exposure to communism. The median number of years of exposure to communism in the analyses that produced this figure was 22 years, while the 90th percentile was 45 years. Where exposure is used as a moderator, it was set at the 5th and 95th percentile of the actual distribution for that particular group of respondents (e.g., CP members).

trast is that the anti-market effects of communist exposure are stronger for individuals with family members who belonged to the Communist Party.

These dynamics are very similar to the effects of parental communist education suggested by Figure 5.4: rather than straight-out communist indoctrination of children in families with CP members, the mechanism appears to have been a reduced resistance to subsequent communist socialization efforts. Or put another way: given that in much of the Soviet bloc CP membership was largely a matter of opportunism/conformism rather than ideological commitment, it should come as no surprise that children from CP families seem to be more likely to adopt the economic orientation du jour. This interpretation explains not only the anti-market zeal of CP member offspring with long communist exposures, but also the (albeit statistically insignificant) pro-market bias of "CP brats" with short communist exposures, who came of age after the fall of communism.[30]

5.6. PARENTAL SOCIALIZATION AND PANEL EVIDENCE FROM HUNGARY

While the analysis in the preceding section addresses parental socialization effects indirectly by inferring unobserved parental attitudes on the basis of observable potential correlates of such attitudes (i.e., the nature and timing of the parents' education or their Communist Party membership), in this section we use a more direct approach that allows us to test the transmission of political attitudes from parents to children by comparing the survey responses of different generations of respondents from the same family. As briefly mentioned in Chapter 3 (Section 3.4.1.3), we were able to locate a valuable source of data for exploring the effect of parental socialization, the Hungarian Household Panel Survey (HHPS).

The HHPS is a yearly panel survey that included over 8,000 respondents from almost 2,700 households in Hungary from 1992 to 1997. Thus it presents a unique opportunity for examining the attitudes of both parents and children from the same household over multiple years. Like many other household panel surveys, the HHPS tends to have a better selection of economic and demographic questions than survey questions tapping into political attitudes, and we were unable to find appropriate questions related to attitudes toward democracy or gender equality. However, respondents were asked one question that arguably taps into market attitudes for a new and highly salient aspect of post-communist political

[30] Note, however, that this positive effect could also reflect the fact that the children of CP members often had better economic opportunities during the post-communist transition.

economy: the rise in unemployment. The question, which was included in the 1992, 1993, 1994, 1996, and 1997 waves, asked respondents to choose between two statements: (1) "unemployment should be avoided by any means," or (2) "economic problems are impossible to solve without facing a certain amount of unemployment." Given the communist emphasis on employment as a right and duty, we would expect communist attitudinal legacies to include opposition to rising unemployment as a crucial component of a broader ambivalence toward market-based economic policies. And while in the absence of a non-communist benchmark it is difficult to establish the extent of post-communist exceptionalism, it is worth noting that about 58% of respondents endorsed the first option.

To capture parental socialization, we code both each respondent's own attitude toward unemployment in the current and previous year and, where applicable, the current and lagged responses of any parent living in the same household. One obvious limitation of our data is that we cannot capture the impact of parental socialization on individuals who do not live in the same household as their parent(s), which precludes us from analyzing the impact of divorced parents and which also means that, particularly for older respondents, the individuals included in our analysis may not be representative of the broader Hungarian population. The proportion of respondents living with at least one of their parents declines from over 90% for minors (up to age 18) to roughly 50% for 22-to-23-year-olds and to about 30% of 25-to-26-year-olds (for more details, see related figure in the electronic appendix.). Therefore, we need to be mindful about the possibility that the parental socialization effects for respondents beyond their early 20s may not be representative of the broader population not just because individuals not living with their parents are likely to be exposed to less parental socialization, but also because the very fact of living with one's parents as an adult may be indicative of closer parental ties.[31] Therefore, we also test whether any of our results are sensitive to restricting our analysis to the age groups where the vast majority of respondents lived with their parent.[32]

Our regressions control for a number of household and individual characteristics that may reasonably be thought to affect individual attitudes toward unemployment, including age, gender, residence, and education levels. Most importantly, we control for changes in logged per capita

---

[31] However, it should be noted that, particularly in the context of the economic crisis of the early 1990s, a key driver of adult children living together with parents were economic constraints and the declining supply of low-cost housing. While this still represents a non-random selection mechanism for adults living with their parents, it is less likely to lead to biased estimates of parental socialization effects.

[32] This means that we reran the analysis using only respondents aged 16–18.

household income between the current and most recent survey. Ideally, this should capture one of the most important sources for spurious correlation between the political attitudes of members of the same household: the possibility that some common economic shock affecting the household could shape the attitudes of both parents and children (e.g., by increasing support for unemployment benefits in response to a sudden loss of income/employment).

Given the dichotomous nature of our dependent variable, we run probit regressions. All models include year-fixed effects to capture possible time-specific shocks in unemployment attitudes. To account for the fact that individuals are grouped in households, we report standard errors clustered at the household level. Finally, to allow for comparability across models we restricted the sample to observations for which we had answers to all the relevant questions from both the respondents and their parents.[33]

The first step, illustrated in Model 1 (of Table 5.4) simply establishes that individual responses are fairly strongly correlated with contemporaneous parental attitudes on the same issue. Not only are the parental attitude indicators statistically significant, but they are fairly large in substantive terms: thus, in Model 1 the difference between a respondent with parents opposed to unemployment and parents supportive of some degree of unemployment corresponds to roughly two-thirds of a standard deviation in the dependent variable.[34] However, these results arguably represent an upper bound of average parental socialization effects: even though the models control for key individual and household demographic characteristics, they ignore the possibility of reverse causation (i.e., children affecting their parents' attitudes) and of spurious correlation (e.g., some unobserved factors, such as media consumption, driving both parents' and children's attitudes).

To deal with these challenges, we run a number of additional model specifications. First, to address concerns of reverse causation, in Model 2 we use the lagged parental responses. While the magnitude of the difference between the two extreme parental views constellations is about 30% smaller in Model 2 than in Model 1, we still find that even lagged parental views are strong predictors of unemployment attitudes among children. However, it appears that using lagged indicators has an asymmetric effect on the size of the coefficients: thus, whereas the coefficients for having two parents who hold "countercurrent" views—that is, who are willing to tolerate unemployment (in Model 2)—are virtually identi-

[33] While this approach resulted in smaller sample sizes, the results were not affected when we ran the individual models on the largest possible samples.

[34] Note that in all models presented in Table 5.4, the excluded category is the neutral category, i.e., in the case where one parent favors some unemployment while the other opposes it.

cal in the lagged and contemporaneous response specifications, the effects of having two parents holding "majoritarian" views is significantly reduced compared to the contemporaneous versions and, in Model 2, even falls short of achieving statistical significance.

As a next step in Model 3 we run an even more conservative specification, which controls for the respondent's attitude toward unemployment in the previous survey. This approach essentially assumes away any contemporaneous effects and thus largely captures whether parental attitudes "anchor" individual responses by either reducing the likelihood of future deviations from the "family line" or by increasing the likelihood of respondents returning to the fold after temporary deviations. While, reassuringly, lagged individual responses are rather strong predictors of current attitudes, the results still reveal a statistically significant and fairly substantial parental influence. Thus, the magnitude of the parental socialization effect corresponds to half the size of the lagged individual response effect in Model 3. However, once again, the impact of parental socialization is asymmetrical, with the effects of having parents who hold minority opinions mattering much more than those of parents with mainstream opinions. In fact, the responses of individuals with conformist parents were statistically indistinguishable from those with neutral/mixed responses, whereas the effects of antiestablishment views were statistically significant and substantively similar to the earlier models.

However, the problem with the approach above is that by viewing parental responses largely as a corrective, it fails to answer the crucial question about where initial individual attitudes come from. Unfortunately the HHPS does not interview individuals under 16, so we do not have the luxury of establishing at what point these views first emerge and how closely they are tied to parental views. Sixteen-year-olds in the HHPS had a noticeably higher share of nonresponses and don't-knows to the unemployment questions (see related figure in the electronic appendix), but over 70% still reported an opinion on the question, and their answers do not seem to be much noisier than for the overall sample.[35] Nonetheless, in Model 4 we focus on respondents where we know the lagged responses of their parents but do not have a prior response to the unemployment questions, either because they were under 16 the last time the question was asked or because they did not answer the question/stated they did not know the answer. While such an approach obviously has its limitations,[36] it nevertheless allows us to test the impact of parental attitudes on a group

[35] Thus, for 17-year-olds the correlation between current and lagged responses was .35, which was not considerably lower than the correlation for respondents age 25 and older (.39).

[36] Besides the longer-standing concerns with how to interpret don't-knows and nonanswers (Berinsky and Tucker 2006), we may worry about the fact that some of the 16-year-olds probably had unemployment views at the time of the previous survey but

Table 5.4. Parental Socialization and Attitudes toward Unemployment in Hungary

	(1)	(2)	(3)	(4)	(5)	(6)	(7)	(8)	(9)
Both parents accept unemployment (t)	-.401** (.124)								
Both parents oppose unemployment (t)	.546** (.112)								
Both parents accept unemployment (t-1)		-.502** (.122)	-.391** (.123)	-.413* (.172)		-.450** (.147)	-.244* (.124)		-.436** (.100)
Both parents oppose unemployment (t-1)		.173 (.115)	.041 (.116)	.386* (.169)		.390** (.144)	.246* (.125)		.187* (.094)
Respondent opposed unemployment (t-1)			.821** (.096)						
Parents more anti-unemployment (t-1→t)					.354** (.094)				
Parents less anti-unemployment (t-1→t)					-.385** (.103)				
Father opposed unemployment (t-1)								.348** (.089)	
Mother opposed unemployment (t-1)								.241* (.095)	
CP member HH × Both parents accept unemployment (t-1)									.028 (.247)

CP member HH × Both parents oppose unemployment (t-1)								.109 (.281)
CP member HH								-.048 (.189)
Year dummies	Yes	Yes	Yes	Yes	Yes	Yes	Yes	Yes	Yes
Demographic controls	Yes	Yes	Yes	Yes	Yes	Yes	Yes	Yes	Yes
Sample	All	All	All	No prior answer	All	Aged 16–18	Aged 19–25	All	All
Observations	1,117	1,117	1,117	465	1,117	664	895	1,299	2,109

Note: This table uses data on multiple members of the same households included in the 1992, 1993, 1994, 1996, and 1997 waves of the Hungarian Household Panel Survey. The dependent variable is based on a question that asked respondents to choose between two statements: "unemployment should be avoided by any means" (coded as 0) or (2) "economic problems are impossible to solve without facing a certain amount of unemployment" (coded as 1). The table reports probit coefficients with standard errors clustered at the household level in parentheses. The results suggest that parental attitudes toward unemployment affect the views of their children, but the effects are stronger when the parents hold minority views (i.e., opposed unemployment). Models 6 and 7 suggest that parental attitudes matter more for younger respondents but are still significant for young adults. The views of fathers seem slightly more influential than those of mothers (Model 8). CP members are slightly more effective at transmitting anti-unemployment attitudes (Model 9) and Catholics are slightly more effective at transmitting pro-unemployment attitudes (Model 10) but the interaction effects are not statistically significant. Note that in Models 1, 2, 3, and 5 we restricted the sample to observations without missing data on any of the variables used in those models ensure that results are comparable across models. However, in Models 6–10 we used the maximum number of observations for each particular model.

of respondents with presumably weaker initial views on the subject. The results reveal statistically significant parental socialization effects with magnitudes broadly comparable to the results in Model 2. Moreover, to the extent that these models are closer to capturing the dynamics of initial parental socialization, it is interesting to note that it appears that the impact of mainstream parental views is broadly similar to that of minority/dissenting views in shaping the initial views of adolescents. In other words, it appears that the greater impact of dissenting views applies primarily to the subsequent anchoring mechanism but does not play as prominent a role in the initial imprinting of parental attitudes.

Finally, in Model 5 we run an additional specification to assess the impact of *changes* in parental attitudes toward unemployment on the corresponding attitudinal *changes* among respondents. While this approach is still vulnerable to the possibility of reverse causation,[37] it has the advantage of reducing concerns about spurious correlation due to unobservable household-level characteristics.[38] The results of this model suggest statistically significant effects of parental attitude changes and the effects are largely symmetric for parental switches toward and away from the mainstream (anti-unemployment) position.

While the discussion so far has revealed rather strong parental socialization effects, there are good theoretical reasons to expect these effects not be uniform across all respondents. Therefore, in the remainder of Table 5.4 we briefly analyze how parental socialization is affected by the age of the respondent, by the gender of the parent holding a given opinion, and by the Communist Party and religious affiliation of a given respondent's household.

First, since we would expect the influence of parental socialization to decline as children get older and correspondingly more independent, we test whether the impact of parental attitudes declines with age. To do so, we compared the effects of lagged parental attitudes for two age groups: respondents aged 16–18 and respondents aged 19–25. Comparing the effects of parental attitudes in Models 6 and 7 suggests that even though parental socialization continues be a statistically significant predictor of

those views were simply not recorded. However, on the latter issue, we were reassured that our results are not significantly affected if we excluded 16-year-olds from the sample.

[37] However, in separate tests (available upon request) we found that the lagged attitudes of children are not significant predictors of the attitudes of parents once we control for the lagged responses of the parents and spouses of the respondents. This suggests that on average we need not be too concerned about reverse causation.

[38] Of course this applies only to time-invariant characteristics, but our models control for what is arguably the most important time-variant factor, changes in the household's economic situation.

unemployment attitudes for young adults, the effects were only about half the magnitude of their younger counterparts. Moreover, given that the proportion of children living with their parents declines from over 90% for 16-to-18-year-olds to about 50% for 19-to-25-year-olds, the overall differences in parental socialization impact would probably be even larger if our surveys had included young adults no longer living with their parents.

The next model separately assesses the impact of paternal and maternal attitudes vis-à-vis unemployment. According to the results in Model 8, the impact of paternal attitudes on overall views about the acceptability of unemployment is somewhat larger, but both paternal and maternal attitudes matter, and the difference between the two coefficients is not statistically significant.[39]

Given our findings in Section 5.5 about the attitudinal effects of having family members who were Communist Party (CP) members, in Model 9 we analyze how parental CP membership moderates the effect of parental socialization. From a straightforward indoctrination perspective, we might expect CP members to have been more willing than average citizens to instill their children with communist values. Alternatively, it is conceivable that given the recent collapse of communism in the region, former Communist Party members might face a credibility deficit not just in the broader society but even in their own families, in which case they might be less effective in shaping the political attitudes of their children. Finally, given that particularly in the case of Hungary's "goulash communism" the Communist Party had lost most of its ideological zeal well before 1989, we may expect CP membership not to matter at all either on its own or as a moderating factor. Judging by the results in Model 9, CP households were indistinguishable from the rest of the country in their ability to socialize their children into accepting unemployment. However, even though the interaction term does not come remotely close to approaching statistical significance, it does appear that the effect of having two parents opposed to unemployment is substantively about 35% larger in CP households than in non-CP households, which offers some modest support to the indoctrination hypothesis. Overall, these results suggest that CP members were no more effective than their non-CP counterparts in transmitting their political attitudes to their children, except (perhaps)

[39] We also checked whether the gender match between parent and child had an effect on socialization but found no such evidence. However, we did find that for both mothers and fathers the effects of socialization grew weaker when the age difference between parent and child increased.

when both parents endorsed values that were broadly in line with communist ideological commitments to full employment.

In separate tests not reported here due to space constraints, we used the HHPS data to probe the micro-foundations of another finding from our earlier analysis: the role of Catholicism in moderating political socialization. Given that in Section 5.4 we found weaker communist socialization effects among Catholics, we wanted to find out whether this lower receptiveness to official propaganda is partly due to the fact that Catholics are more likely to adopt the political attitudes of their parents. While the direction of the interaction effects between Catholicism and parental attitudes points in the direction of Catholics having stronger parental influence effects, the interaction terms were very imprecisely estimated, so these findings need to be treated as highly tentative support for our hypothesis.

Overall, these results confirm the importance of parental socialization in shaping the attitudes toward unemployment of young Hungarians in the early years of the post-communist transition. In line with our expectations, parental socialization is more influential among younger individuals, but we nevertheless still see significant effects well into the early and mid-20s, at least among the individuals who still live with their parents (roughly 50% of the age cohort in our sample). Among moderating factors, it appears that former Communist Party members were less effective in passing on their attitudes to the next generation. More broadly, we find stronger socialization effects among individuals embracing minority/dissenting views (in this case acceptance of unemployment).

5.7. DISENTANGLING COMMUNIST EXPOSURE FROM POST-COMMUNIST RESIDENCE: EVIDENCE FROM GERMANY

In trying to assess the attitudinal impact of communism, large portions of our analysis rely on comparing respondents of ex-communist countries to respondents of non-communist countries. However, this, too, raises two important inferential concerns. The first is a result of the fact that any difference we observe through such comparisons tends to combine (1) the effects of living through communism and (2) the experience of living through post-communism.[40] While our analysis in Table 5.1 of this chapter (and in the corresponding tables in the other empirical chapters) tries to

[40] This latter problem would be somewhat reduced if we were to focus exclusively on surveys from 1990, but even for those we would expect attitudes to be affected by the reverberations of the collapse of communism (see our discussion in Chapter 8 for more details).

account for the potential attitudinal effects of living in an ex-communist country by controlling for a variety of differences between ex-communist and non-communist countries, we may nevertheless worry that these efforts do not fully capture these differences, either because of unobserved factors or because of measurement error in our control variables.

The second problem is rooted in the fact that the two main sources of cross-national surveys we use in this book—the World Values Survey and the EBRD *Life in Transition Survey*—record only respondents' *current place of residence*, but not where they lived prior to the survey. As a result, we do not know whether all our respondents from ex-communist countries have indeed lived under communism prior to its collapse, or, for that matter, whether respondents from non-communist countries could have lived in a communist country before moving to their current country of residence. Given the widespread migration of Eastern Europeans to Western Europe before and especially after the fall of communism, such concerns are not trivial.[41] Such migration may have two—potentially opposite—effects on our estimates. On the one hand, to the extent that migration leads to "contamination" between the two samples, then our cross-national comparisons may understate the true attitudinal effects of communism and perhaps lead to more noise/larger standard errors. On the other hand, however, it is conceivable that migration could introduce selection bias into our analysis if Eastern Europeans were more likely to emigrate if they held anti-communist political attitudes. While this concern is probably less serious for post-communist migration, which seems to have been driven primarily by economic opportunity rather than political convictions,[42] it is likely to apply to a significant subset of those who left the Eastern bloc before 1989.

Fortunately, we are able to address these questions using data from the 1994 wave of the German Election Panel Study. That survey, which included over 2,900 respondents from the territories of the former East Germany along with over 2,500 respondents from the former West Germany, has the unique feature of asking respondents how long they had lived in the Bundesland (state) and where they had moved from—with categories including "other Western Bundesländer," "other Eastern Bundesländer," "other Eastern bloc countries" and "other non–Eastern bloc countries." As a result, we were able to reconstruct (at least partially) the migration

[41] See, for example, Favell (2008), which is the introduction to a special issue of the *Journal of Ethnic and Migration Studies* entitled "The New Face of East–West Migration in Europe."

[42] Levitz and Pop-Eleches (2009) find that Bulgarian citizens who expressed a desire to live/work abroad were no more likely to express pro-democratic attitudes than other Bulgarians with comparable demographic backgrounds.

histories of individual respondents and thus to distinguish between the effects of current residence and those of earlier political socialization. To simplify the interpretation of the results, we created four categories of respondents based on the different possible combinations of socialization and current residence: (1) residents of the territory of the former East Germany who had lived the majority of their adult lives under a communist regime; (2) residents of the territory of the former West Germany who had lived the majority of their adult lives under a communist regime; (3) residents of the territory of the former East Germany who had lived the majority of their adult lives under a non-communist regime; (4) residents of the territory of the former West Germany who had lived the majority of their adult lives under a non-communist regime. While the first version of the variable included international migrants from both communist and non-communist countries, we also created a more restrictive second version, which excludes international migrants and focuses only on internal migrants (i.e., East Germans who had moved to West Germany and vice versa).

To capture attitudes toward markets, we used a five-point agree-disagree survey question focused on the statement that the most important companies need to be nationalized, and recoded it so that higher values indicate greater market support.[43] For ease of interpretation we ran simple OLS regressions, but the results presented below are robust to running ordered probit models as well. In addition to the residence/socialization variables discussed above, the regressions include a standard set of demographic control variables including education, age, residence, occupational status, income, sex, religious denomination, and church attendance. The main results are summarized in Figure 5.6 while the full regression results are available in the electronic appendix.

Figure 5.6 suggests that exposure to communist regimes mattered even once we account for current residence. Thus, compared to the base category (West Germans and other non-communist citizens living in West Germany), respondents who received the majority of their political socialization in a communist country were significantly more likely to endorse the nationalization of important enterprises even if they lived in West Germany at the time of the survey (see row 3 of Figure 5.6).

By contrast, the economic attitude differences were substantively smaller and statistically insignificant for West Germans and other non-communist citizens living in the lands of the former communist East Germany (row 2 of Figure 5.6). This result suggests that simply living in East Germany at a time of relatively pervasive anti-market disenchantment was not sufficient to turn people without significant prior communist so-

---

[43] The variable has a mean of 2.4 and a standard deviation of 1.36.

cialization against markets, or at least not to the levels of Germans who had grown up under communist rule. The final result worth noting in Figure 5.6 is the fact that the anti-market bias was stronger for ex-communist citizens living in the former East German territories than among those who had resettled to West Germany, and the difference was both substantively and statistically significant (row 1 vs. row 3). It is not clear, however, how much of this difference is due to selection (i.e., the fact that East Germans who left to West Germany were more pro-market to begin with), how much of it was due to the experience of worse economic conditions in the former East Germany in the post-communist period, and how much simply reflects the fact that those who migrated to West Germany had their communist socialization truncated earlier.

To address these questions, we next differentiate between three types of migrants from former communist countries: those who migrated relatively early (before 1985, row 4) and had thus lived in a non-communist country for at least ten years, those who had migrated in the final years of communism (1985–89, row 5) and those who left after the collapse of communism (1990 or later, row 6). To the extent that selection is the key driving force, we should observe much weaker (and relatively similar) anti-market biases for the two groups of communist-era migrants than for East German nonmigrants or post-1990 migrants. To the extent that short-term economic experiences affect market support, then the big differences should be between ex-communist residents of East versus West Germany (but with relatively small differences between different types of ex-communist migrants). Finally, to the extent that the timing of the end of communist socialization was decisive, then we should see large (and broadly similar) anti-market biases for East German nonmigrants and post-communist migrants, combined with a monotonic reduction in this bias for earlier migration groups (since communist socialization ended earlier for such individuals).

Judging by the results in the bottom half of the panel in Figure 5.6, the differences between different groups of ex-communist migrants who were living in West Germany by 1994 are most compatible with the third explanation, which focuses on the time that has passed since the respondents were last exposed to communist socialization. Thus, the post-1989 migrants, for whom communist exposure ended at the same time as for individuals who never left East Germany, show a large anti-market bias (row 6) that is comparable in size to, and statistically indistinguishable from, East German nonmigrants (row 1). By contrast, the bias is somewhat smaller but still marginally significant for those who migrated from 1985–89 (row 5) and disappears altogether for earlier migrants (row 6). While the lack of an anti-market bias among pre-1985 migrants is also compatible with the selection story, the same cannot be said of the large

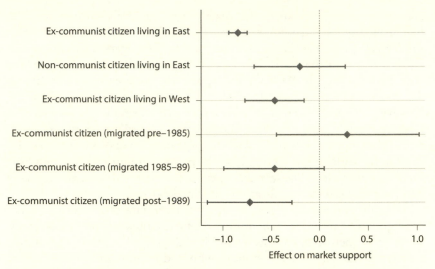

Figure 5.6. Socialization vs. Residence in Germany (1994)
This figure illustrates the differences in market support among German citizens
based on the timing of their experiences of living in East vs. West Germany. The
results in the upper part of the figure suggest that while anti-market attitudes
were the most pronounced among respondents who lived their whole lives in
communist and post-communist Germany, even respondents who moved from
East to West Germany were on average significantly more anti-market than
those who had lived only in West Germany (the excluded baseline category).
The bottom half of the panel shows that Germans who migrated from East to
West Germany post-1989 had much stronger anti-market attitudes than earlier
migrants, especially those from before the mid-1980s. The dependent variable is
a five-category survey question that measures disagreement with the proposition
that economic enterprises should be nationalized. The variable has a mean of
2.4 and a standard deviation of 1.36. Full regression results are in the electronic
appendix. The data utilized in these analyses are from the 1994 wave of the
German Election Panel Study.

and statistically significant difference between the two groups of pre-
1989 migrants: thus, to the extent that anti-communists were overrepresented among communist-era migrants, those two groups should display
similarly weak anti-market biases.[44] Finally, the patterns in Figure 5.6

---

[44]The only way this could hold is if somehow the selection effect was stronger in the
1985–89 period than previously. However, there is nothing in East German history that
suggests to us that anti-communists were suddenly motivated to leave the country more
after 1985 than previously.

are completely at odds with the post-communist economic conditions explanation, which can account for neither the similarity between post-communist migrants and East German nonmigrants, nor for the differences between different groups of ex-communist migrants living in East Germany by the time of the 1994 survey.

Of course, these findings need to be interpreted with some caution given the relatively small number of migrants in the survey[45] and the particular nature of the post-communist transition in East Germany. Nevertheless, our analysis of the 1994 German Election Panel Study confirms our broader findings so far that the attitudinal differences between citizens of ex-communist and non-communist countries are driven by the personal exposure to communist regimes rather than differences from *living in a post-communist country*. Furthermore, the analysis in this section allowed us to address—and largely reject—the concern that post-communist differences in attitudes were driven by a migration-related selection bias whereby individuals with more anti-communist attitudes were more likely to emigrate, thereby exaggerating the socialization effects of communist regimes.

5.7. CONCLUSIONS

In this chapter we have analyzed the attitudinal imprint of communism on the second main ideological pillar that differentiated communist regimes from their Western rivals: support for market-based economic principles. In line with our findings about democratic support in the previous chapter, the empirical evidence from the first two decades of post-communism confirms that despite the extinction of Leninist regimes (Jowitt 1992: 249–83), the effects of the communist socialization project did not simply evaporate overnight. Thus, citizens of ex-communist countries were significantly less supportive of market economics, and these differences persist even when we account for a broad range of features related to *living in a post-communist country*, including pre-communist development differences and post-communist economic and political performance. Furthermore, as in the previous chapter, the attitudinal effects of communism cannot be readily attributed to any of its particular policy outcomes—such as

---

[45] Our analysis included 28 respondents born in the West but living in East Germany and 70 respondents born in an ex-communist country (mostly but not exclusively East Germany) but living in West Germany at the time of the survey (of which 34 had migrated post-1989, 24 between 1985 and 1989, and 12 before 1985). Note that we counted respondents as having been socialized in a communist country only if they had spent at least half of their time before 1990 living in a communist country.

different developmental strategies or welfare spending—but rather seems to reflect a different systemic logic.

This chapter further reinforces the importance of personal exposure to communist regimes and, implicitly, the crucial role of political socialization in shaping the anti-market attitudes of Eastern Europeans well after the demise of communist command economies. As in the case of democracy, the anti-market bias was much more pronounced for individuals who had lived longer under communism, and once again the impact was stronger for adult exposure than for exposure as a child/adolescent. However, unlike in the previous chapter, early communist exposure was not entirely inconsequential: even though by itself it had a relatively modest anti-market effect, it appears to have intensified the attitudinal effects of adult exposure compared to individuals who experienced communism only as adults but not as children.

The analytical utility of the *living through communism* framework is further reinforced by the patterns of factors that *intensify* the effect of, and increase *resistance* to, communist exposure on market support. At the country level, we are reassured by the fact that the anti-market socialization effects of communist exposure were the most pronounced in countries with better overall and late-communist economic growth, that is, precisely in the places where we would expect the economic attractiveness of the communist model to have been the greatest, and, thus, resistance to exposure to have been the lowest. Similarly, homegrown communism, which we also expected to trigger weaker resistance, produced stronger anti-market socialization effects. Compared to Chapter 4 we found somewhat weaker support for resistance rooted in pre-communist developmental differences: while citizens of pre-communist democracies were indeed less receptive to communist-era anti-market influences, pre-communist literacy and economic development played a weaker moderating role (though they pointed in the right direction). The support for country-level intensifying factors was also mixed: on the one hand, socialization effects were indeed stronger in countries with minimal late-communist political liberalization (where economic orthodoxy was reinforced to the bitter end), but the differences across communist regime subtypes did not produce clear evidence that hardline regimes were overall more effective in promoting anti-market attitudes.

At the individual level, the results of the main WVS-based tests confirm the greater intensity of communist socialization among urban residents and—in contrast to the previous chapter but in line with our theoretical expectations—among men. We also confirmed our expectation that socialization effects would be weaker among regular churchgoers. In terms of denominational differences, in line with the democracy support findings in Chapter 4, Catholics again appeared to be more resistant to communist exposure than Protestant and Orthodox respondents, though in this case Muslims exhibited the greatest resistance.

By focusing on a series of unique questions in the LiTS surveys, we were able to explore three additional socialization channels that we had not analyzed in Chapter 4: the effects of communist versus non-communist education, of Communist Party membership, and of parental/family socialization.

While our analysis in Section 5.4 analyzed education as a moderating variable associated with greater resistance to communist socialization, in Section 5.5.1 we focused on the role of education in the transmission of different ideological preferences. Our results confirm that pre-communist (and to a somewhat lesser extent post-communist) education was associated with more pro-market attitudes, but we find weak support for the "communist educational indoctrination" hypotheses, as individuals educated under communism were no more anti-market than those without any education. However, communist education was not inconsequential for shaping post-communist attitudes towards markets: we find that individuals educated under communism experienced noticeably stronger anti-market effects from communist exposure, which suggests that communist education worked primarily by lowering resistance to subsequent ideological indoctrination rather than by actively inculcating anti-market ideas. These patterns closely mirror—albeit using different measures and data—our findings in Section 5.3 about the modest direct effects of early communist exposure combined with the stronger adult socialization effects among individuals who experienced communism in their childhood/adolescence. In other words, the results in this chapter suggests that communist education/early communist exposure mattered not so much because it succeeded in turning children into anti-market zealots but because it "softened them up" for subsequent indoctrination efforts.

The LiTS surveys also allowed us to test the socialization effects of personal Communist Party membership. Given that the anti-market effects were negligible among CP members who were young when communism collapsed, we are able to reject the possibility that any attitudinal differences simply reflect preexisting ideological affinities among those selected for CP membership. By contrast, older CP members were noticeably more opposed to markets than non-CP members from the same age cohorts. This suggests that either CP membership had a direct socializing effect that accumulated over the course of a person's membership or that CP membership lowered people's resistance to other aspects of communist socialization.

The fact that the magnitude of these CP membership effects was not particularly large can be interpreted in two ways. First, we may conclude that the direct ideological indoctrination capacity of the communist parties was fairly limited, perhaps because the (uneven) ideological fervor of the early years had largely given way to an increasingly hollow and ritualistic set of rhetorical exercises after the mid-1950s. Alternatively, however, the aforementioned indirect effects of Communist Party membership on the political attitudes of other family members suggest that perhaps party members did not stand out too much from their compatriots because communist socialization had permeated broad swaths of society fairly effectively.

As expected, parental socialization had an important effect on attitudes toward markets in post-communist countries. However, rather than working as one-time ideological shocks, these effects as well manifested themselves primarily in terms of a lower resistance to communist socialization among individuals whose parents had been educated under communism or whose family members had been members of the Communist Party. As a result, the anti-market effects of growing up in such households were negligible (or even reversed) among those who were young when communism collapsed but were quite substantial for those with extensive subsequent communist exposures.

Our supplementary analysis in Section 5.6 based on the Hungarian Household Panel Survey reveals a robust link between the expressed attitudes of parents and children. In addition to strengthening our confidence in the causal impact of parental socialization, this analysis also adds a number of interesting nuances to the parental socialization dynamics discussed in Section 5.5. First, our tests suggest that while the impact of parental socialization was considerably stronger for younger individuals (the 16-to-18-year-olds in our sample), parents continued to shape the attitudes of their children even for young adults (at least for those still living in the same household). Second, we found that parental socialization effects were significantly stronger when parents held "minority" views (i.e., views diverging from those held by the majority of survey respondents). Third, we found that parents who had been members of the CP were somewhat less likely to shape the attitudes of their children. This finding is in line with our earlier finding that parental CP membership did not result in an ideological shock for young respondents but rather affected attitudes by lowering resistance to subsequent communist socialization (and for the youths in the Hungarian household sample this communist socialization was cut short by the collapse of communism in 1989).

The final empirical contribution of this chapter is that it allowed us to disentangle—at least in the German context—the effects of communist socialization from those of living in a post-communist country. We did so by using data from the 1994 German Election Survey to compare the attitudes of respondents who had lived in East Germany both before and after the collapse of communism (i.e., the typical post-communist respondent in our other surveys) to respondents who had either moved from East to West Germany or from West to East Germany over the course of their lives. Our evidence here strongly suggests that communist socialization is much more important than the current place of residence, at least for respondents for whom communist socialization is not too far removed temporally. In other words, to paraphrase the old saying, "you can take the kid out of East Germany but you can't take East Germany out of the kid."

CHAPTER 6

Social Welfare

The paradoxes of communism:

1. There is no unemployment but nobody works
2. Nobody works but everybody gets paid
3. Everybody gets paid but you can't buy anything
4. You can't buy anything but everybody's taken care of

—Eastern European joke

6.1. INTRODUCTION

If anti-market rhetoric was the stick of communism's Marxist economic message, then a nurturing state providing cradle-to-grave social welfare could be considered the carrot (Cook 1993; Roberts 2010; Lipsmeyer 2003). It is to this topic that we turn in this chapter as we examine attitudes toward social welfare, and, more specifically, the extent to which the state should be responsible for providing for the welfare of its citizens.

There is a rich extant literature on attitudes toward social welfare policies, although the vast majority of this work has featured research from advanced industrialized democracies.[1] Three explanations seem to predominate among the attempts to understand why some people are more supportive of the state providing for social welfare (or more generous social welfare policies). The first—and most prevalent—is that individuals who benefit from social welfare policies (e.g., the poor, unemployed, elderly, disadvantaged, etc.) ought to be the most likely to support social welfare policies (Bean and Papadakis 1998; Hasenfeld and Rafferty 1989; Andreß and Heien 2001; Blekesaune and Quadagno 2003; Busemeyer et al. 2009).[2] The second is that people who live in countries with more

---

[1] And those pieces that do include cases from outside Western Europe and the United States often have only a handful of other countries included in a comparative study, e.g., Blekesaune and Quadagno (2003) and Senik et al. (2009).

[2] In an extension of this argument, Goerres and Tepe (2010) also claim that when people are more closely tied to those who are likely to benefit from social welfare—they examine intergenerational solidarity—support for social welfare policies is likely to be higher.

generous welfare states ought to be more supportive of these policies than people who do not (Svallfors 1997; Andreß and Heien 2001; Jaeger 2006). The final major argument is that attitudes toward social welfare policy ought to be a function of a general left-wing or social-democratic ideological outlook (Bean and Papadakis 1998; Hasenfeld and Rafferty 1989; Blekesaune and Quadagno 2003), although this of course begs the larger question of the role of communist legacies in driving left-right ideological self-placement (Pop-Eleches and Tucker 2010). More recent research—following on earlier studies that examine the effect of race on attitudes toward social welfare policy in the United States (Alesina et al. 2001; Gilens 2009) has also assessed the impact of immigration on attitudes toward social welfare policy in Western Europe (Senik et al. 2009; Eger 2010).

It is worth noting that there appears to be almost no literature on the determinants of attitudes toward social welfare policy specifically in post-communist countries,[3] and certainly no existing work that attempts to disentangle why post-communist citizens might hold different attitudes regarding the state's responsibility for individual social welfare than citizens elsewhere. Moreover, the 2008 global economic crisis—and the subsequent rise in popularity of far-right and far-left movements throughout Europe promising greater state support for individual welfare—again suggests it is important to understand the extent of the communist legacy on post-communist attitudes in this regard. While communist welfare states were quite generous compared to their economic development levels (see, e.g., Haggard and Kaufman 2008), the institutional contrast vis-à-vis the rest of the world may have been less stark than for democracy and markets, so we may expect less pronounced attitudinal differences than in the previous chapters. However, the political centrality of welfare state benefits was driven—particularly starting in the post-Stalinist routinization period—by the unofficial "social contract" of communist regimes that stipulated that the Communist Party would retain a monopoly on power in return for providing economic benefits, and particularly generous (or at least adequate) social welfare benefits (Madison 1968; Cook 1993; Haggard and Kaufman 2008; Inglot 2008). During the growing poverty and economic insecurity of the first post-communist decade we would expect the state's provision of social welfare benefits during the communist period to weigh heavily on people's minds, and indeed this

---

[3] The exception is Lipsmeyer (2003), who examines the extent to which attitudes toward social welfare policies vary across seven different post-communist countries and across different social welfare policies. There is an existing literature on the larger subject of economic preferences among post-communist citizens; see, for example, Kitschelt 1992, 1995; Evans and Whitefield 1993; Markowski 1997; and Gijsberts and Nieuwbeerta 2000.

is undoubtedly a large part of what people refer to when they speak of communist-era nostalgia.

Taken together, this suggests two potentially contradictory predictions for our approach to studying communist-era legacies. On the one hand, we might expect high levels of support for social welfare among post-communist citizens, driven both by memories of the better social welfare provision under communism and by the growing demand for a safety net in the context of the economic downturn and uncertainty of the early post-communist years. On the other hand, we might expect less of a contrast with citizens outside the post-communist world who—at least in some countries—also often experienced generous welfare states (or at least rhetorical commitments by political leaders to provide such benefits) and thus could also be expected to value state provision of social welfare. That being said, our working hypothesis (see Chapter 1) is still that we would expect post-communist citizens to be more supportive of state-provided social welfare than non-post-communist citizens.

As it turns out, we observe a very similar post-communist distinction in the case of support for state-provided social welfare benefits to the ones we did in the previous two chapters in support for democracy and support for market-based economies. More specifically, as Model 1 in Table 6.1 in the following section demonstrates, when we simply examine the bivariate relationship (controlling for the year of the surveys) between living in a post-communist country and attitudes toward state provision of social welfare, citizens of post-communist countries are indeed more likely to agree that it is the state's responsibility to provide for the social welfare of its citizens.[4] Moreover, the size of the effect is the largest we have yet seen in this manuscript: despite the many factors that undoubtedly go into determining one's attitudes toward government responsibility for social welfare, simply living in a post-communist country is associated with a shift of almost one-third of a standard deviation of the distribution of attitudes on the state's role in providing for social welfare.[5]

The remainder of the chapter is organized similarly to the previous two. In the following section, we turn to our large-scale cross-national

[4]The actual survey question reads: "How would you place your views on this scale? 1 means you agree completely with the statement on the left; 10 means you agree completely with the statement on the right; and if your views fall somewhere in between, you can choose any number in between. *People should take more responsibility to provide for themselves* vs. *The government should take more responsibility to ensure that everyone is provided for.*" This is variable e037 on the integrated World Values Survey questionnaire.

[5]We obtained very similar results using an index created from the question above and two additional questions (with much more limited coverage): whether the individual or the state should be responsible for providing pensions (E043) and whether the individual or the state should be responsible for housing (E044).

analysis using the World Values Survey and demonstrate that even after we control for pre-communist conditions and contemporary social-demographic, economic, and political conditions at the time of our surveys, we end up with more support for state-provided social welfare in post-communist countries than elsewhere, and indeed the effect from the fully saturated model is almost 50% larger than the bivariate analysis referenced in the previous paragraph.[6] We then turn to "unpacking communism" at the aggregate level, where we find that citizens in less democratic countries in the years leading up to the collapse of communism are indeed more likely to support state-provided social welfare benefits, which explains a good deal of the post-communist differential.[7]

Once again we find that individual exposure to communism has an important effect on attitudes toward government responsibility for social welfare and that—as we found in the previous chapters—the effect of exposure is stronger for adults than for children (see Table 6.3). Moreover, we continue to find some results of interest from our intensifying and resistance factors that are predicted to moderate the effect of exposure on attitudes toward social welfare, but less so than in previous chapters.

In the final section of this chapter, we again move beyond our standard World Values Surveys analyses to utilize a different source of data, here the Hungarian Household Panel Survey from Hungary. As described in Chapters 3 and 5, this survey included respondents from the same households interviewed annually over a five-year period, thus making it an ideal dataset for estimating the effects of *parental socialization*. And we do indeed find evidence of parental socialization effects on the attitudes of children, although intriguingly these again seem to be stronger when they cut *against* the communist legacy position. Moreover, the study also contains questions regarding past Communist Party membership, thus allowing us to explore the effects of party membership directly, and the effects of party membership on parental transmission of opinions to children. Interestingly, we find that parents who were CP members had more of an effect on their children's attitudes vis-à-vis unemployment benefits than non-communist parents, again raising questions about the role of party membership as a mechanism through which *living through communism* leaves a legacy effect on post-communist citizens' attitudes.

---

[6] The effect within only Germany is also in the same direction, albeit quite a bit smaller.

[7] We also find, somewhat surprisingly, that citizens in countries with more left-wing governments in the decade and a half preceding the collapse of communism were *less* likely to support state-provided social welfare, although this effect ends up being driven more by citizens in democratic countries than those in non-democratic countries. We discuss this finding in more detail in Section 6.3 below.

6.2. LIVING IN POST-COMMUNIST COUNTRIES AND ATTITUDES TOWARD SOCIAL WELFARE

As previously, we begin our analysis with data from four waves of the World Values Survey (1989–93, 1994–98, 1999–2004, and 2005–9), which in the case of attitudes toward social welfare allows us to analyze 207 surveys from 85 countries (including 68 surveys from 24 post-communist countries). For reasons related to the availability of suitable variables, however, instead of relying on an index to ascertain attitudes toward social welfare spending, we instead utilize a single survey question. The question asked respondents to place themselves on a 1–10 scale based on the extent to which they agree more with the statement "People should take more responsibility to provide for themselves" or "The government should take more responsibility to ensure that everyone is provided for." The variable has a mean of 5.9 (6.4 in post-communist countries, and 5.8 elsewhere)—showing an average preference in favor of state-provided social welfare. In line with the previous chapters, we standardize this 1–10 scale so that the mean value is 0 and the standard deviation is 1. Figure 6.1 displays the country averages for this standardized version of the variable (using equalized survey weights).

When we look at the average by country, we find that post-communist countries lean to the right (pro–social welfare) end of the figure, although again we find meaningful variation across the countries. Of particular note is the complete lack of *any* post-communist countries among the collection on the far left side of the figure indicating the lowest level of support for state-provided social welfare. Also interesting is the fact that all the pre-WWII Soviet republics cluster in the upper third of the distribution while the only post-communist countries with below-average support for social welfare are all new Eastern European EU members (Croatia, the Czech Republic, Romania, and Poland).

Turning to the *living in post-communist countries* analysis, the results in Table 6.1 reveal that citizens of the former communist countries were more supportive of a greater state role in providing for the welfare of individuals across a wide range of model specifications.[8] The baseline

---

[8] As in the previous chapters, we use ordinary least squares (OLS) regressions with standard errors clustered at the country-year level and employ equilibrated survey weights in our analysis. While the dependent variable is a 10-point ordinal variable, we present OLS rather than ordered probit/logit results because they are more intuitive to interpret (especially in the case of interaction effects), because the latent variable we are trying to measure is by construct continuous, and because the software package (Stata) that we used to estimate our constrained regressions did not have options for ordered models.

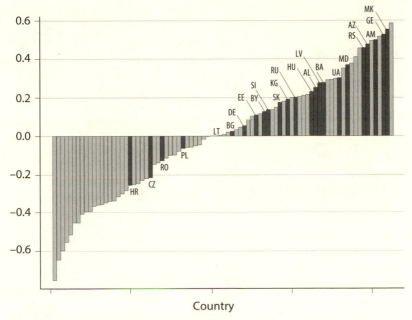

Figure 6.1. Average Support for Social Welfare by Country: Post-communist vs. Non-communist

This figure lists the country-level averages in social welfare support of post-communist countries (dark-gray bars) compared to those of non-communist countries (light-gray bars) based on the 2nd, 3rd, 4th, and 5th waves of the World Values Survey (1990–2008). In calculating the averages we used any individual-level weights, and we also applied equilibrated weights to adjust for different sample sizes across surveys for different years in any given country. The figure shows that the ex-communist countries are significantly over-represented in the upper half of the distribution and make up the majority of countries with the strongest support for state-provided welfare. For the full set of country codes, see the list of country code abbreviations on page xv.

specification in Model 1, which includes only the post-communism indicator and a set of survey year dummies, reveals a statistically significant and substantively sizeable (approximately one-third of a standard deviation) positive effect: thus, citizens of post-communist countries are more likely to think the state is responsible for individual-level welfare. To put the size of this effect in perspective, this difference is slightly larger than the effect of moving from the 10th to the 90th percentile of the household income distribution for the respondents in our sample, and twice the size

Table 6.1. Living in a Post-communist Country and Welfare State Attitudes

	(1)	(2)	(3)	(4)	(5)	(6)	(7)	(8)
Post-communist	.312** (.037)	.411** (.085)	.345** (.126)	.458** (.095)	.527** (.093)	.274** (.095)	.465** (.106)	.274* (.111)
Year dummies	Yes	Yes	No	Yes	Yes	Yes	Yes	Yes
Pre-communist controls	No	Yes	No	Yes	Yes	Yes	Yes	No
Post-communist demographics	No	No	No	Yes	No	No	Yes	Yes
Post-communist econ outcomes	No	No	No	No	Yes	No	Yes	No
Post-communist political institutions	No	No	No	No	No	Yes	Yes	No
Pre-communist & year entropy balancing	No	No	Yes	No	No	No	No	No
Countries	All	All	All	All	All	All	All	Germany
Observations	281,157	281,157	281,157	281,157	281,157	281,157	281,157	9,325
R-squared	.053	.077	.032	.089	.082	.079	.097	.169

Note: This table demonstrates that post-communist citizens are more supportive of state provided social welfare than citizens in the rest of the world, even when controlling for pre-communist conditions (Models 2 and 3) and contemporaneous demographic characteristics, economic conditions, and political institutions (Models 4–7); similar results can be found from analyzing only data from Germany comparing East and West Germans (Model 8). The dependent variable is a question asking respondents to place themselves on a 10-point agreement scale between "People should take more responsibility to provide for themselves" and "The government should take more responsibility to ensure that everyone is provided for," standardized to a mean of 0 and a standard deviation of 1. The list of independent and control variables can be found in Table 3.1 of Chapter 3. Full regression results are in the electronic appendix. The data utilized in these analyses are from the 2nd, 3rd, 4th, and 5th waves of the World Values Survey. Robust standard errors in parentheses: ** p<.01, * p<.05.

of the effect of moving from not completing high school to having a post-secondary degree.[9]

In Model 2, we once again begin the process of assessing whether *living in a post-communist country* can explain these differences by adding pre-communist control variables. As was the case in both the democracy and markets chapters, doing so results in an *increase* in the size of the post-communist differential (although not by as much as in the previous chapters); here, accounting for historical differences between citizens in post-communist countries and those living in other countries increases the gap by approximately one-third. Thus once again controlling for deeper historical differences improves the model fit but, rather than explaining away post-communist distinctiveness, instead further sharpens the attitudinal imprint of communism. As in previous chapters, we replicate the pre-communist control analysis using entropic balancing (Hainmueller 2012) in Model 3 and find a largely similar result (negative, statistically significant, and substantively comparable). While the magnitude of the effect from the non-parametric estimation is somewhat weaker than in Model 2, it is still larger than in Model 1.

In the next four models we explore the impact of adding contemporaneous demographic, economic, and political variables. Adding demographics in Model 4 increases the size of the post-communist dummy variable by approximately 10% relative to including just pre-communist control variables (Model 2); adding contemporary economic conditions increases it by almost 25%. In both cases, the direction of the effect remains the same—post-communist citizens are more supportive of state-provided social welfare—and model fit improves marginally.

By contrast, controlling for post-communist political institutions and outcomes in Model 8 leads to a noticeable reduction in the post-communist indicator effect, which is now almost 30% smaller than in Model 2 (pre-communist controls). Still, though, the post-communist dummy variable continues to be statistically significant at p<.01, and the magnitude is still larger than in the previous two chapters. This suggests that the differential political performance of ex-communist countries is at least partially related to the greater preference of post-communist citizens for state support for social welfare.[10]

---

[9] As suggested by prior research, the more economically vulnerable (those without a high school education) are more supportive of state responsibility for social welfare than those with higher education degrees (Andreß and Heien 2001; Blekesaune and Quadagno 2003).

[10] It is interesting to note that the two most important political factors in Model 6 are age of democracy and corruption (see the electronic appendix for full results), both of which significantly reduce welfare state reliance, and thus help explain why the citizens of newer and more corrupt transition countries are more supportive of state intervention. Perhaps what is going on here is some sort of modern version of the political rights for economic development

In the fully saturated specification in Model 7—including pre-communist conditions and all three sets of contemporaneous indications—the post-communist differential returns to approximately the size it was when including pre-communist conditions and demographics: 10% larger than pre-communist conditions alone, 50% larger than the baseline bivariate model, and still significant ($p<.01$). Thus, it appears that the greater support for welfare state intervention among ex-communist citizens cannot be explained away by differences related to *living in a post-communist country*. This conclusion is further reinforced by the results in Model 8, where we restrict our analysis to Germany. The within-Germany results yield a pro–welfare state bias among East Germans that is somewhat smaller than the results in Model 7 (but still of comparable magnitude to Model 1), in the same direction, and statistically significant ($p<.05$).[11]

6.3. LIVING IN POST-COMMUNIST COUNTRIES: UNPACKING THE EFFECTS OF COMMUNISM

As in the previous chapters, we next add a series of "end of communism" variables to our models and continue to observe the effect of including these variables in our models on the post-communist dummy variable. To reiterate, with these variables we intend to capture the dominant effects of communist rule: developmental legacies, reductions in inequality, non-democratic political rule, and rule by left-wing parties. Model 1 of Table 6.2 is our baseline model, which contains year-fixed effects and pre-communist control variables, and therefore is the same as Model 2 of Table 6.1.

In Model 2, we add a series of variables to attempt to capture communism's developmental legacies. Doing so, however, results in a very minimal decrease in the size of post-communist dummy variable. Moreover, when we add variables to control for inequality and attempts to reduce inequality as of 1989, the size of the post-communist social welfare differential actually increases by about 25% in Model 3. So neither of these

---

of the later Soviet periods (Linz and Stepan 1996) but only updated to a "tolerating corruption vs. provision for social welfare" trade-off. See as well Klašnja and Tucker (2013), who find using a survey experiment that in Moldova respondents punish a mayor for supposed corrupt behavior when the economy is performing badly, but *not* when the economy is performing well.

[11] This Germany specific finding is in line with the results in Alesina and Fuchs-Schündeln (2007).

Table 6.2. Communist System Features and Welfare State Attitudes

	(1)	(2)	(3)	(4)	(5)	(6)
Post-communist	.411**	.398**	.513**	.135	.500**	.062
	(.085)	(.097)	(.084)	(.101)	(.083)	(.101)
Urbanization 1989		.318*				
		(.135)				
Primary school enrollment		.002				
		(.002)				
Literacy 1989		.000				
		(.003)				
Energy intensity		−7.649				
		(5.097)				
Industry as % GDP		.006*				
		(.003)				
Log GDP per capita 1989		−.073#				
		(.043)				
Health & education spending 1989			.012			
			(.012)			
Income inequality 1989			.005			
			(.003)			
State sector size late 1989			−.066**			
			(.022)			
Average regime score 1975–89				−.019**		−.009#
				(.005)		(.005)
Left government share 1975–89					−.251**	−.141**
					(.060)	(.047)
Average regime score 1975–89 × Left government share 1975–89						−.022**
						(.007)
Year dummies	Yes	Yes	Yes	Yes	Yes	Yes
Pre-communist controls	Yes	Yes	Yes	Yes	Yes	Yes
Observations	281,157	281,157	281,157	281,157	281,157	281,157
R-squared	.077	.081	.081	.080	.080	.083

Note: This table demonstrates that post-communist citizens are more supportive of markets than citizens in the rest of the world, even when controlling for most conditions at the time of communism's collapse, including developmental legacies (Model 2), redistributive/egalitarian policies (Model 3), and the leftist orientation of communist regimes (Model 5). However, once we take account of the fact that citizens living in less democratic regimes were significantly more likely to support state responsibility for social welfare, especially in left-wing non-democratic regimes, the post-communist differential is greatly reduced (Models 4 and 6). The dependent variable is a question asking respondents to place themselves on a 10-point agreement scale between "People should take more responsibility to provide for themselves" and "The government should take more responsibility to ensure that everyone is provided for," standardized to a mean of 0 and a standard deviation of 1. The list of independent and control variables can be found in Table 3.1 of Chapter 3. Full regression results are in the electronic appendix. The data utilized in these analyses are from the 2nd, 3rd, 4th, and 5th waves of the World Values Survey. Robust standard errors in parentheses: ** $p<.01$, * $p<.05$, # $p<.1$.

hallmarks of communism appears to be a good candidate for explaining the post-communist preference for state-provided social welfare.

Model 4 of Table 6.2, however, reveals a very different result, and indeed it is a result unlike any that we have come across in the course of analyzing our *living in a post-communist country* model up to this point in the book. Namely, once we control for how democratic the regime was on average from 1975 to 1989, the size of the post-communist differential is substantially cut—here by almost two-thirds—and the statistical significance of the post-communist dummy variable falls below conventional levels.[12] Model 4 suggests that support for social welfare is on average higher in less democratic countries, perhaps because authoritarian regimes are more likely to resort to welfare benefits to shore up legitimacy. Since post-communist citizens live in countries that were—not surprisingly—on average less democratic in the years 1975–89 than citizens in non-post-communist countries,[13] controlling for the level of democracy does indeed explain away a great deal of the post-communist social welfare differential.

However, Model 5 produces a surprising result: citizens in countries with more leftist governments from 1975 to 1989 were actually *less* supportive of state-provided social welfare than those living in countries with more rightist governments. As post-communist countries were by definition run by left-wing governments in the 1970s and 1980s, adding this measure to our model *increases* the size of the post-communist differential.

There are two ways to make sense of this somewhat perplexing finding. The first—which in some ways squares with the finding in Model 3 that people living in countries with smaller state sectors in 1989 were more supportive of state-provided social welfare—is that it is countries that are *lacking* in social welfare that were more likely to vote in left-wing governments in the late 1970s and 1980s.[14]

---

[12] However, with a p-value of .15, a one-tailed significance test would be marginally significant at a level of p<.10. Average regime score is measured using the Polity 2 score from 1975 to 1989, but using Freedom House scores instead produces a similar—albeit a bit weaker—effect, resulting in a coefficient on the post-communist dummy of .21 with a standard error of .13 and a p-value of .11.

[13] The average respondent in the data set used to estimate Model 4 living in a post-communist country was living in a country with a Polity score that averaged –6.8 between 1975 and 1989, while the corresponding average for a citizen living in a non-post-communist country was +3.2.

[14] It is also possible that respondents were cuing off of the "more" in the wording of this question, and that people living in countries with left-wing regimes in power did not think they needed "more" state responsibility for social welfare than currently present. Recall that we discussed this point in greater detail in the previous chapter in Section 5.2. The reason we have not repeated that discussion here is because we think the two sets of questions are different. In previous chapters, respondents were asked whether *more or less* of something

The second, however, is to revisit the finding from Model 4 regarding the relationship between democracy and support for state-provided social welfare, and consider the possibility that something different is going on in more and less democratic governments. Thus in Model 6, we interact average regime type and average governing ideology from 1975 to 1989. This produces two interesting findings. Turning to the direct effects, we find that in democratic regimes (positive Polity scores) having had more leftist governments in the late 1970s and 1980s results in lower support for social welfare, which would make sense from the perspective that people living in democratic regimes with more generous social welfare states would have less of a need to vote in left-wing parties.[15] However, in non-democratic countries (negative Polity scores) having more left-wing governments is correlated with more support for state-provided social welfare. And as post-communist countries were both left-wing and non-democratic in the decade and a half preceding the collapse of communism, controlling for this interaction has a much larger effect on the post-communist social welfare support differential, dropping the size of the coefficient even further and—for the first time in the book— producing a standard error on the post-communist dummy variable that is larger than the coefficient.[16]

We thus arrive at the first time in this book where it looks like we have a candidate for explaining why post-communist citizens may hold different attitudes from citizens elsewhere on the basis of our *living in a post-communist country* approach. Citizens in non-democratic countries with left-wing governments in the 15 years preceding the collapse of communism were more likely to support state-provided social welfare in

---

(privatization, freedom for firms) was desirable, which makes the starting level of that something important. In contrast, in this chapter the word "more" is used for both options: states should be more responsible, or individuals should be more responsible. Thus "more" here is contrasting between the two options (more the responsibility of states or more the responsibility of individuals). Consequently, answers ought to reflect where respondents think the balance between the two ideals should be, not whether changes from the current level is desired. So despite our skepticism that this is what is actually going on here, we thought it prudent to at least flag it as a possible explanation for the unexpected left-wing government finding.

[15] That being said, we would not expect this finding to be particularly robust, and it could be a peculiarity of the particular years for which we included these analyses. It might also be the case that after the recessions of the 1970s, right-wing parties were more willing to increase social welfare spending than they might normally have been, although of course that is not a particularly good description of Ronald Reagan's America or Margaret Thatcher's Britain.

[16] As an aside, this finding is a nice confirmation that our approach to testing our *living in a post-communist country* model is indeed a valid one that can generate positive results.

the 1990s and 2000s across our entire WVS dataset, and post-communist countries were particularly non-democratic and left-wing in those years.[17]

That being said, we still proceed in the following section to examine the effect of exposure to communism on attitudes toward state supported social welfare for two reasons. First, from the point of view of theory testing, we want to make sure that we test the empirical support for both models regardless of the order in which we present our results. But more importantly from a substantive perspective, although we now believe there is something fundamental about leftist non-democratic regimes that encourages citizen support for state-supported social welfare, we still have no idea if the mechanism by which this occurs is related to *living through* these types of regimes. So with that in mind, we turn next to examining the effect of exposure.

6.4. LIVING THROUGH COMMUNISM AND ATTITUDES TOWARD SOCIAL WELFARE

The results in Model 1 of Table 6.3 indicate that once again there is broad support for the *living through communism* model: living longer under a communist regime is associated with higher support for welfare state service provision in the post-communist period.[18] The result is highly statistically significant (at p<.001) and is substantively meaningful; the difference between a respondent with 45 years of communist exposure and one who was six or younger when communism fell (and therefore should be minimally affected by personal exposure) corresponds to almost one-third of a standard deviation in our state-provided social welfare support variable. This is almost identical to the bivariate post-communist dummy variable in Model 1 of Table 6.1, and about three-quarters of the size of the coefficient in our baseline model in Model 1 of Table 6.2.[19] The

[17] Interestingly, the full results for Model 6 in Table 6.1 do not reveal a statistically significant relationship between level of democracy *at the time of the survey* and support for social welfare, and in fact the coefficient here is positive and not negative. Of course, by this point in time many countries that were not democratic in the 1970s and 1980s were now democratic, including much of East-Central Europe. In a sense, this provides yet another reason for looking at the importance of *legacies* as determinants of attitudes as opposed to simply contemporaneous characteristics.

[18] As previously, in an effort to avoid any contamination from post-treatment bias, our baseline model includes only pre-communist control variables at the aggregate level along with individual-level demographic controls, including age.

[19] The predicted effects are obviously larger among residents of interwar Soviet republics, who could have up to 25 years of additional exposure.

results are confirmed by the fixed-effects specification in Model 2, where the size of the exposure coefficient is about 5% larger than in Model 1.[20]

Furthermore, in Model 1 the inclusion of the exposure variable reduces the size of the post-communist coefficient from that in the baseline model (Model 4 in Table 6.1) by more than a third. However, it should be noted that unlike in earlier chapters, the post-communist citizenship effect continues to be large and statistically significant even after we control for individual exposure, which means that even citizens without any personal exposure to communism were still much more likely to support stated-provided social welfare than their counterparts living in non-communist countries.[21] Formal mediation tests suggest that communist exposure explains about 44% of the overall pro–welfare state effect of living in a post-communist country.[22]

When we examine exposure by communist regime type in Models 3 and 4 of Table 6.3, we once again find that the analysis is not robust to including country-fixed effects. Thus, in Model 3 we find very large and substantively significant effects for exposure to communism under post-totalitarian and reformist regimes, but small and statistically insignificant effects for exposure to Stalinism and neo-Stalinism, which was the opposite of what we expected from the *intensifying* exposure perspective.[23] However, in the fixed-effects specification in Model 4, as well as in the HLM models (in the electronic appendix), the patterns are at least partially reversed, with reform communist exposure having slightly smaller effects, especially compared to exposure under Stalinist regimes; in addition, exposure under all four regime types is now statistically significant. On balance, the inconsistent findings across specifications, combined with the fact that in the fixed-effects model all subtypes of communist exposure were associated with statistically significant socialization effects and that the differences between the coefficients of different categories were largely statistically insignificant, suggest that—as was the case in the previous chapters—it is difficult to conclude with much confidence that exposure to different subtypes of communism had different effects.

In Models 5–8 of Table 6.3 we analyze another facet of the intensifying exposure mechanism: the impact of the different timing of communist

[20] As previously, we do not include the post-communist dummy variable in the fixed-effects models because it is a linear combination of the country dummy variables.

[21] Based on our findings from the previous section, we might expect this to be so in part because of communism's non-democratic character.

[22] As in previous chapters we used the medeff command in Stata 13.1 (Hicks and Tingley 2011) to run the tests. Full mediation results are available in the electronic appendix.

[23] From a nostalgia perspective, though, this makes more sense: post-totalitarian and reformist communism are both associated with "gentler" communism (i.e., less political persecution) in an era when the state still provided health care, education, etc.

Table 6.3. Communist Socialization and Welfare State Attitudes

	(1)	(2)	(3)	(4)	(5)	(6)	(7)	(8)
Total communist exposure	.0070** (.0007)	.0073** (.0006)						
Stalinist total exposure			.0022 (.0022)	.0087** (.0013)				
Neo-Stalinist total exposure			.0020 (.0023)	.0073** (.0008)				
Post-totalitarian total exposure			.0151** (.0022)	.0073** (.0013)				
Reform communist total exposure			.0101** (.0018)	.0061** (.0009)				
Early communist exposure					.0035# (.0019)	.0031* (.0015)	.0045 (.0029)	.0031 (.0026)
Adult communist exposure					.0070** (.0007)	.0073** (.0006)	.0073** (.0012)	.0073** (.0010)
Early x Adult communist exposure							-.0000 (.0001)	-.0000 (.0001)

	(1)	(2)	(3)	(4)	(5)	(6)	(7)	(8)
Post-communist citizen	.2586**		.1878*		.2919**		.2834**	
	(.0932)		(.0946)		(.0939)		(.0980)	
Age	-.0029**	-.0028**	-.0028**	-.0028**	-.0029**	-.0029**	-.0029**	-.0029**
	(.0004)	(.0003)	(.0004)	(.0003)	(.0004)	(.0003)	(.0004)	(.0003)
Year dummies	Yes	Yes	Yes	Yes	Yes	Yes	Yes	Yes
Country dummies	No	Yes	No	Yes	No	Yes	No	Yes
Pre-communist controls	Yes	No	Yes	No	Yes	No	Yes	No
Demographic controls	Yes	Yes	Yes	Yes	Yes	Yes	Yes	Yes
Observations	281,157	281,157	281,157	281,157	281,157	281,157	281,157	281,157
R-squared	.0914	.1207	.0936	.1207	.0914	.1208	.0914	.1208

Note: This table demonstrates that additional exposure to communism is correlated with more support for state responsibility for social welfare even after controlling for age. In each pair of models, the first model includes a dummy variable indicating whether the respondent lives in a post-communist country (for comparability with Tables 4.1 and 4.2) as well as pre-communist country-level control variables, while the second table model uses country-fixed effects and, accordingly, drops the dummy variable and pre-communist country-level control variables. Models 3 and 4 examine the differential effect of exposure by type of communist regime, and Models 5–8 examine differential effect of exposure during childhood (age 6–17) and adulthood (18+). The dependent variable is a question asking respondents to place themselves on a 10-point agreement scale between "People should take more responsibility to provide for themselves" and "The government should take more responsibility to ensure that everyone is provided for," standardized to a mean of 0 and a standard deviation of 1. The list of independent and control variables can be found in Table 3.1 of Chapter 3. Full regression results are in the electronic appendix. The data utilized in these analyses are from the 2nd, 3rd, 4th, and 5th waves of the World Values Survey. Robust standard errors in parentheses: ** p<.01, * p<.05, # p<.1.

exposure. The findings are actually fairly consistent across all four models. Adult exposure seems to matter regardless of specification, and indeed the coefficient is very similar to the coefficient on exposure in Models 1 and 2. The coefficient for childhood exposure is always positive (i.e., in the predicted direction), but it achieves marginal statistical significance at best and is of a smaller magnitude than adult socialization. We again tested for the importance of an interaction effect across childhood and adult exposure, but the small and statistically insignificant interaction-effect coefficient suggests that, at least for welfare state preferences, this was not the case. So on balance, the results actually look very similar to those found in Chapter 4 and once again are at odds with what we would expect from a *resistance to socialization* perspective: socialization matters, but it is adult and not childhood exposure that is associated with greater support for state-sponsored social welfare.

6.4.1. Country-Level Moderators of Exposure Intensity and Resistance on Attitudes toward Social Welfare

We next turn to our aggregate-level (this section) and individual-level (next section) hypothesized *intensifying* and *resistance* factors to examine the extent to which there are heterogeneous effects for exposure to communism on attitudes toward state-provided social welfare. As in previous chapters, we relegate the relevant tables to the electronic appendix and include figures of estimated effects of an exposure to a year of communism across different theoretically relevant groups.[24]

What should be immediately apparent from even a quick glance at Figure 6.2 (and at the corresponding table in the electronic appendix) is that there is much more homogeneity across the different intensifying and resistance country-level categories than in the previous two chapters. To begin with, the results in the first three pairs of categories reveal very limited evidence that cross-country differences in pre-communist socioeconomic and political development moderated the effects of individual communist exposure. The effects are practically identical for low-wealth and high-wealth pre-communist countries (pair 2) and for low and high levels of pre-communist democracy (pair 3), and not that far off for low and high levels of literacy (pair 1).

The results are similarly homogenous when we examine countries with low and high levels of overall growth, proportion of years spent under hardline rule, and late-communist political liberalization; in all these

---

[24] As previously, we rely on data only from within post-communist countries for this part of the analysis and consequently used constrained regression analysis; see Chapter 3 for more details.

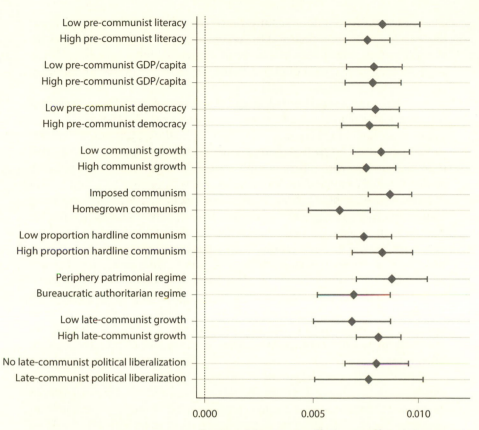

Communist exposure effects on welfare state support

**Figure 6.2. Communist Exposure and Welfare State Support:
Country Moderators**
This figure reports the marginal effects on welfare state support of a single year
of exposure to communism in different types of country contexts. The results
show remarkably consistent positive communist exposure effects on welfare
state support across most types of contexts. The only significant differences are
the stronger exposure effects in imposed communist regimes and in peripheral
patrimonial regimes. In interpreting the substantive size of these effects it is
important to keep in mind that the median number of years of exposure to communism in the analyses that produced this figure was 28 years, while the 90th percentile was 55 years for a resident of the former Soviet Union and 45 years for
a resident of East-Central Europe.

cases—despite some minor separation of the predicted effects—the standard errors of the interaction effects are larger than the coefficients on the interaction effects (see the table in the electronic appendix), which suggests that these cross-country differences had very limited moderating effects.

As it turns out, there is only one variable where we can find a meaningful statistically significant effect: the effect of a year of exposure to communism on favorable state-supported social welfare attitudes is actually more than a third *larger* in countries with externally imposed communism than in countries with native communism. While this effect runs counter to our theoretical expectation about the lower resistance to socialization in more legitimate homegrown communist regimes, this pattern could be consistent with an argument suggesting that in countries where communism was imposed by Soviet troops the communist elites may have relied more heavily on the welfare-based social contract to compensate for their lack of revolutionary legitimacy. A similar but somewhat weaker pattern can be observed in the seventh pair in Figure 6.2, where the pro-welfare effects of exposure appeared to be marginally stronger in what Kitschelt (1999) called periphery patrimonial communist regimes than in bureaucratic authoritarian regimes, arguably also reflecting the greater centrality of welfare benefits in regimes with weaker alternative sources of legitimacy.

Growth in the last decade of communism (eighth pair in Figure 6.2) was the only instance where we see a moderately sized effect with some degree of separation in the correctly predicted direction: exposure in countries where the economy performed well in the 1980s has an 18% larger impact than in post-communist countries with the lowest levels of growth in the 1980s (although even in this case, the standard error is only slightly smaller than the coefficient for the interaction variable—see the related table in the electronic appendix—so this finding should be interpreted very cautiously).

Thus, all told, there is very little evidence of any additional leverage being gained in our understanding of the effect of exposure to communism on attitudes toward state responsibility for social welfare by considering aggregate level indicators of intensifying and resistance variables, which stands in contrast to the previous two chapters.

6.4.2. Individual-Level Moderators of Exposure Intensity and Resistance on Attitudes toward Social Welfare

There is, however, a little more of interest going on with the individual-level moderators, although again not as much as in previous chapters, as displayed in Figure 6.3. Turning first to religion, we find an interest-

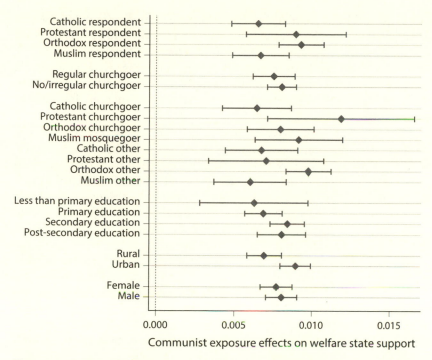

Figure 6.3. Communist Exposure and Welfare State Support: Individual Moderators
This figure reports the marginal effects on welfare state support of a single year
of exposure to communism in different types of individuals. The results indicate
stronger positive communist exposure effects on welfare state support among
Orthodox respondents and among more educated and urban post-communist
citizens. However, neither gender nor church attendance had a significant moderating effect. In interpreting the substantive size of these effects it is important
to keep in mind that the median number of years of exposure to communism
in the analyses that produced this figure was 28 years, while the 90th percentile was 55 years for a resident of the former Soviet Union and 45 years for a
resident of East-Central Europe.

ing amalgam of the previous two chapters when we examine just denomination without considering religious attendance: both Catholics
and Muslims exhibit more resistance to communist socialization than
do Protestants or the Eastern Orthodox.[25] So we once again find support
for the hypothesis that some religions fostered greater resistance to communist socialization efforts. However, unlike in the previous chapters—and

[25] The distinctions are statistically significant between Catholics/Muslims and the Eastern Orthodox with p=.01 and p=.02 levels, respectively, but not between Catholics/Muslims
and Protestants.

especially unlike in the markets chapter—there is no meaningful distinction at all between churchgoers (mosquegoers) and nonattenders. As a result, when we combine the two in our eightfold grouping of effects in Figure 6.3, there is nothing really of interest to report here other than perhaps the somewhat counterintuitive finding that there was actually a *larger* socialization effect for churchgoing Protestants than for non-churchgoing Protestants.[26]

Moving on to education, we find largely homogeneous effects; even the largest distinction between any pair of variables here (exposure effects for those with secondary education vs. less than primary education) does not come close to achieving conventional levels of statistical significance (p=.25). With this caveat in mind, to the extent that we can detect any pattern here, it is in the opposite direction from what we would expect to find: more education is association with a *larger* socialization effect from each additional year of communist exposure.

In contrast, the urban versus rural distinction is very similar to what we found in the previous two chapters, and the interaction effect is statistically significant (at .01). In line with the *intensifying* factors logic, we continue to find larger socialization effects among urban residents: here, an additional year of exposure to communism has an almost 30% larger effect on pro–social welfare attitudes for urban residents than for rural residents.

Finally, unlike in the previous two chapters we find no meaningful distinction between socialization effects on men and women. This suggests that even though men were on average significantly less supportive of generous welfare states (see corresponding table in the electronic appendix), the attitudinal effects of longer communist socialization were very similar for both women and men.

If we take these findings in toto, it is worth raising the question of whether there is something qualitatively different about attitudes toward social welfare compared to democracy and markets. We started this chapter by noting that support for state-provided social welfare—while being a hallmark of communist regimes—was also widespread elsewhere in the world, and was less distinctly "communist" than opposing democracy and markets. Nonetheless, the post-communist differential was even more pronounced vis-à-vis social welfare preferences, and while *living though communism* clearly had an effect—support for state responsibility for social welfare increased with additional years of exposure to communist rule—even individuals who had not personally experienced communist rule continued to be more supportive of state responsibility for social welfare than those living in non-post-communist countries. Moreover, the ex-

[26] p<.07.

posure effects were remarkably consistent across different countries and types of individuals: whereas in the previous two chapters the intensifying and resistance approach to conceptualizing the effects of exposure to communism brought additional nuance and understanding to our analysis and at both the aggregate and individual levels, it almost completely failed to do so in this chapter in the former case and only marginally so in the latter case.[27]

6.5. EXTENSION: PARENTAL SOCIALIZATION AND PANEL EVIDENCE FROM HUNGARY

Given that the analysis so far indicates that the higher propensity of post-communist citizens to support social welfare affects even individuals who had limited or no personal exposure to communist welfare states, one obvious follow-up analysis is to test to what extent these patterns are due to intergenerational transmission of political attitudes within families. Therefore, as in the preceding chapter, we now turn to data from the Hungarian Household Panel Survey (HHPS). As described in Chapters 3 and 5, the HHPS is a yearly panel survey that included over 8,000 respondents from almost 2,700 households in Hungary from 1992 to 1997.

The dependent variable we use in this subsection is based on a survey question that was included in the 1992, 1993, 1994, and 1997 waves and asked respondents whether unemployment benefits should be reduced, kept the same, or increased. While this question does not capture a communist-era welfare policy, since unemployment benefits did not exist under the full-employment command economies, it nevertheless captures the general idea of the state taking care of its citizens. Not surprisingly, the overall balance tilts in the direction of greater state-provided social welfare: thus, 44% thought that benefits should be increased compared to under 24% who favored a reduction of benefits; about a third of respondents supported status quo levels.[28]

As in the previous chapter, we code both the respondent's own responses in the current and previous year and, where applicable, the current and

[27]The only exceptions were rural vs. urban residents and Catholics and Muslims vs. Protestants and Eastern Orthodox.

[28]One could make a case that unemployment is a natural outgrowth of market-based economies and that therefore attitudes toward unemployment belong in the previous chapter as opposed to this one. While this is certainly a legitimate point, we felt there was a more direct connection between unemployment benefits and the idea of a social welfare state. Nevertheless, the analysis should prove equally interesting and relevant regardless of in which chapter it takes place, and anyone who feels particularly strongly about the matter could just read these results as applicable to market attitudes as well.

lagged responses of any parent living in the same household.[29] In addition our regressions control for the same set of household and individual characteristics as in the analysis in Chapter 5 (age, gender, residence, and education levels), and changes in logged per capita household income between the current and the most recent survey.

Given the trichotomous nature of our dependent variable, we run ordered probit models. Once again all models include year-fixed effects, and we report standard errors clustered at the household level.

The first step, illustrated in Model 1 of Table 6.4, simply establishes that individual responses are fairly strongly correlated with contemporaneous parental attitudes on the same issue. Thus, particularly for individuals where both parents favor either lower or higher unemployment benefits, the effects of parental attitudes are both statistically significant and substantively large: thus, the predicted attitude difference between two respondents with parents at the opposite ends of the spectrum in terms of unemployment benefit levels is equivalent to 1.4 times a standard deviation in the dependent variable. When only one parent has a clear opinion, the effect—compared to the baseline of two uncommitted parents—is still in the expected direction but is considerably smaller and falls short of statistical significance.

Since these estimates ignore the possibility of reverse causation and spurious correlation, we run the same set of additional model specifications as in Table 5.4 of Chapter 5. In Model 2 we address reverse causation by using lagged parental responses. While the magnitude of the difference between the two extreme parental views constellations is somewhat smaller in Model 2 than in Model 1, we still find large and statistically significant effects for parental attitudes. However, using lagged indicators once again has an asymmetric effect on the size of the coefficients: thus, whereas the coefficient for having two parents who hold "countercurrent" views—that is, who favor lower unemployment benefits—are virtually identical in the lagged response specifications, the effects of having two parents holding "majoritarian" views is noticeably lower though it continues to be large and statistically significant even in Model 2. Also worth noting is that unlike in Model 1 the real differences are no longer between households with parental unanimity (i.e., the two extreme categories) but between households leaning in one direction or the other.

The even more conservative specification in Model 3, which controls for the respondent's lagged answer to the dependent variable question and thus largely captures whether parental attitudes "anchor" their chil-

---

[29] As a result, our analysis is limited to respondents who still live in the same household as their parents. For a discussion of the inferential problems this poses and our approach for dealing with them, see the discussion in Section 5.6 in Chapter 5.

dren's responses, confirms the robustness of parental influence. However, once again, the impact of parental socialization is asymmetrical, with the effects of having parents who hold minority opinions mattering more than those of having parents with mainstream opinions. In fact, the responses of individuals with conformist parents were statistically indistinguishable from those with neutral/mixed responses, whereas the effects of antiestablishment views were statistically significant and substantively similar to the earlier models.

To address questions related to the source of the original attitudes on unemployment benefits, in Model 4 we focus once again on respondents where we know the lagged responses of their parents but do not have a prior response to the unemployment questions for the respondent him- or herself, either because the respondent was under 16 the last time the question was asked or because the respondent did not answer the question/ stated he or she did not know the answer. Compared to the full sample in Model 2, we find somewhat smaller but still broadly comparable parental socialization effects. The main difference seems to be with respect to having one parent holding the mainstream (i.e., higher unemployment benefits) view, for which the effect is much smaller and no longer statistically significant from the baseline of having two uncommitted parents.

In Model 5 we assess the impact of changes in parental attitudes toward unemployment benefits on the corresponding attitudinal changes among respondents. The results of this model suggest statistically significant effects that are comparable in magnitude to the previous model specifications and thus further reinforce our confidence in the importance of parental socialization. However, it is worth noting that unlike the largely symmetric effects for parental switches toward and away from the mainstream (anti-unemployment) position in Model 5 of Table 5.4 in the preceding chapter, the results from Model 5 in Table 6.4 suggest that only shifts toward a minority/dissenting view have a discernible impact on the attitudes of offspring, which reinforces earlier findings about the importance of contrarian parental views in the socialization process.

To test how the effects of parental socialization are moderated by child age, in Models 6 and 7 we compare the effects of lagged parental attitudes for two age groups: respondents aged 16–18 and respondents aged 19–25. Comparing the effects of parental attitudes in Models 6 and 7 confirms that the role of parental socialization was lower for young adults than for adolescents, particularly for the two extreme categories of parental attitude constellations. Indeed, for young adults (Model 6)—as opposed to adolescents (Model 7)—the effect of having two parents supportive of higher unemployment benefits was no longer statistically distinguishable from the "uncommitted parents" baseline. Nonetheless, the difference between the two extreme constellations continued to be significant even for

Table 6.4. Parental Socialization and Unemployment Attitudes in Hungary

	(1)	(2)	(3)	(4)	(5)	(6)	(7)	(8)	(9)
Both parents lower unemployment benefits (t)	-.443** (.159)								
One parent lower unemployment benefits (t)	-.091 (.231)								
One parent higher unemployment benefits (t)	.206 (.166)								
Both parents higher unemployment benefits (t)	.681** (.126)								
Both parents lower unemployment benefits (t–1)		-.426** (.156)	-.334* (.154)	-.384* (.191)		-.515** (.197)	-.300* (.149)		-.372** (.109)
One parent lower unemployment benefits (t–1)		-.464* (.189)	-.496** (.186)	-.079 (.222)		-.086 (.214)	-.428# (.222)		-.358* (.148)
One parent higher unemployment benefits (t–1)		.272 (.172)	.167 (.176)	.236 (.193)		.246 (.185)	.234 (.160)		.295* (.125)
Both parents higher unemployment benefits (t–1)		.383** (.125)	.193 (.129)	.295# (.156)		.345* (.142)	.222 (.139)		.298** (.093)
Respondent unemployment benefits (t–1)			.431** (.077)						
Parents more unemployment benefits support (t–1→t)					.020 (.115)				
Parents less unemployment benefits support (t–1→t)					-.470** (.114)				
Father lower unemployment benefits (t–1)								-.280* (.122)	
Father higher unemployment benefits (t–1)								.119 (.106)	
Mother lower unemployment benefits (t–1)								-.118 (.129)	
Mother higher unemployment benefits (t–1)								.246* (.104)	

CP member HH* Both parents lower unemployment benefits (t−1)									.175 (.276)
CP member HH × One parent lower unempl benefits (t−1)									.297 (.448)
CP member HH × One parent higher unempl benefits (t−1)									−.602# (.320)
CP member HH × Both parents higher unemployment benefits (t−1)									−.042 (.248)
CP member HH									.060 (.180)
Year dummies	Yes	Yes	Yes	Yes	Yes	Yes	Yes	Yes	Yes
Demographic controls	Yes	Yes	Yes	Yes	Yes	Yes	Yes	Yes	Yes
Sample	All	All	All	No prior answer	All	Aged 16–18	Aged 19–25	All	All
Observations	618	618	618	417	618	462	632	852	1,476

Note: This table uses data on multiple members of the same households included in the 1992, 1993, 1994, 1996, and 1997 waves of the Hungarian Household Panel Survey. The dependent variable is based on a question that whether unemployment benefits should be lowered (coded 0), kept the same (coded 1), or increased (coded 2). The table reports probit coefficients (based on ordered probit models) with standard errors clustered at the household level in parentheses (** p<.01, * p<.05, # p<.1). The results suggest that parental attitudes toward unemployment benefits affect the views of their children, but the effects are stronger when the parents hold minority views (i.e., want lower unemployment benefits). Models 6 and 7 suggest that parental attitudes matter more for younger respondents but are still significant for young adults. The views of fathers and mothers are equally influential (Model 8). CP members are less effective at transmitting attitudes toward unemployment benefits to their children (Model 9), and Catholics are slightly more effective at transmitting their attitudes especially if they favor lower benefits (Model 10), but the interaction effects are not statistically significant. Note that in Models 1, 2, 3, and 5 we restricted the sample to observations without missing data on any of the variables used in those models to ensure that results are comparable across models. However, in Models 6–10 we used the maximum number of observations for each particular model.

young adults, even though the magnitude of the effect was smaller than the corresponding effect for 16-to-18-year-olds in Model 6.

The next model separately assesses the impact of paternal and maternal attitudes vis-à-vis unemployment. According to Model 8, the overall difference between having a parent favoring lower versus higher unemployment benefits is almost identical for mothers and fathers. However, it appears that fathers are more persuasive when they favor lower benefits while mothers are more influential when favoring higher benefits.

In Model 9 we return to the question of how parental Communist Party (CP) membership affects the likelihood of cross-generational attitudinal transmission. We find that whereas in non-CP households parental attitudes had a large impact in the expected direction, in CP households the parental socialization effects were much weaker. Thus, looking at the substantively small and statistically insignificant conditional effects of lagged parental attitudes in CP households, it appears that parents who had been CP members were less capable of getting their children to adopt their political views. The only partial exception occurs in households where both parents favor higher unemployment benefits: under such circumstances children are also more likely to embrace similar preferences, though the effect is only marginally statistically significant and is somewhat smaller than the corresponding effect in non-CP households. Overall, these results suggest that families with CP members were less effective than their non-CP counterparts in transmitting their political attitudes to the next generation, except when both parents endorsed values that were broadly in line with communist ideological commitment to generous welfare benefits. This tracks nicely with prior findings showing stronger parental socialization effects on "countercurrent" attitudes.

As in the case of the analysis in the previous chapter, we also tested whether parental socialization effects were stronger among Catholic respondents (in order to explain the weaker communist exposure effects among Catholics we have found in the cross-national tests). Once again the interaction effects are imprecisely estimated (and are omitted for space reasons), but they all point in the direction of Catholics having stronger parental influence effects.

Overall, these results confirm the importance of parental socialization in shaping the attitudes toward unemployment benefits of young Hungarians in the early years of the post-communist transition. In line with our expectations, parental socialization is more influential among younger individuals, but we nevertheless still see significant effects well into the early to mid-20s, at least among individuals who still live with their parents (roughly 50% of the age cohort in our sample). Among moderating factors, it appears that former Communist Party members were less effective in passing on their attitudes to the next generation. More broadly, we found stronger socialization effects among individuals embracing anti-communist views, as was the case in the previous chapter as well.

6.6. CONCLUSIONS

In this chapter we have analyzed the mechanisms underlying the greater support for an active welfare state among residents of post-communist countries. We began with a post-communist differential of greater support for state responsibility for individual welfare, which, far from being explained away by *living in a post-communist country*, was exacerbated by taking account of pre-communist conditions and contemporaneous demographic and economic conditions; taking account of the political context reduced the gap somewhat, but it still remained substantial.

We then explored the role of aggregate-level conditions at the time of communism's collapse to see if the gap may have been caused by communism's developmental, political, or ideological effects on society. While, as in earlier chapters, accounting for developmental legacies seems to accentuate the gap, we do find that much of the post-communist "surplus" in welfare state support can be explained by the fact that citizens of countries with non-democratic leftist regimes from 1975 to 1989 generally favored greater state responsibility for social welfare.

We then turned to explore the effect of *living through communism*. Overall, we found very strong evidence that additional years of exposure to communist rule were correlated with greater support for state responsibility for social welfare. Furthermore, and in line with the findings from the preceding two chapters, we also show that adult communist exposure has a greater impact on welfare state attitudes than childhood exposure. However unlike in the previous two chapters, it appears that the attitudinal imprint of communism affects not only individuals with long personal exposures to communism but also post-communist citizens with very limited personal exposures to communist regimes (and welfare states).

Also in contrast to the findings in Chapters 4 and 5, we found more limited support for the role of various country- and individual-level factors affecting the resistance to and intensity of communist exposure. Thus, we do not find significant socialization differences between different communist regime subtypes, across countries with different pre-communist political, economic, and developmental legacies, across churchgoers and non-churchgoers, across those with different levels of education, or across men and women. This is not to say we did not find any meaningful factors that either intensified the effects of exposure in the way we expected—for example communist exposure mattered more for urban than rural residents—but it was in a much more limited number of categories, leading to the overall conclusion that exposure effects on attitudes toward social welfare seem to be much more homogeneous than on attitudes toward democracy and markets.

Finally, our supplementary analysis based on the Hungarian Household Panel Survey may help us explain the remarkable cross-generational persistence of pro–welfare state attitudes in post-communist countries. Thus, the analysis in Section 6.5 shows a robust cross-generational correlation between the attitudes toward unemployment benefits of parents and children (even young adults). However, in line with the analysis in Chapter 5, we find that parental socialization effects were once again stronger when parents held "minority" views (i.e., supported lower benefits), which may also explain why parents who had been members of the CP were somewhat less likely to transmit attitudes to their children.

CHAPTER 7

Gender Equality

QUESTION TO RADIO YEREVAN: "Is it possible for a woman to have three
    children in one year?"
RADIO YEREVAN ANSWER: "Not unless they're twins, Comrade Ceauşescu!"

—Romanian joke, late 1980s

7.1. INTRODUCTION

In the previous three chapters, we examined the effect of communist legacies on attitudes toward democracy, markets, and social welfare. In all
three cases, we found clear attitudinal differences—in line with communist ideology—that we could explore to see if *living in a post-communist
country* or *living through communism* could help provide an explanation
for these differences. But communism was more than simply a political
or economic project—it had an explicitly social component as well. Economic equality was to usher in social equality, including in relationships
between the sexes. Nevertheless, as was briefly discussed in Section 1.4 of
Chapter 1, there are reasons to suspect that the effect of communist-era
legacies on gender equality might be more ambiguous than on attitudes
toward democracy, markets, and social welfare.

This ambiguity is due to at least three factors that we discuss briefly
in this introductory section. First, gender issues were more marginal to
the communist ideological project than issues like the dictatorship of the
proletariat or the role of the state in society, and for this reason there was
less emphasis and greater inconsistency in how gender questions were
addressed in official ideology. Second, to an even greater extent than for
other issues, there was a significant gap between the ideological emphasis
on gender equality and the reality of gender policies and gender relations,
which often reinforced traditional patriarchal patterns. Finally, there was
significant variation in the extent to which different communist institutions promoted or undermined gender equality and, therefore, we could
expect very different—and potentially diametrically opposed—effects of
communist exposure on particular individuals depending on the extent

to which they interacted with different institutions during the communist period.[1]

Despite a nominally consistent ideological commitment to gender equality, the treatment of gender in communist ideology underwent a few important transformations. Following the initial influence of a few highly visible proponents of radical gender equality (especially Alexandra Kollontai, see Naiman [1997]), the issue played at best a secondary role in the official ideological discourse of most communist regimes after the 1920s. Thus, while communist ideologues recognized the significant inequalities of traditional gender relations and initially expected to enlist suppressed women as allies for the revolutionary cause (Massell 1974), they largely regarded gender inequality as subordinated to the more fundamental problem of class inequality. Therefore, the expectation was that the "woman problem" would be solved as a side benefit of the process of constructing communism through the equalization of employment and education opportunities (Molyneux 1984; Kamp 2005). Not surprisingly, this approach undermined a clearer focus on the gender-specific roots of gender inequality and provided a basis for complacency about the status of women's issues, which were repeatedly proclaimed to have been solved (Konstantinova 1992; Marsh 1996). Moreover, this approach to gender meant that communist regimes had little use for (and little patience with) Western feminist ideas, which made

---

[1] In Section 1.4 of Chapter 1, we also note that the concept of gender equality may have been less popular among the populations in the countries where communism took root than other hallmarks of communist ideology, such as social welfare provision or state management of the economy. As we lack the data to rigorously assess whether that was indeed the case, in the remainder of this section we instead focus on the three factors noted in this paragraph. However, it is worth noting that in some cases, mistrust of the Communist Party and its rationale for pursuing gender equality interfered with the populations' willingness to embrace the ideal. This was especially so in Central Asia, which consisted of predominantly Muslim populations. The party saw Central Asian nations' partial treatment of women to be emblematic of their backwardness (Suny and Terry 2001). It pursued gender equality forcefully through means such as public unveiling of women, which was at odds with local religious customs (Kamp 2006), in order to fulfill its goal of modernizing these nations (Northrop 2003). The populations regarded the party as a foreign agent and found the party's motivations for their push for gender equality suspect. This in turn may have led these populations to view feminism and nationalism as antagonistic to each other (Edgar 2008). We are grateful for a particularly timely discussion on the PONARS e-mail list for helping make us aware of these sources, as well as to Muthhukumar Palaniyapan, Tucker's undergraduate research assistant at NYU, for synthesizing the key findings from these sources. However, as we will demonstrate later in the chapter, despite starting from a low baseline, it does appear that in categories of countries that include the Central Asian states (e.g., low pre-communist literacy and patrimonial peripheral regimes), exposure had a *larger* effect on inculcating pro–gender equality attitudes than elsewhere, which runs counter to the idea that resistance should have been higher in these countries if there was less original popular support for such ideas.

limited inroads in the largely state-controlled women's movements in the Soviet bloc. Finally, as some observers have argued, communist regimes were less interested in female emancipation than in replacing the traditional hegemony of patriarchal institutions (like the church and the family) with the hegemony of the Communist Party/state (Kukhterin 2000).

Second, there was also a significant gap between the theoretical emphasis on gender equality and the practical reality of "real and existing socialism." While such gaps obviously also existed in the other issue areas discussed in previous chapters, in the case of gender the gap was exacerbated by the fact that gender policies were largely subordinated to other economic and political priorities. The first and most important reason for the gap was the need to boost fertility rates, which was rooted initially in the large population losses incurred by the Soviet Union in the 1920s and 1930s (as a result of a combination of terror and famine) and by the entire communist bloc in World War II, while in later years it was driven by concerns about declining fertility rates. In rhetorical terms these pressures drove the growing emphasis on the role of the woman as a mother, which culminated in the image of the "heroine mother" (Coser 1951: 425), and more broadly fueled an official rhetoric that reinforced the traditional view of the family and childbearing as the primary responsibilities of women (Sanborn 2003). In policy terms, these pronatalist pressures yielded a mix of positive and negative consequences for gender equality: on the one hand, the desire to boost fertility was an important driver in the expansion of a range of welfare policies geared specifically at mothers (Einhorn 1993; Harsch 2006), which not only relieved some of the everyday work pressures on Eastern European women but also strengthened their bargaining position within the household, thereby helping to reduce the continued power imbalance within most marriages. On the other hand, however, the quest for greater fertility was also at the root of more restrictive divorce and abortion policies (Goldfarb 1997; Kligman 1998), which undermined the exit options—and thus the empowerment—of women.

The other key political priority driving the gap between rhetoric and reality in communist-era gender relations was the role of women in the labor market. On the one hand, in their quest to boost industrial production, communist regimes were eager to get women into the labor market, and as a result female participation in the labor force increased dramatically in all communist countries (Lapidus 1978). This trend arguably contributed to women's emancipation both because it integrated them more fully into society and because it gave them sources of income independent of their husbands, and thereby strengthened their power within the family. On the other hand, however, the equalization of paid labor across the sexes was not accompanied by a commensurate adjustment in domestic work and child-rearing duties, which continued to fall overwhelmingly on

the shoulders of women. The result was often known as the "double bur-
den" of wage and domestic labor, which made the everyday lives of women
in communist countries particularly difficult (Einhorn 1993; Wolchik and
Meyer 1985). To make matters worse, domestic work continued to be regarded as lower status than paid work in the public sphere, thereby rein-
forcing one of the key sources of gender inequality.[2]

The third key feature that shaped gender relations during the communist period, and should be reflected in post-communist legacies, was the
highly uneven mix of genuine progress and significant limitations in the
policies affecting the emancipation of women. By far the greatest communist achievement in terms of gender equality was in the sphere of education: not only did the largely successful drives to achieve universal literacy
close the significant gender literacy gap that had existed in most Eastern
European countries, but at least by the early 1970s women had largely
equal access to all levels of education, including secondary and higher
education (Vasileva 1978; Gerber and Hout 1995). Moreover, while societal gender norms still permeated the practice inside the classrooms and
a certain amount of gender-based tracking continued (especially in higher
education, where women were underrepresented in some technical areas
and overrepresented in languages), communist education was nonetheless
the area that came closest to implementing the ideal of gender equality
espoused by the official communist rhetoric.

Labor markets represent another example of the "uneven mix" of progress and limitations for women under communism, although the balance
was less positive than in the educational sphere. As previously noted, communist countries experienced significant increases in female labor participation, including in many areas traditionally reserved for men. However,
significant gender-based differences continued to exist in many industries
based on what was seen by the communist leadership—including early
feminists such as Kollontai (Naiman 1997: 83)—as natural differences in
abilities (Ashwin 2000: 11). In part because of this occupational/sectoral
sorting and in part because of a preferential system of bonuses, women
continued to be paid less than men during the communist period (Lapidus 1978; Harsch 2006), though on balance the situation nevertheless improved compared to the pre-communist period.

Perhaps the clearest communist-era gender disparities were in the
realm of leadership positions, which continued to be dominated to a large
extent by men. Despite the introduction of gender quotas for the leadership of many institutions, the predominance of male leaders persisted

---

[2]For more on the role of women in the labor force in *post*-communist countries, see
Pollert 2003.

at all levels, from economic leadership positions within state-owned enterprises all the way to the upper echelons of the Communist Party apparatus. These differences were rooted in part in the aforementioned gap between the theory and practice of gender equality, but in many ways reflected the fact that even at the rhetorical level communist leaders continued to endorse the dominance of men in leadership positions in the public sphere (Ashwin 2000: 12).

What are the implications of these factors for the expected impact of communist legacies on post-communist gender attitudes? Three expectations seem particularly germane. First, given the tension between the (albeit halfhearted and qualified) rhetorical commitment to gender equality and the mixed and highly uneven institutional and experiential reality, we have good reason to expect that there may be significantly weaker evidence of a post-communist differential in attitudes toward gender equality in the direction we would expect from communist ideology (i.e., more support for gender equality) than we found in previous chapters.[3] Indeed, the ability to even make such a prediction in the first place would depend on the extent to which the rhetoric and the progressive aspects of communist-era institutional changes (especially education, labor market access and women-focused welfare benefits) outweigh the continued gender imbalance in the real-life experience of many key aspects of life under communism, including family relations and the exercise of power in the economic and political leadership structures of communist regimes.

Second, it seems intuitively important to address the possibility of gender-based differences in exposure effects on attitudes toward gender equality, although even here two different sets of expectations can be derived from the discussion so far. On the one hand, in line with the early hopes of communist leaders, we may expect communism to have contributed to the greater attitudinal emancipation of women, armed with greater educational access and reinforced by the independence of higher labor participation and targeted welfare benefits (e.g., Haney 1999), whereas men would have resisted the gender equality rhetoric of communism, instead hanging on to pre-communist attitudes to justify their de facto privileges in both the private and the public sphere. On the other hand, a number of arguments suggest a very different scenario: from this perspective, in their efforts to attain greater control over society, communist regimes stripped men of the traditional sources of privilege of power and therefore destroyed traditional patriarchy, but—unsurprisingly—this power did not benefit women nearly as much as the state (Kukhterin 2000). Conversely, the combination of genuine progress in education, employment, and welfare benefits with a reproduction of traditional gender discourses and practices

---

[3] See as well the discussion in Section 1.4 of Chapter 1.

in other areas appears to have undermined the appeal of feminist ideas in the communist countries, and the problem was exacerbated by the institutional dominance of the fairly traditionalist official women's movement at the expense of independent feminist civil society groups (Einhorn 1993). To the extent that these phenomena were reflected in attitudinal patterns, we could therefore expect the gender equality–promoting communist legacies to be weaker among women than among men.

Finally, one fairly unambiguous prediction seems warranted, which is in the realm of age of exposure. Given that the greatest and most consistent progress toward gender equality occurred in education, we would expect that early exposure to communism (as part of a relatively gender-neutral educational system) to be more likely to promote pro–gender equality attitudes, whereas the effects of adult exposure to the reality of gender-based unequal power dynamics should have a more mixed effect.

The remainder of this chapter proceeds along a similar pattern to the previous three chapters. In Section 7.2 we analyze the effects of *living in a post-communist country* and find that on average citizens of ex-communist countries exhibited a modest (and largely statistically insignificant) *deficit* in support for gender equality (that is, *the opposite* of the prediction that post-communist citizens would be more supportive of gender equality). A similar picture emerges when we add our variables to measures conditions at the time of communism's collapse, although at least we do find that once we control for regime type, we finally observe at least suggestive evidence that post-communist citizens were more supportive of gender equality than countries with a similarly authoritarian experience in the 1970s and 1980s, although other institutional legacies of communism (such as left-wing ideology and socioeconomic development patterns) once again point in the opposite direction. In Section 7.3 we analyze the attitudinal impact of *living through communism*. Our most interesting finding in this section—and one that runs counter to the patterns we found in earlier chapters—is that while early communist exposure strengthened support for gender equality, adult exposure had the opposite effect, thereby confirming our theoretical expectations (and running more in line with the extant literature on political socialization from established democracies). The other noteworthy finding is that communist exposure appears to have promoted more progressive gender attitudes among men but to have had the opposite effect on women. We explore this issue in greater detail in Section 7.5, where we find that whereas childhood exposure is associated with greater support for gender equality among both men and women, for adult exposure the effects are reversed for women (but not for men). Finally, in Section 7.6 we explore the impact of *communist education* and find that while attending primary school under communist rule promoted greater support for gender equality—in line with expectations based on communist ideology—this was not the case for secondary and post-secondary education.

7.2. LIVING IN POST-COMMUNIST COUNTRIES AND ATTITUDES TOWARD GENDER EQUALITY

We continue as in previous chapters by beginning our analysis with data from four recent waves (1989–93, 1994–98, 1999–2004, and 2005–9) of the World Values Survey, which in the case of attitudes toward gender equality allows us to analyze 153 surveys from 77 countries (including 42 surveys from 23 post-communist countries).[4] Our dependent variable in this chapter is an index composed of three questions: one on whether men make better political leaders than women, one on whether university education is more important for a boy than a girl, and one on whether men should be more entitled to a job than women when jobs are scarce; a higher value on the index reflects greater support for gender equality.[5]

Contrary to naive expectations based on official rhetoric, the average support for gender equality is lower for post-communist respondents (–.05) than it is for respondents living in non-post-communist countries (+.06). When we examine the distribution of our gender equality index by country (see Figure 7.1) an interesting pattern emerges. First, the post-communist countries do not cluster at either the right or the left of the scale, as in previous chapters. Instead, post-communist countries are rather tightly grouped around the *center* of the figure: there are few post-communist countries with exceptionally pro–gender equality averages (other than East Germans or Slovenians, there are no other post-communist countries in the top third in terms of pro–gender equality), but then again there are not many on the far left-hand side of the figure either, other than three countries from the Caucasus (Armenia, Azerbaijan, and Georgia) plus Slovakia.[6]

---

[4]This number is lower than in previous chapters featuring the same number of waves because not all the surveys contained the gender equality questions we use to construct our dependent variable in this chapter.

[5]In order to improve the Cronbach's alpha of the index, the job question is entered into the index as two dummy variables (those who agree and those who disagree with the statement) while the questions about political leaders and university education are entered as four-item continuous variables.

[6]Inglehart and Norris (2003) similarly find post-communist countries to be grouped somewhere around the middle in a large cross-national sample of attitudes toward gender equality, also using data from the World Values Survey.

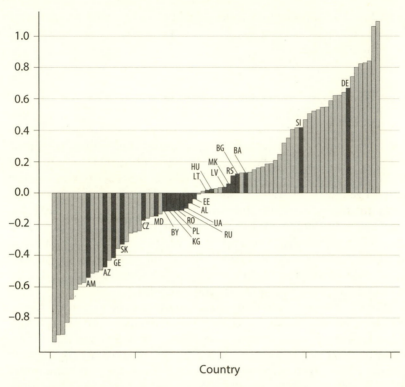

Figure 7.1. Average Support for Gender Equality by Country: Post-communist vs. Non-communist

This figure lists the country-level averages in gender equality support of post-communist countries (dark-gray bars) compared to those of non-communist countries (light-gray bars) based on the 2nd, 3rd, 4th, and 5th waves of the World Values Survey (1990–2008). In calculating the averages we used any individual-level weights, and we also applied equilibrated weights to adjust for different sample sizes across surveys for different years in any given country. The figure shows that ex-communist countries are largely clustered around the middle of the gender equality support distribution, with very few of them in either the upper or lower thirds of the global distribution. The main positive outliers are East Germany and Slovenia, while three countries from the Caucasus (Armenia, Azerbaijan, and Georgia) were relative underperformers. For the full set of country codes, see the list of country code abbreviations on page xv.

With these raw data in mind, it should come as little surprise that for the first time in the manuscript we do *not* find a statistically significant post-communist differential in the predicted direction in Model 1 of Table 7.1, our most basic model featuring only the post-communist dummy variable and year-fixed effects.

Table 7.1. Living in a Post-communist Country and Gender Equality Attitudes

	(1)	(2)	(3)	(4)	(5)	(6)	(7)	(8)
Post-communist	-.080 (.074)	-.223 (.151)	-.364 (.248)	-.271# (.149)	-.288* (.143)	-.024 (.134)	-.216 (.151)	-.058 (.053)
Year dummies	Yes	Yes	No	Yes	Yes	Yes	Yes	Yes
Pre-communist controls	No	Yes	No	Yes	Yes	Yes	Yes	No
Post-communist demographics	No	No	No	Yes	No	No	Yes	Yes
Post-communist econ outcomes	No	No	No	No	Yes	No	Yes	No
Post-communist polit institutions	No	No	No	No	No	Yes	Yes	No
Pre-communist & year entropy balancing	No	No	Yes	No	No	No	No	No
Countries	All	All	All	All	All	All	All	Germany
Observations	215,826	215,826	215,826	215,826	215,826	215,826	215,826	4,049
R-squared	.046	.167	.031	.229	.182	.174	.249	.142

Note: This table demonstrates that post-communist citizens are not more supportive of gender equity than citizens in the rest of the world, despite what we might have expected from communist ideology. This "missing differential" holds even when controlling for pre-communist conditions (Models 2 and 3) and contemporaneous demographic characteristics, economic conditions, and political institutions (Models 4–7); similar results can be found from analyzing only data from Germany comparing East and West Germans (Model 8). The dependent variable is an index of three questions—one on whether men make better political leaders than women, one on whether university education is more important for a boy than a girl, and one on whether men should be more entitled to a job than women when jobs are scarce—standardized to a mean of 0 and a standard deviation of 1. The list of independent and control variables can be found in Table 3.1 of Chapter 3. Full regression results are in the electronic appendix. The data utilized in these analyses are from the 2nd, 3rd, 4th, and 5th waves of the World Values Survey. Robust standard errors in parentheses: ** p<.01, * p<.05, # p<.1.

In fact, not only do we not find a positive and statistically significant coefficient for the post-communist dummy variable, but we actually find a negative effect. While not surprising based on what we just reported regarding the raw data, what is perhaps a little more surprising is the fact that this negative coefficient persists throughout all the different models in Table 7.1. Thus no matter what aspect of *living in a post-communist country* we account for in our analyses, we still find a *negative* post-communist differential: that is, that citizens in post-communist countries are less supportive of gender equality than citizens in the non-communist countries in the World Values Survey dataset, all else equal, albeit almost always with weak levels of statistical confidence.

Of particular interest here are Models 2 and 3, our assessments of the effects of controlling for pre-communist conditions. In both models, the size of the post-communist dummy variable coefficient increases substantially (roughly 3–4 times) relative to the simple bivariate base model. What this means is that conditional on the nature of the countries in which communism took hold, we would actually expect support for gender equality to be higher in post-communist countries relative to the rest of the world. Recall that in Model 2, we are controlling for colonial legacy (i.e., whether countries were part of the Hapsburg empire, Prussian empire, Russian empire, etc) as well as whether countries were Christian or Muslim majority. So our findings cannot be attributed to Prussian, Russian, or Muslim cultural legacies.

The remaining models in Table 7.1 further suggest that neither demographic differences nor the economic and political aspects of *living in post-communist countries* change this broad conclusion. In fact the negative effect gets slightly larger and becomes marginally significant in the models controlling for demographic and economic post-communist differences, and while accounting for political institutional differences in Model 6 erases the post-communist gender equality deficit, none of the models indicate the possibility of a positive communist effect on gender equality support.

To pursue this surprising nonfinding further, we investigated whether any of the components of our gender equality index exhibited different patterns. After all, given our discussion of the uneven rhetorical and policy stance of communist regimes toward gender relations, it could have been possible that the null findings for the index were simply masking countervailing effects on particular dimensions of gender equality support.[7] However, once we replicated the models in Table 7.1 separately for the three index components, we still found no evidence of any post-communist sur-

---

[7] We thank Natalia Forrat for suggesting this possibility.

plus in gender equality support.[8] While the negative impact of communism was—unsurprisingly given the reality of male dominance of political leadership positions under communist rule—the strongest (in terms of both substantive and statistical significance) for believing that women can be equally effective leaders as men, even support for gender equality in the workplace and higher education was on balance weaker in postcommunist countries.

We pursued this idea of heterogeneous communist legacy effects for different aspects of gender equality by analyzing data from the 1994 and 2002 waves of the International Social Survey Programme (ISSP), which focused on gender relations and thus had a broader range of survey questions tapping into different dimensions of gender attitudes. From these questions we created two multiquestion indexes: one that tapped into broad attitudes about marriage and family, and one that captured attitudes toward women's participation in the workplace. While a full replication of our analyses of our WVS surveys was not feasible with the ISSP surveys owing to the smaller number of countries,[9] we nevertheless found similar patterns: post-communist citizens were somewhat less supportive of gender equality/women's emancipation in both the family and the workplace (though the results fell short of statistical significance). The only exception was for a third dimension, captured by a single survey question about support for paid maternity leave: here we found a significantly higher support among post-communist respondents. However, this pattern is arguably more reflective of the strong commitment of post-communist citizens for state-provided social welfare (as discussed in Chapter 6) than of greater support for gender equality.[10]

7.3. LIVING IN POST-COMMUNIST COUNTRIES: UNPACKING THE EFFECTS OF COMMUNISM

Thus the overall takeaway from Table 7.1 is that there is no communist legacy effect at all in terms of providing greater support for gender equality. Indeed, Models 2 and 3 even suggest that the communist experience may have *decreased* support for gender equality among post-communist citizens. Nevertheless, based on our earlier discussion we do want to at least consider the possibility that this may be due to contradictory effects from different aspects of the communist experience. Therefore, as in previous

[8] Full results available in the electronic appendix.

[9] The ISSP surveys in those two waves included eight Eastern European countries (including East Germany) and only one former Soviet republic (Russia).

[10] Results from our ISSP analysis are available in the supplemental appendixes.

chapters, we unpack the effect of communism, here on attitudes toward gender equality, and we begin by turning to our societal-level communist legacies: development, the emphasis on inequality and redistribution, non-democratic rule, and leftist ideology.

As in prior chapters, Model 1 is a replication of Model 2 in the previous table (year-fixed effects and pre-communist controls) and serves as the base model for the remainder of the table. Given that we are starting with what is essentially a null result, Table 7.2 reveals a number of unexpectedly interesting findings. Setting aside regime type for a moment, we find that most of the societal features that we have argued should be associated with communism—development, redistribution, and leftist ideology—should have made citizens in post-communist countries *more* supportive of gender equality. Therefore, it is not surprising that controlling for these factors either *increases* the post-communist gender equality deficit (in Models 2 and 5) or leaves it unchanged (Model 3). Left-wing ideology is particularly striking in this regard: in general, citizens living countries with left-wing governments in the late 1970s and 1980s were more supportive of gender equality, thus increasing the post-communist gender equality deficit in terms of both substantive size (>20% of a standard deviation of the index) and statistical significance (p<.01) compared to Model 1. We find similar patterns in Model 2, where accounting for the higher literacy of ex-communist countries yields a large and statistically significant gender equality support deficit.[11]

Regime type, however, tells a very different story. Living in a more democratic country in the late 1970s and 1980s is associated with a strong and statistically significant positive effect on supporting gender equality. Post-communist countries were of course not democratic in that period of time, so when we control for regime type in the decade and a half before the collapse of communism, we get for the first time a positive coefficient on the post-communist dummy variable. The standard error of this coefficient is quite large, though, suggesting that the most appropriate conclusion is that conditional on living in non-democratic regimes in the 1970s and 1980s, post-communist citizens were not any more likely to oppose gender equality than others living in non-democratic regimes. Finally, Model 6 shows that conditional on living in a *left-wing* non-democratic regime, the coefficient on the post-communist dummy variable returns once again to being negative (although the effect is small and statistically insignificant).

[11] In Model 3, even though all the redistribution/state intervention variables are associated with increased gender equality support, controlling for them leaves the post-communism effect unchanged compared to Model 1.

Table 7.2. Communist System Features and Gender Equality Attitudes

	(1)	(2)	(3)	(4)	(5)	(6)
Post-communist	−.223	−.389**	−.227	.121	−.414**	−.149
	(.151)	(.146)	(.150)	(.147)	(.136)	(.165)
Urbanization 1989		−.319				
		(.205)				
Primary school		−.003				
enrollment		(.002)				
Literacy 1989		.008**				
		(.003)				
Energy intensity		17.40**				
		(4.82)				
Industry as % GDP		−.008*				
		(.004)				
Log GDP/capita 1989		.084				
		(.061)				
Health & education			.031#			
spending 1989			(.016)			
Income inequality 1989			−.010*			
			(.004)			
State sector size			.058#			
late 1989			(.032)			
Average regime score				.027**		.022**
1975–89				(.006)		(.007)
Left gov't share 1975–89					.444**	.363**
					(.085)	(.096)
Average regime score						−.005
1975–89 × Left gov't						(.012)
share 1975–89						
Year dummies	Yes	Yes	Yes	Yes	Yes	Yes
Pre-communist controls	Yes	Yes	Yes	Yes	Yes	Yes
Observations	215,826	215,826	215,826	215,826	215,826	215,826
R-squared	.167	.180	.180	.177	.179	.184

Note: This table demonstrates that post-communist citizens are not more supportive of gender equity than citizens in the rest of the world, despite what we might have expected from communist ideology, even when controlling for conditions at the time of communism's collapse, including developmental legacies (Model 2), redistributive/egalitarian policies (Model 3), and the political orientation of communist regimes (Models 4–6). The dependent variable is an index of three questions—one on whether men make better political leaders than women, one on whether university education is more important for a boy than a girl, and one on whether men should be more entitled to a job than women when jobs are scarce—standardized to a mean of 0 and a standard deviation of 1. The list of independent and control variables can be found in Table 3.1 of Chapter 3. Full regression results are in the electronic appendix. The data utilized in these analyses are from the 2nd, 3rd, 4th, and 5th waves of the World Values Survey. Robust standard errors in parentheses: ** p<.01, * p<.05, # p<.1.

7.4. LIVING THROUGH COMMUNISM AND ATTITUDES TOWARD GENDER EQUALITY

Having failed to find a meaningful distinction in attitudes toward gender equality between post-communist citizens and citizens of countries in the rest of the world, it seems unlikely that *living through communism* would have a strong effect on increasing support for gender equality. The more interesting question would seem to be whether there are particular subgroups of post-communist citizens for which additional exposure to communism indeed resulted in increased support for gender equality (i.e., whether there is support for any of our *intensifying* or *resistance* hypotheses).

Models 1 and 2 of Table 7.3 reveal, for the first time in this manuscript, a lack of robustness when we simply examine exposure to communism without slicing it into mutually exclusive categories. So when we look at the effect of exposure within and across countries (Model 1), we find an—albeit statistically insignificant—negative coefficient, suggesting that each additional year of exposure to communism makes one less supportive of gender equality (even after controlling for an already strong age effect whereby older people are less supportive of gender equality than younger people throughout the entire sample). When we turn to the country-fixed-effects version of the model (Model 2), that is, when we simply look at variation in length of exposure to communism within countries, we actually find the opposite: a marginally significant (p<.10) *positive* effect. So within countries, additional exposure to communism results in more support for gender equality.

While this is indeed the predicted effect based on communist ideology that we would expect from *living through communism*, we want to be very cautious in our interpretation of this finding both because of the lack of robustness across our two specifications (recalling that this estimate was extremely robust across the two different specification in all three of the previous chapters) and because of the high standard errors.[12]

The results from Model 3 are also interesting. Recall that we have argued that among the issues examined in this manuscript gender equality is the area with the greatest disconnect between communist rhetoric and communist reality, *especially as time passed*. If we then suspect that the people who would be most likely to buy into communist rhetoric would be those "true believers" from the early years (and note how this is the opposite of the nostalgia argument), then this ought to be the case where we see the biggest distinction between Stalinist exposure and all other types. Moreover, given that communist regimes put more emphasis on gender equality in their early (largely Stalinist) years, we might expect a stronger effect for greater gender equality support for communist exposure under Stalinism. And indeed, this

---

[12]Note, however, that the HLM results reported in the electronic appendix also yield positive and marginally significant communist exposure effects.

is what we find in Model 3: when we allow for cross-country comparisons, additional years of exposure to Stalinism are associated with significantly greater support for gender equality, which is not the case for exposure to any other type of communism.[13] Furthermore, exposure to both neo-Stalinism and post-totalitarian communism has a negative effect on support for gender equality, which would be expected if in these years either the rhetoric or the reality of a commitment to gender equality diminished. When we look within countries, however, these patterns are much weaker—all the regime types have positive effects, none of them are statistically distinct from zero, let alone from one another, but a year of Stalinist exposure still has a predicted effect that is two times larger than the predicted effect of exposure from any of the other regime types—thus suggesting that a large part of the results in Model 3 is being driven by differences across countries.[14]

Turning to Models 5 and 6 we find one of the most interesting results in the chapter. Recall that in previous chapters, to the extent that there was a difference in the importance of adult versus childhood socialization, it was always in favor of the former, in contrast to the extant US politics literature (although see Mishler and Rose 2007 on Russia). Here, however, we find robust evidence (across both Models 5 and 6) that in the case of gender equality, it is *childhood* socialization that has the relationship originally predicted: more years of early exposure to communism lead to significantly higher levels of support for gender equality. This pattern suggests that communist *education* may indeed have led citizens of communist countries to adopt more pro–gender equality views, while living in a communist *society* did not.[15]

This contrast between early and adult communist exposure effects, to which we return in the supplementary analysis in Section 7.5, makes a lot of sense from the vantage point of the aforementioned distinction between communist rhetoric and reality on the issue of gender equality. Schools were one place where the rhetoric was more pronounced but, even more importantly, one place where *reality* also was in line with that rhetoric, given the significant progress in ensuring equal access for both girls and boys. Finally, the interaction models both suggest that early communist exposure

[13] The coefficient for Stalinist exposure is statistically distinct from all three other coefficients at a level of p<.01 (and from neo-Stalinist and post-totalitarian exposure at a level of p<.001).

[14] Once again, the results for the hierarchical linear models in the electronic appendix are much closer to the patterns in the fixed-effects models.

[15] A supplementary analysis of the gender index subcomponents in the electronic appendix suggests that the positive effects of early exposure primarily affected support for gender equality in the workplace and (to a somewhat lesser extent) higher education, while adult communist exposure undermined support for female political leaders and—somewhat more surprisingly—for higher education gender equality.

Table 7.3. Communist Socialization and Gender Equality Attitudes

	(1)	(2)	(3)	(4)	(5)	(6)	(7)	(8)
Total communist exposure	-.0012	.0017#						
	(.0013)	(.0010)						
Stalinist total exposure			.0121**	.0030				
			(.0025)	(.0022)				
Neo-Stalinist total exposure			-.0093*	.0009				
			(.0041)	(.0025)				
Post-totalitarian total exposure			-.0137**	.0014				
			(.0048)	(.0032)				
Reform comm. total exposure			.0010	.0012				
			(.0023)	(.0016)				
Early communist exposure					.0069*	.0080**	-.0014	.0036
					(.0031)	(.0025)	(.0048)	(.0030)
Adult communist exposure					-.0015	.0015	-.0043#	-.0000
					(.0013)	(.0010)	(.0023)	(.0015)
Early × Adult communist Exposure							.0003*	.0002
							(.0002)	(.0001)

	(1)	(2)	(3)	(4)	(5)	(6)	(7)	(8)
Post-communist citizen	-.2315		-.1996		-.3059#		-.2337	
	(.1614)		(.1537)		(.1627)		(.1687)	
Age	-.0044**	-.0057**	-.0045**	-.0057**	-.0043**	-.0056**	-.0042**	-.0055**
	(.0007)	(.0005)	(.0007)	(.0005)	(.0007)	(.0005)	(.0008)	(.0005)
Year dummies	Yes	Yes	Yes	Yes	Yes	Yes	Yes	Yes
Country dummies	No	Yes	No	Yes	No	Yes	No	Yes
Pre-communist controls	Yes	No	Yes	No	Yes	No	Yes	No
Demographic controls	Yes	Yes	Yes	Yes	Yes	Yes	Yes	Yes
Observations	215,826	215,826	215,826	215,826	215,826	215,826	215,826	215,826
R-squared	.227	.280	.231	.280	.228	.280	.228	.280

Note: This table demonstrates that there is little to support that prediction that additional exposure to communism should be correlated with additional support for gender equity. There is some suggestive evidence that exposure to communism under Stalinist regimes is correlated with greater support for gender equity (Model 3), but this finding is not robust to respecification in a country-fixed-effects model (Model 4). There is, however, strong support for the claim that exposure to communism during *childhood* is related to greater support for gender equity. The dependent variable is an index of three questions—one on whether men make better political leaders than women, one on whether university education is more important for a boy than a girl, and one on whether men should be more entitled to a job than women when jobs are scarce—standardized to a mean of 0 and a standard deviation of 1. The list of independent and control variables can be found in Table 3.1 of Chapter 3. Full regression results are in the electronic appendix. The data utilized in these analyses are from the 2nd, 3rd, 4th, and 5th waves of the World Values Survey. Robust standard errors in parentheses: ** p<.01, * p<.05, # p<.1.

was particularly important in counteracting the negative (anti–gender equality) effects of adult communist exposure: thus, whereas adult exposure had a negative and significant effect on those who had not lived under communism during childhood/adolescence, the effect disappeared completely for those with the full dose (12 years) of early communist exposure.

Taken as a whole, Table 7.3 suggests that while exposure to communism writ large does not have the kind of systematic effect on attitudes toward gender equality as it did in terms of attitudes toward democracy, markets, or social welfare, there are still effects for particular types of exposure, most notably exposure during one's formative years. With this observation in mind, then, we can move on to consider other sources of potentially heterogeneous effects from *living through communism*, including both our intensifying and resistance variables at both the aggregate and individual levels.

7.4.1. Country-Level Moderators of Exposure Intensity and Resistance on Attitudes toward Gender Equality

As in the previous chapters, we relegate the regression tables for our next sets of analyses to the electronic appendix and include in the text figures that illustrate the differential effect of an additional year of exposure to communism at high (95th percentile) and low (5th percentile) levels of the moderating variable in question.[16]

What is immediately apparent from Figure 7.2, which illustrates the effects of the country-level intensifying and resistance variables on the effect of communist exposure, is that there is much more separation in this figure than in any of the earlier chapters. Whereas attitudes toward social welfare told a story of largely homogenous effects for exposure on people in different types of countries, attitudes toward gender equality suggests almost the opposite. Indeed a quick glance at the corresponding table in the electronic appendix reveals that all the interaction effects (save proportion of hardliners and late-communist political liberalization) are actually statistically significant (p<.05).

Perhaps the most interesting set of results is found in the first three pairs of rows containing pre-communist literacy, pre-communist wealth, and pre-communist level of democracy. these factors would normally be associated with more progressive outlooks on social issues, but in the context of our analyses here, these factors were hypothesized to provide "resistance" to communist socialization, which—in this case—would run against the more progressive pro–gender equality views promoted by

---

[16] As previously, we continue at this stage of our analysis to rely only on intra-regional comparisons and utilize constrained regression analysis with regard to respondent age for the reasons described in Chapter 3.

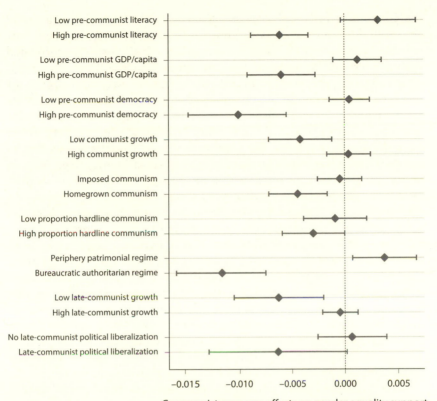

Communist exposure effects on gender equality support

Figure 7.2. Communist Exposure and Gender Equality Support: Country Moderators

This figure reports the marginal effects of a single year of exposure to communism in different types of country contexts. The results indicate that communist exposure had significant negative effects on gender equality support in countries with high pre-communist literacy, GDP/capita, and democracy, but weakly positive effects in countries where weaker pre-communist development reduced resistance to communist socialization. The figure also reveals significantly negative socialization effects in countries with weak overall and late-communist economic growth and in countries with homegrown communism and with bureaucratic authoritarian regimes. The only significantly positive communist socialization regime was in peripheral patrimonial regimes. In interpreting the substantive size of these effects it is important to keep in mind that the median number of years of exposure to communism in the analyses that produced this figure was 28 years, while the 90th percentile was 55 years for a resident of the former Soviet Union and 45 years for a resident of East-Central Europe.

the communist official discourse. That is exactly what the data reveal across all three of these variables: pre-communist literacy, pre-communist wealth, and interwar exposure to democracy are all positively correlated with gender equality support (see corresponding tables in the electronic appendix). However, each additional year of exposure to communism for residents of these countries actually leads to *lower* levels of support for gender equality. So while inclined toward more equitable views, residents of these countries "resisted" communist propaganda by reverting to less equitable views over time. Put another way, our model suggests that in a country with the lowest levels of pre-communist literacy (e.g., Albania or Kyrgyzstan), citizens were unable to "resist" the communist rhetoric in favor of gender equality—despite starting from a lower baseline—and therefore each additional year of exposure is associated with *increased* support for gender equality ($p<.06$), whereas in a high-literacy country like Latvia or Poland, each additional year of exposure is associated with *decreased* support for gender equality ($p<.001$). Taken together, these patterns suggest that communist socialization led to a convergence in gender attitudes among the former communist countries, in the sense that it promoted gender equality in the initially more sexist countries while undermining it in countries with greater initial gender equality support. This may also explain why the ex-communist countries clustered toward the middle of the gender equality distribution in Figure 7.1, with very few outliers among either the best or the worst performers on the issue.

When we move outside the realm of pre-communist conditions, we continue to find similar patterns. To reiterate, we suggested that higher levels of economic growth under communism (either over the entire communist period or in the last decade of communist rule), late-communist liberalization, and homegrown as opposed to imposed communism would all lower the resistance toward communist socialization, and thus we should expect more positive effects for a year of exposure in each of these categories. However, we have also noted that late-communist liberalization might weaken the effect of communist socialization because of lower levels of propaganda, which in the context of gender equality could mean that an additional year of exposure would have a smaller effect on gender equality support. We do indeed find some evidence supportive of our first hypothesis for both overall and late-communist economic growth: whereas exposure had a significant negative effect on support for gender equality in countries with weak growth (and, hence, stronger resistance), for high-growth countries the exposure effects were essentially nil. However, for late-communist political liberalization, the effects are in the opposite direction: exposure effects were more negative in countries that liberalized in the 1980s (albeit only marginally significant at $p=.14$), which supports the "weakened ideology" rather than the "positive nostalgia" argument with regard to late-communist liberalization. The one case in which our findings are at odds with our theoretical expectations is imposed versus homegrown communism, where we find greater resistance to pro–gender equality socialization in countries with homegrown communism than in countries where it was externally imposed (even though we would have expected stronger resistance in the latter).

Interestingly, the largest socialization differential is found when we compare bureaucratic authoritarian regimes with peripheral patrimonial regimes, but it is in the opposite direction from what we expected. Far from intensifying the effect of exposure, living in a bureaucratic authoritarian regime is associated with an additional year of exposure to communism having a strong statistically significant effect on *decreasing* support for gender equality. Conversely, additional years of exposure are associated with *increasing* support for gender equality in the peripheral patrimonial regimes. While counter to our intensifying hypothesis, such a pattern is perfectly consistent with the "equalization of gender equality attitudes" explanation put forward earlier in regard to pre-communist literacy: people living in bureaucratic authoritarian states with no years of exposure to communism have a much higher level of pro–gender equality attitudes than people living in patrimonial peripheral regimes, but additional years of communist exposure serve to mitigate these differences.[17]

Taken together, the aggregate level interaction findings confirm our observation from the previous section regarding the heterogeneous effect of exposure on attitudes toward gender equality: we have yet more evidence that although exposure overall did not seem to have much of a systematic effect on attitudes toward gender equality, exposure is strongly correlated with different attitudes toward gender equality in subcategories of the post-communist population. Moreover, for most of our moderating factors, this effect is as we expected: factors expected to trigger resistance lead to additional years of exposure to communism being associated with decreasing support for gender equality. Conversely, in countries scoring high on intensifying factors, communist exposure is largely not associated with lower support for gender equality. To be clear, in only two categories do we actually find additional years of exposure to communism associated with more of a pro–gender equality outlook—countries with very low pre-communist literacy and patrimonial peripheral regimes (and to a lesser extent low pre-communist wealth)—but the direction of the heterogeneity is mostly in the expected direction.

---

[17]This should not be too surprising, as the two categories have a good deal of overlap (as they do with pre-communist wealth, which also produces similar results in Figure 7.2).

7.4.2. Individual-Level Moderators of Exposure Intensity and Resistance and Attitudes toward Gender Equality

Turning to our individual level moderators in Figure 7.3, we again find a number of expected effects, although with different patterns from the previous chapters.

Beginning with religion, we continue to observe statistically significant evidence of Catholic resistance against exposure effects (p<.001), this time accompanied by Protestants (albeit with less statistical confidence, p<.10). But just to reiterate, more resistance here means that each additional year of exposure to communism is accompanied by *less* support for gender equality. For Muslims and the Eastern Orthodox (who start at *lower* levels of support for gender equality than Catholics or Protestants),[18] in contrast, an additional year of exposure to communism has no real effect on attitudes toward gender equality. Church attendance also appears to have provided some resistance against the communist gender equality message, though the difference is just on the border of conventional measures of statistical significance; moreover, there are no significant exposure differences once we distinguished between religous attendance by different denominations.

Moving to education, we see a new pattern: a very strong distinction between less than primary education and everyone who received at least a primary education. In a way mirroring the finding for highly illiterate pre-communist countries, we find that individuals with the lowest levels of education were the most likely to have *increased* support for gender equality associated with each additional year of exposure for communism, although like Muslims and Eastern Orthodox, the least educated start with a much lower baseline level of support for gender equality (see electronic appendix).[19]

When we look at the effect of residence, for the first time we do not see the predicted more intense effect of exposure on urban residents. Indeed, in this case it is rural residents for whom exposure is more in line with regime ideology, although the difference is small and far from statistically significant.

Perhaps the most surprising effect in the entire set of analyses, however, can be found in the last pairing on Figure 7.3. Here we find two completely different effects for men and women. Again, men—like the less educated, Muslims, and Eastern Orthodox—with no exposure to communism have

---

[18] See the regression results in the corresponding table in the electronic appendix.

[19] Those who have not completed primary education and have no exposure to communism start have a roughly 2/3, 1/2, and 1/3 of a standard deviation lower score on the gender equality index than those with higher, secondary, and primary education completed, respectively.

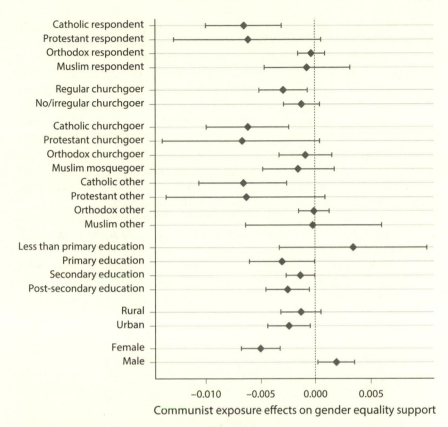

Figure 7.3. Communist Exposure and Gender Equality Support: Individual Moderators

This figure reports the marginal effects on gender equality support of a single year of exposure to communism in different types of individuals. The results indicate negative communist exposure effects among Catholics and Protestants and among regular churchgoers as well as among post-communist citizens with at least primary education. The most striking finding is that communist exposure leads to stronger support for gender equality among men but to weaker support among women in post-communist countries. In interpreting the substantive size of these effects it is important to keep in mind that the median number of years of exposure to communism in the analyses that produced this figure was 28 years, while the 90th percentile was 55 years for a resident of the former Soviet Union and 45 years for a resident of East-Central Europe.

much lower (by more than half a standard deviation of the index) support for gender equality than women do. However, for each additional year of exposure to communism women become *less* supportive of gender equality and men become *more* supportive. In other words, communist exposure makes women less feminist but men less sexist. We can make some sense of this finding from within the rhetoric versus reality framework. If men did indeed come into contact with more regime rhetoric than women, then we might expect them to be relatively more susceptible to incorporating that rhetoric than women. Concurrently, women might naturally be more supportive of gender equality than men, but years of exposure to the reality of communism may have undermined that somewhat, perhaps because state controlled women's movements in the communist bloc largely steered clear of the more assertive feminism adopted by women's organizations in parts of the non-communist world. And to be clear, the model still predicts that even with the full Eastern European dose of exposure to communism (45 years), women would still on average have a .17 higher score on the gender equality index than men.[20]

Overall, even though, unlike in the preceding three chapters, exposure to communism did not have a clear average effect on attitudes toward gender equality, we do find interesting patterns for the effect of exposure when we interact it with the *intensifying* and *resistance* variables. Thus *living through communism*—in some countries, and for some individuals—does seem to have had an effect on attitudes toward gender equality, albeit in a much less consistent way than doing so did in terms of attitudes toward democracy, markets, or social welfare.

7.5. DIFFERENTIAL COMMUNIST EXPOSURE TIMING EFFECTS FOR WOMEN VERSUS MEN

The two most striking findings in the preceding two sections have been the differential effects of early versus adult communist exposure and the uneven impact of exposure to communist rule on the gender equality support of women versus men. While these results are interesting in and of themselves, they nevertheless raise a few additional questions about the sources of this heterogeneity. What aspects of communist exposure triggered these different effects on men and women? Did these differences originate in early communist exposure, or did they only develop once communist citizens entered adulthood?

To answer these questions, we present the results of an extension of our analysis in the preceding two sections. The empirical setup is very similar to the one in the last set of interactions from Figure 7.3—it uses constrained regressions on data for the ex-communist countries from the second through fifth waves of the World Values Survey to explain varia-

---

[20] According to the model, 76 years of exposure would be needed to eliminate the difference altogether, which, ironically enough, is still more than the time from the 1917 Bolshevik revolution until the dissolution of the Soviet Union at the end of 1991.

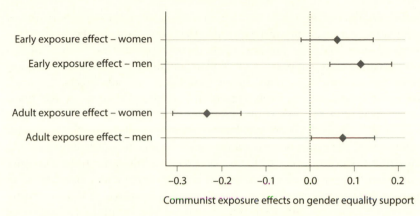

Communist exposure effects on gender equality support

Figure 7.4. Communist Exposure, Sex, and Gender Equality Support
This figure reports the effects of early and adult communist exposure on gender
equality support for women and men. Early exposure is measured as the number
of years between the ages of 6 and 17 that a respondent has lived in a communist
country and the reported effects correspond to a 12-year difference in exposure
(corresponding to a change from the 5th to the 95th percentile of respondents in
the sample). Adult exposure is measured as the number of years after the age of
18 that a respondent has lived in a communist country and the reported effects
correspond to a 44-year difference in exposure (corresponding to a change from
the 5th to the 95th percentile of respondents in the sample, and equivalent to the
full exposure to communism of a resident of an Eastern European ex-communist
country). The results in the top part of the figure suggest that early communist
exposure promoted greater support for gender equality among both women and
men, but the effects were stronger for men. The lower part of the figure suggests
that adult communist exposure moderately promoted gender equality among men
but significantly undermined it among women.

tions in the three-item gender equality index—but now we interact the
respondent's sex with both his or her early and adult communist exposure. This setup allows us to estimate separate early and adult communist
socialization effects for both men and women. The results are once again
presented in graphical form in Figure 7.4, while the full results are available in the electronic appendix. The one difference compared to Figures 7.2
and 7.3 is that the exposure effects are not the marginal effects of one
year, but instead represent the equivalent of the difference between the
5th and the 95th percentile in early exposure (12 years) and adult exposure (44 years).[21]

---

[21] While this is a broader percentile range than typically used in presenting substantive effects, we chose it because these differences are substantively more meaningful than comparisons for the 10th and the 90th percentile. Thus, 12 years of early exposure is the difference

The results in Figure 7.4 offer a more nuanced picture of the drivers of the heterogeneous communist exposure effects on women and men from the former Soviet bloc. The top part of the panel suggests that both boys and girls became more supportive of gender equality as a result of being exposed to communist regimes during childhood and adolescence, though the effects were substantively larger and statistically stronger for boys/young men than for girls/young women.[22] However, while the divergent communist exposure effects may have started to develop during childhood/adolescence, the real contrast occurs with respect to adult exposure. As shown in the bottom part of Figure 7.4, while adult communist exposure continued to have an (albeit somewhat weaker) pro–gender equality effect on men, for women the effects were significantly negative and substantively quite large (about one-quarter of a standard deviation in the DV for those receiving the full dose of adult communist exposure in Eastern Europe).[23]

Taken together, these findings suggest two important qualifications to our earlier findings in Table 7.3 and Figure 7.3. First, while the positive effects of early communist exposure on gender equality support are fairly similar for both sexes, the negative effects of adult communist exposure are driven exclusively by the fact that such exposure weakened feminist attitudes among women rather than by promoting sexist attitudes among men. Second, the negative overall impact of socialization on the gender equality support of Eastern European women is due to experiences during adulthood, which implies that it should have limited effects among the younger generations.

7.6. COMMUNIST EDUCATION AND ATTITUDES TOWARD GENDER EQUALITY

Perhaps one of the most interesting differences between the findings in the previous section and the trends from earlier chapters is that unlike for other types of attitudes, support for gender equality was affected more strongly by *early* rather than *adult* communist exposure. While this find-

---

between having lived all vs. none of one's life between ages of 6–17 in a communist country, while 44 years corresponds roughly to the maximum adult communist exposure for citizens of post–World War II Eastern European communist regimes.

[22] The difference in female vs. male early exposure effects fell just short of being statistically significant (.11 two-tailed).

[23] Furthermore, separate tests for the three components of the gender index (results available in the electronic appendix) indicate that the negative effects of adult communist exposure on women were very similar with respect to support for female political leaders, gender equality in labor markets, and higher education access.

ing is in line with our theoretical discussion about the tension between rhetoric and reality as well as the contrast between genuine communist progress in educating girls and women and the persistence of significant gender inequality in other areas of society, it nevertheless raises some interesting questions about the mechanisms through which this seemingly effective early socialization occurred. Therefore, in this section we briefly address what is one of the most obvious candidates for explaining this pattern: the nature of communist education.[24] Given the earlier socialization findings and the tension between egalitarian rhetoric and the unequal reality of everyday life, we expect the effects of communist education to be more egalitarian the further it is removed from that adult reality, that is, we predict more egalitarian effects for primary and possibly secondary education than for higher education.

Of course, the question is what to use as a counterfactual for assessing the effects of communist education. One possibility would be to judge it against similar types of education in non-communist countries, that is, to compare two people with otherwise similar demographic backgrounds and from otherwise comparable countries with the only difference being that one of them attended secondary school in a communist country, while the other attended it in a non-communist country. However, to disentangle the effects of education from those of other types of communist socialization, such tests would have to control for the length of communist exposure of different individuals. The other option, which sidesteps the concerns about cross-national comparisons, would be to compare individuals from within the former Soviet bloc but to compare the impact of getting a secondary education under communism to that of a secondary education received during either the pre-communist or the post-communist periods. Since once again we need to include communist exposure and age in our models, we ran these tests using the same constrained regression approach we employed for the tests in the previous sections.

In terms of data, we draw on the WVS surveys, but rather than coding the highest educational achievement for any given respondent, we combined the schooling data with information about the respondent's age and country of origin to create a different set of education measures that capture the regime under which a respondent attended different levels of schooling. More specifically, for each respondent from a post-communist country we coded (dichotomously) whether he or she had attended each of three types of education (primary, secondary, and post-secondary) in each of three distinct periods (pre-communist, communist, and non-communist). Note that the resulting nine dummy variables are neither mutually exclusive (since an individual could have attended primary school under both

---

[24] See as well the discussion of this point in Chapter 2, Section 2.3.4.

Table 7.4. Communist Education and Gender Equality Support

	(1)	(2)	(3)	(4)
Pre-communist education	−.044			
	(.043)			
Communist education	.219**		.308**	
	(.028)		(.038)	
Post-communist education	.056**			
	(.017)			
Non-communist education			.212**	
			(.024)	
Pre-communist primary education		−.039		
		(.044)		
Communist primary education		.126**		.217**
		(.028)		(.036)
Post-communist primary education		.071*		
		(.033)		
Pre-communist secondary education		.128*		
		(.061)		
Communist secondary education		.158**		.165**
		(.021)		(.028)
Post-communist secondary education		.084**		
		(.020)		
Pre-communist higher education		.270**		
		(.095)		
Communist higher education		.138**		.170**
		(.021)		(.026)
Post-communist higher education		.126**		
		(.025)		
Non-communist primary education				.148**
				(.023)
Non-communist secondary education				.145**
				(.017)
Non-communist higher education				.164**
				(.014)
Post-communist citizen			−.361*	−.364*
			(.157)	(.160)
Total communist exposure	−.002*	−.001	.001	−.000
	(.001)	(.001)	(.001)	(.001)
Age	−.002	−.002	−.006**	−.004**
	(.000)	(.000)	(.001)	(.001)

Table 7.4. (*continued*)

	(1)	(2)	(3)	(4)
Year dummies	Yes	Yes	Yes	Yes
Other demographic controls	Yes	Yes	Yes	Yes
Pre-communist controls	Yes	Yes	Yes	Yes
Sample	PC	PC	All	All
Observations	52,172	52,172	215,826	215,826

Note: This table demonstrates communist education is associated with greater support for gender equity, and that this effect is for the most part concentrated in the lower educational tiers. The dependent variable is an index of three questions—one on whether men make better political leaders than women, one on whether university education is more important for a boy than a girl, and one on whether men should be more entitled to a job than women when jobs are scarce—standardized to a mean of 0 and a standard deviation of 1. The list of independent and control variables can be found in Table 3.1 of Chapter 3. Full regression results are in the electronic appendix. The data utilized in these analyses are from the 2nd, 3rd, 4th, and 5th waves of the World Values Survey. Robust standard errors in parentheses: ** p<.01, * p<.05, # p<.1.

pre-communism and communism), nor collectively exhaustive (since individuals without any education would score 0 on all measures and thus represent the excluded category when interpreting the results). Based on these indicators we also created different combinations of categories, to capture whether an individual had attended any schooling in a given regime, and, for the regressions on the full set of communist and non-communist countries, we combined pre-communist and post-communist education in a non-communist category to allow for comparisons with non-communist countries.

The results in Table 7.4 largely confirm that communist education had a stronger pro–gender equality effect than non-communist education; note that this comes out of both our intra-regional (Models 1 and 2) and inter-regional (Models 3 and 4) analyses. The contrast is particularly clear when we restrict our focus to the inter-temporal comparison of education in the former Soviet bloc: thus, judging by the results in Model 1, while respondents with at least some communist education received a significant and reasonably large gender equality boost (equivalent to a quarter of a standard deviation), the effects were only about a quarter as large for post-communist education and had an insignificant anti-egalitarian effect for those with pre-communist education. The pattern is confirmed in Model 3 (which includes all the respondents from both post-communist and non-post-communist countries), where we find that while both communist and non-communist education had a positive impact on support for gender equality (compared to the baseline of no education), the effects were about 50% larger for those educated under communism, and the difference between the coefficients is statistically significant.[25]

In Models 2 (only post-communist respondents) and 4 (all respondents) we differentiate education by both regime and level of education. While the results are somewhat noisier,[26] they do provide some support for our expectation that the gender equality boost of communist education would be largely concentrated in the lower educational tiers. Thus, according to Model 2, the impact of communist primary education is substantively larger and statistically stronger than for both pre-communist and post-communist primary education, and the difference in coefficients is statistically significant (at .002 one-tailed) compared to the former and marginally significant (at .09 one-tailed) compared to the latter. Model 2 also suggests that communist secondary education had more egalitarian effects than either pre- or post-communist secondary education, though in this case the difference in coefficients was only significant vis-à-vis the latter. By contrast, even though communist higher education had a positive and significant effect (compared to the reference group of someone without any education), this effect was no stronger than for non-communist higher education.[27] The global comparison in Model 4 confirms that communist primary education was more conducive to gender equality than its non-communist equivalent (and the difference was marginally significant at .05 one-tailed), but this boost did not extend to either secondary or higher education.

Overall, the results of this additional analysis confirm the broad socialization patterns associated with *living through communism* that we identified in Section 7.4 whereby the ideological commitment of communist regimes to greater gender equality was matched by reality only during the early years of the lives of its citizens, during which the massive strides toward ensuring gender equality in education were reflected in the attitu-

---

[25]It is important to note that a post-communist citizen with no education, though, would be over one-quarter of a standard deviation lower on the gender equality index than a commensurate citizen of a non-post-communist country with no education (see the coefficient on the post-communist citizen dummy variable in Model 3). So while the pro–gender equality boost is larger from a communist than non-communist education, the difference in the size of this boost only makes up about a quarter of the original gap in support for gender equality.

[26]This may be due in part to there being relatively few respondents in some of the categories (such as respondents with pre-communist secondary and higher education or respondents with post-communist primary education).

[27]Moreover, it was actually weaker than for those with pre-communist higher education. That being said, people with pre-communist higher education make up less than 0.5% of our respondents from post-communist countries.

dinal effects of individuals exposed to the school system. However, these gender-egalitarian effects of communist education were already somewhat weaker during secondary education and disappeared completely for higher education, a pattern that mirrors the weaker (and even reversed) impact of adult communist exposure.

7.6. CONCLUSIONS

In this chapter, we examined attitudes toward gender equality as our fourth issue area for assessing the effect of communist legacies. We did so fully acknowledging that compared to the previous three areas—support for democracy, markets, and the welfare state—there was a much greater disconnect between rhetoric in favor of gender equality and reality, which was quite a bit more complicated, as well as the fact that we were moving into an area that was less central to communist ideology and (likely) less popular among the citizenry (especially compared to welfare benefits).

Nevertheless, the baseline finding from our initial examinations of the raw data, the bivariate analyses, and just about all our *living in a post-communist country* analysis was still somewhat surprising: not only were we unable to find any evidence of a "pro–gender equality" attitudinal differential in post-communist countries, but we quite often found exactly the opposite. To the extent that post-communist citizens held different attitudes toward gender equality from those of citizens elsewhere, they were likely to be *less*, not more, supportive of gender equality. This was particularly the case when controlling for historical effects (such as where communism took root), economic conditions, socioeconomic development patterns, and the fact that communism featured rule by left-wing governments.

At the same time, however, we did find some evidence that the effect of communist education may have played a role in inculcating pro–gender equality views in line with communist rhetoric. Two sets of findings point in this direction. First, unlike in previous chapters, we found that early communist exposure led to greater gender equality support, but adult exposure did not. This was the first time we observed this pattern, which is in line with the idea of schools shaping the development of a particular attitude. Second, in Section 7.5, we examined the direct effect of communist education on pro–gender equality attitudes and did indeed find that *communist education* had a larger effect on gender equality support than either pre-communist or post-communist education (when looking within post-communist countries) or than non-communist education (when comparing with non-communist countries). Moreover, when contrasting different levels of communist education to their non-communist counterparts, it is primary education that seems to have the strongest pro–gender equality effect.

Why is this important? We argued at the beginning of the chapter that the one place where communist rhetoric in support of gender equality matched reality was likely to be in the educational sphere, and, within the educational sphere, probably most clearly at lower levels of education, where girls were educated on a par with boys. In other words, while the overall effects of communist socialization on gender equality were at odds with the official discourse and less central to the communist project, communism left the expected attitudinal imprint in the one area where reality most closely reflected rhetorical commitments: primary education. While far from the last word on the matter, these findings do suggest that actions speak louder than words when it comes to communist-era legacies due to *living through communism*. Simply being a tenet of communist ideology may not be enough to create a legacy effect if that guiding principle is not reflected in reality. Clearly, communist societies were less democratic, featured more centralized economic planning, and more state-provided social welfare than most of their non-communist counterparts. Whether these societies were actually more hospitable toward women, however, varied greatly across different societal spheres, and our findings do indeed reflect this difference.

CHAPTER 8

■ ■ ■ ■ ■

Temporal Resilience and Change

An American, a Russian, and a Romanian are sitting at breakfast talking about their dreams.

The American says: "I had the worst nightmare last night. I dreamt that it was 2030, I turned on NBC, and they had a report on the record corn crop at some kolhoz in Indiana."

The Russian responds: "My dream was even worse. I dreamt that it was 2030, and I turned on Russian TV, and I couldn't even understand anything because the whole news report was in Chinese."

The Romanian chimes in: "But I had the worst nightmare of all. I also dreamt that it was 2030, and I turned on Romanian TV, and there was Ceauşescu giving a speech to some guys in a factory!"

—Romanian joke, late 1980s

8.1. INTRODUCTION

The preceding four chapters have revealed significant attitudinal differences between citizens of post-communist and non-communist countries on a number of crucial political and economic issues during the first two decades after the collapse of Eastern European and Soviet communism. Moreover, despite important variations across different types of countries and individuals, we have consistently found substantively and statistically significant effects of individual exposure to communist regimes on attitudes toward democracy, markets, and social welfare (as well as a more nuanced set of findings regarding gender equality). The relative stability of this result reinforces the idea that despite its ultimate geopolitical and ideological defeat, communism left a lasting legacy not only in institutional terms but also in the hearts and minds of its former subjects.

Nonetheless, our analysis up to this point has largely identified average attitudinal effects over the first twenty years of transition without addressing the temporal dynamics of public opinion during a particularly tumultuous period of Eastern European and Eurasian history. This has followed from our decision to conduct primarily pooled analysis of all our data, although we have always controlled for the year of the survey. While there were good theoretical reasons to ground our analyses in this manner, doing so leaves many interesting questions unanswered. There- fore, in this final empirical chapter we address what is perhaps the most important follow-up question raised by our analysis so far: how tempo- rally resilient are the attitudinal effects of the communist socialization project and of communist regimes more broadly? Put another way: are the effects we have identified in the previous chapters largely constant over time or do they vary in meaningful ways as time passes?

The answers to these questions are important from a number of dif- ferent perspectives. Perhaps most obviously, they can contribute to the ongoing debates in the literature about the end of the transition and the continued theoretical relevance of the "post-communist" label and im- plicitly about the raison d'être of post-communist studies as a political science subfield.[1] Along the lines of Shleifer and Treisman's (2004, 2014) argument about the normalization of ex-communist countries, for our purposes we may ask at what point we can consider post-communist citizens "normal," not in some normative or clinical sense, but rather in the sense of holding political attitudes that are indistinguishable from those held by citizens of developmentally comparable countries.[2] From this perspective our analysis has the advantage of offering an objective criterion for judging whether normalization is occurring and if so how quickly.

The analysis in this chapter also contributes to broader debates about the dynamics of political socialization by bringing evidence from the post- communist transition to bear on questions about the durability of par- ticular socialization episodes and the interaction between prior social- ization and subsequent political shocks/aging processes (Krosnick and Alwin 1989; Visser and Krosnick 1998; Sears and Valentino 1997; Prior 2010; D. Osborne et al. 2011). By looking at the temporal evolution of post-communist legacies in Eastern Europe and Eurasia, we can begin to assess the extent to which the timing of socialization affects its durability, thereby testing the importance of the "impressionable years" highlighted by the literature on partisanship formation in the United States. Further- more, our focus on a variety of different political attitudes lends itself to testing the extent to which socialization is uniformly resilient across issue

---

[1] See, e.g., Nodia (2000); Bernhard and Jasiewicz (2015); Ekiert (2015); Hozić (2015); Kubik (2015), Pop-Eleches (2015); and Tucker (2015).

[2] To reiterate points made in the introductory chapter, this would not necessarily mean that in the aggregate attitudes would be identical in post-communist countries to attitudes elsewhere, but rather that attitudes would be a function of characteristics such as demo- graphics, politics, and economics in the same way as elsewhere.

areas, or whether certain attitudes remain more deeply ingrained than others. For example, are attitudes toward more concrete issues affecting everyday life (such as the availability of welfare services) more or less malleable than more abstract questions about political regimes? Similarly, are attitudes about areas in which there was a consistency across rhetoric and action (e.g., social welfare provision) more durable than those where the rhetoric was more divorced from reality (e.g., gender equality)? Finally, the significant variation in post-communist economic and political trajectories among the countries of the former Eastern bloc offers a fascinating opportunity for testing how the resilience of communist socialization patterns is affected by the nature and magnitude of subsequent attitudinal shocks. For example, are people more likely to hang on to the anti-market ideology of communism in countries where the post-communist transition to a market economy has been particularly painful? Conversely, do the effects of communist socialization disappear in ex-communist countries with successful transitions to market economies? The answers to these questions are not only interesting in their own right for our understanding of post-communist politics, but also allow us to test the scope conditions of our findings about the continued importance of communist attitudinal legacies.

8.2. THEORETICAL EXPECTATIONS

While a full-fledged theory of the temporal evolution of communist attitudinal legacies and the durability of political socialization effects more broadly would go far beyond the scope of the theoretical arguments laid out in Chapters 1 and 2 of this book, we of course want to have some theoretical grounding for our discussion of the temporal evolution of post-communist attitudes. We therefore introduce three heuristics for thinking about the different types of factors that we would expect to shape the resilience of post-communist exceptionalism in political attitudes, which we will call the "fleeting legacies," "generational replacement," and "temporary divergence" models. Or, to put it more concretely, in the first model there is a gap initially but it disappears fairly quickly, in the second model it persists as long as there are people alive socialized under communism, and in the final model the size of the gap may even *increase* in size, at least initially.

Given our findings in earlier chapters, our starting point for this discussion is the fact that with the partial exception of gender equality attitudes, we have found that the political views of post-communist citizens were visibly shaped by exposure to communist rule in the sense that—at least on average—they were less supportive of markets and democracy and more supportive of welfare states than their non-communist counter-parts, and these effects were more pronounced for individuals who had lived longer under communist regimes.

Given that for much of the extant literature the primary question related to the temporal resilience of communist legacies has been when rather than whether communist legacies would cease to matter (e.g., Shleifer and Treisman 2004; Bernhard and Jasiewicz 2015; Pop-Eleches 2015) we begin by discussing two stylized models of attitudinal convergence. The first model, which we will call the *fleeting legacies* model, assumes the half-life of individual communist socialization to be fairly short and therefore predicts a fairly rapid convergence of both ex-communist countries to the rest of the world (i.e., the "normalization" hypothesis) and a fairly quick attitudinal convergence across individuals with different degrees of communist exposure within ex-communist countries. The most straightforward theoretical justification of such an expectation would be the collapse of the communist ideological project in the last decade (or more) of communist rule, which paved the way for the ideological domination of economic neoliberalism starting in the late 1980s (Williamson 1990) and the growing sense of liberal democracy as "the only game in town" in the 1990s.[3]

Alternatively—and possibly in combination with the first view—we may have expected to see a gradual weakening of the common Leninist legacies following from the significant and highly heterogeneous economic political shocks experienced by post-communist citizens (at both the individual and the country levels). Given that the trajectories of part of the region—driven by the dynamics of Western integration—moved fairly quickly in the direction of (albeit fragile and imperfect) market economies, liberal democracies, and economic recovery while other ex-communist countries struggled with new forms of authoritarianism, hybrid economic systems, and poor economic performance (Hellman 1998; Frye 2002; Vachudova 2005; Pop-Eleches 2007), it seems reasonable to expect economic and political attitudes to reflect increasingly these new post-communist realities rather than an increasingly distant shared communist past.[4] Note, however, that from this perspective, we may expect

[3] To be sure, both of these effects weaken as one moves from Central Europe further east through the Caucasus region and Central Asia, especially in terms of liberal democracy. Moreover, given recent events in the post–Great Recession era in terms of the rise of populism throughout Europe and the United States, we might expect both of these effects to now be weakening generally as well. This, of course, remains a subject for future research requiring analysis of data beyond what we have collected for this book.

[4] Note that even though in Chapters 4–7 we have found post-communist economic conditions and political institutions to have a fairly modest overall effect in explaining post-communist exceptionalism, such average effects could theoretically mask heterogeneous

to see greater heterogeneity in the half-life of communist legacies, and, in particular, we should expect post-communist exceptionalism to persist longer in countries whose post-communist economic and political performance has been more disappointing.[5]

The second post-communist attitudinal convergence model, which we will call the *generational replacement* model, relaxes the assumption of diminishing individual socialization effects. According to this framework, even if communist socialization efforts produced lasting effects on the individuals subjected to them, we should expect former communist countries to converge gradually to the attitudinal patterns of non-communist countries through a generational replacement process, whereby older generations with stronger communist mentalities are gradually replaced by new generations born shortly before or even after the fall of communism. While such a process should still be detectable with our data (especially given the declining life expectancy in many ex-communist countries), complete convergence would obviously take several decades, and could be further delayed to the extent that the type of intergenerational attitude transmission discussed in Chapters 5 and 6 is sufficiently strong. Moreover, under such a scenario, we would expect to see very limited convergence among different age cohorts within the countries of the former communist bloc: whereas the older generations are "stuck" in their old mentalities, the youngest generations with limited or no direct communist exposure should be very different from their parents and grandparents and at the same time be virtually indistinguishable from their non-communist counterparts. Obviously these trends will also be attenuated to the extent that intergenerational transmission is fairly effective.

The third (and final) model questions the very assumption of post-communist "normalization" and allows for the possibility that (at least for a while) the effects of communist socialization could *increase* over time. We will refer to this scenario as the *temporary divergence* model in order to highlight (a) that the gap is getting larger (i.e., attitudes are diverging as opposed to converging) and that (b) we expect this effect to eventually reverse (i.e., that is, it will be temporary in nature).[6] While a systematic theory (and empirical test) of the psychological and political

---

temporal effects, with communist legacies mattering greatly at the outset but vanishing after a few years.

[5] Relatedly, we may expect individuals who have fared poorly during the post-communist period, i.e., transitional losers, to be more likely to hang on to political preferences linked to the communist regimes (e.g., Tucker 2006).

[6] On one level, this is purely definitional: attitudes cannot diverge forever without hitting some sort of ceiling effect. However, we intend this in a slightly stronger way—such that we expect the dynamics of transition to result in the divergence coming to a close eventually— for reasons we lay out in the rest of the paragraph.

underpinnings of this phenomenon is beyond the scope of our efforts here, we can test for observable implications of this framework. The logic of this model can be summarized as follows: despite the shortcomings of the ideological appeal of communism in the late-communist period, the widespread disappointment with the economic trauma of the post-communist transition, characterized by deep recessions, growing inequality, and collapsing welfare states, created the political context for an ideological reassessment of communism. To the extent that this reevaluation happens fairly uniformly across different cohorts—perhaps because of a strong elite-driven communist nostalgia discourse at the national level (Ganev 2014)—then we should expect to see a significant growth in country-level post-communist exceptionalism, combined with a relatively constant difference across age cohorts (as a function of the length of personal communist exposure).

Alternatively, however, it is conceivable that this reevaluation could be concentrated among particular groups, either because the communist nostalgia discourse resonates more strongly with individuals who experienced more extensive personal communist socialization, or because certain groups suffered disproportionately during the post-communist transition and therefore embraced communist values as part of a straightforward "retrospective pocketbook" logic. Given that the individuals affected by the latter scenario have tended to be disproportionately older, both of these dynamics should be expected to have similar observable implications from the perspective of our analysis, in the sense that they should lead to a rather sharp polarization of political attitudes across different age cohorts within the former communist countries.

While our primary goal in this chapter is to establish empirically which of these three models best describes the public opinion patterns during the first two decades of the post-communist transition, it is nevertheless worth noting that based on our discussion of particular attitudes in earlier chapters, we can formulate some tentative hypotheses about which models we would expect to apply in particular issue areas. Thus, given our discussion in Chapter 7 about the ambiguous communist legacy vis-à-vis gender equality questions, combined with the fact that gender issues have generally not figured prominently in the communist nostalgia discourse of the last two decades, we should expect the rapid convergence patterns of the *fleeting legacies* model to apply most clearly to post-communist gender equality attitudes.

At the other extreme, given the much greater consistency between communist rhetoric and reality vis-à-vis welfare state services, we expect communist socialization to have been much more effective—and therefore more resilient—in this area, which should translate into a longer half-life of post-communist exceptionalism. The strong effects of personal exposure in Chapter 6 (Table 6.3) imply that pro–welfare state attitudes should be more pronounced among the older cohorts, and these differences were probably exacerbated by the lack of economic opportunities—and hence the higher reliance on welfare state support—among the older post-communist cohorts. What is less clear is to what extent younger generations would still be affected by the communist attitudinal imprint: on the one hand, the analysis in Chapter 6 suggests that the higher post-communist support for welfare states also applied to younger individuals with more limited personal experiences with communist welfare states. Furthermore, the analysis of unemployment attitudes in Hungary in Chapter 6 revealed significant cross-generational transmission of welfare state preferences, which is likely to reduce cross-generational differences and to extend the half-life of communist-era pro–welfare state preferences. On the other hand, pro–welfare state socialization may have been shallower among the younger cohorts, which, combined with the greater economic opportunities during the post-communist transition, could lead to a shorter half-life of communist legacies.

Based on our earlier analysis, we expect attitudes toward markets to be characterized by fairly significant cohort differences within the former communist countries: thus, given the strong anti-market effect of personal communist exposure, older generations should be considerably more hostile toward markets than post-communist citizens born shortly before (or even after) the fall of communism. Moreover, as in the case of welfare state preferences, these differences are likely to be exacerbated by the fact that in general younger individuals were more likely to benefit from the opportunities created by capitalism and less likely to suffer from its downsides than their parents and grandparents, particularly during the steep economic decline of the early post-communist period. From this perspective, the *temporary divergence* model seems to be a promising candidate for capturing the temporal dynamics of attitudes toward markets, especially with respect to attitudinal differences across cohorts. On the other hand, the abject failure of communist command economies during their final two decades (Kornai 1992) arguably meant that the communist ideological dictums about the inherent inferiority of market economies were probably less persuasive and therefore anti-market convictions should be less ideologically resilient than welfare state preferences. As a result, as the post-communist capitalist systems started to stabilize and even grow, their (albeit unevenly distributed) benefits may have started to reverse the anti-market ideological shock of the early transition years and should therefore contribute to a gradual convergence of market attitudes among post-communist citizens (along the lines of the fleeting legacies model). However, the strength of this rebound should vary considerably across both countries and individuals, depending on the strength of the recovery and how widely its benefits are distributed.

Finally, we expect the temporal dynamics of democratic attitudes to be fairly similar to those vis-à-vis markets. This expectation is based on the fact that—as in the case of markets—the ideological appeal of communist "people's democracies" was not particularly strong but the region's largely disappointing early post-communist political trajectory, marked by growing corruption, considerable political instability (including violent conflict), and weak democratic representation, may have provided—at least in the early transition years—additional ideological credibility to communist nostalgia arguments about the putative political advantages of communist regimes over Western-style democracies. Moreover, to the extent that for many post-communist citizens the concepts of markets and democracy were closely intertwined for a variety of reasons (see, e.g., Bunce 1998; Fish 1997; Kitschelt 1992), democratic attitudes were likely also affected by some of the same generational dynamics discussed above with respect to markets, with older cohorts turning more anti-democratic than their younger compatriots as a result of their disaffection with the post-communist transition and the resonance between this experience and their prior communist political socialization. However, by the same token, we expect this initial divergence in democratic attitudes (across both cohorts and countries) to give way to a gradual convergence in subsequent years, owing to a combination of generational replacement and—possibly—some degree of pro-democratic "updating" as at least some of the region's economies and political systems started to function more effectively.[7]

Before proceeding to our findings, one final methodological point is in order. To the extent that we are tracing the evolution of a gap in attitudes between post-communist citizens and those in other countries over time (e.g., Figures 8.1, 8.4)—as opposed to the change over time in our estimate of the effect of exposure to communism on post-communist citizens (e.g., Figures 8.2, 8.3)—it remains possible that the change is coming from the comparison category as opposed to post-communist citizens; that is, we could see the democracy gap shrink because people elsewhere are becom-

---

[7]Of course, this also implies that post 2008 there could be a similar anti-democratic updating as the region reacts to economic shocks associated with the Great Recession. However, any such analysis trying to test hypotheses related to this expectation would need to wrestle carefully with the question of whether such an updating represented a communist era legacy or, alternatively, represents a convergence with other non-post-communist countries having a similar reaction to a similar economic shock. While a very interesting—and important—subject for future research, it is again beyond the analysis of the current book.

ing less enamored with democracy, not because post-communist citizens are becoming more supportive.[8] Such a scenario would not invalidate our analysis in this chapter—since post-communist countries are no longer isolated from global political and economic trends, the fact that they eschew broader global attitudinal trends would still be worth investigating and could well be rooted in communist legacies—but it would affect our interpretation of the temporal evolution of the attitudinal gaps between ex-communist and non-communist countries. Therefore, we analyzed the temporal patterns of attitudes in the non-communist countries in our WWS sample. For two of the four attitudes—democracy and gender equality support—we found no clear temporal trend, so any temporal differences in the post-communist gap can be interpreted as being largely driven by attitudinal change in the ex-communist countries. For the other two attitudes, the temporal trends suggest a *decline* in market support and an *increase* in welfare state support among the citizens of non-communist countries, which means that our estimates of the persistence of communist anti-market and pro–welfare state attitudes in this chapter are—if anything—likely to be conservative.[9]

8.3. EMPIRICAL RESULTS

As a first step toward understanding the resilience of post-communist attitudinal legacies we employ the empirical setup from the baseline analyses used in Model 4 of the first table in Chapters 4–7—a cross-national sample using WVS data from 1989 to 2009 and controlling for pre-communist conditions and individual demographic indicators—but in addition to the dichotomous post-communist country indicator, we also included interaction terms between this variable and the year of the survey (as well as year squared, to capture nonlinear time trends).[10] While the full regression results are available in the electronic appendix, given the difficulty of interpreting quadratic interaction terms on the basis of regression coefficients, in our discussion of these (and subsequent) results we rely almost exclusively on the graphical illustration of the predicted

[8] We thank Timothy Frye for raising this point.

[9] Time will tell if these patterns hold post–Great Recession, but for now it is sufficient to note that any such changes should not effect the interpretation of the results presented in this chapter.

[10] Recall that the democracy questions were not asked in Wave 2 of the WVS, and therefore our democracy analysis begins in 1995. Readers will also note that none of the figures in this chapter contain estimates for 2008 and 2009; this is simply because there were too few surveys in these years to reliably calculate year-specific estimates.

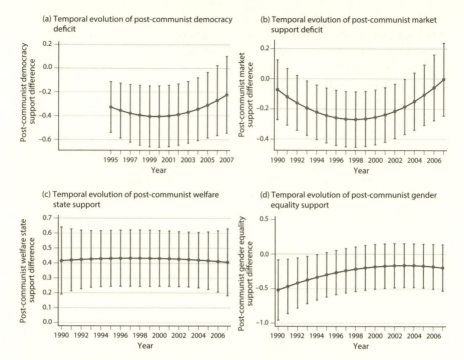

Figure 8.1. (a) Temporal Evolution of Post-communist Democracy Deficit;
(b) Temporal Evolution of Post-communist Market Support Deficit; (c) Temporal
Evolution of Post-communist Welfare State Support; (d) Temporal Evolution of
Post-communist Gender Equality Support

The four panels in this figure show the temporal evolution of the difference between post-communist and non-communist countries for the four types of political
attitudes discussed in Chapters 4–7. The first two panels show that for democracy
and market support, the size and statistical significance of the post-communist
exceptionalism increased until the late 1990s but then declined noticeably and was
no longer significant by 2007. The third panel shows a virtually unchanged and
substantively large post-communist surplus in support for the welfare state. The
fourth panel shows an initially significant post-communist deficit in support for
gender equality in the early 1990s, which gradually declined in substantive and
statistical significance over the first transition decade. For comparability, all dependent variables are standardized to have a mean of 0 and a standard deviation of 1.
All statistical models control for pre-communist country differences and individual
demographic characteristics. For full regression results, see the electronic appendix.

values of the four political attitude indicators we used in our earlier empirical chapters.

    Figure 8.1 illustrates the size of the gap between attitudes in post-
communist countries and non-communist countries by year (controlling
for pre-communist conditions and individual demographic indicators) on

our standardized scale where all indexes/indicators have a mean of 0 and a standard deviation of 1. The overall temporal patterns in the four figures are broadly in line with our theoretical expectations in the preceding section. Most strikingly, Figure 8.1c reveals that both the magnitude and the statistical significance of the pro–welfare state post-communist effect are virtually unchanged from 1990 to 2007. These findings confirm that at least on average the demand of post-communist citizens for a paternalist welfare state has been largely unaffected by the almost two decades of tumultuous post-communist transformations and highlight the resilience of the communist legacy in this respect.

By contrast, Figure 8.1d suggests that attitudes toward gender equality are compatible with either the *fleeting legacies* or the *generational replacement* model: an initially significant post-communist sexist bias in the early 1990s declines by roughly 60% over the course of the first transition decade and is no longer even close to statistical significance by the end of the 1990s. While this pattern confirms the more inconsistent communist stance on gender issues discussed in Chapter 7, it is worth noting briefly that the convergence trend seems to have largely stopped after 2000, and there is even some (admittedly weak) evidence of a renewed move in the direction of divergence by 2007. Moreover, the gender equality patterns show that rather than being completely irrelevant—as we may have concluded from the analysis in Table 7.1 in Chapter 7—communist legacies also affected gender equality attitudes, but the effects were more fleeting than for other indicators and are therefore washed out in the pooled analysis. Again, though, it is worth reiterating that the direction of this effect—while it lasted—was the *opposite* of what we originally expected based on communist rhetoric regarding gender equality, if not actual practices on the ground.

Finally, according to Figures 8.1a and 8.1b post-communist support for democracy and markets initially exhibited the type of pattern associated with the *temporary divergence model* discussed in the previous section. However, after bottoming out in the late 1990s, we notice a fairly significant convergence after 2000 for both democratic and market support, and by 2007 the post-communist exceptionalism was no longer significant at conventional levels. However, we should note that whereas for market support the post-communist effect had (at least on average) disappeared completely in 2007, the anti-democratic legacy of communism was somewhat more resilient, in the sense that by 2007 the deficit was only about a third smaller than in 1995, and was at least marginally significant at .10 (one-tailed). Nonetheless, for these two indicators of attitudes toward the two central elements of the post-communist economic and political transition, the cross-national survey evidence suggests that rather than experiencing a more or less rapid convergence to "normality," the political attitudes of former communist subjects initially underwent a radicalization process, before exhibiting the type of convergence predicted (implicitly or explicitly) by the transition paradigm.

Overall, the analysis so far suggests that post-communism—to the extent that we conceptualize it in terms of divergent average political and economic attitudes—seemed to be "over" with respect to market support,[11] and to a somewhat lesser extent for attitudes toward democracy and gender equality, but that the communist legacy of welfare state reliance had been largely unaffected by the first two decades of the post-communist transition. To understand the micro-dynamics of these aggregate patterns in greater detail, our next two sets of figures turn to the question of how the impact of personal communist exposure has changed over time since 1990. This approach can help us begin to understand the nature of the initial divergence process in support for markets and democracy. Moreover, it allows us to test whether the aggregate convergence trends with respect to gender equality in the 1990s and vis-à-vis markets and democracy after 2000 were driven primarily by generational replacement (as predicted by the *generational replacement* model) or reflect a weakening of communist socialization effects, and if so, whether these changes affected post-communist publics uniformly or were concentrated among particular age cohorts.

Figures 8.2a–d illustrate the results of Models 1–4 in related tables in the electronic appendix, which are based on the specifications of Model 1 in Tables 4.3–7.3 respectively, but in addition to the demographic and precommunist controls also include an interaction term between the years of communist exposure (after age six) and survey year and year squared (to allow for nonlinear temporal effects). The results confirm patterns from the earlier country-level comparisons, in that they once again show different temporal evolutions for different political attitudes.

However, the temporal trends in individual exposure also add a number of interesting nuances to the earlier analysis. Perhaps the most striking difference is with respect to the comparison between democracy and market support: whereas in Figures 8.1a and 8.1b we had found that the average (negative) post-communist country effect had been somewhat more resilient for democratic support, the situation is reversed for individual exposure effects. Thus, even though for both indicators the effects of exposure declined by about 50% from around 1997 to 2007, for market support exposure continues to be statistically significant even by the end of our study period, whereas for democracy the effect is both substan-

---

[11] Or at least was over prior to the advent of the 2007–8 global economic crisis. Whether it returned following the crisis is an important subject for future research.

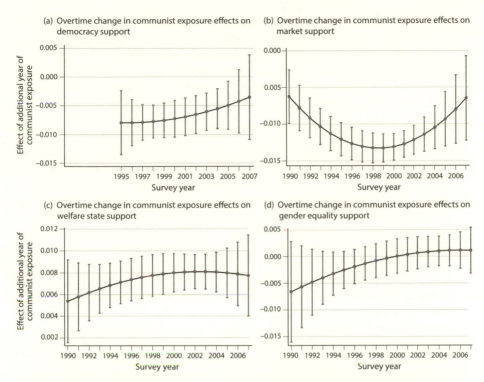

Figure 8.2. (a) Over-Time Change in Communist Exposure Effects on Democracy; (b) Over-Time Change in Communist Exposure Effects on Market Support; (c) Over-Time Change in Communist Exposure Effects on Welfare State Support; (d) Over-Time Change in Communist Exposure Effects on Gender Equality Support

The four panels in this figure show the temporal evolution of a year of personal communist exposure for the four types of political attitudes discussed in Chapters 4–7. The top left panel shows that for democracy support, the size and statistical significance of the communist exposure effects declined gradually after the mind-1990s and were no longer significant by 2008. According to the top right panel exposure effects on market support increased until the late 1990s but then declined noticeably, though they were still significant by 2008. The bottom left panel shows an initially increasing and then largely stable positive exposure effect on support for the welfare state. The bottom right panel shows an initially noticeable but statistically insignificant negative exposure effect on support for gender equality in the early 1990s, which completely disappeared by 2000. For comparability, all dependent variables are standardized to have a mean of 0 and a standard deviation of 1. All statistical models control for precommunist country differences and individual demographic characteristics. For full regression results, see the electronic appendix.

tively weaker[12] and statistically insignificant by 2007. In other words, it appears that exposure effects on market attitudes, which had been stronger than for democracy even at the height of divergence around 1996–98, continued to be more pronounced a decade later. Moreover, the effects of the initial divergence/radicalization are much clearer in Figure 8.2b, where we can see that the overall growth in the post-communist anti-market bias in Figure 8.1b was accompanied by a roughly twofold increase in the effects of communist socialization.[13] However, Figures 8.2a and 8.2b also reflect an important commonality in that they suggest that the post-1997 country-level convergence was driven not only by generational replacement but also by a significant attenuation of individual communist exposure effects. What is less clear—and represents an interesting area of future research—is whether this decline in socialization effects represents part of a longer-term process of legacy decline or merely a return to the "steady-state" level from the early 1990s as post-communist citizens recovered from the shock of the early transition period.[14]

By comparison, it appears that at least on average post-communist welfare state preferences were much less affected by the vagaries of the transition. According to Figure 8.1c, the effects of communist exposure increased moderately during the crisis of the 1990s[15] and then broadly stabilized after 2000. Combined with the steady country-level post-communist exceptionalism effect in Figure 8.1c, these findings suggest that the aggregate stability was a result of two parallel and opposite processes—a slight strengthening of communist exposure effects and the gradual generational replacement process—cancelling each other out. While extrapolating beyond the current data is obviously risky, especially given the unpredictable effects of the shock of the global financial crisis after 2008, these patterns suggest that in the next decades welfare state attitudes may evolve along the lines of the *generational replacement* model in our theoretical discussion.

---

[12]Thus, based on Figure 8.2b, an additional 40 years of communist exposure in 2007 (i.e., the effect of having been exposed to 40 years of communism as opposed to zero years on someone taking a survey in 2007) was equivalent to .26 of a standard deviation in the market support index, whereas for democracy in Figure 8.2a the effect of a similar 40 years of exposure in 2007 was about .14 of a standard deviation.

[13]For democratic attitudes the patterns are less clear, but this is due largely to the fact that the democracy questions were not asked in WVS before 1995, and we did not feel comfortable extrapolating from the post-1995 data.

[14]Indeed it is worth noting that in Figure 8.2b the exposure effects on market support are almost identical at the starting and end point of our study period (1990 and 2007).

[15]The increase during the first post-communist decade was nontrivial (about 50%), but the magnitude of the increase was less than half the corresponding increase for market support in Figure 8.2b.

Finally, Figure 8.2d nicely complements the earlier aggregate-level patterns of fairly rapid convergence in gender equality attitudes. Whereas in the early 1990s we can detect an (albeit only marginally significant) negative communist exposure effect, the legacy of communism appears to decline quite rapidly in the first transition decade and the effect disappears completely by the end of the 1990s. This finding suggests that the rapid aggregate-level convergence reflected in Figure 8.1d was not simply the result of generational replacement but rather reflects genuine attitudinal change along the lines of the *fleeting legacies* model (though it should be noted again that the starting point was in the opposite direction of what we would have expected from the perspective of the communist rhetorical commitment to gender equality).

As a next step, mirroring our analysis in Chapters 4–7, we address the corollary question of whether the resilience of communist socialization depends not only on the particular issue area but also on the timing of socialization. While in the earlier analysis we saw that on average adult socialization left a larger attitudinal footprint on attitudes toward democracy, markets, and welfare states—only gender equality was an exception with a stronger effect for childhood socialization—we now turn to the question whether these average effects over the first two decades of post-communism were driven primarily by differences in starting points at the outset of the transition or by the greater resilience of adult socialization to the attitudinal shocks of the transition process. To do so, we use the same setup as in the regressions underlying Figures 8.2a–d, but instead of overall exposure we interact early and adult exposure separately with survey year (and year squared).

While largely confirming the findings from Chapters 4–6 about the greater importance of adult communist socialization and the broad temporal trends discussed above in the context of overall communist exposure, the patterns in Figures 8.3a–d nevertheless provide a more nuanced and dynamic picture of the temporal dimension of communist legacies in the post-communist period. Thus, whereas in Figure 8.2d we saw that the impact of total communist exposure on attitudes toward gender equality disappeared over the course of the first post-communist decade, Figure 8.3d shows a more interesting mix of trends. More specifically for adult exposure we see a very similar pattern of the gradual disappearance of an initial sexist bias. However, for early exposure the roughly parallel temporal trend means that while in the early 1990s early communist exposure (between ages 6 and 17) had no effect on gender equality preferences, over the course of transition we can detect a growing *positive* effect, which achieves statistical significance after 2000. This suggests that the relative gender equality of communist education systems is reflected in the longer-term gender attitudes of individuals who have gone

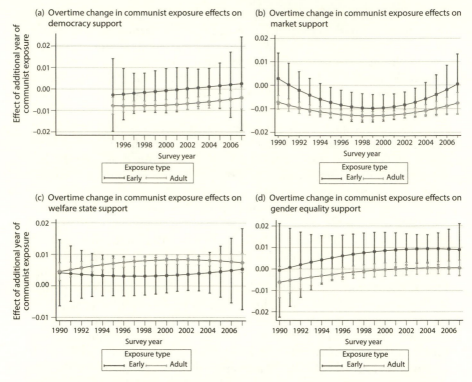

Figure 8.3. (a) Over-Time Change in Communist Exposure Effects on Democracy Support; (b) Over-Time Change in Communist Exposure Effects on Market
Support; (c) Over-Time Change in Communist Exposure Effects on Welfare
State Support; (d) Over-Time Change in Communist Exposure Effects on Gender Equality Support
The four panels in this figure show the temporal evolution of a year of early vs.
adult personal communist exposure for the four types of political attitudes discussed in Chapters 4–7. The first three panels show that adult exposure had
consistently negative effects on democracy and market support and positive effects on welfare state support, and even though the size of the effect diminished
after 2000 for all three attitudes, it nevertheless continued to be significant. By
contrast, early socialization had smaller, less significant, and more temporary
effects on economic and regime attitudes. The bottom right panel shows a gradually declining negative adult exposure effect and a growing positive early exposure effect on support for gender equality, which achieved statistical significance
around 2000. For comparability, all dependent variables are standardized to
have a mean of 0 and a standard deviation of 1. Early exposure measures the
years lived under communist regimes between the ages of 6 and 17, while adult
exposure captures years under communism experienced at ages 18 and above.
All statistical models control for pre-communist country differences and individual demographic characteristics. For full regression results, see the electronic
appendix.

to school under communism, which may bode well for the generations that experienced only early communist socialization but were spared the more sexist reality of adult life under communism.

A roughly comparable picture emerges with respect to democratic attitudes: as illustrated in Figure 8.3a, the negative impact of adult socialization gradually declined after the mid-1990s, though its effect was still at least marginally significant (at .06 one-tailed) in 2007. Meanwhile, the impact of early communist socialization switched (from negative to positive) over the course of the transition, but its effects were far from achieving statistical significance at any point during the 1995–2007 period. Nonetheless, given that the anti-democratic effects of communist socialization seem to be limited to individuals with adult communist exposure, these findings suggest that the post-communist convergence in democratic norms is likely to continue because of a combination of gradually declining socialization effects and a slow but steady process of generational replacement. An important caveat here is that we are again discussing only an attitude *gap* between post-communist citizens and non-post-communist citizens: should later data reveal a general global trend away from support of democracy in the era following the global economic crisis, these data suggest little reason to expect that the post-communist countries would be an exception to such a trend.

The temporal evolution of early versus adult communist exposure effects was somewhat more heterogeneous for market and welfare state attitudes. As we can see in Figures 8.3b and 8.3c, adult exposure roughly replicates the earlier temporal patterns, whereby the communist socialization effects doubled during the first decade and declined subsequently. However, the decline was more significant with respect to anti-market attitudes, where the exposure effect in 2007 declined to 1990 levels, as opposed to the much more modest fall-off in adult exposure effects on welfare state preferences, providing yet again further evidence of the resilience of post-communist attitudes toward social welfare.

The more interesting dynamics are with respect to early socialization, where we discover reversed temporal trends for market versus welfare state attitudes. Thus, as illustrated in Figure 8.3b, the anti-market effects of early communist exposure increased sharply during the early 1990s; by the late 1990s they were statistically significant and of comparable magnitude to those of adult exposure. However, these effects proved to be much more transitory, and by 2007 the early exposure effects had once again vanished completely, while the adult exposure effects continued to be negative and statistically significant. Meanwhile, the early communist exposure effects on welfare state attitudes not only failed to achieve statistical significance during the entire 1990–2007 period, but they actually weakened slightly during the crisis in the 1990s. However, Figure 8.3c also reveals an (albeit modest and imprecisely estimated) uptick in early exposure effects on welfare state attitudes and hints at a growing convergence of communist exposure effects irrespective of its timing.

8.4. AGE COHORT ANALYSIS

The next set of figures addresses the same set of questions through a slightly different methodological approach by analyzing the temporal evolution of attitudes among different age cohorts in post-communist and non-post-communist countries. In this analysis, we divided respondents into nine different ten-year age cohorts based on their year of birth and then analyzed the interaction between the post-communism dummy variable, the survey year and year squared, and these nine age cohorts (analyzed as a nominal rather than a continuous variable to allow for maximum flexibility in analyzing cohort differences). As in the previous analyses, the regressions on which the figures were based include our standard demographic and pre-communist developmental controls. While such an approach is not without its drawbacks,[16] it does have the advantage of allowing us to synthesize in a single set of figures information about both the differences between citizens of post-communist countries and those living elsewhere in the world, and the within-country differences between cohorts with different degrees of communist exposure.

Since including all nine age cohorts on a single figure would have made the figure practically impossible to read (especially without color illustrations), we have chosen to focus on three cohorts (separated by 30-year intervals) that can be seen as representing three different generations affected in different ways by the communist experience. Individuals from the first cohort, who were born between 1915 and 1924, experienced the full dose of adult communist exposure but—at least in the case of the post-WWII communist regimes of Eastern Europe—were not subjected to early communist exposure. Members of the second cohort were born between 1945 and 1954 and thus had all their early socialization under communism while also experiencing communism as adults for between two and three decades. The final cohort, born between 1975 and 1984,

---

[16] In addition to the perennial question about how to define the length and start/end years of particular cohorts, for our analysis such an approach has the added disadvantage that the different start and end dates of the communist regimes across the former Soviet bloc means that for some cohorts the actual exposure to communism for individuals from a given cohort might vary significantly across different post-communist countries.

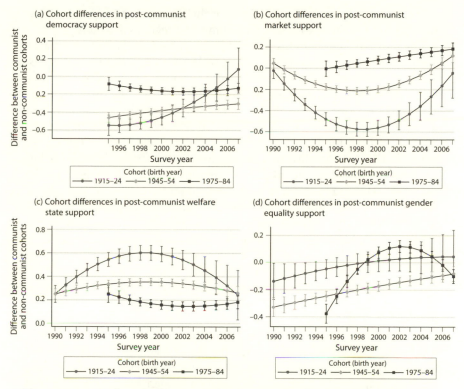

Figure 8.4. (a) Cohort Differences in Post-communist Democracy Support;
(b) Cohort Differences in Post-communist Market Support; (c) Cohort
Differences in Post-communist Welfare State Support; (d) Cohort Differences
in Post-communist Gender Equality Support

The four panels in this figure show the temporal evolution of the difference
between three post-communist and non-communist age cohorts for the four
types of political attitudes discussed in Chapters 4–7. The top left panel suggests
that the initial post-communist democratic deficit was primarily driven by the
significantly less democratic older cohorts, but by 2007 the age differences had
been reduced and even partially reversed for the oldest cohort. The top right
and bottom left panels show that the increase in post-communist anti-market
and pro–welfare state attitudes in the 1990s was driven by the older cohorts,
while the youngest cohort actually turned more pro-market. However, in both
panels we see significant attitudinal convergence between different age cohorts
by the end of the time periods. The bottom right panel shows a gradually declining negative effect among the older cohorts, while the youngest cohort showed
rapid relative increases in gender equality support until 2002 followed by a
noticeable decline. For comparability, all dependent variables are standardized
to have a mean of 0 and a standard deviation of 1. All statistical models control
for pre-communist country differences and individual demographic characteristics. For full regression results, see the electronic appendix.

typically had at least a few years (but not the full dose) of early communist socialization but did not experience communist regimes as adults.[17]

The most striking findings are with respect to the relative cohort evolution of attitudes toward markets and welfare states. For these attitudes, which are most closely connected to the economic trauma of the early transition period, Figures 8.4b and 8.4c indicate that the growing postcommunist exceptionalism of the 1990s was driven by a radicalization of the oldest cohorts, rather than by a uniform societal rejection of capitalism.[18] Indeed, for both indicators, the youngest cohort in our figure moved in the opposite direction in response to this crisis, thereby further exacerbating the generational divergence in economic preferences by the end of the 1990s. However, it should be noted that while in the case of welfare state preferences this shift merely amounted to a relatively modest reduction in the cohort's enduring pro–welfare state bias (that continued to be statistically significant throughout this period), in the case of attitudes toward markets, the 1975–84 cohort actually developed a statistically significant pro-market bias after 1998.

The temporal evolution of democratic support in Figure 8.4a also reveals a fair bit of convergence between different age cohorts after the mid- to late 1990s, but this convergence has a darker side in the sense that it was driven not only by the reduction in the anti-democratic bias in the older cohorts but also by a significant worsening of the democratic deficit of the younger cohort. This pattern helps explain why despite the declining impact of communist exposure revealed in Figures 8.2a and 8.3a, the country-level democratic deficit of post-communist countries did not completely disappear during the first two transition decades. And while the democratic attitude reversal of the oldest cohort is impressive—and may reflect the anti-communist effects of pre-communist early socialization discussed in Chapter 4—its implications for the future of democratic support in the ex-communist countries is modest because it means that in this case generational replacement is starting to be at odds with attitudinal convergence given the deteriorating democratic support among the younger cohorts.

The cohort trajectories in Figure 8.4d further reinforce the earlier findings about the complicated and uneven dynamics of communist legacies with respect to gender equality support. First, even though the two older generations broadly follow the overall trend of a diminishing post-

[17]Note that since the oldest individuals from this cohort turned 18 only in 1993, we did not have enough respondents from the cohorts in the WVS before 1995 to make us feel confident about presenting estimates for this cohort in these figures prior to 1995.

[18]This result of a particularly large gap in support for social welfare among the older cohort is consistent with Alesina and Fuchs-Schündeln (2007)'s findings regarding differences being especially pronounced between the older cohorts of East and West Germans.

communist sexist bias, it is worth noting that the oldest cohort in the figure (born in 1915–24) actually exhibited a consistently weaker sexist bias that the generation of their children. This difference, which is consistent with the findings in Chapter 7 about the greater gender equality effects of Stalinist exposure compared to other subtypes of communism, also means that—in the short term—the positive impact of weakening negative exposure effects are likely to be counteracted by generational replacement dynamics. Finally, the evolution of the youngest cohort in Figure 8.4d is somewhat puzzling in the sense that the initial sexist bias of the cohort in the mid-1990s was reversed by the early 2000s, only to dip back into significantly negative territory by 2007. While we need to be careful about extrapolating from the evolution of this cohort over the course of just a bit more than a decade, the continuation of this downward trend would undermine the prospects for more progressive attitudes on gender equality in the post-communist world.

8.5. INDIVIDUAL-LEVEL ATTITUDE CHANGE: PANEL EVIDENCE FROM GERMANY

In the analysis so far, we have analyzed the temporal evolution of post-communist political and economic attitudes using cross-national data from successive waves of the World Values Survey. As discussed in Chapter 3, this approach has the advantage of drawing on a broad range of countries and thereby expanding the external validity of our analysis. However, this data source also has certain limitations due to the changing mix of countries in different waves and survey years, and these limitations may be particularly relevant when studying temporal change.[19] Moreover, even if we were to focus on successive surveys from the same set of countries, we may be concerned that temporal changes in attitudes could be affected by differences in samples across successive waves,

---

[19] Thus, we may worry that what we interpret as over-time attitudinal change is simply an artifact of the fact that different countries make up both the post-communist and the non-communist groups of countries in different years. Of course, these concerns should be at least partially alleviated by our individual and country-level controls, and we are reassured by the fact that we find very similar results using fixed-effects specifications for Figures 8.2a–d and 8.3a–d, which suggests that our findings are not driven primarily by changing sample compositions. However, fixed-effects specifications are not really feasible for the models involving the post-communist dummy variable (which varies only across but not within countries); as Figures 8.1 and 8.4 are measuring the gap in attitudes between post-communist and non-post-communist countries/cohorts, the analysis by definition includes the post-communist dummy variable.

thereby limiting our ability to isolate genuine attitudinal changes from other confounding factors.[20]

Therefore, in this section we analyze data from the three-wave German Election Panel Study (GEPS) around three successive national elections in 1994, 1998, and 2002.[21] As discussed in Chapter 3, these within-Germany comparisons have the additional advantage of minimizing cultural/linguistic sources of survey response heterogeneity. At the same time, however, it is also important to bear in mind some of the external validity limitations of analyzing intra-German variation, both because East German communism differed in some respects from communism elsewhere in Eastern Europe, and because Germany's pre- and especially post-communist experience differed from the rest of the region.

While the German election surveys did not use the same survey questions as the ones we used in our WVS analyses in the preceding sections, they nevertheless included useful questions for two of the attitudes analyzed in this book. Thus, we used a survey question that asked respondents to agree or disagree (on a five-point scale) with the statement that dictatorship is better than democracy in some circumstances, which we coded so that higher values indicate stronger disagreement and therefore stronger support for democracy. To capture attitudes toward markets, we used another five-point agree-disagree question focused on the statement that the most important companies need to be nationalized, and similarly coded it so that higher values indicate greater market support.

To capture the dynamics of post-communist attitudinal change for individuals with different levels of communist exposure, our statistical models use a very similar cohort variable as the one used in the WVS analysis, with individuals placed into 10-year cohorts based on their birth year.[22] We then interact this eight-category cohort variable with the post-communism dummy and focus on the attitudinal differences between post-communist and non-communist (i.e., East and West German) cohorts. All the regressions include a standard set of demographic control variables including education, age, residence, occupational status, income,

---

[20] Such changes could be driven by the use of different sampling frames by the survey firms running successive surveys, but they may also reflect certain demographic changes (e.g., migration or mortality patterns) that could be correlated with political attitudes. Thus, if many young people leave the country and pro-market young people are more likely to seek work abroad, then even with well-designed national samples we may find an artificial decline in pro-market attitudes in certain age cohorts even if individual-level attitudes remain unchanged.

[21] See Chapter 3, Section 3.4.1.3 for details on this survey.

[22] The only difference is that since the German data stopped in 2002 we did not include the youngest cohort we had used in the WVS data (post-1985 births), since such individuals were not represented in the German panel surveys.

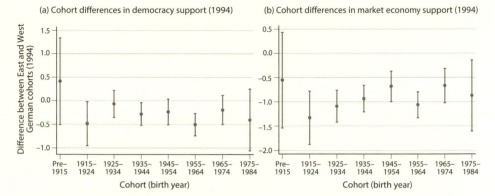

Figure 8.5. (a) Cohort Differences in Democracy Support (1994); (b) Cohort Differences in Market Economy Support (1994)
The two figures illustrate the differences in democratic attitudes (Figure 8.5a) and market attitudes (Figure 8.5b) between East and West Germans for different age cohorts. The first figure does not show any clear patterns of cross-cohort democratic support differences, except for an imprecisely estimated democratic surplus among East Germans born pre-1915. The second panel shows that East German anti-market attitudes were somewhat stronger among respondents born between 1915 and 1934, but there were once again no clear patterns for those born in the post-1945 period. The data utilized in these analyses are from the 1994 wave of the German Election Panel Study. All statistical models control for individual demographic characteristics. For full regression results, see the electronic appendix.

sex, and religious denomination and attendance (see the electronic appendix for complete details).

As a first step in Figures 8.5a and 8.5b, we establish an attitudinal baseline reflecting the degree to which the democratic and market preferences of different cohorts from post-communist East Germany differed from their West German counterparts in the first survey wave of 1994. The two figures represent the predicted value and the 95% confidence intervals of the difference between East and West German respondents for the different age cohorts. As expected based on the within-Germany analysis in Chapters 4 and 5, East German respondents were overall more anti-democratic and anti-market than their West German compatriots.

In terms of cohort differences, Figure 8.5a does not reveal very significant cross-cohort differences that can be obviously traced to differences in communist exposure. The most striking difference is between the two oldest cohorts—East Germans born between 1915 and 1924 appear to be significantly less democratic than their West German counterparts while their compatriots born a decade earlier (pre-1915) exhibit a democracy surplus—albeit a statistically insignificant one—but given

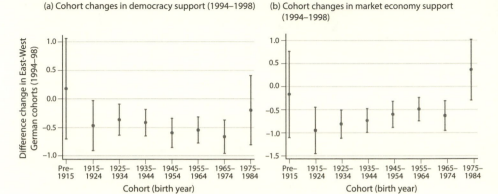

Figures 8.6. (a) Cohort Changes in Democracy Support (1994–98); (b) Cohort
Changes in Market Economy Support (1994–98); (c)

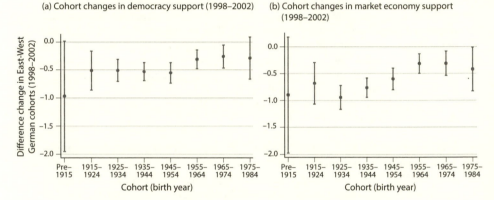

Figures 8.7. (a) Cohort Changes in Democracy Support (1998–2002);
(b) Cohort Changes in Market Economy Support (1998–2002)

The four panels in figures 8.6 and 8.7 illustrate the relative changes in democratic attitudes (Figures 8.6a and 8.7a) and market attitudes (Figures 8.6b and
8.7b) between East and West Germans from different age cohorts. The estimates
show the change in the East-West attitudinal differences 1994–98 (Figures 8.6a
and 8.6b) and 1998–2002 (Figures 8.7a and 8.7b). The first two figures confirm
the growing anti-democratic and anti-market gap among post-communist respondents during the mid-1990s while the second two figures indicate that the
trend continued into the late 1990s and early 2000s in Germany. The only exceptions to this trend were the oldest (pre-1915) and oldest (post-1975) cohorts,
for which the negative effects were weaker in terms of both substantive and
statistical significance 1994–98. The data utilized in these analyses are from the
1994, 1998, and 2002 waves of the German Election Panel Study. All statistical
models control for individual demographic characteristics. For full regression
results, see the electronic appendix.

that both these cohorts had identical communist exposure, the difference cannot be readily traced to communist socialization differences. Instead, the difference may be due to the fact that the older cohort came of age in Weimar Germany (they were 18 or older in 1933) and so the experience of Germany's democratic interlude may have inoculated this cohort against the anti-democratic influence of communist socialization, whereas the slightly younger (1915–24) cohort spent its early adulthood in Nazi Germany and thus did not get the same democratic education. Beyond that, the only partially significant difference is the greater democratic deficit of the 1955–64 cohort, though again it is unclear how this difference can be explained from a straightforward communist exposure perspective given that the two adjacent cohorts had significantly smaller democratic deficits.

Judging by Figure 8.5b, cohort differences in market attitudes exhibited some important similarities, including the pronounced difference between the two oldest cohorts and the clear "dip" for the 1955–64 cohort, which appears to have been more deeply affected by communist socialization than the two adjacent age cohorts. However, the monotonic decline in the anti-market communist bias between the 1915–24 and 1945–54 cohorts is consistent with the importance of adult communist socialization in driving anti-market attitudes. But given that this trend does not continue for the three youngest cohorts, we need to be careful about placing too much weight on this explanation.

We now turn to analyzing the temporal change patterns that are our core theoretical interest in this chapter. For these models, we take advantage of the study's panel structure and regress an individual's attitude at time t on that same respondent's attitude at time $t-1$ and on the interaction between cohorts and the post-communism dummy variable discussed above.[23] Therefore, the estimated effects in Figures 8.6a and 8.6b capture the change in the post-communist attitudinal difference between 1994 and 1998 (while Figures 8.7a and 8.7b repeat the analysis for the 1998–2002 period). Thus, a negative value in Figures 8.6a and 8.6b means that between 1994 and 1998 post-communist respondents from a given cohort have become more anti-democratic/anti-market than West German respondents from that same cohort, while positive values indicate a reduction in the post-communist democracy/market support deficit for that cohort from 1994 to 1998.

Overall, Figures 8.6a and 8.6b confirm our cross-national findings that the post-communist democracy and market deficits became more pronounced during the mid-1990s. Moreover, given that these changes are measured at the individual level, we have greater confidence that these

---

[23] As in the regression analysis used to generate Figures 8.5a and 8.5b, these models include demographic controls and the year of the survey.

trends capture genuine radicalization rather than the changing composition of different cohorts across successive survey waves. According to Figures 8.7a and 8.7b, this divergent trend seems to have continued at roughly comparable rates from 1998 to 2002, which suggests that post-communist divergence lasted somewhat longer in Germany than elsewhere in the Eastern bloc, where an albeit slow convergence had started around 2000 (see Figures 8.1a and 8.1b).

The other broad pattern worth noting in the four figures is that as long as we ignore the oldest cohort (pre-1915) we can identify some interesting differences between democracy and market support in the attitudinal changes by cohort. Thus, in both Figure 8.6b (1994–98) and Figure 8.7b (1998–2002) the anti-market turn of East Germans was more pronounced in the older cohorts, which is consistent with the broader regional patterns we identified in Figure 8.4b and suggests the role of longer adult communist exposure in driving anti-market radicalization. In contrast, Figure 8.6a reveals that the anti-democratic turn was more pronounced for the younger cohorts from 1994 to 1998.[24] While this finding is in line with the broader regional patterns in Figure 8.4a about the weakening democratic support among the younger post-communist cohorts in the mid-1990s,[25] it is at odds with our theoretical expectation that individuals with longer communist exposure would be more likely to radicalize in response to the crisis of the 1990s. However, Figure 8.7a suggests that this pattern was reversed from 1998 to 2002, when, in line with our theoretical expectations, the post-communist anti-democratic bias grew faster among the older cohorts.

Finally it is worth noting that the pre-1915 generation, which already stood out in terms of its baseline market and democratic support patterns in Figures 8.5a and 8.5b, also exhibited distinctive change patterns as compared to their slightly younger counterparts. Thus during the 1994–98 period, the pre-1915 cohort defied the general radicalization trend of other East German cohorts, while in 1998–2002 they experienced greater democratic backsliding, although these effects were very imprecisely estimated (and not statistically significant from zero). While a more detailed analysis of the mechanisms underlying this greater immunity to communist socialization among the "Weimar" cohort is beyond the scope of the current analysis, it nevertheless echoes our earlier findings about the

[24]The youngest cohort is a partial exception from this trend, but this estimate needs to be treated with caution because most individuals from that cohort were too young to be included in the 1994 survey, so we have few observations for that cohort in the 1994–98 analysis.

[25]Note, however, that in Figure 8.4a the democracy deficit for the older cohorts was already gradually improving by the mid-1990s, whereas in Germany it was merely growing more slowly than for the younger cohorts.

greater resistance to communist socialization in regard to both democracy and markets (see Figures 4.2 and 5.3 in Chapters 4 and 5, respectively) in countries with pre-communist democratic experiences.

Overall, our analysis of the German panel data confirms our earlier findings about the growth in anti-democratic and anti-market communist socialization effects in the mid-1990s and suggests that in Germany this divergence process continued until at least part of the 1998–2002 period. Moreover, our panel analysis suggests that for market attitudes this radicalization was much more pronounced for older cohorts than for their younger compatriots. Taken together, these findings confirm that communist socialization affected the temporal evolution of attitudes towards democracy and markets during the first decade of transition.

8.6. ECONOMIC PERFORMANCE AND THE RESILIENCE OF COMMUNIST SOCIALIZATION EFFECTS

In this final empirical section we analyze the moderating influence of economic performance on the resilience of communist socialization effects. In particular, we examine the extent to which the anti-market and pro–welfare state attitudes of post-communist citizens, and particularly those with extensive personal exposures to communism, were shaped by the differential economic trajectories of their countries during the post-communist transition. Such an analysis is warranted for a number of reasons. First, it permits us to get a clearer understanding of the mechanisms underlying the radicalization phenomena during the first decade of the transition revealed by the analysis in Section 8.3 of this chapter. Was the growing anti-market and pro–welfare state sentiment of the older cohorts primarily driven by the catastrophic economic performance of new (at least semi)capitalist institutions in some ex-communist countries, and if so, which aspects were particularly salient? Or was the disenchantment with markets and the even stronger embrace of the welfare state part of a broader regional phenomenon affecting even citizens of countries that had enjoyed fairly successful post-communist economic trajectories?

Second, understanding the extent to which post-communist attitudinal exceptionalism and the resilience of communist exposure effects are driven by the vagaries of economic performance could have important implications for the future prospects of attitudinal "normalization" in the ex-communist countries. To the extent that the radicalization of the 1990s was driven by the post-communist economic decline, then we may expect subsequent crises—including the post-2008 global financial crisis—to trigger a revival of communist legacies. If, however, the initial decline was not affected by economic conditions—perhaps because it reflected a more generalized realization of the limitations of new economic and political institutions to bring about rapid progress—then we might expect the gradual decline of communist attitudinal legacies to continue and eventually produce the long-expected normalization of post-communist politics.

Finally, this analysis can help us establish another set of scope conditions for arguments about the importance of communist exposure. In particular, we can test whether the strength and resilience of exposure effects in our earlier analyses were primarily driven by the disappointing economic performance of most post-communist countries, particularly during the first decade of the transition. If we are able to observe a much quicker normalization of political attitudes in countries with more favorable economic trajectories, then we would need to be more careful in our assessment of the strength of communist socialization effects. Instead, it might be more warranted to conclude that the resilience of a communist imprint was driven by a "perfect storm" of long-term communist socialization efforts combined with very disappointing post-communist economic reform results that reinforced the (initially compromised) credibility of communist ideological teachings.[26]

To test the moderating effects of post-communist economic performance, we return to the empirical setup from Section 8.3 using data from the World Values Survey for 1989–2009 and analyzing the temporal evolution of age cohort differences between post-communist and non-post-communist countries. However, in line with our theoretical interests, for the analysis in this section we included an additional interaction effect with one of two economic performance indicators: the size of GDP as a percentage of 1989 levels and the level of economic inequality (both measured in the year preceding the survey). While other indicators of economic performance could obviously be important, these two indicators capture two of the most important aspects of the post-communist crisis—the deep and lasting economic decline and the rapid growth of inequality—while at the same time offering significant contrasts between countries that recovered quickly and experienced limited inequality growth (such as Poland) and others stuck in the high-inequality low-growth trap of the transition J-curve for much of the first two post-communist decades (Hellman 1998). Given our focus on economic conditions, we limit our analysis to the two indicators that we would expect to be affected most directly by economic performance: attitudes toward the market and the welfare state.

[26]Note that this analysis supplements our earlier findings in Chapters 4, 5, and 6 that merely controlling for economic conditions does not explain away the various post-communist attitudinal gaps. Our analysis here should therefore be construed as an attempt to dig deeper into this question to see if there is other evidence consistent with such our earlier findings that we can illustrate with a somewhat less blunt statistical tool.

The results of these tests are once again presented graphically in Figures 8.8a–d, while the full regression results are available in the electronic appendix. Note that given the complicated nature of the interaction effects[27] in this analysis, we limit our simulations to two values for the interacted variables in each model. Thus we focus on two age cohorts, 1935–44 and 1965–74, separated by three decades and, more importantly, by large differences in adult communist socialization. For the economic indicators we also choose two values, representing the lower and higher range of economic output change (+25% vs. –25% compared to 1989 levels) and economic inequality (Gini coefficient of 30 vs. 44).[28]

The most important pattern that emerges from the four figures is that even though economic conditions played a moderating role in the expected direction—that is, anti-market/pro–welfare state views were more pronounced in countries experiencing economic decline and high income inequality—the differences between age cohorts in countries with similar economic performances are much larger and have higher levels of statistical significance than the differences between well-performing and poorly performing countries for any given age cohort. Moreover, members of the older post-communist cohort (who had extensive adult exposure to communism) displayed a significant anti-market and pro–welfare state bias compared to their non-communist peers of the same age for most of the transition period, even in countries with solid post-communist growth and modest inequality increases. In other words, the older cohorts of post-communist citizens differed in how they reacted not only when they faced particularly severe crises, but even when they experienced relatively benign economic environments. Given that the differences between the older and the younger post-communist cohorts were also mostly significant in these economic star performers,[29] we interpret these findings as providing additional evidence about the robustness of the communist exposure effects during the post-communist period.

[27] To properly test our theory, we had to run what amounted to a quadruple interaction (post-communist × age cohort × economic performance (GDP as % of 1989 or economic inequality) × year) with a quadratic function for year.

[28] Note that for both economic indicators we were somewhat constrained by the fact that there was fairly limited overlap in the distribution of values between early and late years (e.g., very few countries in the early 1990s were as unequal as even the most equal countries in the mid-2000s). As a result, we had to choose values that balanced the need for getting significant variation in economic performance with avoiding to present simulations based on out-of-sample values. Nonetheless, given that there were no post-communist countries in our sample with a Gini coefficient of 44 or higher before the 1997 surveys, we do not report standard errors for the pre-1997 estimates for the high inequality cases.

[29] The only partial exceptions were the insignificant (though correctly signed) differences for high economic growth countries in the 1990s in Figures 8.8a and 8.8b.

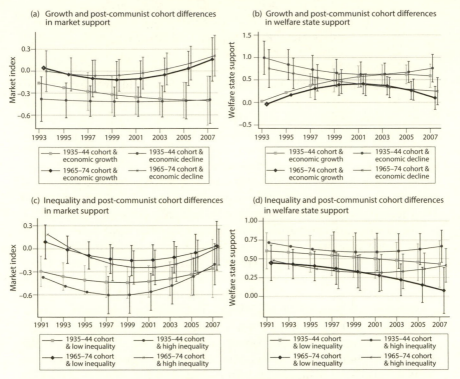

Figure 8.8. (a) Growth and Post-communist Cohort Differences in Market Support; (b) Growth and Post-communist Cohort Differences in Welfare State Support; (c) Inequality and Post-communist Cohort Differences in Market Support; (d) Inequality and Post-communist Cohort Differences in Welfare State Support
The four panels in this figure show the temporal evolution of the difference in market and welfare state attitudes between two post-communist and non-communist age cohorts in countries with varying post-communist economic growth and income inequality. The top left panel suggests that differences in market support were driven primarily by attitudinal differences between age cohorts while economic growth differentials had a negligible effect, especially toward the end of the period. The top right panel suggests that while welfare state support was initially stronger in countries with steeper economic declines, after 2000 cross-country economic differences were once again less important than differences across age cohorts. The bottom left panel also shows greater cross-cohort differences in market support than cross-country differences rooted in economic inequality differences, though high inequality mattered at least marginally in the late 1990s for the older cohorts. The bottom right panel suggests that both socialization-based cohort differences and economic conditions drove welfare state support in the 2000s: the post-communist pro–welfare state differential declined sharply among the younger cohorts in low-inequality countries but was largely unchanged in high-inequality contexts. The values for the moderating variables are as follows: –25% cumulative economic GDP change from 1989 for economic decline, +25% cumulative economic GDP change from 1989 for economic growth, an income Gini coefficient of 30 for low inequality, an income Gini coefficient of 44 for high inequality. To reflect that not all these values were represented in all years, we do not report standard errors for years where the moderating variable was out of sample. For comparability, all dependent variables are standardized to have a mean of 0 and a standard deviation of 1. All statistical models control for pre-communist country differences and individual demographic characteristics. For full regression results, see the electronic appendix.

While most of these findings were in general remarkably consistent across different types of economic indicators and different types of economic attitudes, it is still worth highlighting some interesting temporal differences we did identify in the moderating role of different economic indicators. Thus, as illustrated most strikingly in Figure 8.8b, the differences in post-communist output trajectories initially mattered a great deal in shaping preferences for welfare state protection: at least in the early to mid-1990s, the primary differences in welfare state attitudes were between countries with good versus bad GDP trajectories, whereas the differences between cohorts in economically similar countries were substantively small and statistically insignificant. However, over the course of the next decade we observe a striking pattern change: the welfare state preferences converge for members of the same age cohort irrespective of their countries' output performance, while diverging within countries for different cohorts. As a result, by the mid- to late 2000s output trajectories no longer predict welfare state support, but there are large and statistically significant attitudinal differences *across* age cohorts. The older cohorts converge on large and significant pro–welfare state biases. However, for the younger cohorts the differences diminished over time and are no longer statistically significant at conventional levels by 2007.

A similar if somewhat more muted pattern can also be seen in Figure 8.8a: whereas cohort differences were substantively smaller and only partially statistically significant during the mid to late-1990s, these differences became much clearer after 2000. At the same time, cross-country differences due to economic performance differentials, which had been at least partially visible (but statistically insignificant) in the mid-1990s, disappeared altogether. Taken together, the findings in Figures 8.8a and 8.8b suggest that the political salience of economic output differentials declined over the course of the post-communist transition and that once the dust settled, what mattered were *cohort differences* rooted in different levels of personal communist exposure.

Turning to the political fallout of the region's growing economic inequality, Figures 8.8c and 8.8d confirm that cohort differences were more important than inequality in driving attitudes toward both markets and welfare states. The growth in the initially negligible impact of inequality differences at first affected primarily market attitudes, as illustrated by the sharper growth of anti-market attitudes in the older cohorts of more unequal countries in Figure 8.8c, but these differences never achieved statistical significance, and the effect had disappeared completely by 2007. For welfare state attitudes, inequality differences started to matter only after 2000, but by 2007 they had resulted in substantial attitudinal differences in the expected direction for both the older and the younger post-communist cohorts. While these inequality-based differences were significant only for the younger cohort and their magnitude was still somewhat smaller than differences between cohorts, it nevertheless reveals a growing salience for inequality in driving post-communist attitudes. While this growing importance of inequality is compatible with its greater resonance with communist ideology—capitalism had been primarily been criticized for being unjust rather than inefficient—the contrast between Figures 8.8c and 8.8d suggests that, at least before 2008, growing post-communist inequality primarily promoted calls for a gentler form of capitalism with more generous welfare benefits rather than a rejection of capitalism altogether.

8.7. CONCLUSIONS

In this final empirical chapter of the book we have addressed the question of the temporal resilience of communist socialization effects. To do so, we first developed three stylized models of attitudinal change, which carry very different implications for the temporal evolution of both aggregate-level post-communist exceptionalism and within-country attitudinal differences between different age cohorts.

The first model, *fleeting legacies*, based on theories about the ideological bankruptcy of communism at the time of its collapse, predicted a fairly rapid attitudinal convergence of post-communist citizens toward the views of their non-communist counterparts, while at the same time suggesting a quick reduction in the large generational differences based on the large communist exposure effects revealed in the earlier chapters. Not surprisingly, the issue area that most closely conformed to this model was support for gender equality, where, as discussed in greater detail in Chapter 7, communist regimes had left the weakest overall legacy. As a result, we observed a fairly rapid reduction of an initially significant gender equality deficit, along with the disappearance of the early negative communist exposure effect (which had been concentrated among those exposed to communism as adults).

The second model, *generational replacement*, entails a much slower process of attitudinal convergence based on the gradual dying-off of the older and more heavily exposed age cohorts and the coming of age of new cohorts with shorter or no direct communist exposure. In contrast to the *fleeting legacies* approach, under this scenario individual attitudes are quite sticky, and as a result exposure-based differences across cohorts are very persistent. Judging by the results of this chapter, it appears that support for the welfare state most closely approximates this scenario: the significant post-communist bias in support for the welfare state barely declined over the first two decades of the transition, and the effects of communist exposure also seem quite resilient. Taken together, these two patterns confirm that the communist attitudinal imprint was the strongest in an issue area (support for state-provided welfare) where communist ideology was fairly appealing and where the reality of socialist societies (fairly generous welfare benefits) matched the official rhetoric to a greater extent than in other areas.

The third model, *temporary divergence*, allowed for the possibility that the attitudinal legacies of communism could actually increase, at least temporarily, over the course of the post-communist transition. We expected these patterns to apply primarily in areas where communism was not particularly popular at the outset of the transition, but where the disappointing economic and political performance of much of the first transition decade may have triggered an updating process that reinforced (at least temporarily) some of the communist socialization effects that had been obscured in the revolutionary euphoria of 1989–90. This chapter reveals that these patterns indeed applied to support for both democracy and markets, areas in which communist regimes were unpopular by 1989—hence the lack of a post-communist deficit in 1990—but where the economic costs and political disappointments of early reform efforts led to a significant spike in nostalgia for the economic and political institutions of the old regime. These divergence patterns based on data from the World Values Survey are also confirmed at the individual level using panel data comparisons of East and West Germans' attitudes toward markets and democracy in the German Election Panel Study surveys from 1994 to 2002. However, this chapter also confirms that this initial divergence was indeed temporary, and in the context of gradually improving economic and political performance after 2000 we observe not only a significant reduction in the overall post-communist exceptionalism (which disappears entirely for market attitudes by 2007), but also a significant weakening of exposure effects, which suggests a gradual erosion of individual-level communist socialization legacies.

The comparative analysis of the temporal evolution of different post-communist age cohorts in this chapter provides a number of additional nuances to our understanding of communist legacies in the first two post-communist decades, as well as about the likely future trajectory of these legacies. In terms of future trajectories, we found fairly significant differences in the extent to which the younger post-communist cohorts, who were children or adolescents when communism fell, still exhibited different attitudes than their counterparts in non-post-communist countries. Thus, whereas these younger cohorts were not affected by the anti-market bias of their older post-communist compatriots—and in fact appear to have developed a pro-market bias by the mid- to late 2000s—with respect to democracy and welfare state support, they still exhibited significant and temporally resilient post-communist "signature" patterns, which suggest that in these areas not even generational replacement will be sufficient to eliminate the distinctive public opinion patterns in the countries of the former Eastern bloc. Our analysis in Chapter 6 (Section 6.5) suggests that at least with respect to welfare state support this extended half-life of communist legacies is due to strong intergenerational transmission, and these mechanisms are likely reinforced by the nostalgic way in which the communist era is described in the political discourse of many ex-communist countries (Ganev 2014).

Nostalgia arguably played an even more important role for the older age cohorts in the post-communist countries. These cohorts, who were disproportionately affected by the economic downturn and upheavals of the 1990s, exhibited much steeper declines in democracy and market support and much sharper increases in welfare state support in the early years of the transition than their younger compatriots. However, in all three areas, these trends were reversed starting in the late 1990s, and by the end of our period of analysis we observe a pronounced convergence pattern across different age cohorts in the context of the improving economic and political conditions in much of the region. Of course, our analysis stops in 2008, which raises the obvious question as to whether the renewed economic and political malaise of the post-2008 period would once again reopen this cross-generational gap.

While the period of attitudinal divergence broadly coincided with the trough of the J-curve of post-communist economic output, simply focusing on the temporal evolution of post-communist attitudinal exceptionalism does not necessarily prove that these patterns were indeed driven by the economic disappointments of the early transition period. To test this link more directly, in the final part of this chapter we take advantage of the wide variation in economic performance between different ex-communist countries to analyze the interplay between economic performance, time, and different age cohorts more explicitly. When doing so we confirm that both weaker economic output and higher inequality exacerbate the post-communist bias against markets and in favor of welfare states, and that these effects tend to be somewhat stronger for the older cohorts (with more extensive communist exposure). However, as time passes, the cross-country differences in market and welfare state attitudes between low- and high-performing transition countries are both substantively and statistically weaker than the differences between cohorts, which further reinforces our findings in Chapters 4–7 that the post-communist attitudinal differences are better explained by *living through communism* than *living in post-communist countries*.

Overall, the analysis in this chapter has shown that while the resilience of communist attitudinal legacies varies significantly across issue areas, in a number of important areas, including democratic support and welfare state preferences, the effects of communist socialization are still clearly visible even 20 years after the collapse of communism. Furthermore, these differences are visible even among individuals with short personal exposures to communist regimes, which means that we have reason to expect communism to continue to cast its shadow on the political preferences of post-communist citizens for many years to come.

CHAPTER 9

■ ■ ■ ■ ■

Legacies and Communism

NEWS REPORT ON ROMANIAN TV IN THE LATE 1980S.

FIRST ANNOUNCER: "Capitalist countries have reached the edge of the abyss!"
SECOND ANNOUNCER CHIMES IN: "Meanwhile, communist countries are,
as usual, two steps ahead of them!"

—Romanian joke, late 1980s

9.1. INTRODUCTION

Soviet communism was arguably history's greatest experiment in trying to reorganize the fundamental tenets of political, economic, and social life in a radical fashion. Moreover, the "treatment" was of a long and continuous duration: over 40 years in East-Central Europe, and close to 70 years in most of the republics of the former Soviet Union. At the time of this writing, we are witnessing perhaps the dawn of a new Cold War between the West and Russia, as well as erstwhile poster children of successful democratic transitions in Eastern Europe wrestling with challenges to democracy from right-wing national-populist parties (e.g., Hungary and Poland), while at the same time over 600,000 Romanians have taken to the streets and succeeded in forcing the government to back down from efforts to weaken anticorruption legislation. All of which leads to the question: how much does this communist "treatment" still affect the manner in which people approach politics in the post-communist years?

In the earliest days after the collapse of communism, the idea of communist society as a tabula rasa seemed tantalizing, one in which the rules of communism could be replaced by different laws reflecting different ideological predispositions with the belief that changes in behavior and outcomes would surely follow. In more recent years, however, the tabula rasa idea has gradually given way to an almost uniform belief (at least among political scientists who study post-communist politics) that *legacies* need to be taken into account in an attempt to understand the realities of post-communist politics and political behavior.[1] Prior to our own work, though, the vast majority of scholarly research on the topic of legacies has focused on institutional outcomes: democracy, corruption, bureaucratic procedures, and so on.

In this book, we extend the study of communist-era legacies to the realm of political behavior by examining the effect of these legacies on fundamental *attitudes* toward politics, economics, and social relations. More specifically, we examine the effect of legacies on attitudes toward democracy, markets, social welfare, and gender equality. We did not pick these topics randomly: in addition to representing fundamental components of modern public opinion, they also allow us tap into a great deal of what we would have expected to be a communist legacy: a distrust of multiparty democracy; a belief in the superiority of central planning as opposed to markets for allocating economic production; a sense that the state was responsible for providing for the welfare of the people; and a desire to eradicate inequality, which included sexism and gender inequality. Furthermore, these categories also present us with issue areas that varied in terms of ideological centrality to the communist project, gaps between rhetoric and reality, and popularity with the mass public.

In order to explore the extent to which differences in opinions in these areas between post-communist citizens and those in the rest of the world (a) exist and (b) are the result of communist-era legacies, we developed both a theoretical approach and a methodological framework. Theoretically, we have argued that there are two—quite different—types of explanations for why we might find divergent attitudes between post-communist citizens and non-post-communist citizens. First, it could be the case that differences in opinions are due to conditions in the countries in which people are living, or, to use the language of this book, to the fact that they are *living in post-communist countries*. To put another way, it is not that *living through communism* changed people's attitudes, but rather than when exposed to condition A (e.g., high unemployment), people are more likely to hold attitude B (e.g., distrust of the market), and there is simply more of condition A in post-communist countries than elsewhere.

We investigate a number of different types of *living in post-communist countries variables*, some of which are clearly not legacies of communism, some of which largely are legacies of communism, and some of which are likely legacies both of communism and post-communism (and maybe even pre-communism as well). To begin with, we explore whether

[1]See for example Kitschelt et al. 1999; Grzymała-Busse 2002, 2006; Howard 2002, 2003; Ekiert and Hanson 2003; Tucker 2006; Wittenberg 2006; Pop-Eleches 2007; Nalepa 2010; Pop-Eleches and Tucker 2012; Ekiert and Kubik 2015; and Rosenfeld 2016.

pre-communist conditions might explain the differences between attitudes (e.g., if condition A was literacy before the advent of communism); any effects due to pre-communist conditions would clearly not be legacies of communism. Next, we examine whether *contemporary conditions* (defined as conditions at the time respondents were queried about their attitudes) could explain attitudinal divergence; here we focused on sociodemographic characteristics, economic conditions, and political institutions. To the extent that any of these factors could explain differences in attitudes, they would reflect some combination of communist-era legacies and post-communist developments depending on the particular variable in question.[2] Finally, in an attempt to pin down more clearly the effect of communism independent of post-communist developments, we also consider the effect of *conditions at the end of the communist era* while controlling for pre-communist conditions. Furthermore, we identify variables for the end-of-communism measures that are most closely associated with major characteristics of communist rule: development, redistribution/egalitarianism, non-democratic rule, and leftist ideology. To the extent that these factors might explain divergence in attitudes (while controlling for pre-communist conditions), they would represent the strongest evidence of a direct legacy effect of communism from within our *living in post-communist countries* framework.

Our theoretical approach, however, also accounts for an alternative pathway by which legacies of communism could affect post-communist political attitudes by focusing on the actual experience of *living through communism*. This approach builds on the existing literature on political socialization to suggest that when regimes attempt to inculcate a set of views among the citizenry, greater exposure to the regime ought to lead to more congruence with the regime's position. We argue that the simplest observable implication of this proposition is that people with more *years of exposure* to the regime ought to be more likely to hold the attitude congruent with the regime's position than those with fewer years of exposure. Of course, such a blunt measure would miss the possibility that all years of exposure might not have the same effect. Some years of exposure might be more *intense* in terms of socialization effects, and we might also expect variation in *resistance* to the regime's message in different years of exposure; further, these *intensity* and *resistance* effects could vary at both the country and individual levels. Recall that in Chapter 1 we invoked the analogy of exposure to the sun and sunburn: exposure to

[2]For example, given the relatively slow change in sociodemographic characteristics, these would lean more toward communist-era legacies; conversely, political institutions adopted during the post-communist period such as electoral rules would be correspondingly less likely to be considered legacies of communism. In contrast, economic conditions in the post-communist years might be said to be more of a combination of communist legacies and post-communist policies.

the sun in summer is more likely to cause sunburn than in the winter, but regardless of the time of year, wearing sunscreen makes one less likely to be burned as well.

Both the *living in post-communist countries* and *living through communism* theoretical arguments were laid out in much greater detail in Chapters 1 and 2. In Chapter 3, we explained the methodological approaches we used to test the empirical support for each of these arguments as well as, crucially, the set of results that would falsify both of these arguments. (For reasons of space we are not going to revisit these methodological considerations here, but we invite interested readers to return to Chapter 3 for details.) In Chapters 4–7, we then considered in detail the extent to which each of these theoretical approaches could explain differences in attitudes between post-communist citizens and non-post-communist citizens. This analysis was organized by the attitude in question (e.g., Chapter 4 examined attitudes toward democracy, Chapter 5 toward markets, etc.); each chapter also presented some supplementary analysis drawing on different data and/or new specification of models specific to that particular topic. For readers interested in what we learned on a topic-by-topic basis, we recommend the conclusions of each chapter where we attempted to summarize concisely what we had learned in that chapter about the issue in question.

In this final concluding chapter, however, we want to return to the type of cross-topic analysis that we began in the previous chapter. Chapter 8 is the only chapter in the book so far to consider simultaneously findings across attitudes toward democracy, markets, social welfare, and gender equality, but it was focused a specific topic: how did these attitudes—and the "gap" in attitudes between post-communist citizens and non-post-communist citizens—change over the two decades covered by our surveys? In this chapter, however, we want to broaden the scope even further and examine what we have learned from our results in toto. With that in mind, the remainder of the chapter is organized along the following lines. First, in Section 9.2, we summarize our key results not by topic but by theoretical approach: what are the findings across the different components of the *living in a post-communist country* overall? What support is there for the *living through communism* model, and are there consistent results across the different *intensity* and *resistance* hypotheses? With these overall findings in hand, in Section 9.3 we consider what lessons the results offer for the study of comparative political behavior generally, that is, what have we learned about regime legacies that may not be specific to the post-communist context? Finally, in Section 9.4, we return to the question with which we began this manuscript: what have we learned about the legacies of communism on post-communist political, economic, and social attitudes, and what can this (potentially) tell us about the nature of post-communist politics today?

9.2. SUMMARY OF FINDINGS BY
THEORETICAL APPROACHES

The major finding of this manuscript is that we find much stronger empirical support for the *living through communism* model than we do for the *living in a post-communist country* model.[3] Accounting for all our different *living in a post-communist country* characteristics does *not* eliminate the gap in attitudes between post-communist citizens and non-post-communist citizens (conditional on a gap existing); if anything, accounting for these conditions generally *increases* the size of the gap.[4] Moreover, with the exception of gender equality—which differs from the other three issue areas across many of our findings—there is consistently strong support for the *living through communism* model. Simply reporting these headline results, though, misses the insight from the numerous ways in which we probed these findings and came to these conclusions, which we therefore now systematically summarize in the remainder of this section.[5] To aid in this process, we have prepared a visual summary of our findings in Table 9.1.

9.2.1. Living in a Post-communist Country

As mentioned in the previous section, there are three primary components of the *living in a post-communist country* analysis: accounting for pre-communist conditions; contemporaneous conditions (which are in turn divided into sociodemographic, economic, and political conditions), and conditions at the end of the communist era that are most closely associated with the communist project. We consider our findings from each set of factors in turn, drawing on the results presented in the first and second tables in Chapters 4–7. As we do so, however, it is important to reiterate that we did not originally find a gender equality "gap," and, to the extent that one appears after we account for particular blocks of variables, it is in the *opposite* direction from what we expected to find based on communist ideology: there is *less* support for gender equality among post-communist citizens than non-post-communist citizens. For this reason,

---

[3] Again in the spirit of research transparency, we do want to note that this was not necessarily our expectation going into the project: at least one of us fully expected to find stronger empirical support for the *living in a post-communist country* model than for the *living through communism* model.

[4] The only exception is with respect to the HLM tests of democracy support in the electronic appendix, where the post-communist deficit is reduced, though not fully eliminated, by controlling for living in a post-communist country.

[5] See Chapter 1, Section 1.7 for a less systematic summary of what we found to be the most interesting findings across all the different results.

in the remainder of this particular part of the discussion we focus our remarks on comparative findings between the democracy, markets, and social welfare results.[6]

Somewhat surprisingly, in all three issue areas where there is a gap—democracy, markets, social welfare—controlling for pre-communist conditions *increases* the size of the communist deficit, and sometimes dramatically so. In the case of attitudes toward democracy and markets, the size of the gaps approximately doubles; for social welfare, the gap increases by a third.[7] So, rather than pre-communist conditions explaining why post-communist citizens were less supportive of democracy and markets, and more supportive of social welfare, it turns out that conditional on pre-communist conditions post-communist citizens should have been more supportive of democracy and markets, and less supportive of social welfare! Thus, for example, once we take account of the "favorable for democracy" pre-communist characteristics in the societies that would become communist countries, the deficit in support for democracy in the post-communist era appears even larger.

Turning to contemporary conditions, our findings here are a bit more issue dependent. In some cases (democracy, markets), the attitudinal differences that appear when we add the contemporaneous variables are smaller than those that appear when we control simply for pre-communist conditions—suggesting they do account for some of the existing gap. In other cases (social welfare), the contemporary variables tend to *increase* the size of the gap relative even to the pre-communist control variables. But in not a single model do we find that accounting for contemporaneous conditions eliminates the gap entirely. Furthermore, we have very similar findings when we replicate our analysis using only citizens from Germany.[8]

---

[6] As there is no gap in gender equality to explain away, we leave it out of the current discussion (and label it not applicable (n/a) on Table 9.1); we do return to discussing gender equality comparatively when discussing the *living through communism* model.

[7] Although the size of the gender equality gap did increase substantially (again in the wrong direction), it is important to note that neither the bivariate nor the pre-communist models produced statistically significant effects (see Table 7.1 for details). However, because of the double negative here (increasing the gap in the wrong way), one way to interpret this finding is to say that communism did indeed mitigate the amount of anti–gender equality sentiment one would have expected to find in post-communist societies on the basis of pre-communist conditions alone.

[8] Gender equality is again a bit of an exception, as there is not statistically significant gap to eliminate, although most model specifications do result in an increase in the size of the (still statistically insignificant) gap. In two cases—including contemporary demographic indicators and including contemporary economic conditions—the gap actually approaches statistical significance ($p<.10$), albeit again in the *wrong* direction (i.e., less support for gender equality).

Table 9.1. Summary of Results

	Democracy	Markets	Social welfare	Gender equality
Living in . . .				
Pre-communism	**(Pre-communism)**	**(Pre-communism)**	(Pre-communism)	n/a
Demographics	Demographics	Demographics		n/a
Economic			(Economic)	n/a
Political		Political	Political	n/a
All	All			n/a
Unpacking				
Development				n/a
Welfare state		(Welfare state)		n/a
Authoritarian		Authoritarian	Authoritarian	n/a
Leftist				
Left-authoritarian	(Left-authoritarian)	(Left-authoritarian)	Left-authoritarian	n/a
Exposure				
Total	**Total**	**Total**	Total	
Youth		Youth	Youth	Youth
Adult	**Adult**	**Adult**	Adult	
Country-level				
Pre-communist literacy	Pre-communist literacy			Pre-communist literacy
Pre-communist GDP/capita	Pre-communist GDP/capita			Pre-communist GDP/capita
Pre-communist regime	Pre-communist regime	Pre-communist regime		Pre-communist regime

Overall communist growth		Overall communist growth		Overall communist growth
Native communism		Native communism	Native communism	(Native communism)
Proportion hardliners				
Bureaucracy type	(Bureaucracy type)		(Bureaucracy type)	(Bureaucracy type)
Late-communist growth		**Late-communist growth**		**Late-communist growth**
Late-communist liberalization		Late-communist liberalization		(Late-communist liberalization)
Individual				
Denomination	Catholic	Catholic, Muslim	Orthodox	Catholic
Attendance	Churchgoer	**Churchgoer**		Churchgoer
Education	**Education**			Education
Urban v. rural	Urban	Urban	Urban	
Gender/Sex		Male		Male

Note: This table presents a visual summary of our primary findings from Chapters 4–7. Each column represents one chapter, indicated by the heading at the top of the column. Each row represents a set of analyses. In each case, we list the name of the analysis if the effect is in the correctly predicted direction, with the text **bolded** if it is a strong effect. If there is an effect in the wrong direction, we put the name of the analysis in parentheses (as on a balance sheet), continuing bolding particularly strong effects. If there is no effect one way or another, we leave the name of the analysis out of that column. For our living in a post-communist country analyses, a correctly predicted effect is one that reduces the size of the predicted post-communist differential; given that there is no evidence of the predicted post-communist differential for gender equality, we mark those results as not applicable (n/a). For our living through communism exposure analyses, a correctly predicted effect is one where more exposure leads to more support for the position on the attitude associated with communism. Note that we do not include communist regime type on this table because the analysis does not lend itself to yes/no summarizing. For the intensifying and resistance hypotheses, a correctly predicted effect is one where the interaction is in the hypothesized direction. Note that strong vs. weak effects do not correspond to any particular statistical threshold; the table is simply intended as a quick visual summary of our findings. Readers interested in any particular findings should see the relevant tables and figures in Chapters 4–7 and the electronic appendix.

Looking across the different contemporary factors, for the most part there are no particular patterns that stand out. Taking account of demographic characteristics reduces the size of the deficit by about a third for attitudes toward democracy and a quarter for attitudes toward markets but increases it for social welfare. Taking account of economic conditions surprisingly has no effect on the gap in support for markets and actually increases the gap in support for social welfare.

There is one interesting exception in this regard, which is that adding *political* institutions into the analysis reduces the size of the gap relative to the pre-communist models for both markets and social welfare. Moreover, these reductions are substantively meaningful: the gap decreases by about a third for markets, by close to half for social welfare, and even decreases the gap for democracy a bit too. Thus it seems safe to say that part of the difference in attitudes between citizens in post-communist countries and non-post-communist countries is due to *political* institutions, though the extent to which these institutions should be considered communist legacies, the result of post-communist policy (or constitutional) decisions, or even "accidents of chance" varies greatly across institutions and is beyond the scope of this discussion.[9] Of course, it is possible that some of these institutional choices could be endogenous to levels of support for democracy; this would be an interesting subject for future research.[10]

Our final set of *living in a post-communist country* variables measures conditions at the end of the communist period, and specifically conditions designed to tap into communism's most prevalent policies and characteristics: development, redistribution, non-democratic rule, and leftist political orientation. The conclusions from these analyses are fairly similar to those from the contemporaneous variables—most of these variables have no effect on the post-communist attitudinal gap—with one noticeable exception. In the case of markets and social welfare (but not democracy), adding the average Polity scores (i.e., level of democracy) in the country in the decade and a half leading up to the collapse of communism to the model did systematically reduce the size of the attitudinal gap. This was particularly striking in the case of attitudes toward social welfare. In that case, simply controlling for the level of democracy in the country in the last fifteen years of communist rule dropped the size of the

[9] Thus, differences in Freedom House democracy scores may well be (at least in part) a communist legacy (Pop-Eleches 2014), but for other institutions the answer is less obvious. For example, should we think of the decision to have a presidential as opposed to parliamentary system of government as a legacy of communism? Similar questions could be posed regarding corruption. For more, see Pop-Eleches and Tucker (2012).

[10] For example, if people do not care about democracy, then perhaps they would be more willing to accept strong presidencies or violations of political rights or civil liberties.

social welfare attitude gap by two-thirds (and below conventional levels of statistical significance). One way to think of this is that conditional on having lived in a less democratic regime in the last years of the Cold War, post-communist citizens did not have all that different attitudes toward belief in the appropriate level of state responsibility for providing for the social welfare of its citizens; this was especially true for non-democratic leftist regimes. Gender equality is also very interesting in this regard: controlling for level of democracy, we see the only post-communist *pro–gender equality* gap (although not statistically significant) in any of our *living in a post-communist country* models. What this suggests is that conditional on having lived in non-democratic regimes in the 1970s and 1980s, post-communist citizens were no less likely to have harbored anti–gender equality attitudes than citizens living in other non-democratic, but non-post-communist, countries.

9.2.2. Living through Communism

In contrast, the primary empirical results regarding the *living through communism* model are supportive of the model's predictions. Controlling for age, attitudes toward democracy, markets, and social welfare are all affected by additional exposure to communist rule in the direction we would expect: additional years of exposure to communist rule leads to less support for democracy, less support for markets, and more support for state responsibility for social welfare. To be clear, these effects are all present in even the most naive models that essentially assume each year of exposure is equal to any other year of exposure (see Models 1–2 in Table 3 of Chapters 4–7). The one exception in this case is in terms of gender equality, although here it is important to remember that there is no "gap" in attitudes to explain away in the first place. Further, we do find results consistent with the model's predictions in terms of gender equality once we begin to take account of *intensifying* and *resistance* factors. Finally, it is important to note that all the baseline exposure estimates were essentially the same when we reestimated the models with country-fixed effects, as well as using hierarchical linear models (see electronic appendix).

In the remainder of this section, we summarize the findings regarding our *intensifying* and *resistance* hypotheses. Recall that we have essentially carried out three types of tests for both of these categories of hypotheses: individual-level effects that we tested across all four chapters using the World Values Survey (WVS) data; country-level effects that we tested across all four chapters using the WVS data; and individual-level effects we tested only in particular chapters using supplementary data. In the individual chapters, we considered these hypotheses sequentially by the type of test; here we instead examine the *intensifying* and *resistance* hypotheses in turn. Note that summaries of the results we discuss from the WVS analyses can be found in Table 9.1.

Among the *intensifying* variables, perhaps the theoretically most interesting one—and certainly so when judged by the number of questions we received during presentations of earlier versions of this research—is communist regime type (Stalinism, neo-Stalinism, post-totalitarian, and reformist). Somewhat surprisingly, the results regarding type of communist regime are much less informative than we expected. First, unlike our baseline overall exposure (and our adult vs. child exposure) estimates, these communist regime type findings are generally not robust to using country-fixed-effects models. While the direction of the effects remains the same, the magnitude and significance of the coefficients frequently change. This makes reporting general patterns trickier. That being said, it is safe to note that we do *not* find strong evidence in support of the general hypothesis that effects of exposure decrease from Stalinist to neo-Stalinist to post-totalitarian to reformist exposure. However, there are some instances that fit this model: the country-fixed-effects models for attitudes toward democracy and attitudes toward social welfare do show this general pattern (see Tables 4.3 and 6.3, Model 4), although the differences in most of the pairs of coefficients were fairly small.[11] Perhaps the most interesting finding in this regard, however, comes from the gender equality analyses which—for the non-fixed-effects model—does reveal that years of exposure to Stalinism led to an *increase* in support for gender equality, thus being consistent with the idea of Stalinism being a time of true believers adopting the rhetoric of the party[12] and cutting against the grain of our general finding that post-communist citizens are less supportive of gender equality. Nevertheless, even this finding is not particularly robust to adding country-fixed effects to the model.

While none of our *intensifying* hypotheses that we test with WVS data generate empirical support across all four issue areas, both *late-communist growth* and *living in an urban area* are associated with a stronger effect for exposure in three out of our four issues areas. Being a male also results in a stronger exposure effect in two of the four areas, suggesting at least some support for the idea that increased exposure to regime messages could be enhancing the effect of exposure. Interestingly, we also find a stronger exposure effect on attitudes toward markets for people living in families where at least one parent was a member of the Communist Party.

On the other hand, there are a number of hypothesized intensifier variables where the predicted effects fail to materialize. Most strikingly,

---

[11] These patterns were also confirmed in the corresponding HLM tests; see the electronic appendix for details.

[12] Alternatively, it might reflect that the rhetoric of gender equality more closely matched actual policy in the earlier days of communism.

having bureaucratic authoritarian regimes under communism is associated with *weaker* exposure effects, as opposed to *intensified* effects, in three of the four issue areas. Additionally having a higher proportion of communist rule occur under Stalinist or neo-Stalinist communist regimes only seems to intensify the effect of exposure in terms of attitudes toward democracy, but not any of the other variables. That being said, with the exception of bureaucracy type, when we do find significant *intensifying* effects, they are almost always in the correctly predicted direction.

Turning to our *resistance* variables, we begin with our estimates of the effects of time of life exposure.[13] In contrast to our measure of exposure by regime type, the estimates for time of life exposure are quite robust across the two different forms of model specification and lead to very interesting cross-issue patterns. In contrast to the extant literature on political socialization from the United States discussed in Section 1.2 of Chapter 1, we find that *adult* communist exposure has a stronger effect on attitudes toward democracy, markets, and social welfare than *early* exposure. Indeed, for attitudes toward democracy, childhood exposure has no effect on increasing the democracy gap, and for markets and social welfare the effect of a year of childhood exposure appears to have about half the effect of a year of adult exposure. Interestingly, though, the pattern reverses (again robust to model specification) for gender equality, with only *childhood* exposure having an effect on *pro–gender equality* views, which is the direction in which we originally expected the regime socialization to occur. As we have mentioned throughout this chapter, we actually find a gap in the opposite direction (less support for gender equality) among post-communist citizens in many of our model specifications. However, as we note in Chapter 7, the one place that this gap is either nonexistent, or at least significantly smaller, is in the schools. Thus, to the extent that the rhetoric of gender equity matched the reality of childhood experiences under communist rule, perhaps we should not be surprised to see a socialization effect for childhood exposure.

There are number of other instances of relatively strong *resistance* effects at the individual level. Two of these are related to religion: we find both Catholics and those who attend religious services more frequently to have had higher *resistance* to the effects of an additional year of communist socialization across three of the four issue areas. Additional years of education also provide *resistance* largely as predicted in two of the four issue areas. Moreover, in our supplemental analysis in Chapter 5, we find two additional education effects consistent with our *resistance* hypotheses: individuals who received a communist education had a stronger

---

[13] The period of life (adult vs. childhood) in which one is exposed to communist rule is classified as a resistance effect because it is based on the idea that resistance to communist socialization should be lower among school-aged children.

exposure effect than those not educated under communism; and individuals with a parent educated under communism had a stronger exposure effect.[14]

At the country level, we find relatively strong support for the idea that *pre-communist* development provided *resistance* to communist socialization. Both higher pre-communist literacy and higher pre-communist GDP per capital are associated with reduced exposure effects on attitudes toward democracy and gender equality, and higher levels of pre-communist political pluralism are associated with smaller exposure effects on democracy, gender equality, and attitudes toward markets. Having a communist system imposed from abroad also provides additional resistance to communist exposure on attitudes toward markets and social welfare. Finally, living in countries with higher levels of overall economic growth under communist rule is associated with a strong reduction in *resistance* (i.e., a stronger exposure effect) for attitudes toward markets and gender equality.

Taken together, three conclusions seem important with respect to the *resistance* and *intensifying* hypotheses component of the *living through communism* model. First, we can definitely find many instances where intensifier or resistance variables moderate the extent to which communist exposure promote political attitudes in line with communist ideology. Further, when these effects are present, they are usually—although not always—in the direction that we expected. Indeed, perhaps the strongest finding from these analyses is—with the exception of bureaucratic governing type—just how infrequently we find effects that are in the wrong direction.[15] So conditional on finding an *intensifying* or *resistance* effect, it is almost always in the correct direction. Thus, by taking account of these factors, one can get a more nuanced picture of the manner in which exposure affects any of the attitudes we have examined in this manuscript. To put it another way, if the goal is a more accurate account of the effects of exposure on any particular attitude, then these intensifier and resistance variables are the way to go.

The second conclusion, however, is that in terms of general findings across issue areas, the approach did not yield a clear set of "silver bullet" factors that consistently amplified or diminished the socialization ef-

---

[14] Moreover, individuals who had a parent who was educated in a pre-communist school setting were more likely support markets, thus showing support for the parent socialization hypothesis. However, to be clear, this was a direct effect and *not* an interaction effect with exposure.

[15] Setting aside the effects in the wrong direction of the three bureaucratic governing types, of the remaining effects that we identified as strong enough to warrant inclusion in Table 9.1, only 2 out of 32 are in the wrong direction; including bureaucratic type brings this ratio to 5 out of 35.

fects of communist exposure. None of the variables that we examined had strongly consistent results in the expected direction across all four issues. While a few variables—late-communist economic growth and urban residence increasing intensity, Catholicism and interwar democracy increasing resistance—generally have the predicted moderating role (i.e., are correct in most issue areas and not wrong in the others), many other moderating factors either produced weak results or yielded different effects across issue areas (as in the case of homegrown versus native communism).

Another way to interpret these results, is that while our tests confirm that certain subsets of communist citizens were indeed noticeably more/ less affected by communist exposure, it is also true that the effects of exposure were strikingly similar across a surprisingly large number of individual-level and country-level differences that we might have expected to have moderated the effects of exposure. This phenomenon was most obvious in the case of welfare state support, which appears to have been uniformly high among most post-communist citizens. But even for attitudes toward democracy and markets, where there was greater intensity/ resistance-induced heterogeneity in exposure effects, across the many tests we conducted we found virtually no subgroup of ex-communist citizens whose attitudes were completely unaffected by having lived under communism. Indeed, except for the market support effects for Muslims who attend mosque frequently in Figure 5.3, all the other conditional exposure effects in Figures 4.2, 4.3, 5.2, 5.3, 6.2, and 6.3 were significantly different from 0 in the direction predicted by communist ideology. In other words, except for gender equality, it appears that *communist regimes were overall remarkably effective in shaping the political attitudes of their subjects.*

Finally, as Table 9.1 visually demonstrates, it is interesting that it is the issue of gender equality—the one issue area where we do not find a statistically significant effect for exposure writ large—that we find the most support for the *intensity* and *resistance* hypotheses. Two lessons seem germane from this finding. First, simply finding an insignificant effect for years of exposure in a *living through* legacy framework should not be taken as sufficient evidence to close the books on whether there are relevant legacy effects due to *living through* that regime: it may be the case that there are legacy effects of this type, but that they are relevant only among certain subsections of the population or that they act in opposite directions for different sets of individuals or countries. Second, it is possible that because gender equality was less central to communist ideology, socialization effects related to gender equality were more likely to be concentrated in certain subsections of the population (or in particular countries). If this is correct—and this remains nothing more than speculation at the moment—then it might suggest that it is particularly important to look for heterogeneous evidence of *living through* exposure effects on attitudes related to more peripheral components of a regime's ideology.

9.3. CONTRIBUTIONS TO THE STUDY OF LEGACIES AND ATTITUDES

With these findings in hand, we can now turn to the task of discussing the broader implications of what we have learned. In the following section (9.4), we will return to the question that originally motivated this book by assessing the implications of our results for understanding the effect of communist legacies on post-communist attitudes specifically and post-communist politics more generally. Before doing so, though, we wish to pause briefly to address the implications of our work for scholars and students of comparative political behavior more generally who may be less interested in the peculiarities of the post-communist case. We focus on three main conclusions here: the implications of greater empirical support for our *living through communism* versus *living in post-communist countries* models; our findings regarding child versus adult socialization; and the fact that we get such different findings in one issue area (attitudes toward gender equality).

The first finding with broader importance is the fact that post-communist attitudinal exceptionalism is consistently better explained by *living through communism* than by *living in a post-communist country*. Thus to the extent that communist legacies have shaped attitudes in post-communist countries, it is more through the experiences of the people who lived through communism than it is through reshaping the society in which those people are currently living. This suggests that the *length of time* a regime has been in power is an important determinant of the legacy effects that regime will have on the attitudes of its citizenry once the regime itself is gone. While hardly an earth-shattering conclusion, it does point to reasons why, for example, we might expect that it would take Russians after 1991 longer to shed attitudes associated with communism than it took Germans post-1945 to shed attitudes inculcated by the Nazis, even if the "societal transformation" brought out by Nazism was similar to that brought about by communism.[16] Similarly, based on our findings in this book we might expect that in countries where military regimes and democratic regimes alternated in office (e.g., Turkey, Pakistan, and parts of Latin America) we will find weaker legacy effects than

---

[16] To be clear, we are not claiming that it was but instead simply highlighting the consequences of finding more support for a model based on time of exposure.

in countries where regimes remained in power continuously for longer periods of time (e.g., Spain, Taiwan or Mexico).

Perhaps even more importantly, our findings suggest that skepticism may be warranted regarding claims that simply changing institutional arrangements may change underlying beliefs in the efficacy of those institutions. Recent events in Egypt may prove illustrative: despite the euphoria that initially seemed to greet the fall of Mubarak, many Egyptians seemed comfortable with the idea of returning to military rule shortly thereafter when the ascent of the Muslim Brotherhood threatened stability. While we have obviously not studied attitudes in Egypt in this book, it seems consistent with what we have found here that for people who had lived many years of their lives under military rule, the military in Egypt could have come to be seen as a force for stability.[17] This is not to say the failure of democracy in Egypt was in any way preordained by the previous experience of military rule (indeed, Tunisia for now provides contrary evidence), but only that it might have been wrong to assume that once democratic elections were in place the mass populace would have shed their affinity for authoritarian rule. To put this another way, we do not in any way want to claim that citizens who have lived under a particular non-democratic regime type for an extended period of time are somehow "unsuited" for democratic rule—indeed, the post-1989 history of much of East-Central Europe shows the fallacy of such a view—but rather that we need to take a realistic view of the underlying support that is likely to be present for new institutions that are at odds with those found under the old regime. Further, our findings suggest that these attitudes are likely to be a function of the number of years individuals spent living under the previous regime, which points again to the importance of the longevity of the regime.

The second general point we want to highlight, in particular for scholars of political socialization, is our findings regarding the effects of exposure among children as opposed to adults. To the best of our understanding, the extant literature—especially but not exclusively in the United Sates—has focused primarily on the question of whether political socialization occurs exclusively in childhood or occurs throughout one's lifetime (Krosnick and Alwin 1989; Visser and Krosnick 1998; Sears and Valentino 1997; D. Osborne et al. 2011). We have not, however, seen any studies suggesting that socialization might occur *only* in adulthood and not in childhood, or even that the effect might be stronger in adulthood than in childhood. And yet, that is exactly what we found in three of our

---

[17] See, for example, the following two Pew Global reports: http://www.pewglobal .org/2013/05/16/egyptians-increasingly-glum/ and http://www.pewglobal.org/2014/05/22 /chapter-3-democratic-values-in-egypt/.

issue areas: an effect only in adulthood in the case of attitudes toward democracy, and an effect that was roughly twice as strong in adulthood than in childhood for attitudes toward markets and social welfare. Only in the case of gender equality was the effect stronger in childhood. Why might this be the case?

The first answer to this question lies in our theoretical distinction between *intensifying* and *resistance* factors that moderate the impact of political socialization. Thus, as laid out in Chapter 2, we interpret the "impressionable years" explanation for the importance of early socialization as based on the idea that children and adolescents have weaker *resistance* to political indoctrination efforts than adults, and are therefore more likely to internalize these messages and incorporate them into their political attitudes. However, our empirical results are clearly at odds with such an interpretation, and it seems hard to come up with a persuasive resistance-based explanation for why adults would be affected to a greater extent than children. By contrast, these patterns may be easier to explain if instead we focus on variation in the *intensity* of political socialization to which communist citizens were exposed at various stages of their lives. Thus, it could be the case that even though most children were exposed for years to ideologically infused curricula in communist education systems, communist socialization on topics such as political regimes, markets versus central planning, and welfare services may have been much more intense—and perhaps more intelligible—once communist citizens turned 18 and entered the work force, began to take part in the political process, and began to appreciate the importance of state-provided welfare in the context of starting their own families.

Such an *intensity*-based explanation may also be helpful in accounting for the difference between the socialization patterns of gender equality and the other three types of attitudes discussed in this book: by focusing on variation in the nature and intensity of the message rather than the receptiveness of the recipient, such an account may also explain why we find different adult versus childhood exposure effects across issue areas. Thus, arguably the gender-egalitarian facets of communist ideology may have been more prominent in primary and secondary schools (given that the majority of teachers were women) than in universities and factories, where those in charge were more likely to be men. Of course, since we arrived at this argument inductively in order to explain the unexpected socialization patterns in Chapters 4–6, it cannot be tested with the same data but will require some "out-of-sample" confirmation in future work. Nevertheless, this explanation suggests that our intensity-resistance framework for understanding the effects of communist exposure may be fruitfully applied to a broader range of research questions about political socialization processes.

A second possible answer to the puzzle raised by our unexpected adult versus childhood socialization results—and here too we are largely entering tentative hypothesis-building territory that will hopefully be explored in greater detail in future work—focuses on the role of education in driving political socialization in authoritarian regimes. Our speculation is that the key factor here may be the role of primary and secondary education in non-democratic regimes. Suppose it is the case that the purpose of this education is not actually to teach children a set of complex political values, but rather simply to break down any resistance to the very idea that it is possible to challenge the position of the state. Simply receiving this type of an education might not, for example, build up a belief that markets are inherently bad, but they would decrease the capacity of an individual as an adult to question state proclamations regarding markets. Thus, if an individual is educated under communism and then lives most of her life under communist rule, over time she will be more likely to adopt an anti-market position as an adult. Conversely if she is educated under communism but then lives in a post-communist world where markets are no longer reviled by the new post-communist state, she will be less likely to develop an anti-market viewpoint. To be clear, we are suggesting this possibility—that non-democratic ideologically oriented states may use primary and secondary education not to indoctrinate so much as to create citizens willing to accept the dictates of the state as an adult— based not on any evaluation of educational practices under communist rule (or any other non-democratic regime for that matter), but rather as a conjecture based on our surprising findings regarding adult and childhood exposure effects in our analysis. Nevertheless, we intend to investigate this in our own research in the future.

Combining the two findings, though, leads to an interesting and potentially new way to think about indoctrination/socialization under authoritarian regimes: the real value of having access to children (i.e., controlling education) is that the state can teach students not necessarily a specific doctrine, but rather the more basic fact that the state is always right. This is potentially even more valuable to the state that inculcating any particular doctrine, because it gives the state flexibility in the future. If the state is always correct, then the state can change its message in the future without contradicting the core tenet of regime ideology (i.e., the state is correct). Thus the actual attitudinal indoctrination—for example, opposition to markets, democracy—takes place only later in one's adult life, but the early childhood exposure plays a crucial role in setting the stage for this process. Again, this is not a theory we have tested, but rather a conjecture based on our results that we think is an interesting avenue for study in the future.

But what of the findings regarding gender equality, which do not fit the patterns described in the preceding paragraphs? In addition to our earlier points about variation in the intensity of socialization efforts across different issue areas, this puzzle can also be addressed from a different perspective, which also may be of interest for future studies of political socialization: for a wide variety of regimes (including liberal democracies) there are some aspects of regime ideology that are matched by reality, and then there are aspects of ideology to which the regime pays lip service but that may not be reflected in reality. There are also aspects of regime ideology that are more and less central to any given regime. As we have mentioned previously, it would be hard to deny that communist regimes featured single-party political rule, central planning over much of the economy, and generous social welfare benefits, or that any of these characteristics of communist rule—and in particular single-party rule and state management of the economy—were more central to communist ideology than gender equality. Meanwhile, gender equality may have been part of official communist dogma, but it was not matched—at least not thoroughly—by reality for the wide variety of reasons we describe in Chapter 7. We suspect that there are many non-democratic regimes that have particular policies stressed as part of the ideological justification for the regime but where related promises are not met in reality, and where there is variation in how prominent these ideas feature even in regime ideology. Our research here would suggest that unless the rhetoric is matched by actual policies and outcomes, attitudinal legacy effects in that particular issue area are likely to be weaker following the collapse of the regime. The same holds for ideas that are less prominently featured in—or central to—regime ideology and for ideological aspects that are less popular in a given society.

Combining the last two points, then, one reason we might not see adult gender equality socialization effects is precisely because the societies in which adults lived in communist countries did not—for the most part—reflect gender equality, regardless of what communist ideology might suggest. Thus, while education might have made people more receptive to state policy in terms of gender equality, these effects were undermined by the lack of gender equity in many other parts of communist societies. In school, by contrast, children were arguably exposed to a more gender-equal context, thus leading to the observed childhood socialization effect.

Before moving on to our conclusions regarding legacies and postcommunist politics specifically, we do want to mention one more general contribution of this manuscript, namely the theoretical and methodological approach we have developed to the study of legacies on political behavior. There is nothing in either the *living in* or *living through* model that is specific to the post-communist context as opposed to any other "post-X regime type" context. Of course, the variables we use for some parts of our analysis are driven by the nature of communism—especially in "unpacking communism" and in terms of the particular *intensity* and *resistance* hypotheses—but the basic setup could be exported to other contexts. The same is true for the statistical methods we have proposed for testing these models. While the particular intensifying and resistance factors are specific to communism, the general approach of identifying factors that could intensify exposure or provide resistance to exposure in the case of regime X is itself generalizable. Further, while we have looked at the effects of legacies on attitudes, there is no reason the method could not be applied to other aspects of political behavior including evaluation and participation (e.g., Pop-Eleches and Tucker 2013) or other attitudes beyond the four considered in this manuscript (e.g., Pop-Eleches and Tucker 2010). Thus we very much hope that not just our findings, but our methods as well, will inspire research on legacy effects on political behavior broadly outside of the specific attitudes and context featured in this manuscript.

9.4. CONTRIBUTIONS TO THE STUDY OF POST-COMMUNIST POLITICS

In this final section we discuss how the findings in our manuscript contribute to debates about the role of historical legacies in explaining the politics of post-communist Eastern Europe and Eurasia. We will start by placing our book in the broader context of scholarly debates about the nature, mechanisms, and scope conditions of historical legacy effects. Next, we take a brief empirical detour to discuss in greater detail how our analysis helps explain one of the more puzzling empirical regularities of the post-communist transition: the gap between the countries emerging from the republics of the pre-WWII Soviet Union and the countries where communist regimes came to power only at the end of WWII. Finally, we briefly discuss the implications of our findings for the debates about the "end of the post-communist transition" and for understanding some of the recent political developments in the region, including concerns about authoritarian backsliding.

9.4.1. *Varieties of Legacy Arguments and Different Contributions*

As mentioned previously, in this book we have been focused primarily on developing a theoretical framework for understanding the effects of communism on political attitudes, proposing a methodological approach for testing the theoretical predictions of this model, and then applying this method to establish the extent and the nature of communist legacy effects on four important dimensions of post-communist political attitudes. As such, we hope that this book will provide an impetus for future work on these important and surprisingly understudied questions by encouraging research that would apply the framework to other questions related to post-communist political behavior.[18]

Given that the literature on communist attitudinal legacies is still in its infancy, we now also discuss how our findings speak to two separate but related strands of the literature on historical legacies in Eastern Europe (and beyond). The first strand is a group of studies that have analyzed the effects of "deeper" pre-communist historical legacies in explaining individual political attitudes and behavior in post-communist Eastern Europe (Darden and Grzymała-Busse 2006; Wittenberg 2006; Darden 2011; Peisakhin 2015).[19] While there is an obvious tension between the emphasis in these works on the survival of important pre-communist differences and our focus on the common legacies of the shared communist experience, we agree with Ekiert and Ziblatt (2013) that the two approaches are best seen as complementary, not as alternatives. In part this complementarity is rooted in the very logic of the two types of arguments, given that they both take the role of historical legacies seriously and rely on similar transmission mechanisms. But the findings in our book suggest an additional interesting source of complementarity, rooted in the interaction between pre-communist and communist legacies in shaping post-communist attitudes. Thus, we find significant evidence that country-level pre-communist socioeconomic and political development, and individual-level pre-communist education (and religious denomination) played an important role in helping us understand the varying degrees of resistance toward communist political socialization efforts. In other words, even though pre-communist differences do not account for post-communist attitudinal exceptionalism, our understanding of communist legacies is enriched by accounting for the significant pre-communist differences between the countries that ended up behind the Iron Curtain. Conversely, we would argue that our focus on communist-era socialization can help elucidate the mechanisms through which pre-communist legacy differences

---

[18] One important extension, for example, would be to expand the scope of analysis to contribute to the small but growing literature on the post-communist deficit in civic and political participation (Howard 2002, 2003; Pop-Eleches and Tucker 2013; Ekiert and Kubik 2014; Rosenfeld 2016).

[19] Technically, both Darden and Grzymała-Busse (2006) and Wittenberg (2006) focus on aggregate outcomes, but the logic of the argument is largely rooted in individual attitudes and behavior, which is why we reference them as part of this discussion here.

were able to survive the sustained and often violent efforts of communist regimes to erase all vestiges of the pre-communist past.[20]

The second comparison set consists of studies of post-communist politics that use historical legacy arguments to explain a broad range of macro-level (typically country-level) economic and political outcomes. As in the case of individual-level legacy work, we can make a further distinction between works emphasizing post-communist diversity rooted in pre-communist legacies (e.g., Janos 2000) and those emphasizing the distinctive and fairly uniform post-communist imprint of Leninist legacies (e.g., Jowitt 1992, Tismăneanu et al. 2006). Given our emphasis on shared communist legacies, our book obviously speaks more directly to the second set of studies, especially those concerned with the continued existence of a post-communist democratic deficit (Pop-Eleches 2014) or with the nature of Eastern European welfare states (Haggard and Kaufman 2008). For such studies our manuscript potentially provides some of the micro-foundations underlying variation in macro-level outcomes. While even in democracies the translation of individual political preferences into policy and institutional outcomes is by no means straightforward (Gilens 2012), public opinion can nevertheless create varying political opportunities and constraints for political elites and thereby influence political outcomes even in non-democracies.[21] Similarly, the growing resistance to market economics in the mid-1990s (discussed in Chapter 8) may help explain why the initially rapid privatization progress of the first transition years slowed down considerably by the mid- to late 1990s despite the fact that state sectors in most ex-communist countries are still significantly larger than in much of the rest of the world (Pop-Eleches 2015). While the congruence of macro- and micro-level patterns is reassuring, our understanding of these linkages between the two levels would undoubtedly be improved if future work on the topic would analyze in a more integrated fashion how historical legacies affect both individual attitudes and aggregate institutional outcomes and the processes through which macro- and micro-level factors shape each other.

While the second subtype of macro-level historical legacy work, which emphasizes variation in institutional outcomes across different ex-communist countries, is somewhat further removed from the focus of the present book, there are nevertheless a number of areas in which the findings in this book can help clarify some of the mechanisms underlying the differences in macro-institutional outcomes highlighted by earlier studies. For example, our finding in Chapter 4 regarding the greater

---

[20] See, for example, Wittenberg 2006.

[21] For example, Rosenfeld (2016) shows that countries with larger shares of democrats tended to be more democratic even among post-Soviet non-democratic regimes.

resistance among Catholics to the anti-democratic socialization effects of communist exposure may help explain why at the aggregate level several studies have found better democratic outcomes in countries with Western Christian majorities (Fish 1998; Pop-Eleches 2007). Moreover, our finding about the greater resistance among Catholics than Protestants suggests that aggregate studies should differentiate between Catholics and Protestants, at least when analyzing post-communist democracy and authoritarianism.

In the following subsection we address how our findings in this book can help illuminate one of the more striking (but largely undertheorized) findings in the literature on historical legacies in post-communist politics: the divergence between the successor states of the pre-WWII Soviet republics and the countries that became communist only in the wake of World War II.

9.4.2. Reassessing the Differences between Eastern Europe and the Pre-WWII Soviet Republics

Even a cursory look at the economic and political trajectories of the former communist countries during the first decade of the transition reveals a stark contrast between the significant (albeit uneven) progress toward democracy and market economies among the former Eastern European Soviet satellite states (plus the Baltic states) and the greater resilience of authoritarianism and statist economics in the "core" pre-WWII Soviet republics. These patterns were confirmed by a number of studies that revealed significant democratic reform deficits among the pre-WWII Soviet republics (Pop-Eleches 2007, 2014). This contrast raises an interesting challenge to our analytical approach in this book, where we lump together as post-communist citizens any resident of a country of the former Soviet bloc, irrespective of the timing of the onset of communist rule in a particular country. This raises an important question: does it really make sense to talk about "post-communist" citizens, or should we differentiate between the two types of countries based on the length of their communist regime spells?

While in the preceding chapters of this book we opted for the lumping approach for both theoretical reasons—we were interested in testing the extent to which various pre-communist and communist country characteristics moderated the attitudinal impact of communism—and practical reasons—the presentation of results would have been much more complicated had we used two different types of communist countries—in this section we will nevertheless briefly present for each of our four types of political attitudes a series of statistical models that differentiate between pre- and post-WWII communist countries. The first set of models simply includes the two communist regime indicators along with a series of survey-year dummies to establish the bivariate attitudinal differences between the two types of ex-communist citizens (along the lines of the results presented in Model 1 of the first tables in Chapters 4–7). The second set of models presents the fully saturated specifications used in Model 7 of these tables, and thus controls for the full set of pre-communist controls, demographic controls, and post-communist economic and political performance indicators. These *living in a post-communist country* control variables are important to help us disentangle the effects of longer communist regime durations in the pre-WWII Soviet republics from the significant developmental differences that separated them from many of the Eastern European satellite states (Pop-Eleches 2007). Finally, in the third set of models we simply add the individual-level personal communist exposure to the previous model specification. Doing so allows us to test to what extent any remaining differences in average political attitudes between pre- and post-WWII communist countries (and between them and non-post-communist countries) can be explained by the differences in the length in communist individual exposure (which was capped at about 45 years in Eastern Europe and over 70 years in the pre-WWII Soviet Union).

In Table 9.2 we present the coefficients for the two types of communist regimes (compared to the baseline of non-communist countries) and—for ease of interpretation—the difference between the two coefficients. For the bivariate models, the results suggest that the extent of the post-communist exceptionalism was indeed stronger in the pre-WWII Soviet republics across all four attitude types (and the differences were significant at p<.1 in Model 1 and p<.01 or better in Models 4, 7 and 10). By comparison, the average effects in post-WWII communist regimes, while still pointing in the same direction, were substantively smaller and fell short of reaching statistical significance for market and gender equality support.

However, once we turn to the fully specified models that account for pre-communist structural differences and post-communist economic and political conditions, a very different picture emerges. Along all dimensions, the magnitude of the coefficients for post-WWII communist countries increases, and it is now significant at .05 or better for democracy, markets, and welfare states and at .1 (two-tailed) for gender equality compared to the non-communist country baseline. Just as importantly, once we control for their pre-and post-communist developmental disadvantages, the pre-WWII Soviet republics no longer stand out as the key drivers of post-communist exceptionalism. In fact, for two of the dimensions— democracy and gender support (Models 2 and 11 respectively) the difference is now *greater* for the Eastern European countries, although these differences are at best marginally significant (at .1 in Model 11). For

Table 9.2. Attitudinal Differences between Eastern Europe and the Pre-WWII Soviet Union

Variables	(1)	(2)	(3)	(4)	(5)	(6)	(7)	(8)	(9)	(10)	(11)	(12)
	Democracy support			Market support			Welfare state support			Gender equality support		
Eastern Europe	-.213**	-.275*	-.081	-.070	-.189*	.130	.285**	.465**	.260*	-.009	-.274#	-.259#
	(.072)	(.132)	(.129)	(.049)	(.096)	(.097)	(.039)	(.107)	(.106)	(.075)	(.151)	(.156)
Pre-WWII Soviet Union	-.444**	-.164	.035	-.326**	-.435**	-.102	.400**	.464**	.251*	-.261*	-.057	-.041
	(.128)	(.162)	(.156)	(.069)	(.112)	(.109)	(.063)	(.126)	(.125)	(.104)	(.173)	(.178)
Difference	.231#	-.111	-.117	.256**	.246**	.232**	-.116#	.002	.009	.252**	-.217#	-.217#
	(.136)	(.105)	(.104)	(.074)	(.090)	(.089)	(.062)	(.080)	(.080)	(.103)	(.110)	(.110)
Year dummies	Yes	Yes	Yes	Yes	Yes	Yes	Yes	Yes	Yes	Yes	Yes	Yes
Pre-communist controls	No	Yes	Yes	No	Yes	Yes	No	Yes	Yes	No	Yes	Yes
Demographics	No	Yes	Yes	No	Yes	Yes	No	Yes	Yes	No	Yes	Yes
Post-communist economic & political controls	No	Yes	Yes	No	Yes	Yes	No	Yes	Yes	No	Yes	Yes
Communist exposure	No	No	Yes	No	No	Yes	No	No	Yes	No	No	Yes
Observations	227,373	227,373	227,373	262,299	262,299	262,299	281,157	281,157	281,157	215,826	215,826	215,826
R-squared	.031	.156	.158	.025	.086	.091	.054	.097	.099	.049	.249	.249

Note: This table shows the attitudinal differences for Eastern European countries and pre-WWII Soviet republics compared to the baseline of non-post-communist countries for the four types of political attitudes discussed in Chapters 4–7. There results show that with the exception of market attitudes, where pre-WWII Soviet republics have a larger and more persistent anti-market bias, for the other three types of political attitudes the differences between the two types of communist countries disappear once we control for pre-communist legacies. For comparability, all DVs are standardized to have a mean of 0 and a standard deviation of 1. For full regression results, see the electronic appendix.

welfare state support, Model 8 reveals a much larger post-communist bias once we control for pre- and post-communist conditions but the difference between different types of ex-communist countries disappears completely. The only area where the post-communist "signature" effect was still stronger for pre-WWII Soviet republics was for the anti-market bias in Model 5. This suggests that once we account for the significant developmental differences between the older and newer communist regimes, the attitudinal contrast between the two sets of countries is much less pronounced than in the bivariate models. This pattern is in line with the aggregate-level findings from prior work by one of us (Pop-Eleches 2007), where the negative effects of prewar Soviet Union membership on post-communist regime outcomes were highly sensitive to the inclusion of other historical legacy indicators.

Arguably the most interesting finding comes from the last set of models. Once we control for individual-level differences in personal communist exposure, both groups of ex-communist countries are no longer statistically distinguishable at conventional significance levels from their non-communist counterparts for three of the four types of attitudes we analyzed in this book: democracy, markets, and gender equality.[22] The only area where we continue to see a clear post-communist bias even net of personal exposure differences is in support for state provided social welfare, but even here the magnitude of the effect was reduced by 50% and there were essentially no differences between pre- and post-WWII communist regimes.

Overall, this analysis indicates that once we account for developmental differences, the attitudinal differences between Eastern Europeans and citizens of pre-WWII Soviet republics are noticeably reduced (and even partially reversed), which suggests that our decision to analyze them jointly in the preceding chapters was justified. Just as importantly, the fact that neither pre- nor post-WWII communist countries were statistically distinguishable from their non-communist counterparts once we account for exposure to communism (in addition to residence in a post-communist state) further confirms the importance of communist exposure for explaining attitudes toward democracy, markets, and welfare state support. However, it appears that the length of communist exposure is more important in explaining differences between post-communist and non-communist countries than between the pre- and post-WWII communist regimes.

[22] It should be noted that even in Model 6, which controls for communist exposure and thus for the different lengths of living under command economies, citizens of pre-WWII communist countries were still significantly more anti-market than their Eastern European counterparts, but, interestingly, neither of them were significantly different from the non-communist baseline.

9.4.3. What Next?

While prediction in the social sciences is a notoriously risky endeavor, in this final section we speculate at least briefly on a few of the implications of our findings both for the analytical utility of "post-communism" as a category for understanding political phenomena in Eastern Europe and the former Soviet Union and, more broadly, for the political prospects of the post-communist region.

From the perspective of the ongoing debates about the end of the transition/end of post-communism/end of Eastern Europe (e.g., Bernhard and Jasiewicz 2015), the obvious starting point is our analysis of temporal trends in Chapter 8. At least as far as the era before the global financial crisis is concerned, our analysis suggests that the answer to the question about the end of the post-communist transition depends to a large extent on the issue area under consideration. Thus, for democratic commitments and especially for welfare state support, post-communist citizens still differ markedly from their non-communist counterparts in the time period under consideration (1989–2009). Given that in both issue areas these differences are also visible for the younger cohorts with limited personal communist exposure, this suggests that cross-generational transmission of these attitudes is sufficiently strong that we should expect to see a recognizable communist legacy for at least the short-to-medium term, a finding that is further supported by the evidence about parental transmission effects with regard to social welfare in our supplemental analysis in Chapter 6. By contrast, for market and gender equality support the ex-communist countries had largely converged by 2008—at least on average—to the "normality" of non-communist countries, which could be interpreted as marking the end of the transition (Shleifer and Treisman 2004).[23]

However, given that the WVS surveys analyzed above end in 2009, we may need to be cautious about interpreting the partial convergence in terms of democratic support and the almost complete convergence with respect to market attitudes as irreversible trends. Given our findings in Chapter 8 about the growing deficit in democracy and market support in the context of the economic and political malaise of the early to mid-1990s, it is conceivable that the renewed recessions combined with the often disappointing political response by Eastern European governments could have already triggered a renewed widening of the post-communist

---

[23] We also find evidence of some parental socialization effects in attitudes toward markets, but these are either in terms of strengthening exposure effect for parents with communist education or who were members of the Communist Party—and thus would not be relevant for people with no exposure to communism—or are in the pro-market direction (for people who had a parent with pre-communist education).

gap. Thus, it is not hard to imagine that in the context of increasingly influential critiques about the inequities of capitalist systems (Piketty 2014) and parallel concerns about the abilities of Western liberal democracies to cope with the global economic crisis (Bermeo and Bartels 2013)—and the more recent refugee crisis—these attitudes would resonate with the ideological priors of individuals who had been socialized by communist regimes to distrust Western capitalism and liberal democracy. However, it is important to keep in mind that during the 1990s the bulk of the divergence in post-communist democracy and market support was driven by the older cohorts with extensive personal exposures to communism. Given that these cohorts account for a smaller and rapidly shrinking share of post-communist populations two decades later, the findings in our book suggest that the magnitude of any such renewed divergence could be significantly smaller in the post-2008 period. While these are interesting questions that could be fruitfully analyzed within our theoretical framework, answering them in a systematic fashion is beyond the scope of the present book and should be the subject of future research.

Another interesting question is how the attitudinal gaps we have identified in this book can shed light on a number of worrisome political developments that have questioned not only the prospects of further democratization in the largely non-democratic former Soviet republics, but also the stability and even survival of liberal democratic institutions among some of the region's erstwhile democratic frontrunners (especially Hungary but more recently also Poland). While the democratic backsliding in Putin's Russia and several other pre-WWII former Soviet republics was obviously driven to a large extent by elite politics (Taylor 2011; Petrov et al. 2014), the weak popular commitment to democracy combined with a broader communist nostalgia in many of these countries has undoubtedly facilitated such backsliding.

Among the post-WWII communist countries, many of which have been democratic since the early to mid-1990s, the recent democratic challenges raise a different set of questions. At a basic level, the fact that our analysis in the preceding section shows that the post-communist deficit in democratic support also affected these relative democratic frontrunners suggests that the real puzzle may not be the recent fragility of democracy in Eastern Europe, but rather its resilience during the crises of the 1990s. In a sense the spread of democracy to most of East-Central Europe and the Baltics in the early 1990s and then to a growing number of Balkan countries can be interpreted as approximating Di Palma's (1990) model of "democracy without democrats." While this model worked reasonably well in the 1990s owing in large part to the strong incentives of European integration at both the mass and the elite level (Vachudova 2005), the lack of strong normative commitments to democracy among a large part of the Eastern European publics could potentially undermine the resilience of these democracies in the face of subsequent anti-democratic challenges.

Even though the extent and the reasons for this democratic backsliding continue to be debated (Levitz and Pop-Eleches 2009; Sedelmeier 2014; Orenstein 2015) what is striking is the weak societal reaction toward the anti-democratic moves in several Eastern European countries. Thus, neither Orban's power grab in Hungary nor the attempted constitutional coup in Romania were met by significant popular protests, and while it may be tempting to blame this weak response on the general weakness of post-communist civil society (Howard 2003; Pop-Eleches and Tucker 2013), the validity of this explanation could be called into question by the fact that in recent years we have seen an uptick of protests on different topics, ranging from anti-mining protests in Romania to protests against a proposed Internet tax in Hungary. In other words, perhaps the problem is not the lack of mobilization in general, but rather the fact that in neither country did the desire to defend constitutional checks and balances evoke sufficiently strong passions among citizens, which, in turn, may be rooted at least in part in the lukewarm democratic support revealed by the analysis in our manuscript. None of this is to say that weak democratic commitments are either necessary or sufficient explanations of post-communist democratic backsliding,[24] but they nevertheless provide potentially important constraints on the actions of political leaders, especially in the context of the weaker external democratic conditionality of the post-EU accession period. From this perspective, the massive recent anti-corruption protests in Romania may be an important turning point because of their emphasis on defending the rule of law against encroachments by the ruling elites.

Compared to the continued democratic support deficit, the greater convergence of post-communist market attitudes may help explain why in the wake of the global economic crisis we have not seen a radical shift in the economic policies of most post-communist countries despite the high economic costs of the austerity measures adopted in response to this crisis. In fact, it appears that many post-communist governments actually adopted tougher adjustment measures than their Western European counterparts, and while many of the governments were subsequently punished at the

---

[24] Thus, Hungarian politics would have arguably looked quite different without Orban's particular personality and leadership style and the "perfect storm" of the implosion of the Hungarian Socialist Party after 2006. Similarly, the ultimate failure of the Romanian constitutional coup attempt of 2012 was due primarily to external pressures from the United States and EU rather than the democratic commitments of either Romanian elites or the general public. Nevertheless, events in Poland—long considered the bedrock of post-communist democracy—in the months preceding the completion of this book make it increasingly challenging to sustain a narrative of idiosyncratic explanations.

polls in post-crisis elections, it did not produce a rise in the vote shares of radical left parties (especially compared to Greece and Spain). In fact, quite possibly the greatest challenge against neoliberal economic policies came from the strongly anti-communist Hungarian Fidesz, and more recently from the equally anti-communist Polish Law and Justice (PiS) party, which suggests that the legacy of communist anti-market appeals may have either faded or morphed into a very different phenomenon.

Perhaps the biggest outstanding "real-world" puzzle raised by the findings in our book concerns the political reverberations of the large and resilient post-communist bias in favor of welfare states providing for individual needs. This question is particularly salient in the context of the significant decline in welfare provision in much of the post-communist world, which has led to a large and growing gap between the communist legacy–based expectations and the stark reality of actual provision in most ex-communist countries. This gap is arguably one of the underlying reasons for the widespread dissatisfaction of most Eastern Europeans with successive post-communist governments and in the long run has the potential to undermine support both for democracy, to the extent that democratic regimes prove unable to fulfill these demands, and for markets, whose uncertainties and inherent inequalities heighten the demand for a more generous welfare state.

9.5. LAST THOUGHTS

In 1989 a series of (largely) unexpected changes ushered in a remarkably fast and (mostly) peaceful end to perhaps the longest and most ambitious experiment in reordering the political, economic, and social rules of society. Affecting hundreds of millions of people, Soviet-style communism created a particular political and economic order that was based on the idea of fundamentally reorienting social relations in line with theoretical works by Marx, Engels, Lenin, and others. By the end of 1990, single-party rule in Eastern Europe was largely over, replaced by (often chaotic) multiparty democratic elections in country after country. By the start of 1993, the Soviet Union had ceased to exist, replaced by 15 new independent states. Within a decade and a half, NATO and the EU would expand to encompass most of Eastern Europe. Communism in Europe was dead. And yet . . .

Scholars of post-communist politics have recognized for many years now that communism may be dead, but its legacy lives on. Most of the prior research on this topic, however, has focused on the effects of legacies on post-communist *institutions*. While institutional legacies are unquestionably theoretically interesting and practically important, in this book we have tried to broaden the focus of the historical legacy debates to include a more systematic discussion of how communism has shaped—

and continues to shape—a broad range of political attitudes and preferences for hundreds of millions of citizens from the countries of the
former Soviet bloc. To paraphrase Max Weber, our intention here is not
to replace an (almost) exclusive focus on institutional legacies with an exclusive focus on mass political attitudes, but instead to bridge the divide
between scholars studying communist legacies (and historical legacies
more broadly) and those interested in understanding political attitudes
in post-communist countries (and elsewhere). We think that in addition
to offering interesting insights into the dynamics of attitude formation
and change, such an "attitudinal turn" in the study of historical legacies
can contribute to a better understanding of post-communist politics in
the last quarter century and arguably for years to come. Of course, political attitudes are only one part of the much larger and more complicated
equation of post-communist politics, and their impact on political outcomes is circumscribed by a variety of factors, including poorly functioning democratic representation mechanisms, external policy constraints,
and significant collective action problems. Nonetheless, political attitudes,
and the historical legacies that shape them, play at the very minimum
a "parameter-setting" role in constraining the actions of political elites
(Beissinger and Kotkin 2014), and during periods of popular mobilization—be they protests or elections—they can shape political outcomes in
much more consequential ways. Therefore, we hope that the theoretical
framework and the empirical results we have discussed in this book can
be a starting point for a broader discussion about how the past shapes
contemporary politics through its impact not just on institutions, but on
political attitudes and behavior as well.

Bibliography
■■■■■

Abarca, Jamie. F, Claudio C. Casiccia, and Felix D. Zamorano. 2002. "Increase in Sunburns and Photosensitivity Disorders at the Edge of the Antarctic Ozone Hole, Southern Chile, 1986–2000." *Journal of the American Academy of Dermatology* 46 (2) (February): 193–99.

Abbott, Pamela, and Roger Sapsford. 2006. "Trust, Confidence and Social Environment in Post-communist Societies." *Communist and Post-communist Studies* 39 (1): 59–71.

Acemoglu, Daron, Simon Johnson, and James A. Robinson. 2001. "The Colonial Origins of Comparative Development: An Empirical Investigation." *American Economic Review* 91 (5): 1369–401.

———. 2002. "Reversal of Fortune: Geography and Institutions in the Making of the Modern World Income Distribution." *Quarterly Journal of Economics* 118: 1231–94.

Achen, Christopher. 1992. "Social Psychology, Demographic Variables, and Linear Regression: Breaking the Iron Triangle in Voting Research." *Political Behavior* 14 (3): 195–211.

———. 2002. "Parental Socialization and Rational Party Identification." *Political Behavior* 24 (2): 151–70.

Achen, Christopher H., and Larry M. Bartels. 2016. *Democracy for Realists: Why Elections Do Not Produce Responsive Government*. Princeton, NJ: Princeton University Press.

Adorno, Theodor W. 1950. *The Authoritarian Personality*. New York: Harper.

Alesina, A., E. Glaeser, and B. Sacerdote. 2001. *Why Doesn't the US Have a European-Style Welfare System?* No. w8524. National Bureau of Economic Research.

Alesina Alberto, and Nicola Fuchs-Schündeln. 2007. "Good Bye Lenin (or Not?)—the Effect of Communism on People's Preferences." *American Economic Review* 97: 1507–28.

Almond, Gabriel, and Sidney Verba. 1965. *The Civic Culture: Political Attitudes and Democracy in Five Nations*. Newbury Park: Sage.

Anderson, Christopher, and Kathleen O'Conner. 2000. "System Change, Learning and Public Opinion about the Economy." *British Journal of Political Science* 30 (1): 147–72.

Andreß, H. J., and T. Heien. 2001. "Four Worlds of Welfare State Attitudes? A Comparison of Germany, Norway, and the United States." *European Sociological Review* 17 (4): 337–56.

Appel, Hilary. 2004. *A New Capitalist Order: Privatization and Ideology in Russia and Eastern Europe*. Pittsburgh: University of Pittsburgh Press.

Arel, Dominique. 1995. "Language Politics in Independent Ukraine: Towards One or Two State Languages?" *Nationalities Papers* 23 (3): 597–622.

Ash, Timothy Garton. 1990. *Polska Rewolucja: Solidarność 1980–1981*. Warsaw: Res Publica.

———. 1993. *The Magic Lantern: The Revolution of '89 Witnessed in Warsaw, Budapest, Berlin, and Prague*. New York: Vintage.

Ashwin, Sarah. 2000. *Gender, State and Society in Soviet and Post-Soviet Russia*. New York: Routledge.

Aslund, Anders. 2002. *Building Capitalism: The Transformation of the Former Soviet Bloc*. New York: Cambridge University Press.

Avis, George. 1983. "Access to Higher Education in the Soviet Union." In Janusz Tomiak, ed., *Soviet Education in the 1980s*, 199–239. New York: St. Martin's.

Bădescu, Gabriel, and Paul Sum. 2005. "Historical Legacies, Social Capital and Civil Society: Comparing Romania on a Regional Level." *Europe-Asia Studies* 57 (1): 117–33.

Bahry, Donna, Cynthia Boaz, and Stacy Burnett Gordon. 1997. "Tolerance, Transition, and Support for Civil Liberties in Russia." *Comparative Political Studies* 30 (4): 484–510.

Baron, Reuben, and David Kenny. 1986. "The Moderator-Mediator Variable Distinction in Social Psychological Research: Conceptual, Strategic, and Statistical Considerations." *Journal of Personality and Social Psychology* 51 (6): 1173–82.

Barrington, Lowell W. 2002. "Examining Rival Theories of Demographic Influences on Political Support: The Power of Regional, Ethnic, and Linguistic Divisions in Ukraine." *European Journal of Political Research* 41 (4): 455–91.

Bean, C., and E. Papadakis. 1998. "A Comparison of Mass Attitudes towards the Welfare State in Different Institutional Regimes, 1985–1990." *International Journal of Public Opinion Research* 10 (3): 211–36.

Beck, Paul Allen, and M. Kent Jennings. 1991. "Family Traditions, Political Periods, and the Development of Partisan Orientations." *Journal of Politics* 53 (3): 742–63.

Beissinger, Mark. 2002. *Nationalist Mobilization and the Collapse of the Soviet State*. New York: Cambridge University Press.

Beissinger, Mark, and Stephen Kotkin, eds. 2014. *Historical Legacies of Communism in Russia and Eastern Europe*. New York: Cambridge University Press.

Berinsky, Adam, and Joshua A. Tucker. 2006. "'Don't Knows' and Public Opinion towards Economic Reform: Evidence from Russia." *Communist and Postcommunist Studies* 39 (1): 1–27.

Berkhoff, Karel C. 2012. *Motherland in Danger: Soviet Propaganda during World War II*. Cambridge, MA: Harvard University Press.

Bermeo, Nancy, and Larry Bartels, eds. 2013. *Mass Politics in Tough Times: Opinions, Votes and Protest in the Great Recession*. Oxford: Oxford University Press.

Bernhard, Michael. 1993. "Civil Society and Democratic Transition in East Central Europe." *Political Science Quarterly* 108: 307–26.

Bernhard, Michael, and Krzysztof Jasiewicz. 2015. "Whither Eastern Europe? Changing Approaches and Perspectives on the Region in Political Science." *East European Politics and Societies* 29: 311–22.

Bernhard, Michael, and Ekrem Karakoc. 2007. "Civil Society and the Legacies of Dictatorship." *World Politics* 59 (4): 539–67.

Birch, Sarah. 2000. "Interpreting the Regional Effect in Ukrainian Politics." *Europe-Asia Studies* 52 (6): 1017–41.

Blanchflower, David G., and Richard B. Freeman. 1997. "The Attitudinal Legacy of Communist Labor Relations." *Industrial and Labor Relations Review* 50 (3): 438–59.

Blekesaune, M., and J. Quadagno. 2003. "Public Attitudes toward Welfare State Policies: A Comparative Analysis of 24 Nations." *European Sociological Review* 19 (5): 415–27.

Brady, Henry E., and Cynthia S. Kaplan. 2012. "Political Opinion in the Collapse of the USSR: A Reassessment Twenty Years Later Using a New Consolidated and Linked Data Set." APSA 2012 annual meeting paper. https://ssrn.com/abstract=2106422.

Brambor, Thomas, William Roberts Clark, and Matt Golder. 2006. "Understanding Interaction Models: Improving Empirical Analyses." *Political Analysis* 14 (1): 63–82.

Brzezinski, Z. K. 1989. *The Grand Failure: The Birth and Death of Communism in the Twentieth Century*. New York: Scribner.

Bunce, Valerie. 1995. "Should Transitologists Be Grounded?" *Slavic Review* 54 (1): 111–27.

———. 1998. "Regional Differences in Democratization: The East versus the South." *Post-Soviet Affairs* 14 (3): 187.

———. 1999. *Subversive Institutions: The Design and the Destruction of Socialism and the State*. New York: Cambridge University Press.

———. 2003. "Rethinking Recent Democratization: Lessons from the Postcommunist Experience." *World Politics* 55 (2): 167–92.

———. 2005. "The National Idea: Imperial Legacies and Postcommunist Pathways in Eastern Europe." *East European Politics and Society* 19 (3): 406–42.

Busemeyer, M. R., A. Goerres, and S. Weschle. 2009. "Attitudes towards Redistributive Spending in an Era of Demographic Ageing: The Rival Pressures from Age and Income in 14 OECD Countries." *Journal of European Social Policy* 19 (3): 195–212.

Campbell, Angus, Philip E. Converse, Warren E. Miller, and Donald E. Stokes. 1960. *The American Voter*. New York: Wiley.

Campbell, David E. 2006. "What Is Education's Impact on Civic and Social Engagement?" In Richard Desjardins and Tom Schuller, eds., *Measuring the Effects of Education on Health and Civic/Social Engagement*, 25–126. Paris: Centre for Educational Research and Innovation/Organisation for Economic Cooperation and Development.

Carter, Jeff, Michael H. Bernhard, and Timothy Nordstrom. 2016. "Communist Legacies and Democratic Survival in a Comparative Perspective Liability or Advantage." *East European Politics and Societies* 30 (4): 830–54.

Chen, Cheng, and Rudra Sil. 2004. "State-Legitimacy and the (In-)Significance of Democracy in Post-communist Russia." *Europe-Asia Studies* 56 (3): 347–68.

Chu, Yun-han, Michael Bratton, Marta Lagos, Sandeep Shastri, and Mark Tessler. 2008. "Public Opinion and Democratic Legitimacy." *Journal of Democracy* 19 (2): 74.

Cioroianu, Adrian. 2007. *Pe umerii lui Marx: O introducere în istoria comunismului românesc*. Bucharest: Curtea Veche.

Codrescu, Andrei. 2009. *The Posthuman Dada Guide: Tzara and Lenin Play Chess*. Princeton, NJ: Princeton University Press.

Collier, David, et al. 1979. *The New Authoritarianism in Latin America*. Princeton, NJ: Princeton University Press.

Collier, Paul, and Anke Hoeffler. 2003. "Greed and Grievance in Civil War." *Oxford Economic Papers* 56: 563–95.

Conquest, R. 1986. *The Harvest of Sorrow: Soviet Collectivization and the Terror-Famine*. New York: Oxford University Press.

Cook, Linda. 1993. *The Soviet Social Contract and Why It Failed: Welfare Policies and Workers' Politics from Brezhnev to Yeltsin*. Cambridge, MA: Harvard University Press.

Coser, Lewis A. 1951. "Some Aspects of Soviet Family Policy." *American Journal of Sociology* 56 (5): 424–37.

Cox, James, and Denise Powers. 1997. "Echoes from the Past: The Relationship between Satisfaction with Economic Reforms and Voting Behavior in Poland." *American Political Science Review* 91 (3): 617–33.

Craumer, Peter R., and James I. Clem. 1999. "Ukraine's Emerging Electoral Geography: A Regional Analysis of the 1998 Parliamentary Elections." *Post-Soviet Geography and Economics* 40 (1): 1–26.

Crawford, Beverly, and Arend Lijphart, eds. 1997. *Liberalization and Leninist Legacies: Comparative Perspectives on Democratic Transitions*. Berkeley, CA: International and Area Studies.

Dalton, Russell. 1994. "Communists and Democrats: Democratic Attitudes in the Two Germanies." *British Journal of Political Science* 24 (4): 469–93.

Darden, Keith. 2011. *Resisting Occupation: Mass Literacy and the Creation of Durable National Loyalties*. New York: Cambridge University Press.

Darden, Keith, and Anna Grzymała-Busse. 2006. "The Great Divide: Precommunist Schooling and Postcommunist Trajectories." *World Politics* 59 (1): 83–115.

Davies, Christie. 2007. "Humour and Protest: Jokes under Communism." *International Review of Social History* 52 (S15): 291–305.

de Melo, Martha, Cevdet Denizer, Alan Gelb, and Stoyan Tenev. 2001. "Circumstance and Choice: The Role of Initial Conditions and Policies in Transition Economies." *World Bank Economic Review* 15 (1): 1–31.

Dennis, Jack. 1968. "Major Problems of Political Socialization Research." *Midwest Journal of Political Science* 12 (1): 85–114.

Deutscher, Isaac. 1967. *On Socialist Man*. New York: Merit.

Di Palma, Giuseppe. 1990. *To Craft Democracies: An Essay on Democratic Transitions*. Berkeley: University of California Press.

Djankov, Simeon, Elena Nikolova, and Jan Zilinsky. 2016. "The Happiness Gap in Eastern Europe." *Journal of Comparative Economics* 44 (1): 108–24.

Dolenec, Danijela. 2013. *Democratic Institutions and Authoritarian Rule in Southeast Europe*. Colchester: ECPR.

Donnelly, Michael J., and Grigore Pop-Eleches. 2016. "Income Measures in Cross-National Surveys: Problems and Solutions." *Political Science Research and Methods*, pp. 1–9. https://doi.org/10.1017/psrm.2016.40.

Duch, Raymond. 1993. "Tolerating Economic Reform: Popular Support for Transition to a Free Market in the Former Soviet Union." *American Political Science Review* 87 (3): 590–608.

Earle, John, and Scott Gehlbach. 2003. "A Spoonful of Sugar: Privatization and Popular Support for Reform in the Czech Republic." *Economics and Politics* 15 (1): 1–32.

Easter, Gerald. 1997. "Preference for Presidentialism: Postcommunist Regime Change in Russia and the NIS." *World Politics* 49 (1): 184–211.

Easterly, William, and Ross Levine. 2003. "Tropics, Germs, and Crops: How Endowments Influence Economic Development." *Journal of Monetary Economics* 50 (1): 3–39.

Ebon, Martin. 1987. *The Soviet Propaganda Machine*. New York: McGraw-Hill.

EBRD. 2008. *Structural and Institutional Change Indicators*. London: European Bank for Reconstruction and Development.

———. 2011. *Life in Transition Survey II*. London: European Bank for Reconstruction and Development.

Eckstein, K., P. Noack, and B. Gniewosz. 2013. "Predictors of Intentions to Participate in Politics and Actual Political Behaviors in Young Adulthood." *International Journal of Behavioral Development* 37: 428–35.

Edgar, Adrienne. 2008. "Bolshevism, Patriarchy, and the Nation: The Soviet 'Emancipation' of Muslim Women in Pan-Islamic Perspective." *Slavic Review* 65 (2): 252–72.

Eger, M. A. 2010. "Even in Sweden: The Effect of Immigration on Support for Welfare State Spending." *European Sociological Review* 26 (2): 203–17.

Einhorn, Barbara. 1993. *Cinderella Goes to Market: Citizenship, Gender, and Women's Movements in East Central Europe*. New York: Verso.

Ekiert, Grzegorz. 1996. *The State against Society: Political Crises and Their Aftermath in East Central Europe*. Princeton, NJ: Princeton University Press.

———. 2015. "Three Generations of Research on Post-communist Politics—a Sketch." *East European Politics and Societies* 29: 323–37.

Ekiert, Grzegorz, and Stephen Hanson. 2003. "Time, Space, and Institutional Change in Central and Eastern Europe." In Grzegorz Ekiert and Stephen Hanson, eds., *Capitalism and Democracy in Central and Eastern Europe*, 15–48. New York: Cambridge University Press.

Ekiert, Grzegorz, and Jan Kubik. 1998. "Contentious Politics in New Democracies: East Germany, Hungary, Poland, and Slovakia, 1989–93." *World Politics* 50 (4): 547–72.

———. 1999. *Rebellious Civil Society: Popular Protest and Democratic Consolidation in Poland, 1989–1993*. Ann Arbor: University of Michigan Press.

———. 2014. "Myths and Realities of Civil Society." *Journal of Democracy* 25 (1): 46–58.

Ekiert, Grzegorz, Jan Kubik, and Milada Anna Vachudova. 2007. "Democracy in the Post-communist World: An Unending Quest?" *East European Politics and Societies* 21 (1): 7–30.

Ekiert, Grzegorz, and Daniel Ziblatt. 2013. "Democracy in Central and Eastern Europe One Hundred Years On." *East European Politics and Societies* 27 (1): 90–107.

Ellman, M. 2014. *Socialist Planning*. 3rd ed. New York: Cambridge University Press.

Ericson, R. E. 1991. "The Classical Soviet-Type Economy: Nature of the System and Implications for Reform." *Journal of Economic Perspectives* 5 (4): 11–27.

Estrin, Saul. 2007. "Organizations in Economy and Society: Firms and the State." Lecture slides available at http://personal.lse.ac.uk/estrin/Presentations/Organi zations%20in%20Economy%20and%20Society.ppt.

Evans, Geoffrey. 2006. "The Social Bases of Political Divisions in Post-communist Eastern Europe." *Annual Review of Sociology* 32: 245–70.

Evans, Geoffrey, and Stephen Whitefield. 1993. "Identifying the Bases of Party Competition in Eastern Europe." *British Journal of Political Science* 23 (4): 521–48.

———. 1995. "The Politics and Economics of Democratic Commitment: Support for Democracy in Transition Societies." *British Journal of Political Science* 25 (4): 485–514.

———. 1999. "Political Culture versus Rational Choice: Explaining Responses to Transition in the Czech Republic and Slovakia." *British Journal of Political Science* 29 (1): 129–54.

Falter, Jürgen W., Oskar W. Gabriel, Hans Rattinger, and Klaus Schmitt. 2012. *Political Attitudes, Political Participation and Voting Behavior in Reunified Germany (Panel 1994–2002)*. Cologne: GESIS Data Archive, ZA4301. Data file version 1.1.0, doi:10.4232/1.11408.

Favell, Adrian. 2008. "The New Face of East–West Migration in Europe." *Journal of Ethnic and Migration Studies* 34 (5): 701–16.

Fearon, James D. 2003. "Ethnic and Cultural Diversity by Country." *Journal of Economic Growth* 8: 195–22.

Fidrmuc, Jan. 2003. "Economic Reform, Democracy and Growth during Post-communist Transition." *European Journal of Political Economy* 19 (3): 583–604.

Finkel, Steven, Stan Humphries, and Karl-Dieter Opp. 2001. "Socialist Values and the Development of Democratic Support in the Former East Germany." *International Political Science Review* 22 (4): 339–62.

Fish, Steven. 1995. *Democracy from Scratch: Opposition and Regime in the New Russian Revolution*. Princeton, NJ: Princeton University Press.

———. 1997. "The Determinants of Economic Reform in the Post-communist World." *East European Politics and Societies* 12 (1): 31.

———. 1998. "Democratization's Requisites: The Postcommunist Experience." *Post-Soviet Affairs* 14 (3) (July–September): 212–47.

Franco, Annie, Neil Malhotra, and Gabor Simonovits. 2014. "Social Science: Publication Bias in the Social Sciences; Unlocking the File Drawer." *Science* 345 (6203): 1502–5.

Frye, Timothy. 2002. "The Perils of Polarization: Economic Performance in the Post-communist World." *World Politics* 54 (3): 308–37.

———. 2010. *Building States and Markets after Communism*. New York: Cambridge University Press.

Gabel, Matthew J. 2009. *Interests and Integration: Market Liberalization, Public Opinion, and European Union*. Ann Arbor: University of Michigan Press.

Gaidar, Yegor. 2012. *Russia: A Long View*. Cambridge, MA: MIT Press.

Gal, Susan, and Gail Kligman. 2000. *The Politics of Gender after Socialism: A Comparative-Historical Essay*. Princeton, NJ: Princeton University Press.

Ganev, Venelin. 2014. "The Inescapable Past: The Politics of Memory in Postcommunist Bulgaria." In Michael Bernhard and Jan Kubik, eds., *Twenty Years after Communism: The Politics of Memory and Commemoration*, 213–32. Oxford: Oxford University Press.

Gans-Morse, Jordan. 2004. "Searching for Transitologists: Contemporary Theories of Post-communist Transitions and the Myth of a Dominant Paradigm." *Post-Soviet Affairs* 20 (4): 320–49.

Geddes, Barbara. 1997. "A Comparative Perspective on the Leninist Legacy in Eastern Europe." In Beverly Crawford and Arend Lijphart, eds., *Liberalization and Leninist Legacies: Comparative Perspectives on Democratic Transitions*, 142–83. Berkeley, CA: International and Area Studies.

Gelman, Andrew, and Jennifer Hill. 2007. *Data Analysis Using Regression and Multilevel/Hierarchical Models*. Cambridge: Cambridge University Press.

Gerber, Alan S., Gregory A. Huber, David Doherty, Conor M. Dowling, Shang E. Ha. 2011. "Personality Traits and Participation in Political Processes." *Journal of Politics* 73: 692–706.

Gerber, Alan S., Gregory A. Huber, David Doherty, Conor M. Dowling, Connor Raso, Shang E. Ha. 2010. "Personality and Political Attitudes: Relationships across Issue Domains and Political Contexts." *American Political Science Review* 104 (1): 111–33.

Gerber, Theodore P., and Michael Hout. 1995. "Educational Stratification in Russia during the Soviet Period." *American Journal of Sociology* 101: 611–60.

Gibson, James, Raymond Duch, and Kent Tedin. 1992. "Democratic Values and the Transformation of the Soviet Union." *Journal of Politics* 54 (2): 329–71.

Gibson, James L. 1995. "The Resilience of Mass Support for Democratic Institutions and Processes in the Nascent Russian and Ukrainian Democracies." In Vladimir Tismăneanu, ed., *Political Culture and Civil Society in Russia and the New States of Eurasia*, 53–111. Armonk, NY: M. E. Sharp.

———. 1996. "Political and Economic Markets: Connecting Attitudes toward Political Democracy and a Market Economy within the Mass Culture of Russia and Ukraine." *Journal of Politics* 58: 954–84.

———. 2003. "Russian Attitudes towards the Rule of Law: An Analysis of Survey Data." In Denis J. Galligan and Marina Kurkchiyan, eds., *Law and Informal Practices: The Post-communist Experience*, 77–91. Oxford: Oxford University Press.

Gibson, James L., and Raymond N. Duch. 1993. "Political Intolerance in the USSR: The Distribution and Etiology of Mass Opinion." *Comparative Political Studies* 26: 286–329.

Gijsberts, Merove, and Paul Nieuwbeerta. 2000. "Class Cleavages in Party Preferences in the New Democracies in Eastern Europe: A Comparison with Western Democracies." *European Societies* 2 (4): 397–430.

Gilens, Martin. 2009. *Why Americans Hate Welfare: Race, Media, and the Politics of Antipoverty Policy*. Chicago: University of Chicago Press.

———. 2012. *Affluence and Influence: Economic Inequality and Political Power in America*. Princeton, NJ: Princeton University Press.

Goerres, A., and M. Tepe. 2010. "Age-Based Self-Interest, Intergenerational Solidarity and the Welfare State: A Comparative Analysis of Older People's Attitudes towards Public Childcare in 12 OECD Countries." *European Journal of Political Research* 49 (6): 818–51.

Goldfarb, Jeffrey. 1997. "Why Is There No Feminism after Communism?" *Social Research* 64 (2): 235–57.

Gorlach, Krzystof. 1989. "On Repressive Tolerance: State and Peasant Farm in Poland." *Sociologia Ruralis* 29 (1): 23–33.

Gould, John. 2011. *The Politics of Privatization: Wealth and Power in Postcommunist Europe*. Boulder, CO: Lynne Rienner.

Grabbe, Heather. 2014. "Six Lessons of Enlargement Ten Years On: The EU's Transformative Power in Retrospect and Prospect." *JCMS: Journal of Common Market Studies* 52 (S1): 40–56.

Graham, Carol, and Sandip Sukhtankar. 2004. "Does Economic Crisis Reduce Support for Markets and Democracy in Latin America? Some Evidence from Surveys of Public Opinion and Well Being." *Journal of Latin American Studies* 36 (2): 349–77.

Green, Donald P., Bradley Palmquist, and Eric Schickler. 2002. *Partisan Hearts and Minds: Political Parties and the Social Identities of Voters*. New Haven, CT: Yale University Press.

Greenberg, Edward. 1973. *Political Socialization* Chicago: Aldine Transaction.

Greene, Samuel A., and Graeme Robertson. Forthcoming. "Agreeable Authoritarians: Personality and Politics in Contemporary Russia." *Comparative Political Studies*.

Greenstein, Fred. 1971. *A Source Book for the Study of Personality and Politics*. London: Markham.

Gregory, P. 1990. *Restructuring the Soviet Economic Bureaucracy*. Cambridge: Cambridge University Press.

Gregory, P. R., and A. Tikhonov. 2000. "Central Planning and Unintended Consequences: Creating the Soviet Financial System, 1930–1939." *Journal of Economic History* 60 (4): 1017–40.

Grzymała-Busse, Anna. 2002. *Redeeming the Communist Past: The Regeneration of Communist Parties in East Central Europe*. New York: Cambridge University Press.

———. 2006. "Authoritarian Determinants of Democratic Party Competition." *Party Politics* 12 (3): 415–37.

———. 2007. *Rebuilding Leviathan: Party Competition and State Exploitation in Post-communist Democracies*. Cambridge: Cambridge University Press.

———. 2015. *Nations under God: How Churches Use Moral Authority to Influence Policy*. Princeton, NJ: Princeton University Press.

Haerpfer, Christian, and Richard Rose. 1997. "The Impact of a Ready-Made State." *German Politics* 6 (1): 100–21.

Haggard, Stephan, and Robert Kaufman. 2008. *Development, Democracy, and Welfare States: Latin America, East Asia, and Eastern Europe*. Princeton, NJ: Princeton University Press.

Hainmueller, Jens. 2012. "Entropy Balancing for Causal Effects: A Multivariate Reweighting Method to Produce Balanced Samples in Observational Studies." *Political Analysis* 20 (1): 25–46.

Hainmueller, Jens, and Yiqing Xu. 2013. "Ebalance: A Stata Package for Entropy Balancing." *Journal of Statistical Software* 54 (7): 1–18.

Hall, Robert E., and Charles I. Jones. 1999. "Why Do Some Countries Produce So Much More Output per Worker Than Others?" *Quarterly Journal of Economics* 114 (1): 83–116.

Haney, Lynne. 1999. "'But We Are Still Mothers': Gender, the State, and the Construction of Need in Post-socialist Hungary." In M. Burawoy and K. Verdery, eds., *Uncertain Transition: Ethnographies of Change in the Post-socialist World*, 151–87. Oxford: Rowman and Littlefield.

Harsch, Donna. 2006. *Revenge of the Domestic: Women, the Family, and Communism in the German Democratic Republic*. Princeton, NJ: Princeton University Press.

Hasenfeld, Y., and J. A. Rafferty. 1989. "The Determinants of Public Attitudes toward the Welfare State." *Social Forces* 67 (4): 1027–48.

Hayo, Bernd. 2004. "Public Support for Creating a Market Economy in Eastern Europe." *Journal of Comparative Economics* 32 (4): 720–44.

Hellman, Joel. 1998. "Winners Take All: The Politics of Partial Reform in Post-communist Transitions." *World Politics* 50 (2): 203–34.

Herzog, Alexander, and Joshua A. Tucker. 2010. "The Dynamics of Dissent: The Winners-Losers Gap in Attitudes towards EU Membership in Post-communist Countries." *European Political Science Review* 2 (2): 235–67.

Hicks, Raymond, and Dustin Tingley. 2011. "Causal mediation analysis." *Stata Journal* 11.4: 609–615.

Hoffman, David. 2011. *Cultivating the Masses: Modern State Practices and Soviet Socialism, 1914–1939*. Ithaca, NY: Cornell University Press.

Horowitz, Shale. 2003. "Sources of Post-communist Democratization: Economic Structure, Political Culture, War, and Political Institutions." *Nationalities Papers* 31 (2): 119–37.

Howard, Marc. 2002. "The Weakness of Post-communist Civil Society." *Journal of Democracy* 13 (1): 157–69.

Howard, Marc Morjé. 2003. *The Weakness of Civil Society in Post-communist Europe*. Cambridge: Cambridge University Press.

Howard, Marc Morjé, Rudra Sil, and Vladimir Tismăneanu, eds. 2006. *World Order after Leninism*. Seattle: University of Washington Press.

Hozić, Aida. 2015. "East European Studies: A Question and Some Ambivalence." *East European Politics and Societies* 29: 433–39.

Hunter, H. 1988. "Soviet Agriculture with and without Collectivization, 1928–1940." *Slavic Review* 47 (2): 203–16. http://doi.org/10.2307/2498462.

Imai, Kosuke, Luke Keele, Dustin Tingley, and Teppei Yamamoto. 2009. "Causal Mediation Analysis Using R." In H. D. Vinod, ed., *Advances in Social Science Research Using R*, 129–54. New York: Springer.

Inglehart, Ronald. 1990. *Culture Shift in Advanced Industrial Society*. Princeton, NJ: Princeton University Press.

Inglehart, Ronald, and Pippa Norris. 2003. *Rising Tide: Gender Equality and Cultural Change Around the World*. New York: Cambridge University Press.

Inglot, Tomasz. 2008. *Welfare States in East Central Europe*. Cambridge: Cambridge University Press.

Jaeger, Mads M. 2006. Welfare Regimes and Attitudes towards Redistribution: The Regime Hypothesis Revisited. *European Sociological Review* 22 (2): 157–70.

Janos, Andrew C. 1996. "What Was Communism: A Retrospective in Comparative Analysis." *Communist and Post-communist Studies* 29 (1): 1–24.

———. 2000. *East Central Europe in the Modern World: The Politics of the Borderlands from Pre- to Postcommunism*. Stanford, CA.: Stanford University Press.

———. 2001. "From Eastern Empire to Western Hegemony: East Central Europe under Two International Regimes." *East European Politics and Societies* 15 (2): 221–49.

———. 2006. "What Was Communism? A Retrospective in Comparative Analysis." *Communist and Post-communist Studies* 29 (1): 1–24.

Jennings, M. Kent, et al. 2009. "Politics across Generations: Family Transmission Reexamined." *Journal of Politics* 71: 782–99.

Jennings, M. Kent, and Richard Niemi. 1968. "The Transmission of Political Values from Parent to Child." *American Political Science Review* 62 (1): 169–84.

Jones Luong, Pauline. 2002. *Institutional Change and Political Continuity in Post-Soviet Central Asia*. Cambridge: Cambridge University Press.

Jowitt, Ken. 1992. *New World Disorder: The Leninist Extinction*. Berkeley: University of California Press.

Kamp, Marianne. 2005. "Gender Ideals and Income Realities: Discourses about Labor and Gender in Uzbekistan." *Nationalities Papers* 33 (3): 403–22.

———. 2006. *The New Woman in Uzbekistan: Islam, Modernity, and Unveiling under Communism*. Seattle: University of Washington Press.

Karl, Terry L., and Philippe C. Schmitter. 1991. "Modes of Transition in Latin America, Southern and Eastern Europe." *International Social Science Journal* 128 (2): 269–84.

Katchanovski, Ivan. 2006. "Regional Political Divisions in Ukraine in 1991–2006." *Nationalities Papers* 34: 507–32.

Kenez, Peter. 1985. *The Birth of the Propaganda State: Soviet Methods of Mass Mobilization, 1917–1929*. New York: Cambridge University Press.

King, Gary. 2010. "A Hard Unsolved Problem? Post-treatment Bias in Big Social Science Questions." Hard Problems in Social Science Symposium, Harvard University, April 4.

King, Gary, Christopher J. L. Murray, Joshua A. Salomon, and Ajay Tandon. 2003. "Enhancing the Validity and Cross-Cultural Comparability of Measurement in Survey Research." *American Political Science Review* 97 (4): 191–207.

Kitschelt, Herbert. 1992. "The Formation of Party Systems in East Central Europe." *Politics and Society* 20: 7–50.

————. 1995. "Formation of Party Cleavages in Post-communist Democracies." *Party Politics* 1 (4): 447.

————. 1999. "Accounting for Outcomes of Post-communist Regime Change. Causal Depth or Shallowness in Rival Explanations." Presented at the 1999 Annual Meeting of the American Political Science Association.

————. 2003. "Accounting for Post-communist Regime Diversity: What Counts as a Good Cause?" In G. Ekiert and Stephen Hanson, eds., *Capitalism and Democracy in Central and Eastern Europe: Assessing the Legacy of Communist Rule*, 49–88. New York: Cambridge University Press.

Kitschelt, Herbert, and Lenka Bustikova. 2009. "The Radical Right in Post-communist Europe: Comparative Perspectives on Legacies and Party Competition." *Communist and Post-communist Studies* 42 (4): 459–83.

Kitschelt, Herbert, Zdenka Manfeldova, Radosław Markowski, and Gabor Toka. 1999. *Post-communist Party Systems: Competition, Representation, and Interparty Cooperation*. Cambridge: Cambridge University Press.

Klašnja, Marko. 2015. "Corruption and the Incumbency Disadvantage: Theory and Evidence." *Journal of Politics* 77 (4): 928–42.

Klašnja, Marko, and Joshua Tucker. 2013. "The Economy, Corruption, and the Vote: Evidence from Experiments in Sweden and Moldova." *Electoral Studies* 32 (3): 536–43.

Kligman, Gail. 1998. *The Politics of Duplicity: Controlling Reproduction in Ceausescu's Romania*. Berkeley: University of California Press.

Konstantinova, Valentina. 1992. "The Women's Movement in the USSR." In Shirin Rai, Hilary Pilkington, and Annie Phizacklea, eds., *Women in the Face of Change: The Soviet Union, Eastern Europe, and China*, 200–17. London: Routledge.

Kopstein, Jeffrey. 2003. "Postcommunist Democracy: Legacies and Outcomes." *Comparative Politics* 35 (2): 231–50.

Kopstein, Jeffrey, and David Reilly. 2000. "Geographic Diffusion and the Transformation of the Postcommunist World." *World Politics* 53 (1): 1–37.

Kornai, János. 1992. *The Socialist System: The Political Economy of Communism*. Oxford: Oxford University Press.

————. 1994. "Transformational Recession: The Main Causes." *Journal of Comparative Economics* 19 (1): 39–63. http://dx.doi.org/10.1006/jcec.1994.1062.

Kotkin, Stephen. 2010. *Uncivil Society: 1989 and the Implosion of the Communist Establishment*. Vol. 32. New York: Modern Library.

Krosnick, Jon, and Duane Alwin. 1989. "Aging and Susceptibility to Attitude Change." *Journal of Personality and Social Psychology* 57: 416–25.

Kubicek, Paul. 2000. "Regional Polarisation in Ukraine: Public Opinion, Voting and Legislative Behaviour." *Europe-Asia Studies* 52 (2): 273–94.

Kubik, Jan. 2015. "Between Contextualization and Comparison: A Thorny Relationship between East European Studies and Disciplinary 'Mainstreams.'" *East European Politics and Societies* 29: 352–65.

Kukhterin, Sergei. 2000. "Fathers and Patriarchs in Communist and Postcommunist Russia." In Sarah Ashwin, ed., *Gender, State, and Society in Soviet and Post-Soviet Russia*, 71–89. London: Routledge.

Kulyk, Volodymyr. 2011. "Language Identity, Linguistic Diversity and Political Cleavages: Evidence from Ukraine." *Nations and Nationalism* 17 (3): 627–48.

Kurtz, Marcus J., and Andrew Barnes. 2002. "The Political Foundations of Post-communist Regimes—Marketization, Agrarian Legacies, or International Influences." *Comparative Political Studies* 35 (5): 524–53.

Lapidus, Gail Warshofsky. 1978. *Women in Soviet Society Equality, Development, and Social Change*. Berkeley: University of California Press.

Lenin, Vladimir Il'ich. 1999 [1902]. *Imperialism: The Highest Stage of Capitalism*. Sydney: Resistance Books.

Letki, Natalia. 2004. "Socialization for Participation? Trust, Membership, and Democratization in East-Central Europe." *Political Research Quarterly* 57 (4): 665.

Levitsky, Steven, and Lucan Way. 2002. "Elections without Democracy: The Rise of Competitive Authoritarianism." *Journal of Democracy* 13 (2): 51–66.

———. 2013. *Competitive Authoritarianism: Hybrid Regimes after the Cold War*. New York: Cambridge University Press.

Levitz, Philip, and Grigore Pop-Eleches. 2009. "Why No Backsliding? The European Union's Impact on Democracy and Governance before and after Accession." *Comparative Political Studies* 43 (4): 457–85.

Linz, Juan, and A. Stepan. 1996. *Problems of Democratic Transition and Consolidation: Southern Europe, South America and Post-communist Europe*. Baltimore: Johns Hopkins University Press.

Lipsmeyer, C. S. 2003. Welfare and the Discriminating Public: Evaluating Entitlement Attitudes in Post-communist Europe. *Policy Studies Journal* 31 (4): 545–64.

Lipton, David, and Jeffrey Sachs. 1992. *Privatization in Eastern Europe: The Case of Poland*. London: Palgrave Macmillan UK.

Lupu, Noam, and Leonid Peisakhin. 2016. "The Legacy of Political Violence across Generations." Paper presented at the Order, Conflict and Violence Workshop, Yale University.

Maddison, Angus. 2009. *Historical Statistics of the World Economy: 1–2008 AD*. www.ggdc.net/maddison/.

Madison, Bernice Q. 1968. *Social Welfare in the Soviet Union*. Stanford, CA: Stanford University Press.

Manove, M. 1971. "A Model of Soviet-Type Economic Planning." *American Economic Review* 61 (3): 390–406.

Markowski, Radosław. 1997. "Political Parties and Ideological Spaces in East Central Europe." *Communist and Post-communist Studies* 30 (3): 221–54.

Marsh, Rosalind J. 1996. *Women in Russia and Ukraine*. Cambridge: Cambridge University Press.

Marx, Karl. 2012 [1867]. *Das Kapital: A Critique of Political Economy*. Washington, DC: Regnery.

———. 2008. *Critique of the Gotha Program*. Rockville, MD: Wildside.

Marx, Karl, and Friedrich Engels. 2002 [1848]. *The Communist Manifesto*. London: Penguin.

Mason, David. 1995. "Attitudes toward the Market and Political Participation in the Post-communist States." *Slavic Review* 54 (2): 385–406.

Massell, Gregory J. 1974. *The Surrogate Proletariat: Moslem Women and Revolutionary Strategies in Soviet Central Asia, 1919–1929*. Princeton, NJ: Princeton University Press.

Matito, Cecilia, Neus Agell, Susana Sanchez-Tena, Josep L. Torres, and Marta Cascante. 2011. "Protective Effect of Structurally Diverse Grape Procyanidin Fractions against UV-Induced Cell Damage and Death." *Journal of Agricultural and Food Chemistry* 59 (9): 4489–95.

Mayer, Thierry, and Soledad Zignago. 2011. "Notes on CEPII's Distances Measures: The GeoDist Database." MPRA Paper No. 36347. https://mpra.ub.uni-muenchen.de/36347/.

McDevitt, Michael, and Steven Chaffee. 2002. "From Top-Down to Trickle-Up Influence: Revisiting Assumptions about the Family in Political Socialization." *Political Communication* 19 (3): 281–301.

Millar, J. R. 1974. "Mass Collectivization and the Contribution of Soviet Agriculture to the First Five-Year Plan: A Review Article." *Slavic Review* 33 (4): 750–66.

Miller, Arthur H., Vicki L. Hesli, and William M. Reisinger. 1994. "Reassessing Mass Support for Political and Economic Change in the Former USSR." *American Political Science Review* 88: 399–411.

Mishler, William, and Richard Rose. 1994. "Support for Parliaments and Regimes in the Transition toward Democracy in Eastern Europe." *Legislative Studies Quarterly* 19 (1): 5–32.

———. 1996. "Trajectories of Fear and Hope: Support for Democracy in Post-communist Europe." *Comparative Political Studies* 28 (4): 553–81.

———. 1997. "Trust, Distrust, and Skepticism: Popular Evaluations of Civil and Political Institutions in Post-communist Societies." *Journal of Politics* 59: 419–51.

———. 2001. "Political Support for Incomplete Democracies: Realist vs. Idealist Theories and Measures." *International Political Science Review/Revue internationale de science politique* 22 (4): 303–20.

———. 2007. "Generation, Age, and Time: The Dynamics of Political Learning during Russia's Transformation." *American Journal of Political Science* 51 (4): 822–34.

Molyneux, Maxine. 1984. "Women in Socialist Societies: Problems of Theory and Practice." In Kate Young, Carol Wolkowitz, and Roslyn McCullagh, eds., *Of Marriage and the Market: Women's Subordination Internationally and Its Lessons*, 55–90 London: Routledge and Kegan Paul.

Mondak, Jeffery J. 2010. *Personality and the Foundations of Political Behavior.* New York: Cambridge University Press.

Mondak, Jeffrey J., et al. 2010. "Personality and Civic Engagement: An Integrative Framework for the Study of Trait Effects on Political Behavior." *American Political Science Review* 104 (1): 85.

Mondak, Jeffery J., and Karen D. Halperin. 2008. "A Framework for the Study of Personality and Political Behaviour." *British Journal of Political Science* 38: 2335–62.

Mullinix, Kevin J., Thomas J. Leeper, James N. Druckman, Jeremy Freese. 2015. "The Generalizability of Survey Experiments." *Journal of Experimental Political Science* 2 (2): 109–38.

Murrell, Peter. 1993. "What Is Shock Therapy? What Did It Do in Poland and Russia?" *Post-Soviet Affairs* 9 (2): 111–40.

Naiman, Eric. 1997. *Sex in Public: The Incarnation of Early Soviet Ideology*. Princeton, NJ: Princeton University Press.

Nalepa, Monika. 2010. *Skeletons in the Closet: Transitional Justice in Post-communist Europe*. Cambridge: Cambridge University Press.

Nalepa, Monika, and Grigore Pop-Eleches. 2015. "Religion and Anti-authoritarian Resistance: Evidence from Communist Poland." Working paper, September.

Neundorf, Anja. 2009. "Growing Up on Different Sides of the Wall—a Quasi-experimental Test: Applying the Left-Right Dimension to the German Mass Public." *German Politics* 18 (2): 201–25.

———. 2010. "Democracy in Transition: A Micro Perspective on System Change in Post-Soviet Societies." *Journal of Politics* 72 (4): 1096–108.

Neustadt, I. 1947. Review of *The Development of the Soviet Economic System: An Essay on the Experience of Planning in the U.S.S.R.* by Alexander Baykov. *Slavonic and East European Review* 25 (65): 594–97.

Nodia, Ghia. 2000. "Chasing the Meaning of 'Post-communism': A Transitional Phenomenon or Something to Stay?" *Contemporary European History* 9 (2): 269–83.

Northrop, Douglas Taylor. 2003. *Veiled Empire: Gender and Power in Stalinist Central Asia*. Ithaca, NY: Cornell University Press.

Nove, A. 1990. *An Economic History of the U.S.S.R.* 2nd rpt. ed. Harmondsworth: Penguin Books IX.

O'Dwyer, Conor. 2012. "Does the EU Help or Hinder Gay-Rights Movements in Post-communist Europe? The Case of Poland." *East European Politics* 28 (4): 332–52.

Olcott, Martha B. 1993. "Central Asia on Its Own." *Journal of Democracy* 4 (1): 92–103.

Orenstein, Mitchell A. 2001. *Out of the Red: Building Capitalism and Democracy in Postcommunist Europe*. Ann Arbor: University of Michigan Press.

———. 2015. "Geopolitics of a Divided Europe." *East European Politics and Societies* 29 (2): 531–40.

Osborne, Danny, David O. Sears, and Nicholas A. Valentino. 2011. "The End of the Solidly Democratic South: The Impressionable-Years Hypothesis." *Political Psychology* 32 (1): 81–108.

Pacek, Alexander C., Grigore Pop-Eleches, and Joshua A. Tucker. 2009. "Disenchanted or Discerning? Turnout in Post-communist Elections, 1990–2004." *Journal of Politics* 71 (2): 473–91.

Peisakhin, Leonid. 2015. "Cultural Legacies: Persistence and Transmission." In Norman Schofield and Gonzalo Caballero, eds., *The Political Economy of Governance: Studies in Political Economy*, 21–39. Basel, Switzerland: Springer International.

Petrov, Nikolay, Maria Lipman, Henry Hale. 2014. "Three Dilemmas of Hybrid Regime Governance: Russia from Putin to Putin." *Post-Soviet Affairs* 30 (1): 1–26.

Pierson, Paul, and Theda Skocpol. 2002. "Historical Institutionalism in Contemporary Political Science." *Political Science: The State of the Discipline* 3: 693–721.

Piketty, Thomas. 2014. *Capital in the Twenty-First Century*. Cambridge, MA: Harvard University Press.

Pollert, A. 2003. Women, Work and Equal Opportunities in Post-communist Transition. *Work Employment and Society* 17 (2): 331–57.

Pop-Eleches, Grigore. 1999. "Separated at Birth or Separated by Birth? The Communist Successor Parties in Romania and Hungary." *East European Politics and Societies* 13 (1): 117–47.

———. 2007. "Historical Legacies and Post-communist Regime Change." *Journal of Politics* 69 (4): 908–26.

———. 2009. "The Post-communist Democratic Deficit: Roots and Mechanisms." Annual meeting of the American Association for the Advancement of Slavic Studies, November 12–15, Boston, MA.

———. 2010. "Throwing Out the Bums: Protest Voting and Anti-establishment Parties after Communism." *World Politics* 62 (2): 221–60.

———. 2013. "Learning from Mistakes: Romanian Democracy and the Hungarian Precedent." *APSA European Politics and Society Newsletter*, Winter, 9–12.

———. 2014. "Communist Development and the Post-communist Democratic Deficit." In Mark Beissinger and Steven Kotkin, eds., *The Historical Legacies of Communism*. New York: Cambridge University Press.

———. 2015 "Pre-communist and Communist Developmental Legacies." *East European Politics and Societies* 29: 391–408.

Pop-Eleches, Grigore, and Joshua A. Tucker. 2010. "After the Party: Legacies and Left-Right Distinctions in Post-communist Countries." Center for Advanced Study in the Social Science. Fundación Juan March, Madrid, Spain, Working Paper Series, Estudio/Working Paper 2010/250.

———. 2011. "Communism's Shadow: Postcommunist Legacies, Values, and Behavior." *Comparative Politics* 43 (4): 379–408.

———. 2012. "Post-Communist Legacies and Political Behavior and Attitudes." *Demokratizatsiya: The Journal of Post-Soviet Democratization.* 20(2): 157–66.

———. 2013. "Associated with the Past? Communist Legacies and Civic Participation in Post-communist Countries." *East European Politics and Societies* 27 (1): 45–68.

———. 2014. "Communist Socialization and Post-communist Economic and Political Attitudes." *Electoral Studies* 33: 77–98.

Popov, Vladimir. 2007. "Shock Therapy versus Gradualism Reconsidered: Lessons from Transition Economies after 15 Years of Reforms." *Comparative Economic Studies* 49 (1): 1–31.

Powell, Eleanor Neff, and Joshua Tucker. 2014. "Revisiting Electoral Volatility in Post-communist Countries: New Data, New Results and New Approaches." *British Journal of Political Science* 44 (1): 123–47.

Preda, Marin. 1967. *Moromeţii.* Vol. 2. Bucureşti: Editura Pentru Literatura.

Prior, Markus. 2010. "You've Either Got It or You Don't? The Stability of Political Interest over the Life Cycle." *Journal of Politics* 72 (3): 747–66.

Pryor, F. 2014. *The Red and the Green the Rise and Fall of Collectivized Agriculture in Marxist Regimes*. Princeton, NJ: Princeton University Press.

Przeworski, Adam. 1991. *Democracy and the Market*. Cambridge: Cambridge University Press.

Remington, Thomas. 1989. *Politics and the Soviet System: Essays in Honour of Frederick C. Barghoorn.* New York: Palgrave Macmillan.

Rigobon, Roberto, and Dani Rodrik. 2005. "Rule of Law, Democracy, Openness, and Income: Estimating the Interrelationships." *Economics of Transition* 13 (3): 533–64.

Roberts, Andrew. 2004. "The State of Socialism: A Note on Terminology." *Slavic Review* 63 (2): 349–66.

———. 2008. "Hyperaccountability: Economic Voting in Eastern Europe." *Electoral Studies* 27 (3): 533–46.

———. 2010. *The Quality of Democracy in Eastern Europe: Public Preferences and Policy Reforms.* New York: Cambridge University Press.

Robertson, Graeme. 2010. *The Politics of Protest in Hybrid Regimes.* Cambridge: Cambridge University Press.

Roeder, Philip G. 1993. *Red Sunset: The Failure of Soviet Politics.* Princeton, NJ: Princeton University Press.

Rohrschneider, Robert. 1999. *Learning Democracy: Democratic and Economic Values in Unified Germany.* Oxford: Oxford University Press.

Rose, Richard. 2009. *Understanding Post-communist Transformations: A Bottom Up Approach.* Abingdon-on-Thames: Routledge.

Rose, Richard, and William Mishler. 1996. "Testing the Churchill Hypothesis: Popular Support for Democracy and Its Alternatives." *Journal of Public Policy* 16 (1): 29–58.

Rose, Richard, William Mishler, and Christian Haerpfer. 1998. *Democracy and Its Alternatives: Understanding Post-communist Societies.* Baltimore: Johns Hopkins University Press.

Rosen, S. M. 1964. "Problems in Evaluating Soviet Education." *Comparative Education Review* 8 (2): 153–65.

Rosenfeld, Bryn. 2016. "The Middle Class, the State, and Democratization." Unpublished book manuscript.

Rupnik, Jacques. 2007. "Is East-Central Europe Backsliding? From Democracy Fatigue to Populist Backlash." *Journal of Democracy* 18 (4): 17–25.

Sachs, Jeffrey, and David Lipton. 1990. "Poland's economic reform." *Foreign Affairs* 69 (3): 47–66.

Sachs, Jeffrey D., and Andrew M. Warner. 1997. "Fundamental Sources of Long-Run Growth." *American Economic Review* 87 (2): 184–88.

Sapiro, Virginia. 2004. "Not Your Parents' Political Socialization: Introduction for a New Generation." *Annual Review of Political Science* 7: 1–23.

Sakwa, Richard. 1990. *Gorbachev and His Reforms, 1985–1990.* New York: Prentice Hall.

Sanborn, Joshua A. 2003. *Drafting the Russian Nation: Military Conscription, Total War, and Mass Politics, 1905–1925.* DeKalb: Northern Illinois University Press.

Schimmelfennig, Frank. 2007. "European Regional Organizations, Political Conditionality, and Democratic Transformation in Eastern Europe." *East European Politics and Societies* 21 (1): 126–41.

Schimmelfennig, Frank, and Ulrich Sedelmeier. 2005. *The Europeanization of Central and Eastern Europe.* Ithaca, NY: Cornell University Press.

Schmitter, Philippe, and Terry Karl. 1994. "The Conceptual Travels of Transitologists and Consolidologists." *Slavic Review* 53 (1): 173–85.

Sears, David. 1993. *Symbolic Politics: A Socio-psychological Theory*. Durham, NC: Duke University Press.

Sears David, and Nicholas Valentino. 1997. "Politics Matters: Political Events as Catalysts for Preadult Socialization." *American Political Science Review* 91 (1): 45–65.

Sedelmeier, Ulrich. 2014. "Anchoring Democracy from Above? The European Union and Democratic Backsliding in Hungary and Romania after Accession." *Journal of Common Market Studies* 52 (1): 105–21.

Senik, Claudia, H. Stichnoth, and Karina Van der Straeten. 2009. "Immigration and Natives' Attitudes towards the Welfare State: Evidence from the European Social Survey." *Social Indicators Research* 91 (3): 345–70.

Shabad, Goldie, and Kazimirez M. Slomczynski. 1999. "Political Identities in the Initial Phase of Systemic Transformation in Poland: A Test of the Tabula Rasa Hypothesis." *Comparative Political Studies* 32 (6): 690–723.

Shlapentokh, Vladimir. 1989. *Public and Private Life of the Soviet People*. New York: Oxford University Press.

———. 2006. "Trust in Public Institutions in Russia: The Lowest in The World." *Communist and Post-communist Studies* 39 (2): 153–74.

Shleifer, Andrei, and Daniel Treisman. 2004. "A Normal Country." *Foreign Affairs* 83 (2): 20–38.

———. 2014. "Normal Countries: The East 25 Years after Communism." *Foreign Affairs* 93: 92–103.

Slezkine, Yuri. 1994. "The USSR as a Communal Apartment; or, How a Socialist State Promoted Ethnic Particularism." *Slavic Review* 53 (2): 414–52.

Snijders, T.A.B., and R. J. Bosker. 1999. *Multilevel Analysis: An Introduction to Basic and Advanced Multilevel Modeling*. London: Sage.

Stan, Lavina, and Lucian Turcescu. 2000. "The Romanian Orthodox Church and Post-communist Democratisation." *Europe-Asia Studies* 52 (8): 1467–88.

Stark, David, and Laszlo Bruszt. 1998. *Postsocialist Pathways: Transforming Politics and Property in East Central Europe*. New York: Cambridge University Press.

Stokes, Susan C. 1996. "Public Opinion and Market Reforms: The Limits of Economic Voting." *Comparative Political Studies* 29 (5): 499–519.

Stoner, Kathryn, and Michael McFaul. 2013. *Transitions to Democracy: A Comparative Perspective*. Baltimore: Johns Hopkins University Press.

Suny, Ronald Grigor, and Terry Martin. 2001. *A State of Nations: Empire and Nation-Making in the Age of Lenin and Stalin*. Oxford: Oxford University Press.

Svallfors, S. 1997. Worlds of Welfare and Attitudes to Redistribution: A Comparison of Eight Western Nations. *European Sociological Review* 13 (3): 283–304.

Svejnar, Jan. 2000. "Firms and Competitiveness in Central Europe: Accomplishments and Challenges." *Economic and Business Review* 2 (1): 5–28.

———. 2002. "Transition Economies: Performance and Challenges." *Journal of Economic Perspectives* 16 (1): 3–28.

TARKI. 1997. Hungarian Household Panel Survey (HHPS). Budapest: Social Research Informatics Center (TARKI).

Taylor, Brian D. 2011. *State Building in Putin's Russia: Policing and Coercion after Communism*. New York: Cambridge University Press.

Thelen, Kathleen. 1999. "Historical Institutionalism in Comparative Politics." *Annual Review of Political Science* 2 (1): 369–404.

Ticktin, H. H. 1973. "Towards a Political Economy of the USSR." *Critique* 1 (1): 20–41.

Tismăneanu, Vladimir. 1998. *Fantasies of Salvation: Democracy, Nationalism and Myth in Post-communist Societies*. Princeton, NJ: Princeton University Press.

———, ed. 2009. *Stalinism Revisited: The Establishment of Communist Regimes in East-Central Europe*. Budapest: Central European University Press.

Tismăneanu, Vladimir, Marc Morjé Howard, and Rudra Sil, eds. *World Order after Leninism*. University of Washington Press, 2006.

Todosijevic, Bojan, and Szolt Enyedi. 2008. "Authoritarianism without Dominant Ideology: Political Manifestations of Authoritarian Attitudes in Hungary." *Political Psychology* 29 (5): 767–87.

Torcal, Mariano, and José Ramón Montero. 2006. *Political Disaffection in Contemporary Democracies: Social Capital, Institutions and Politics*. New York: Routledge.

Tucker, Joshua A. 2001. "Economic Conditions and the Vote for Incumbent Parties in Russia, Poland, Hungary, Slovakia, and the Czech Republic from 1990–1996." *Post-Soviet Affairs* 17 (4): 309–31.

———. 2002. "The First Decade of Post-communist Elections and Voting: What Have We Studied, and How Have We Studied It?" *Annual Review of Political Science* 5: 271–304.

———. 2006. *Regional Economic Voting: Russia, Poland, Hungary, Slovakia, and the Czech Republic, 1990–99*. New York: Cambridge University Press.

———. 2015. "Comparative Opportunities: The Evolving Study of Political Behavior in Eastern Europe." *East European Politics and Societies and Cultures* 29 (2): 420–32.

Tucker, Joshua A., Alexander Pacek, and Adam Berinsky. 2002. "Transitional Winners and Losers: Attitudes toward EU Membership in Post-communist Countries." *American Journal of Political Science* 46 (3): 557–71.

UNICEF. 2014. *TransMonEE 2014 Database*. Geneva: UNICEF Regional Office for CEE/CIS. www.transmonee.org.

United Nations University, World Institute for Development Economics Research. 2007. *World Income Inequality Database: User Guide and Data Sources*. Vol. 2.0b. Helsinki: UNU/WIDER.

Vachudova, Milada Anna. 2005. *Europe Undivided: Democracy, Leverage, and Integration after Communism*. Oxford: Oxford University Press.

———. 2008. "Tempered by the EU? Political Parties and Party Systems before and after Accession." *Journal of European Public Policy* 15 (6): 861–79.

———. 2009. "Corruption and Compliance in the EU's Post-communist Members and Candidates." *JCMS: Journal of Common Market Studies* 47 (S1): 43–62.

Vachudova, Milada Anna, and Tim Snyder. 1996. "Are Transitions Transitory? Two Types of Political Change in Eastern Europe since 1989." *East European Politics and Societies* 11 (1): 1–35.

Varshney, Ashutosh. 2001. "Ethnic Conflict and Civil Society: India and Beyond." *World Politics* 53 (3): 362–98.

Vasileva, E. K. 1978. *Sotsial'no-Ekonomicheskaia Struktura Naseleniia SSSR* (The social-economic structure of the population of the USSR). Moscow: Statistika.

Verdery, Katherine. 1996. *What Was Socialism and What Comes Next.* Princeton, NJ: Princeton University Press.

Visser, Penny, and John Krosnick. 1998. "The Development of Attitude Strength over the Life Cycle: Surge and Decline." *Journal of Personality and Social Psychology* 75: 1388–409.

Walder, Andrew G., Andrew Isaacson, and Qinglian Lu. 2015. "After State Socialism: The Political Origins of Transitional Recessions." *American Sociological Review* 80: 444–68.

Williams, Kieran. 1997. *The Prague Spring and Its Aftermath: Czechoslovak Politics, 1968–1970.* New York: Cambridge University Press.

Williamson, John. 1990. "What Washington Means by Policy Reform." In John Williamson, ed., *Latin American Adjustment: How Much Has Happened*, 7–20. Washington, DC: Institute for International Economics.

Wimmer, Andreas, and Brian Min. 2006. "From Empire to Nation-State: Explaining War in the Modern World, 1816–2001." *American Sociological Review* 71 (6): 867–97.

Wittenberg, Jason. 2006. *Crucibles of Political Loyalty: Church Institutions and Electoral Continuity in Hungary.* Cambridge: Cambridge University Press.

———. 2015. "Conceptualizing Historical Legacies." *East European Politics and Societies* 29 (2) (May): 366–78.

Wolchik, Sharon L., and Alfred G. Meyer. 1985. *Women, State and Party in Eastern Europe.* Durham, NC: Duke University Press.

World Values Survey Association. 2009. "World Values Survey 1981–2008 Official Aggregate V.20090901." Madrid: ASEP/JDS.

Zuckerman, Alan, Josip Dasovic, and Jennifer Fitzgerald. 2007. *Partisan Families: The Social Logic of Bounded Partisanship in Germany and Britain.* New York: Cambridge University Press.

Index

■■■■■